THE COMMON LOT

*Sickness, Medical Occupations and the Urban Poor
in Early Modern England*

THE COMMON LOT
*Sickness, Medical Occupations and the Urban Poor
in Early Modern England*

Essays by
MARGARET PELLING

LONGMAN
London and New York

Addison Wesley Longman Limited
Edinburgh Gate,
Harlow, Essex CM20 2JE, United Kingdom
and Associated Companies throughout the world.

Published in the United States of America by Addison Wesley Longman, New York.

First published 1998

ISBN 0–582–23183–3 CSD
ISBN 0–582–23182–5 PPR

Visit Addison Wesley Longman on the world wide web at http://www.awl-he.com

British Library Cataloguing in Publication Data

A catalogue entry for this title is available from the British Library

Library of Congress Cataloging-in-Publication Data

A catalogue entry for this title is available from the Library of Congress

Set by 35 in 11/12pt Garamond
Produced by Addison Wesley Longman Singapore (Pte) Ltd.,
Printed in Singapore

To
the Hiltons
and
the Matthews

Contents

List of Figures and Tables

Figures

Tables

Preface and Acknowledgements

It is to be hoped that a volume of essays of this kind rarely emerges without the encouragement of friends and colleagues. This is certainly true in the present case, although no responsibility is thereby transferred. I am grateful for support from, at different stages, Jonathan Barry, Sandra Cavallo, Trish Crawford, Cathy Crawford, Penelope Gouk, Ludmilla Jordanova, Anne Laurence, Ross McKibbin, Charles Webster, Paul Weindling, and those whose names are specifically mentioned in connection with each of the essays. The students taking my MSc/MPhil paper on health, medicine and social conditions in early modern England provided salutary and informative responses, as did my doctoral students. I also owe a great deal to audiences at various conferences held by the Society for the Social History of Medicine. Because of institutional circumstances, I was doubly appreciative of the understanding shown by the Director of my Unit, Jane Lewis, and by Unit staff. Outside the Unit, Frances White showed unexampled patience, especially during computer crises, as well as her usual meticulousness. Peter Humphrey of the Modern History Faculty was also extremely helpful. Of the many libraries concerned I wish particularly to mention the Bodleian Library, Oxford, the Corporation of London Record Office, the Guildhall Library, London, and the Archivist and staff of the Norfolk Record Office, Norwich. Like many other scholars who owe a special debt to Norwich records, I was forcibly reminded of that debt by the fire that destroyed Norwich's library (but fortunately not all its holdings) in 1994. Over the period during which these essays were written I have been supported by the Wellcome Trust, and I am grateful for the opportunity thus offered. I should also like to thank Andrew MacLennan and his colleagues at Addison Wesley Longman, who have been both civilised and encouraging, as well as tolerant when the project was affected by circumstances outside my control. My greatest debt over many years is to the dedicatees, in particular Mary Hilton.

Chapter 1 first appeared as 'Medicine and Sanitation', in J. F. Andrews (ed.), *William Shakespeare: His World, His Work, His Influence*, 3 vols (Charles Scribner's Sons, New York, 1985), vol. 1, pp. 75–84; Chapter 3 as 'Illness among the Poor in an Early Modern English Town: the Norwich Census of 1570', *Continuity and Change*, 3 (1988), 273–90; Chapter 4 under its present title in *Medical History*, 29

(1985), 115–37; Chapter 5 under its present title in *Social History of Medicine*, 1 (1988), 135–64; Chapter 6 under its present title in M. Pelling and R. M. Smith (eds), *Life, Death and the Elderly: Historical Perspectives* (Routledge, London and New York, 1991), pp. 74–101; Chapter 9 as 'Occupational Diversity: Barbersurgeons and the Trades of Norwich, 1550–1640', *Bulletin of the History of Medicine*, 56 (1982), 484–511; and Chapter 10 as 'Medical Practice in Early Modern England: Trade or Profession?', in W. Prest (ed.), *The Professions in Early Modern England* (Croom Helm, London, 1987), pp. 90–128.

The essays have been edited as follows: overall, I have tried to eliminate repetitions, and to include cross-referencing instead. To save space, I have in a number of cases (Pound's edition of the Norwich census, for example) adopted short titles which are used throughout the volume. I have also used short titles for the chapters themselves. Full references for these will be found under Abbreviations (p. xii), rather than in each chapter's footnotes. For those chapters already published, except Chapter 1, I have restricted the changes mainly to clarifications and stylistic and factual corrections, while doing as much as possible in the limited space to bring their references up to date. From the reader's point of view it seemed more convenient to include new references in the chapter to which they are most relevant, rather than scattering them throughout the Introduction. Chapter 1 was originally published with only a short bibliography, and has now been provided with footnotes; I have made only minor changes to the text. This first chapter is intended to serve as an overview, although it also makes reference to the use of literary sources. Each of the essays includes general and historiographical discussion by way of introduction and conclusions. Chapter 10 also considers general issues, which are tackled in greater historical detail in the preceding chapters. The purpose of the Introduction is to explain the overall intentions of the volume, to single out unifying themes and approaches, and to connect the findings of the essays to wider debates.

Margaret Pelling
Wellcome Unit for the History of Medicine
University of Oxford

The publishers would like to thank the following for permission to reproduce copyright material:

Cambridge University Press for Margaret Pelling, 'Illness among the Poor in an Early Modern English Town: the Norwich Census of 1570', *Continuity and Change*, 3 (1988), 273–90 and for Figure 5.2 from E. A. Wrigley and R. S. Schofield, *The Population History of England 1541–1871* (1981), p. 216; Johns Hopkins University Press for Margaret Pelling, 'Occupational Diversity: Barbersurgeons and the Trades of Norwich, 1550–1640', *Bulletin of the History of Medicine*, 56 (1982), 484–511. Routledge and Croom Helm for Margaret Pelling, 'Old Age, Poverty, and Disability in Sixteenth-Century Norwich: Work, Remarriage, and Other Expedients', in M. Pelling and R. M. Smith (eds), *Life,*

Death and the Elderly: Historical Perspectives (Routledge, 1991), pp. 74–101 and Margaret Pelling, 'Medical Practice in Early Modern England: Trade or Profession?', in W. Prest (ed.), *The Professions in Early Modern England* (Croom Helm, 1987), pp. 90–128; Simon & Schuster for Margaret Pelling, 'Medicine and Sanitation', in J. F. Andrews (ed.), *William Shakespeare, His World, His Work, His Influence*, 3 vols (1985), vol. I, pp. 75–84; the Society of the Social History of Medicine for 'Child Health as a Social Value in Early Modern England', *Social History of Medicine*, 1 (1988), 135–64; The Wellcome Trust for Margaret Pelling, 'Healing the Sick Poor: Social Policy and Disability in Norwich, 1550–1640', *Medical History*, 29 (1985), 115–37 (Copyright The Trustee, The Wellcome Trust, reproduced with permission).

Abbreviations

Beier and Finlay, *London 1500–1700*	A. L. Beier and R. Finlay (eds), *London 1500–1700: The Making of the Metropolis* (London, 1986)
Bull. Hist. Med.	*Bulletin of the History of Medicine*
Bull. SSHM	*Bulletin of the Society for the Social History of Medicine*
CPL, Annals	London, Royal College of Physicians, Annals*
CLRO	Corporation of London Record Office, London
Eco. Hist. Rev.	*Economic History Review*
DNB	*Dictionary of National Biography*
DSB	*Dictionary of Scientific Biography*
Furnivall, *Vicary*	F. J. Furnivall and P. Furnivall (eds), *The Anatomie of the Bodie of Man by Thomas Vicary*, Early English Text Society Extra Ser. LIII (1888)
Hudson and Tingey, *Records*	W. Hudson and J. C. Tingey (eds), *The Records of the City of Norwich*, 2 vols (Norwich and London, 1906–10)
Marland and Pelling, *Task of Healing*	H. Marland and M. Pelling (eds), *The Task of Healing: Medicine, Religion and Gender in England and the Netherlands 1450–1800* (Rotterdam, 1996)
NCC	Norwich Consistory Court
NRO	Norfolk Record Office, Norwich
OED	*Oxford English Dictionary*
P & P	*Past and Present*
PCC	Prerogative Court of Canterbury
Pelling, 'Appearance and Reality'	M. Pelling, 'Appearance and Reality: Barber-surgeons, the Body and Disease', in Beier and Finlay, *London 1500–1700*, pp. 82–112
Pelling, 'Apprenticeship'	M. Pelling, 'Apprenticeship, Health and Social Cohesion in Early Modern London', *History Workshop Journal*, 37 (1994), 33–56
Pelling, 'Child Health'	Chapter 5 in the present volume; see also Acknowledgements[†]

Pelling, 'Compromised by Gender'	M. Pelling, 'Compromised by Gender: The Role of the Male Medical Practitioner in Early Modern England', in Marland and Pelling, *Task of Healing*, pp. 101–33
Pelling, 'Food, Status and Knowledge'	Chapter 2 in the present volume
Pelling, 'Healing the Sick Poor'	Chapter 4 in the present volume; see also Acknowledgements[†]
Pelling, 'Illness among the Poor'	Chapter 3 in the present volume; see also Acknowledgements[†]
Pelling, 'Medicine and the Environment'	Chapter 1 in the present volume; see also Acknowledgements[†]
Pelling, 'Nurses'	Chapter 8 in the present volume
Pelling, 'Occupational Diversity'	Chapter 9 in the present volume; see also Acknowledgements[†]
Pelling, 'Old Age, Poverty and Disability'	Chapter 6 in the present volume; see also Acknowledgements[†]
Pelling, 'Older Women'	Chapter 7 in the present volume
Pelling, *Strength of the Opposition*	M. Pelling, *The Strength of the Opposition: The College of Physicians and Irregular Medical Practice in Early Modern London* (Macmillan, Basingstoke, forthcoming)
Pelling, 'Trade or Profession'	Chapter 10 in the present volume; see also Acknowledgements[†]
Pelling and Webster, 'Medical Practitioners'	M. Pelling and C. Webster, 'Medical Practitioners' in Webster, *H, M & M*, pp. 165–235
PHE	Wrigley and Schofield, *Population History*
Phythian-Adams, *Desolation of a City*	C. Phythian-Adams, *Desolation of a City: Coventry and the Urban Crisis of the Late Middle Ages* (Cambridge, 1979)
Pound, *Census*	J. F. Pound, *The Norwich Census of the Poor 1570*, Norfolk Record Society XL (1971)[‡]
PRO	Public Record Office, London
Slack, *Impact of Plague*	P. Slack, *The Impact of Plague in Tudor and Stuart England* (London, 1985)
Webster, *Great Instauration*	C. Webster, *The Great Instauration: Science, Medicine and Reform 1626–1660* (London, 1975)
Webster, *H, M & M*	C. Webster (ed.), *Health, Medicine and Mortality in the Sixteenth Century* (Cambridge, 1979)

Wrigley and Schofield, *Population History*	E. A. Wrigley and R. S. Schofield, *The Population History of England 1541–1871* (London, 1981)
Young, *Annals*	S. Young, *Annals of the Barber-Surgeons of London* (1890; repr. New York, 1978)

All dates are given in New Style.

* All quotations and page numbers are from the translation/transcription of the Annals produced in the 1950s and now available on microfilm.

† References to the previously published essays give the original page numbers first, followed by the equivalent page numbers in the present volume in brackets.

‡ All quotations are from Pound's edition of the census. Outside quotations, first names of individuals have been modernised, while surnames are as transcribed by Pound.

Introduction

The first part of the title of this book is intended to signify two things. First, I want to indicate the extent to which early modern people, especially in towns, had reason to believe that their lives would be affected by illness, disability, and disease. These dangers were felt, although not equally, by all groups in society. Although the structure and practice of medicine was often as hierarchical as other social structures of the period, the perceived threats to bodily integrity, term of life, and physical existence of the self, family, and friends were present enough to bridge social divisions and to create something like a common sense of human frailty. Such fears, it should be stressed, were levelling without being democratic. Social barriers remained intact, but networks of information about cures and practitioners ramified across divisions of gender, age, and class. When it came to illness, a Privy Councillor could learn from his laundress, a husband from his wife, a philosopher from an old woman, a gentleman from his servant, a bishop from a cunning man, an empiric from a collegiate physician, a Protestant from a Catholic, an Englishwoman from an Italian. This did not imply real or lasting tolerance, nor would one party to the exchange of information necessarily refrain from taking advantage of the other. However, something about the imperative to communicate on such matters was recognised by all parties, and proved a major obstacle to attempts by medical corporations at restriction and regulation.

Awareness of a common fate can be seen as particularly acute at a time when, following the Reformation, religious consolations for the degradation and death of the body seemed to have been removed further from the individual's reach. At the same time, God seemed to be devising new punishments for new levels of sin and disobedience. Rampant new diseases (syphilis or the French pox, the English sweat), and increased devastation from old enemies, such as plague, added troubling new dimensions to all forms of human contact, including sexual behaviour. Contact with other people became, during the sixteenth century, both a curse and a blessing. Contemporary awareness of this dilemma burst out in black humour, satire and cynicism, fascination with disguise and display, and an extreme and inventive physicality of language which has probably never been equalled since the Jacobean period for its wit and lack

1

of prurience. The same dilemma was very evident in attitudes to the poor, and can be inferred from increased ambivalence, as expressed across much of the social spectrum, towards spaces, things, and even people (alehouses, baths, prostitutes) which were consolations and yet involved indiscriminate sharing with strangers.

In spite of recent interest in topics like gender and the history of the body, these aspects of early modern life have generally been regarded as peripheral. British historians of the postwar period have been persuaded of the importance of plague as one cause of the restructuring of social policy and social obligation, but they have generally been less willing than earlier generations of continental scholars to allow other disease conditions to have had such a role. Today's cultural historians, whom one might expect to be more interested in such phenomena, have seen it as part of their ideological brief to disengage from the material, or at least from the material as other than symbolic. 'Real' causes, along with 'real' changes, have been somewhat devalued. If early modern people seemed to see change and to fear disaster, rather than the continuity and stability carefully constructed by many historians, then we are asked to seek the explanation in changing meanings, rather than real events. My own view is that the cultural and the material, attitudes and 'reality', should if possible be brought together, just as it is desirable to bring together the findings of historical demography, and the issues of human agency and human suffering which lie behind them. Urban historians have moved away from controversies over crisis and decline, but I would like to suggest that the evidence which led some to locate decline in the period before 1570, and others in the period after this date, has still to be taken into account.[1] I survey some aspects of the environment in which Shakespeare's contemporaries found themselves, and their responses to it, in Chapter 1.

The drive to communicate mentioned earlier was of course a broadly based impulse; information on medical matters was usually conveyed within a religious or moral framework. Communication of this kind was represented in the well-documented upsurges in the sixteenth century of medical and health-related publications in the vernacular. Although it should not be exaggerated, 'commonness' was also something happening to medical ideas and practices in the Tudor and Stuart period.[2] Particularly in towns, the circulation of 'bills' (prescriptions) was probably close to universal, even in a period when illiteracy was still a significant factor. Other forms of communication were more exclusive, so that medical knowledge was held in common – and fought for – at a number of different levels. The competing natural philosophies on which learned medicine could be based were shared by significant groups among the laity. Even academic medicine had to share its basic skills with other groups who attended the universities; others in this period besides those intending to qualify

1. J. Barry, 'Introduction', in Barry (ed.), *The Tudor and Stuart Town: A Reader* (London and New York, 1990), pp. 6–7.
2. On this theme see also Pelling, 'Knowledge Common and Acquired: the Education of Unlicensed Medical Practitioners in Early Modern London', in V. Nutton and R. Porter (eds), *The History of Medical Education in Britain* (Amsterdam and Atlanta, GA, 1995), pp. 250–79.

in medicine were interested in the medical ideas which circulated as part of the 'informal curriculum'. In response to this situation, the College of Physicians of London was by 1600 trying to insist upon criteria for qualification which were not only recondite, but also (given the mode of examination) subjective.[3] Increasingly however the College was obliged, not least by the interests of some of its own members, to compromise with rival systems of medical knowledge. Recently, historians have given prominence to the need for physicians to 'share a language' with their elite clients. We should not lose sight of the fact that physicians in particular were also dependent for self-definition on forms of knowledge which were *not* held in common. Chapter 2 suggests that academically qualified physicians of this period gradually abandoned one form of intellectual capital, Galenic dietetics, which was becoming 'common', for another, the physiology of the Scientific Revolution. Unlike Galenic dietetics, Harveian physiology, widely acclaimed for its intellectual qualities, had, at least at this time, relatively little significance for medical practice. This point, which arguably helped to preserve the physicians' monopoly over their intellectual resources, was generally appreciated by seventeenth-century commentators.

The second message of my title is that the essays in this book are concerned primarily with the middling to lower sorts in early modern society. Historians regularly deplore the comparative neglect of these groups. It is true also for the medical occupations that elite physicians, and their polar opposites, the least orthodox among the irregulars, have received more attention than the far more numerous practitioners occupying the artisanal middle ground, or practising informally in everyday obscurity. One reason for this bias has been the historiography constructed by medical practitioners themselves as part of their urgent need to acquire credentials as a learned profession. Chapter 10 discusses why professionalisation as defined in the nineteenth and twentieth centuries is far too narrow a construct to be applicable to early modern English medicine, and further suggests that the same process of professional self-definition also devalued the crafts and trades. It is necessary to acknowledge that, from its foundation in the early sixteenth century, the London College of Physicians began evolving an ideology closely related to modern professional ideals. In other respects, however, early modern medicine is better seen in terms of a combination of craft and trade, with the important proviso that we should restore to our definition of craft and trade the concern for standards and brotherhood disparaged by the later world of *laissez faire*. For all these reasons, my title refers to 'medical occupations', rather than to the medical profession, or simply to medicine.

Beginning with an interest in medical practitioners at or below the level of the artisan, I have also sought for information about the health status of the poor, defined here as a numerous group including up to one-third of a given population. This line of investigation, although sometimes frustrating because of the terseness of many of the sources, has led to an awareness of the place

3. The College is given more attention in Pelling, 'Compromised by Gender' and *The Strength of the Opposition.*

of health and medicine in the social institutions, especially poor relief and apprenticeship, which most affected the lives of the poor and middling sorts outside the family. That ample evidence exists for this position is, I hope, demonstrated by Chapters 3 and 4 in Part I, and all of the chapters in Part II. There is still much to do on health practices within the early modern family, but the importance of health issues in this period is shown particularly by the way in which they are structured into institutions fundamental to early modern society. Such structuring was far from static: the ebb and flow of disease, or consciousness of disease, needs to be built into our analysis of family relations, and extra-familial institutions such as apprenticeship, and can help explain why such institutions changed over time.[4]

The poor rarely speak for themselves, but it is possible, at least to some extent, to deduce from the information gathered by town authorities something about the expedients the poor themselves adopted in trying to survive. In Chapters 4, 5, and 6, I argue that these expedients included forms of marriage, types of household, and 'exchanges' of family members. Such restructuring was however in no way limited in scope to the kin group. Apparently unrelated individuals were included in a household, or transferred to another household, in order to improve its chances of survival. Marriage between ostensibly ineligible partners – the aged, the disabled, those with large families – can be similarly interpreted. A major element in these forms of restructuring, and the one which has been most overlooked by historians, is disability. Other expedients aimed at survival included forms of work, including work carried out by older people or the severely disabled. These employments deserve to be taken seriously, both with respect to the poor themselves and as part of the essential underpinning of urban life, however marginal they may appear in broad-brush economic terms. Many such employments were 'women's work', or closer in character to women's work, and some of them, like charring, were health-related.

A further theme of these essays, and particularly of Chapter 9, is that medicine has been neglected as an economic activity, because it has been defined too narrowly in professional terms. While it is essential, I believe, to consider work done for and by the poor in this discussion, it would be crass to suggest that illness and disease provided 'opportunities' for the poor. It is likely, for example, that parish women had little real choice when appointed to be searchers for the plague, just as many poor people were subjected to compulsory medical treatment by municipal authorities. The lazarhouse-keepers, the women practitioners, the 'keepers' and helpers, the washers and scourers, the nursekeepers, and the active young children who can be discerned among poor populations are best seen as mirroring the needs of the poor, rather than as providing the means of escape from deprivation. The early modern authorities discussed in Chapter 4 were observing the same symmetry in seeking to solve two problems at once by paying poor people to look after others in an equally vulnerable position. As Chapter 3 suggests, the poor may appear to define their own state of health in terms congruent with the limited terms used by poor-law

4. See also Pelling, 'Apprenticeship'.

authorities: that is, the poor were accounted able-bodied not according to any ideal standard, lack of symptoms, or even to the absence of disability or disease, but according to the ability to work. We need however to recognise that this limited kind of description is not a true measure of the extent of disadvantage, but an indication of low expectations and a shared recognition of the place of work during the whole lifecycle of the poor – men, women, and all but the youngest children.

Nonetheless, as already indicated, there were at this period no 'separate spheres' of rich and poor as far as medical practice was concerned. Lazarhouse-keepers were not necessarily poor themselves; the same may be true of some nursekeepers, just as many midwives have been found on closer investigation to be relatively prosperous. Older writers took for granted that most of the population before the nineteenth century had no access to medical services worthy of the name; medical care was necessarily confined to the rich. The existence of relatively elaborate systems of medical poor relief in some early modern towns has been overlooked even by more recent accounts, because it has been assumed that 'the profession' was insufficiently developed, or too small in numbers and too exclusively devoted to its patrons among the elite, for such systems to be feasible before the eighteenth century. This is a faulty deduction on several counts. Whatever their motivation, some late sixteenth- and early seventeenth-century urban authorities at least were prepared, as Chapter 4 shows, to employ the whole range of practitioners, including physicians and expensive specialists, to treat the poor. The same authorities, in a climate of increasing restriction on begging and vagrancy, continued to allow individuals to travel and to beg in order to pay for expensive cures. Although such policies might in many cases represent a resort to desperate measures, they should be seen as evidence of a relatively balanced faith in medical effectiveness. In general, the 'public' as well as the 'private' consumer of medical services was sceptical and highly selective. Ultimately, however, as was universally recognised, a selection had to be made; however far one travelled, or however widely one compared notes among family and friends, the imperative of need would force a decision to consult this practitioner or that. Early modern people had a clear understanding of the impulse towards faith in one's own chosen practitioner, but took care to hedge this about with as many worldly precautions as possible, including a system of contracts.

It is a basic premise of this book that early modern people were obsessed with health, its fragility, and with the means for preserving it. This set of attitudes was, I would maintain, matched in scale if not in specifics by what we can judge to be the 'reality' of everyday experience. For many historians, these are contentious statements, not so much for their content, which might be accepted without being given particular prominence, as for their implied methodology. In the first place, as I have already suggested, it is currently more usual for cultural and material phenomena to be dealt with by historians of contrasting persuasions, except, curiously enough, in the context of consumerism. Thus, for some cultural historians, civic ceremonies do not decline because they can no longer be paid for, as an economic historian might claim; or, sexual mores do not change because of the effects of venereal disease. Secondly, some would deny the possibility of attaining to *any* kind of historical 'reality', given our own prepossessions and the selectivity of the historical record. Such views have been asserted partly as a desirable corrective to the deeply rooted empiricism of Anglophone historians, and partly as an antidote to 'present-centred' historiography. These issues are felt particularly acutely by social historians of medicine, who hold to the social construction of knowledge, and, more controversially, to the social construction of disease, as bulwarks against the ahistorical approaches of the past.[5] The *bêtes noires* of social historians of medicine include the urge to diagnose retrospectively, to ascribe an historical actor's abilities or decisions primarily to some physical condition, to construct 'what if' hypotheses on the basis of the death or disablement of a major historical figure, to contrast the futile agonies of the past with the life-saving achievements of the present, to define present knowledge by past ignorance, or to build a reassuring chronology of milestones, discoveries, unsung heroes and great men, all according to modern interpretations and priorities.

It is arguable that many of these are now more truly described as straw men, rather than *bêtes noires*. Opinions undoubtedly differ as to whether the social history of medicine has 'come of age', but most of its practitioners would agree that the subject has gained sufficient maturity in historiographical terms not to need entrenched and defensive positions.[6] This also means, of course, that there are no easy targets any more. Social historians of medicine can no longer distinguish their own work simply by distancing it from hagiography or positivist chronologies. Very soon it will no longer be possible to catch the attention of generalists merely by the novelty or fairground appeal of our subject matter, or to impress historians of medicine by importing the frameworks used by generalists. It is only fair to add to this that social historians of medicine have been readier than generalists to experiment with new methodologies, or to import concepts from other disciplines, in particular philosophy, sociology, and anthropology. The liveliness and interest of the field owes much to its interdisciplinary character. Once the gap between generalists and social historians of medicine is bridged, however, this willingness to experiment may have to work much harder to justify itself.

Lyndal Roper has recently argued, with considerable subtlety, that respect for the priorities of the past may entail seeing categories such as gender, and attitudes of mind such as witchcraft beliefs, as having an absolute dimension rather than being wholly socially constructed.[7] Her argument may well apply *a fortiori* in the present context. In my own view, the social construction of disease,

5. These problems are lucidly explored in T. Ashplant and A. Wilson, 'Whig History and Present-centred History', *Historical Journal*, 31 (1988), 1–16; 'Present-centred History and the Problem of Historical Knowledge', ibid., pp. 253–74; L. J. Jordanova, 'The Social Construction of Medical Knowledge', *Social History of Medicine*, 8 (1995), 361–81.

6. Cf. A. Wear, 'Introduction', in Wear (ed.), *Medicine in Society: Historical Essays* (Cambridge, 1992), p. 1; L. Jordanova, 'Has the Social History of Medicine Come of Age?' [essay review], *Historical Journal*, 36 (1993), 437–49.

7. L. Roper, 'Introduction', in idem, *Oedipus and the Devil: Witchcraft, Sexuality and Religion in Early Modern Europe* (London and New York, 1994), pp. 1–34.

whatever its value as a defensive principle, cannot be applied universally. To put it baldly, even though any disease may be interpreted in a period-specific way in a given historical context, some diseases are more socially constructed than others. If it is applied universally, social constructionism runs into the danger of becoming anthropocentric. That is, it implies that no entities can be allowed an existence except as an extension of the human observer. Given the relatively brief span of recorded human consciousness, this seems radically to underestimate the potential for biological constancy (however interpreted). It is indeed of the first importance to respect the priorities and meanings expressed in a given historical period; some disease conditions certainly appear to have been entirely ephemeral and period-specific. But this should not mean, for example, denying that smallpox appears to have had a consistent character over many centuries, even though there were shifts in the way it was interpreted.

Consistently with this, it is hoped that the essays which follow give expression to a definition of 'social history of medicine' which is inclusive rather than exclusive. According to this definition, social history of medicine is not a 'soft' subject, or a history of medicine with medicine and science left out. Rather, it includes an obligation to consider medical ideas like any others, that is historically; and secondly, it recognises the need to make the subject both intelligible and interesting to generalists. This is a comprehensive and demanding approach which involves both moving on to the ground favoured by others, and at the same time redefining the territory. Many scholars have of course met us halfway, having become interested in subjects like mortality, women's bodies, philanthropy, or disease metaphors in literature. The 'social history of medicine' is now researched by many who would never define themselves in such terms either intellectually or institutionally. This is a tribute to the intrinsic interest of the subject, to the refusal of social history itself to lie down and die during what amounts to a little ice age, and to the intellectual zest of the interdisciplinary approach which social historians of medicine, rightly, feel impelled to adopt in order to deal with their problematic subject matter.

It may seem to contradict what I have just said that most of the essays in this volume make some reference to twentieth-century viewpoints, or use twentieth-century comparisons. My justification is partly pragmatic: the field is still – if not increasingly – dominated by those working on the most recent periods. This weighting against the early modern period, defined here as between 1500 and 1700, is evidenced even in the activities of the Society for the Social History of Medicine, to which many of these essays were first presented. It therefore seemed desirable to make some connection with prevailing concerns. In addition, my own first research was in the disease theories dominating nineteenth-century British public health, and I have continued to be intrigued by parallels and contrasts between the later and the earlier periods. Beyond such pragmatism, however, I would also like to claim a justification in principle. In spite of the comparative maturity of the subject, social historians of medicine have still to face the fact that even the academic audiences they wish to reach are imbued with preconceptions about health and medicine in the past in a way that is scarcely true of other historical subjects (a possible exception being the congruent area of the history of the family). To this extent there is still some life in the straw men previously referred to. However little they understand their own bodies, modern people tend to think they know what the experience of past bodies has been. The trend of such views is teleological: medicine goes on being able to do better and better, just as it goes on being more and more expensive. These preconceptions are a reflection both of current beliefs about what was 'the common lot' in past societies, and of the hegemony of scientific and medical ideas in modern western society. The scientifically trained minority today regularly deplores the ignorance of science among even educated people, but there can be no doubt that this same under-informed audience thinks it knows what science is, however limited its knowledge of what science contains. Twentieth-century laypeople may regard scientists as a breed apart, but the authority of science itself is not seriously questioned.

With medicine, the picture is somewhat modified. Regardless of how successful the 'scientising' of medicine in the present century has been, it remains, to use the traditional binaries, an art as well as a science. The period during which laypeople have lacked effective control over its ideas and institutions has been relatively brief in historical terms. Laypeople still – perhaps increasingly – claim some rights over their own bodies and lives, and therefore bring a mindset to bear on historical material relevant to the field, whether consciously or not. As already indicated, this is equally true of historians, and it seems better to confront this directly, rather than to pretend that there is no significant degree of prepossession about matters to do with medicine and health. Moreover, given the history of the history of medicine – which, as Chapter 10 suggests, includes extended service in the cause of the professionalisation of medicine itself – many of our ideas about earlier periods are descendants, recognised or not, of nineteenth-century historiography. Again, it seems better to have this out in the open. Finally, there is the vexed issue of how 'useful' history should be. The 'safe' position is that history is valuable for its own sake. While more than ready to defend this position, I do not see why history should not also inform the present, especially since the subjects we choose, and the ways in which we write about them, undeniably reflect current concerns. Similarly, given that medicine is an area in which modern society is disposed to be complacent with reference to the past, there seems no harm in occasionally questioning such complacency.

Some readers may be surprised, given the constant reference in the discussion so far to social history, by the extent to which all the chapters place emphasis on economic issues. An obvious point to make first is that social issues need not – perhaps should not – be considered separately from economic issues. There is currently a divide between qualitative and quantitative methodologies in economic history. Econometric history, in concentrating on what it can quantify, seeks to take on many of the attributes of a science, which means in ideological terms (it is assumed) an abandonment of social territory as pathless and soggy underfoot. Historians of science are perhaps well placed to judge whether this attempt is well-founded and whether it will sacrifice more than it gains. The essays here do not pretend to contribute to this debate. However, the economic issues with which they connect are also those which were found most interesting by the generations of historians associated with Fabian circles and the London School of Economics in the early decades of this century. At this time, as is well known, economic history was a radicalising force and included many areas which would now be regarded as belonging to social history. Quantification was important, but qualitative evidence was freely used. More recently, the works by these earlier generations of economic historians have enjoyed a revival, especially those by women scholars such as Dorothy George, Eileen Power, and Alice Clark, and many of them have been reissued.[8] Readers of the essays here will find repeated reference to these early studies, which I first began to find valuable when trying, as in Chapters 9 and 10, to look at medicine in the context of the guild structure. Interest in the guilds and companies has now revived considerably, although much less attempt has been made to reappraise their economic functions. Many of the older studies have not been superseded. They are cited for this reason, but also because it seems necessary to recognise how many current historiographical issues are reinventions rather than new departures.

Stress on economic issues was, in addition, one method of wresting medicine out of the isolated haven of professionalisation and back into relationship with other areas of economic activity. Given constantly-repeated reference in recent work by social historians of medicine to the concept of the 'medical marketplace', this may now seem like a work of supererogation. The claim by Harold Cook that practitioners perforce sold their skills in what he called the medical marketplace was based on conditions in early modern London.[9] It was primarily a claim about the ineffectiveness of medical regulation, the comparative inability of medical institutions to serve the interests of their members, and the difficulty experienced by regular practitioners in distinguishing themselves from the irregular, or of selling their services to patients on this basis. However, although presented in meticulous detail by Cook, the medical marketplace has, since its introduction, almost always been applied simply as a label, without any examination of its wider implications. While Cook himself cannot have had any such intention, the concept has merely come to reinforce traditional sceptical stereotypes about medicine, and has done little to connect medicine with other areas of economic life. The medical marketplace is assumed to represent the practice of *laissez-faire* in medicine without any consideration of whether this is generally applicable to the period in question, just as the 'market' itself is assumed always to be of one kind, that is, unregulated. Overall, the concept has been used by social historians to puncture the pretensions of early modern medicine, if not of medical practitioners in general. This may have been necessary and even desirable, but it adds no further historical depth to the discussion, may have few lasting effects, and will no doubt breed a form of revisionism which is likely to be equally self-referential.

8. For background, see P. Sharpe, 'Continuity and Change: Women's History and Economic History in Britain', *Eco. Hist. Rev.*, 48 (1995), 353–69; M. Berg, *A Woman in History: Eileen Power, 1889–1940* (Cambridge, 1996); J. Lewis, *Women and Social Action in Victorian and Edwardian England* (Aldershot, 1991).

9. H. Cook, *The Decline of the Old Medical Regime in Stuart London* (Ithaca, NY, 1986).

A convincing account of medicine as an economic activity must move outside the professionally-related criteria of interest versus disinterest, to prove in detail *how* medicine was an economic activity, to what parts of the contemporary economy it was most closely related and why, what congruence there was of skills and materials, how transactions between patient and practitioner actually took place, and to what extent such transactions still remained outside the system of exchange. I attempt to take up these issues in Chapters 9, 10 and 2. Medicine itself presented so varied a picture that no single economic formulation is adequate. Further, restoring an economic dimension to medicine should not be primarily a derogatory process, especially as many early modern economic institutions recognised the need for an ethical dimension. If contemporary economic practices and principles are the reference point, rather than those of the present day, there is far less danger of isolating the discussion from other important influences, such as religion or philanthropy.[10]

A starting point for these essays was the finding that medical practitioners, however various, were far more substantial as an occupational group than previously supposed, and therefore of greater significance economically.[11] However, abandoning exclusive professional definitions as essentially anachronistic, and modifying the usual terms of occupational analysis, also led me to take a fresh look at how the medical occupations were followed. As Chapter 9 shows, taking Norwich as a case-study, a great many different practitioners can be found. But, although the ratio of practitioners to population was surprisingly favourable, and demand for their services never less than high, this was balanced by a part-time, piecework, and patchwork mode of earning a living. This 'occupational diversity' is alien to professional and even occupational ideals. It has been recognised mainly as an increasing aspect of rural occupations in this period, as a long-standing if not definitive characteristic of the work of women, or as an indication of the early collapse of guild restrictions under the pressure of the emergent capitalist economy. Increasing evidence suggests, however, that it was typical of the reality of early modern lives, regardless of the constant contemporary emphasis on (male) occupational identity. Such emphasis may indeed have been prompted more by the fragility of fixed occupational identity for men, than by its strength. The form of occupational identity which is now emerging is more one of process, than of structure.[12]

The lifecycle version of occupational diversity, in which a man might over a lifetime follow various occupations according to age and circumstances, is perhaps more generally accepted by historians than the version in which a man followed more than one occupation simultaneously. Chapter 9 provides a number of examples of the latter kind. Such shifts were possibly as common among the

10. On religion and medicine, see most recently O. P. Grell and A. Cunningham (eds), *Religio Medici: Medicine and Religion in Seventeenth-Century England* (Aldershot, 1996); D. Harley, 'Anglo-American Perspectives on Early Modern Medicine: Society, Religion and Science' [essay review], *Perspectives on Science*, 4 (1996), 346–86. On philanthropy, see J. Barry and C. Jones (eds), *Medicine and Charity before the Welfare State* (London and New York, 1991).

11. Pelling and Webster, 'Medical Practitioners'.

12. P. J. Corfield, 'Defining Urban Work', in idem and D. Keene (eds), *Work in Towns 850–1850* (Leicester, etc., 1990), pp. 216ff; Barry, 'Introduction', pp. 14, 9.

highly educated as they were among the illiterate poor. Joan Thirsk, whose work has done so much to illuminate by-employments in the countryside, has placed a positive emphasis on the period between 1500 and 1700 as one in which occupations became fluid and innovation could flourish.[13] The medical occupations in many ways confirm this. Certainly, as examples in Chapter 9 from a range of locations suggest, many medical practitioners can be found who appear to have taken full advantage of this kind of flexibility to move in and out, not only of the different medical crafts, but also of other branches of manufacturing and entrepreneurial activity. It is undoubtedly wrong, as already indicated, to interpret such interdigitation simply as an effect of poverty, low status, and failure to achieve recognition as a craft. It also seems clear that medicine provides confirmation of a kind of closure of opportunities in the later seventeenth century, when educational criteria for entry began to become more demanding, and medicine itself both more dynastic and more generally respectable. The 'occupational diversity' of medical practitioners between 1500 and 1700 has many facets, but can undoubtedly be seen, at least in the cities, as part of the early growth of consumerism suggested by Thirsk.

There is nonetheless a negative side to this burgeoning activity. For example, the issue of status of medical practitioners is a particularly complicated one for historians, given the extremely various character of the occupational group (something which is increasingly recognised for many other occupational groups), and the need to counteract preconceptions essentially based on later polemic. Thus, the status of apothecaries has tended to be underestimated, except by historians of pharmacy, and barber-surgeons have been too readily dismissed as a manual craft. Overall, on the other hand, the social status of medical practitioners was probably lower in the early modern period than has been assumed. The dilemmas and aspirations of the academically qualified physicians, hardly then admitted to the ranks of the learned professions, and hovering uneasily on the outskirts of gentry status, epitomise the troubled consciousness of the middling sort. For physicians, most forms of occupational diversity were full of pitfalls and undesirable associations, and it is this view which helped to shape their definitions of what a profession should be, however diversified they may have been themselves. Physicians put a great deal of effort into creating an acceptable social identity, which in the end was remarkably successful.[14] It is no accident, I would like to suggest, that demand for the services of physicians has come to be associated with a relatively agreeable picture of urban life – improved towns, urban sociability, the growth of leisure, greater prosperity, and gentrification.

Although physicians, and probably apothecaries to an even greater extent, unquestionably felt some of the mild but determined glow of the 'urban renaissance', the essays in this volume mainly seek to convey a different and complementary emphasis. I would see a high level of consumption of medical care not as by definition a measure of prosperity, but also as an aspect of economic

13. J. Thirsk, 'Plough and Pen: Agricultural Writers in the Seventeenth Century', in T. H. Aston, P. R. Coss, C. Dyer and J. Thirsk (eds), *Social Relations and Ideas* (Cambridge, 1983), pp. 299, 318.
14. See Pelling, 'Compromised by Gender'.

disadvantage. As Chapter 4 indicates, early modern society provided some means whereby the poor gained access to expensive medical care, and also retained, in a variety of contexts statutory and otherwise, the convention that medicine practised out of charity was both laudable and free from penalty regardless of outcome. This convention was in part a recognition of the fact that, just as sickness could bring ruin, so the better-off would beggar themselves, and the poor resort to socially undesirable measures like selling their clothing or the tools of their trade, in order to pay for medical care. Those who gave medical services for nothing were therefore performing a public service, regardless of the interests of qualified practitioners who charged their patients. Historically, as indicated earlier, there is little evidence to suggest that poor people refrained from seeking medical care simply because they were poor. Rather, poverty determined the forms of care they were able to afford, in terms of cash or kind. Hence, in early modern society, the enormously wide range of forms and scales of payment for medical services, as well as the existence of many forms of practice disliked either by orthodox practitioners or by the elite. Although the poor had more reason than any other group in society to hope that their chosen remedy would be effective, it is also probable that medical care was consumed in excess, like alcohol and tobacco in the same period, as a kind of consolation for insecurity and disadvantage.

Insecurity was not of course confined to the poor. Modern critics have characterised the medical profession as 'anxiety makers'; present-day clinicians, on their own behalf, see uncertainty as an inevitable part of confronting those aspects of the individual case which remain unique, unpredictable, and impossible to explain.[15] However, I would also argue as others have done that, for modern as well as for earlier periods, medicine has a major role to play in the 'management of uncertainty'. Was medicine, then, yet another means of ensuring stability in early modern society? This seems a somewhat perverse reading, at least in so far as it stresses stability rather than the social and economic conditions prompting the search for stability. A study of health, disease and medicine in this period does little to encourage the more optimistic view now current in the literature on early modern towns. The essays here do, of course, tend to concentrate on poorer groups in society, and the conditions threatening their survival; the medical occupations could also perhaps be seen as peculiarly related to uncertainties connected to social mobility and social change. As I have suggested elsewhere, the crisis in gender relations suggested by many historians for this period can be plausibly connected not only to the incidence of particular diseases, particularly venereal disease, but also to the status difficulties of practitioners themselves.[16] However, this does not mean that it is right to see issues of health and medicine as a special case which tends to overstress uncertainty, crisis, death, and decay.

There can be little doubt that the constant presence of disability and disease in society and in the minds of individuals has been underestimated as an aspect

15. A. Comfort, *The Anxiety Makers: Some Curious Preoccupations of the Medical Profession* (London, 1967); J. A. Barondess, 'The Impossible in Medicine', *Perspectives in Biology and Medicine*, 29 (1986), 521–9.
16. Pelling, 'Compromised by Gender'.

of contemporary experience, partly because of the conventional divisions of labour observed by historians, and partly because it has seemed that a sophisticated historical approach of the traditional kind could at most make some reference to filth or smells and then pass on. What is being urged here is not any return either to dwelling on horrors for the sake of it, or to simplistic explanations in terms of the total lack of hygiene of early modern environments. Rather, the full spectrum of disease and disability should be recognised as a potential factor in all our historical calculations; secondly, contemporary consciousness of health and disease, which was pervasive, should be recognised as a means of expression of other forms of doubt and uncertainty. There is of course a kind of circularity about this, which can nonetheless be defended as being in fact part of the historical picture. This becomes evident as soon as (for example) one tries to disentangle the use of medical metaphors in virtually any form of contemporary literature, from satire to sermons.[17]

I have tried in many of these essays to give recognition to the pervasiveness of health issues by dealing with groups or populations, rather than individuals. This is also another way of trying to arrive at what was 'the common lot'. None of the chapters is demographical, but several draw on the findings of historical demographers, and suggest variants of some demographic generalisations. My intention here is to link demographical factors with the social and the economic. I have given less attention to mortality than to morbidity, partly for this reason. Only the most preliminary estimates can be provided for morbidity, but it is some comfort that the nature and incidence of sickness is equally difficult to measure in the present day. As Chapter 3 in particular illustrates, early modern authorities themselves attempted to measure the extent of sickness, recognising its importance in creating poverty and undermining social cohesion. As historians we have yet to catch up with contemporary perceptions. The minorities involved in crime and disorder are counted and studied minutely, but the disabled and the infectious are overlooked except in the context of poor relief and plague. It is necessary, at the least, to recognise that a minimum of 10 per cent of the population, at any one time, would be physically or mentally disqualified from attending school, leaving home, entering service or apprenticeship, migrating, taking communion, turning up at musters, becoming freemen, governing a household or family, taking parochial office, and any number of other activities which concerned the bulk of the population. Of course there are modifications to this, as mortality rates among the sick and disabled were presumably high, and the contemporary definition of 'impotent' was a comparatively narrow one. However this is more than compensated for by the figure of 10 per cent, which is low even in modern terms.

Obviously, the sick and disabled do not deserve attention simply so that they can be counted out of our calculations. They also merit attention as a group in their own right. Moreover, if the sick and disabled were not necessarily excluded from social and economic life, as seems to have been the case, then

17. See for example S. C. Lorch, 'Medical Theory and Renaissance Tragedy' (University of Louisville PhD thesis, 1976); D. Harley, 'Medical Metaphors in English Moral Theology, 1560–1660', *Journal of the History of Medicine*, 48 (1993), 396–435.

we have even more reason to take into account the nature and effects of their interactions with others. Sources dealing with the sick in any systematic way are extremely rare, which is why considerable use has been made in these essays of the 1570 Norwich census of the poor. Especially after the full version was unearthed and edited by Pound, this census was mentioned by a number of historians, but in general they were content with the extensive forms of analysis Pound provided.[18] The census had few attractions for historical demographers because the centre in question (Norwich) was too large for the purposes of reconstitution, and the census itself was of only a selected part (albeit a significant part) of the population. For present purposes on the other hand, as I hope these essays show, the census is invaluable.

Aside from the census, the account of health, sickness, and medical practice given here is one which emerges from the use of as wide a range of sources as possible. In the past, disproportionate attention has been paid to the literary remains of practitioners themselves; these sources are indeed valuable, but they are also very often tendentious, and there is a great deal that they exclude. Although it is hardly sensible to overlook obvious sources, such as the records of the London medical corporations (most of the provincial equivalents are lost), there is much to be gained from a realisation that there is scarcely any kind of source for this period which does not provide evidence relating to medicine and health. At the same time, of course, we have to remember in regard to *all* sources the need (of which social historians of medicine are only too well aware) to bear in mind the purpose for which such sources were produced. The obvious point is that most early modern records, like the Norwich census, were produced by men. The use of a wider range of sources has promoted a much more realistic picture of the occupation of medicine itself, and of the importance of health-related issues in early modern society. A variety of sources, together with a peculiarly rich single source, also makes it possible to look closely at less visible social groups: not just the sick and disabled, but different agegroups, including children (Chapter 5) and old people (Chapters 6 and 7), and thoroughly submerged groups, such as poor working wives and widows (Chapter 7). These can be glimpsed, by turns, as at risk from sickness and disability, and as looking after the sick and disabled, as well as in their own right as wage-earners. A further reason why a range of sources is necessary is that the great bulk of this activity took place without benefit of institutions, except in the broader sense of administrative institutions such as the parish, the guild, quarter sessions, or the town council. Institutionalisation in terms of bricks and mortar tends to attract our attention automatically, and, from Bentham to Foucault, has tended to dominate ideologically. But for early modern England, most common experience of life's chances and changes, even in towns, lay outside institutions, not inside them.

The intention of looking at as broad a range of sources as possible is also what determined the emphasis evident in these essays on Norwich, London, and East Anglia. In attempting to ask relatively new questions, it seemed

18. See Pound, *Census*.

sensible to look first at where record survival was best.[19] The Norwich records proved to be particularly fertile ground for the topics tackled here. This means that the essays concentrate on a part of the country which was, comparatively, both well-populated and prosperous, in spite of experiencing its share of epidemic outbreaks and a high rate of immigration. Norwich was in addition a town (also known as a city, and a provincial capital) which, even if too large and too variegated to be described as 'godly', was at least influenced by Puritan ideas.[20] As might be expected, there is considerable compatibility between Norwich and London. Whether or not the findings here are representative for different parts of the country remains an open question. However, there are some grounds for confidence that comparable areas – such as the southwest – would produce a similar picture. In the meantime, it is hoped that these essays together provide a close case-study of a particular location, as well as some indication of different forms of metropolitan influence.

A final justification for use of the Norwich records in particular is the access they provide to information about women's work. As far as possible, males and females are considered evenhandedly in these essays, both among the sick and as medical practitioners. Gender is also an integral factor in the discussion of medical knowledge in Chapter 2. But it is hoped too that the use of a more flexible definition of employment, which has proved fruitful in analysing the medical occupations, has also helped to reveal more about the varied nature of women's work. As Merry Wiesner has shown for early modern Germany, the medical occupations are well suited to provide links between gender studies and economic history. Many of the women workers considered in the chapters that follow, especially Chapters 6 and 7, are both elderly and poor: I would like to argue, however, that even in this supposedly extreme case, women can qualify, in Pamela Sharpe's terms, as independent economic agents.[21] In this sense women's work, even outside the household, is something more than a set of negations of the characteristics defining the work of men. Medical or health-related occupations also supply specific case-studies which illuminate the issue of the *longue durée* as an aspect of the depressed status and menial character of women's work. One can see evidence of lack of change in the low-status, low-reward area of cleaning and laundrywork, and even in the stereotypes attached to it. Sicknursing, on the other hand, which is discussed in detail in Chapter 8, was an area of work related to cleaning and washing which was nonetheless subject to considerable change in the course of the seventeenth century, so much so that the problems of defining the occupation of the sicknurse are as complex as they are interesting. This occupation is decidedly a neglected topic for this period, apparently not because of the problems of definition, but because it has been taken for granted. Although, as I argue, not confined to women, sicknursing appears to have been a woman's task which changed its public profile, if not

19. See Pelling and Webster, 'Medical Practitioners', p. 167.
20. For a recent assessment see P. Slack, "'Great and Good Towns'", in P. Clark (ed.), *Urban History of Britain, Vol. 2: 1540–1840* (Cambridge University Press, forthcoming).
21. M. E. Wiesner, *Working Women in Renaissance Germany* (New Brunswick, 1986); idem, *Women and Gender in Early Modern Europe* (Cambridge, 1993); Sharpe, 'Continuity and Change', p. 363.

its content, quite markedly over the period in question. At the same time, however, sicknursing no sooner emerged into the public arena than it attracted a pejorative gender-related stereotype which, whatever its specificities (such as a connection with infectious disease), is a reminder of the constant features adversely affecting the value placed on women's work in the public realm.

In summary, my main hope for these essays is that together they will help to build bridges – between specialists and generalists, and between areas of scholarship such as economic history, social history, historical demography, English literature, and gender studies. I would also like to contribute to comparisons between men's work and women's work. As my title implies, I wish to capture something of the experience of early modern people from the middling and lower orders, which nonetheless had intimate connection with the concerns of the whole society. Most of all, perhaps, my aim is to suggest that health and medicine, with their constant effects on the minds and bodies of early modern people, should be regarded by generalists not as intriguing or repellent technicalities, but as an integral part of the subject matter of their own histories.

PART I

THE URBAN ENVIRONMENT

CHAPTER ONE

Medicine and the Environment in Shakespeare's England

The relationship between human beings and their physical environment is an area of great historical interest and wide extent, which has only recently begun to attract its due share of attention from early modern historians.[1] It has fairly consistently been assumed that Elizabethan people were closer to the natural world, the soil, the seasons, and even to death than their twentieth-century western counterparts. This greater intimacy has been made to look alternately romantic or primitive, just as the mentality of the period itself has been seen as vibrant or melancholy. Shakespeare's contemporaries were perhaps better able than modern people to comprehend, if not to resolve, contradictory experience, to express the sense of spring as well as the bitterness of winter, to describe beauty as well as degradation.[2]

Their relationship with the natural world was at once closer and more casual. Thus, an early modern woman might suckle a young puppy to keep herself in milk until it was proper to put her baby to the breast.[3] A continuity in raw materials still linked production with both the kitchen and the outside world.[4] Animal (including human) excrements, properly treated, were used in medicine as well as agriculture and industry (urine, for example, being traditionally used as a bleach).[5] But the greater proximity of the natural world was also an object

1. Recent trends are incisively surveyed by M. Jenner, 'Early Modern English Conceptions of "Cleanliness" and "Dirt" as Reflected in the Environmental Regulation of London, *c.* 1530–*c.* 1700' (University of Oxford DPhil thesis, 1991), forthcoming as a monograph published by Oxford University Press.

2. In intellectual terms, this is a long-standing topic among historians of ideas, literature, and art: see R. Colie, *Paradoxia Epidemica: The Renaissance Tradition of Paradox* (Princeton, NJ, 1966). More recently, historians have attempted to demonstrate such habits of mind within social practice itself.

3. The most extensive discussion is K. Thomas, *Man and the Natural World: Changing Attitudes in England 1500–1800* (London, 1983). On the interpretation of suckling practices, see G. Paster, *The Body Embarrassed: Drama and the Disciplines of Shame in Early Modern England* (Ithaca, NY, 1993), chaps 4 and 5, esp. p. 233.

4. Pelling, 'Medicine and Economic Incentives in the Early Modern Period', *Bull. SSHM*, 41 (1987), 59–61.

5. R. Reynolds, *Cleanliness and Godliness, or the Further Metamorphosis* (London, [1946]), pp. 33, 199. D. Woodward, '"An Essay on Manures": Changing Attitudes to Fertilization in England, 1500–1800', in J. Chartres and D. Hey (eds), *English Rural Society, 1500–1800* (Cambridge, 1990), pp. 251–78. For significantly 'distant' references by collegiate physicians to the prescription of excrements, see Francis Herring, *Certaine Rules . . . for this Time of Pestilential Contagion* (London, 1625), sig. B2; Nathaniel Hodges, *Loimologia* [1665], trans. J. Quincy (London, 1720), p. 216. See also Pelling, 'Compromised by Gender', pp. 107–9.

of fear, as in the suspicion of small animals kept as pets, or in the notion of many sick people that their symptoms were akin to, or even caused by, the invasion of their bodies by worms, insects, or even small mammals such as moles.[6] Living and organic matter of all kinds was thus at once more useful and more intrusive. This situation aptly bears out the contention of anthropologists that pollution can often be defined as material in the wrong place, and is thus not only relative to the society in which it occurs but also likely to vary within that society.[7] However, it also tends to challenge any assumption of absolute relativism with respect to certain crucial substances such as human excrement.

Shakespeare's England was still largely a rural society, including hinterlands such as the forest and fenlands.[8] Even the largest provincial towns, such as Norwich, and London itself, included open space, river meadows, orchards and walled gardens, although these more natural areas were not necessarily idyllic.[9] While Elizabethans used colour lavishly, most interiors were plain, dark and sparsely furnished.[10] Living space for the most part did not as yet show a material artificiality that implied a necessary separateness from the unadorned world outside. By contrast, the dress of the wealthier classes displayed an extreme artificiality that distinguished individuals from their surroundings. At the same time, the style of dress and accessories adopted was one in which most of the body was concealed from view unless it could be satisfactorily presented. Some habits were becoming less communal; in the case of eating habits this may have been, at least in part, a response to the prevalence of venereal disease.[11]

The Elizabethan period was markedly one of change and of conscious awareness of mutability. The artificial environment was being transformed as the result of the 'great rebuilding' which became evident towards the end of the sixteenth century. For certain classes, and certain regions, there was a rising standard of material comfort and even luxury. The classical theme of the dichotomy between urban and rural life was finding a new relevance with the enormous growth of London, which was among the four largest cities in Europe by 1600.[12]

6. See for example M. MacDonald, *Mystical Bedlam: Madness, Anxiety and Healing in Seventeenth-Century England* (Cambridge, 1981), pp. 203–4. See also the empathetic discussion of Piero Camporesi: *The Incorruptible Flesh*, trans. T. Croft-Murray (Cambridge, 1988).

7. The locus classicus here is Mary Douglas, *Purity and Danger. An Analysis of Concepts of Pollution and Taboo* (1966; 2nd impr. London, 1976).

8. D. M. Palliser, *The Age of Elizabeth* (London and New York, 1983), p. 4; J. Thirsk (ed.), *The Agrarian History of England and Wales, Vol. IV: 1500–1640* (Cambridge, 1967). On urbanisation in general in this period, see P. Clark (ed.), *The Urban History of Britain, Vol. 2: 1540–1840* (Cambridge University Press, forthcoming).

9. Like other such accounts, Simon Forman's autobiography contains many references to incidents in London gardens and orchards: A. L. Rowse, *The Case Books of Simon Forman* (London, 1976), pp. 65–6, 294, 296, 299, 301 and *passim*. See also Thomas Dekker, *Villanies Discovered by Lanthorne and Candle-light* (London, 1620), sig. I2. Norwich was perhaps unusually well provided: P. Corfield, 'A Provincial Capital in the Late Seventeenth Century: the Case of Norwich', in P. Clark and P. Slack (eds), *Crisis and Order in English Towns 1500–1700* (London, 1972), p. 270.

10. P. Thornton, *Seventeenth-Century Interior Decoration in England, France and Holland* (New Haven, CT, and London, 1978), p. 4.

11. See Pelling, 'Appearance and Reality', esp. pp. 89–95. This last conclusion contrasts with the interpretations of N. Elias, *The Civilizing Process. Vol. 1: The History of Manners* (1939), trans. E. Jephcott (Oxford, 1983).

12. R. Machin, 'The Great Rebuilding: a Reassessment', *P & P*, 77 (1977), 33–56; C. Platt, *The Great Rebuildings of Tudor and Stuart England* (London, 1994). Beier and Finlay, *London 1500–1700*, p. 2, fig. 1.

Contemporaries were disturbed by evidence of social mobility and rifts in the social order.[13] As a whole, the population was much more mobile than is customarily believed, travelling on business, to marry, in search of work or subsistence, and for or during apprenticeships or service.[14] Although adolescents and young adults were the most mobile, both the very young and the very old could become rootless, and young children habitually changed households even – or perhaps especially – among the less prosperous. Pressure from substantial population growth gave a new dimension to this situation, increasing the gulf between rich and poor. By the end of Elizabeth's reign, England's population may have been 35 per cent higher than at its beginning. The Elizabethan Poor Law evolved to meet apparent threats to economic and social stability from resident as well as vagrant poor. Sickness and disability were perceived as creating poverty as well as danger from contagious disease; and local authorities invested in a wide range of medical services, as well as in clothing and diet, to alter the physical state and dependency of the poor.[15]

The easy impression that public and private standards of cleanliness were especially low during this period has been challenged but, except for Jenner's work on London, not systematically investigated.[16] Older writers often made a comparison with the middle ages, drawing attention to evidence such as the decline of communal bathing in the sixteenth century. For other historians, comparisons drawn between the eighteenth and nineteenth centuries from conflicting points of view, and, more recently, the notion of an eighteenth-century 'urban renaissance', have overshadowed the investigation of earlier periods, but it is clear that the element of public provision in early modern towns of relevant services such as street cleaning and paving should not be underestimated.[17] We should no longer assume that the development of these amenities was necessarily dependent upon the emergence of strong centralised government. Many commentators on the Tudor and early Stuart period have accepted

13. London was the focus of many of these anxieties: see I. Archer, *The Pursuit of Stability: Social Relations in Elizabethan London* (Cambridge, 1991). In general, see A. Fletcher and J. Stevenson (eds), *Order and Disorder in Early Modern England* (Cambridge, 1987); J. Boulton, 'The Quest for Stability in the Early Modern City' [essay review], *Journal of Urban History*, 19 (1993), 110–15.

14. See P. Clark and D. Souden (eds), *Migration and Society in Early Modern England* (London, 1987).

15. Palliser, *Age of Elizabeth*, p. 37; P. Slack, *Poverty and Policy in Tudor and Stuart England* (London and New York, 1988); Pelling, 'Healing the Sick Poor'.

16. Jenner, 'Early Modern English Conceptions', expands on many of the points that follow. Besides the work of the Webbs, J. H. Thomas, *Town Government in the Sixteenth Century* (London, 1933), is still useful. See also T. Atkinson, *Elizabethan Winchester* (London, 1963), chap. 11, and G. Mayhew, *Tudor Rye* (Falmer, 1987), pp. 42–8 (for sources); D. Palliser, 'Civic Mentality and the Environment in Tudor York', *Northern History*, 18 (1982), 78–115. On personal cleanliness, see V. Smith, 'Cleanliness: the Development of Idea and Practice in Britain 1770–1850' (University of London PhD thesis, 1985), currently being expanded for publication; Pelling, 'Appearance and Reality', pp. 93–4; G. Vigarello, *Concepts of Cleanliness: Changing Attitudes in France since the Middle Ages*, trans. J. Birrell (Cambridge, 1988); A. Labisch, *Homo Hygienicus. Gesundheit und Medizin in der Neuzeit* (Frankfurt and New York, 1992); K. Thomas, 'Cleanliness and Godliness in Early Modern England', in A. Fletcher and P. Roberts (eds), *Religion, Culture and Society in Early Modern Britain* (Cambridge, 1994), pp. 56–83. See in general G. Rosen, *A History of Public Health*, enlgd edn (1958; Baltimore, MD, 1993).

17. L. Mumford, *The Culture of Cities* (London, 1940), pp. 119–20; P. Borsay, *The English Urban Renaissance: Culture and Society in the Provincial Town, 1660–1770* (Oxford, 1991); see the debate between Borsay and A. McInnes in *P & P*, 126 (1990), 189–202.

uncritically, and extrapolated backwards from, the denunciation of prevailing urban conditions by late-seventeenth-century reformers of manners who aimed at a 'polite society'. The assertions of these reformers built upon the plague literature, which harped upon the concentration of sources of putrefaction.

Local geography – the state of natural drainage, rivers, brooks, types of soil, and even prevailing winds – had, and were seen as having, a major influence on local conditions, in particular the sources and degree of contamination of water supply.[18] In many respects, sixteenth-century urban life merely provided variations on problems inherent in any extensive human settlement, problems that were consequently provided for from an early period. The detailed regulation of markets included constant attention to the quality of provisions exposed for sale – especially meat, grain, bread, and ale or beer. In spite of the growth of inland trade, crafts and trades, especially those related to food and clothing, were still producing locally for local consumption, and municipal authorities were concerned by the effects on the public health of the activities of butchers, dyers, glovers, curriers, fishmongers, tanners, and the like.[19] These tradesmen were normally restricted in different ways, being required to operate outside the city walls, to burn their waste only at night, to divide it into a form suitable for disposal at certain sites, or to filter their contaminated effluents in sumps, or 'sinkers'. Some domestic industries (such as brewing, soap boiling, and sugar refining) were beginning to move on to an industrial scale of operation, to use coal rather than wood as fuel, and thus to change the nature of urban pollution.[20]

The economic situation of a town could mean considerable variation in its physical condition, and some major sixteenth-century towns felt themselves to be less populated, less well paved and cleaned, and generally less well 'edified' than at earlier periods.[21] Many of the larger corporate towns undertook more thorough paving in the course of the century, which provided raised footways and a central drainage channel.[22] In legal terms, the cleaning of all but the widest streets was effected by some variation on the ancient device of responsibility of the householder or tenant for that part of the highway coextensive with the house frontage. Like other responsibilities, the duty of overseeing street cleaning

18. On English geography and health, see the work of Mary Dobson, esp. her *Contours of Death and Disease in Early Modern England* (Cambridge, 1997). On the relevant concepts, see C. Hannaway, 'Environment and Miasmata', and M. Pelling, 'Contagion/Germ Theory/Specificity', both in W. F. Bynum and R. Porter (eds), *Companion Encyclopedia of the History of Medicine*, 2 vols (London and New York, 1993), vol. 1, pp. 292–308, 309–34; A. Wear, 'Making Sense of Health and the Environment in Early Modern England', in idem (ed.), *Medicine in Society: Historical Essays* (Cambridge, 1992), pp. 119–47.

19. See E. L. Sabine, 'Butchering in Mediaeval London', *Speculum*, 8 (1933), 335–53; H. T. Riley, *Memorials of London . . . 1276–1419* (London, 1868). On 'social topography', including noxious trades, see Phythian-Adams, *Desolation of a City*, pp. 158–69.

20. See M. Jenner, 'The Politics of London Air: John Evelyn's *Fumifugium* and the Restoration', *The Historical Journal*, 38 (1995), 535–51.

21. The definitive study of urban 'decline' in both physical and mental terms remains Phythian-Adams, *Desolation of a City*; see also his 'Urban Decay in Late Medieval England', in P. Abrams and E. A. Wrigley (eds), *Towns in Societies* (Cambridge, 1978), pp. 159–85. See J. Barry, 'Introduction', in idem (ed.), *The Tudor and Stuart Town: A Reader* (London and New York, 1990), pp. 14, 6–7, 10–11; A. Dyer, *Decline and Growth in English Towns 1400–1640* (Cambridge, 1995).

22. See Thomas, *Town Government*, chaps 5 and 6.

tended in the later sixteenth century to devolve on to parish officials. The more feudal system of contributed labour was being replaced by contracts with individuals or by the direct employment of labour by the municipality. But (as in the case of medical relief for the poor) many sixteenth-century experiments of this kind were short-lived. Sweeping and refuse collection could take place weekly or even twice as often, financed by rates paid to 'scavengers', with tradesmen having to make special arrangements. Charitable bequests for municipal improvements sometimes provided for services like a 'common cart' for rubbish removal.[23]

Whereas gardens or open spaces remained within cities, rubbish was disposed of in fenced-off private tips as well as 'common laystalls', which were usually, for health reasons, outside the city walls. Often dungheaps were located so that they could be drawn upon for agricultural purposes. Present-day commentators should be well placed to appreciate the possibility that more waste was recycled – or was at least biodegradable – in the early modern period than in later phases of industrialisation.[24] Animal hair, bone, dung, decaying fish, offal, blood, sawdust, malt dust, soot, soap ashes, leather scraps and rags were all applied to the land. In London this occurred systematically: dung was carried by barge to the market gardens which supplied the capital. In smaller towns, contaminated water from the streets was fed by ditches into the fields. In some rural areas road repair and agriculture were linked: bracken, cut to preserve pasture, was laid on the roads in autumn and put on the fields in the spring after it had been broken down by traffic.[25] Because of the dominance (and proximity) of agriculture, towns are unlikely to have festered passively in their own wastes, even though the active use of waste materials could itself have unwanted effects.

It would seem inevitable that for Shakespeare's contemporaries odour was as ubiquitous as defect and sickness; in neither case, however, should it be assumed that this led to crassness or indifference. In the medical theory and natural philosophies of the time, odour had a substantial existence and was consequently taken seriously both as a cause of disease and as a means of its prevention or cure.[26] Thus, when there was a threat of epidemic disease, municipal authorities prohibited the normal cleaning and dredging of ditches and

23. See for example the bequest by a mayor of Norwich in the 1540s, citing 'the manner and custom of London': B. Cozens-Hardy and E. A. Kent, *The Mayors of Norwich 1403 to 1835* (Norwich, 1938), p. 53.

24. Although a few historians, such as Jean-Paul Aron, Carolyn Sargentson and Beverly Lemire, have begun to look at trade in second-hand goods as an aspect of consumerism or of women's work, wider issues, and the period before 1700, remain to be tackled. See the pioneering D. Woodward, '"Swords into Ploughshares": Recycling in Pre-Industrial England', *Eco. Hist. Rev.*, 38 (1985), 175–91.

25. Thirsk, *Agrarian History*, pp. 52, 167–8, 180, 196–7, 654; Jenner, 'Early Modern English Conceptions', pp. 86–100. On market gardens, see F. J. Fisher, 'The Development of the London Food Market, 1540–1640', reprinted in idem, *London and the English Economy 1500–1700*, ed. P. J. Corfield and N. B. Harte (London and Ronceverte, 1990), pp. 66–70.

26. Pelling, 'Contagion/Germ Theory/Specificity', pp. 312–14, 318–21; R. Palmer, 'In Bad Odour: Smell and its Significance in Medicine from Antiquity to the Seventeenth Century', in W. F. Bynum and R. Porter (eds), *Medicine and the Five Senses* (Cambridge, 1993), pp. 61–8; Jenner, 'Early Modern English Conceptions', pp. 150ff; for post-1700, A. Corbin, *The Foul and the Fragrant: Odour and the Social Imagination*, trans. M. Koshan (London, 1994); for a twentieth-century response, S. Taylor, *Good General Practice* (London, 1954), pp. 209, 424–43, 543 (I owe the last reference to a seminar by Marshall Marinker).

rivers, to prevent the corruption of the air by ill odours. For the same reason, they were especially vigilant about the quality of foodstuffs exposed for sale in markets. The quality of the stuffings of mattresses and pillows was a matter of concern, because, if inferior, these stuffings released foul odours when warmed by sleeping bodies. It is not surprising that odour often formed the major part of the definition of a nuisance, which was the main concept involved in legal proceedings against unsanitary conditions.[27]

In terms of legislation, Elizabethan codifications were to dominate means used for the maintenance of highways to at least 1800, as they did methods of poor relief. It is significant, however, that national bodies were created not for the maintenance of roads but for the proper management of rivers and harbours.[28] Freely running water was still of the greatest economic as well as social importance.[29] Any scheme to tap rivers and brooks met with opposition from those dependent upon the flow for transport, power or fishery. Apart from diversion to agriculture, the main vehicle of waste disposal was still running water. River banks were carefully maintained and divided into areas specified for transport, waste disposal, manufacturing processes, and washing.[30] Householders were responsible for brooks and ditches, as they were for highways, and could be persuaded to take on this responsibility in exchange for a cheap lease; but, as with rubbish removal, sixteenth-century urban authorities also experimented with special taxes and direct labour. An inability to maintain rivers and harbours could be, or could be seen as, an important part of a vicious cycle of economic decline, and it often prompted direct intervention on a major scale.[31]

Although the water supply of towns varied, it was probably better than is usually imagined. The different projects culminating in the practically (but not economically) successful New River, which brought water to the northern parishes of London, are well known, but by 1600 most provincial towns had some kind of extramural supply, usually from springs; this water was brought in to a few centrally sited cisterns or conduit heads.[32] Some towns, in confiscating monastic property, also acquired a relatively sophisticated system of water supply. Direct connection to private houses (by 'quills', or pipes of lead) was fairly unusual and, where wells were plentiful, not sought after even by the

---

27. See most recently on nuisance, Jenner, 'Early Modern English Conceptions', pp. 29ff, 181ff.

28. That is, commissioners of sewers were placed on a permanent centralised footing in 1532; a national (rather than parochially administered) approach to highways dates only from the 1650s: S. and B. Webb, *English Local Government: Statutory Authorities for Special Purposes* (London, 1922), pp. 21–4; idem, *English Local Government: The Story of the King's Highway* (London, 1913), pp. 14, 20–1.

29. T. S. Willan, *River Navigation in England 1600–1750*, new edn (London, 1964); J. and C. Bord, *Sacred Waters: Holy Wells and Water Lore in Britain and Ireland* (London, 1985). The importance of free flow was stressed by contemporary writers like Robert Burton: see *The Anatomy of Melancholy*, ed. T. C. Faulkner, N. K. Kiessling and R. L. Blair, 3 vols (Oxford, 1989–94), vol. 1, pp. 218–19. See also Jenner, 'Early Modern English Conceptions', pp. 351ff, 358ff, 375ff, 382–95.

30. See also the inhibitions built up against the pollution of wells and springs: Bord and Bord, *Sacred Waters*, pp. 79, 85.

31. See for example Mayhew, *Tudor Rye*, pp. 233ff, 262–9; Phythian-Adams, 'Urban Decay', p. 165; D. Sacks, 'Ports', in Clark, *Urban History*.

32. Thomas, *Town Government*, chap. 7. On the New River project, begun in 1609, see J. W. Gough, *Sir Hugh Myddleton, Entrepreneur and Engineer* (Oxford, 1964); B. Rudden, *The New River. A Legal History* (Oxford, 1985).

prosperous; trade and public-health purposes, and especially fire prevention, were paramount. The Plymouth 'Leat', which antedated London's New River, was intended primarily to victual, clean, and prevent fire in the fleet.[33] Nonetheless, Shakespeare's contemporaries were served with water by an increasing body of entrepreneurs, or 'projectors', as well as by wells, water carriers, waterbutts (in which roof water could be collected), and domestic cisterns.

Many commentators on the physical conditions of sixteenth-century life have allowed themselves to be influenced partly by the robustness of contemporary description and partly by the incidence of devastating outbreaks of epidemic disease, which contemporaries tended to associate with corruption and thence with poverty. Interestingly, condemnation of local habits or conditions still tends to be taken literally, and negatively, by historians, at a time when much else is interpreted as rhetoric.[34] The almost over-scrupulous care taken with other forms of evidence produced by attempts at regulation or punishment has not yet been extended to more mundane aspects of physical life and environment. However, even if some of this commentary is discounted for literal purposes, it is still necessary to pay attention to the vexed issue of the causes of death in infancy, which tend to be unspecific and closely related to environmental conditions.[35] It should nonetheless be noted that the 'sweating sickness', bubonic plague, and syphilis are not 'filth diseases' in the nineteenth-century sense.[36] It is also important in the present context to reiterate the familiar observation that the England of Shakespeare's time consisted of a large number of small settlements; increased human contact inevitably heightened mortality, at least until a new equilibrium was reached, but it was probably only in the largest towns and in London that traditional methods of sanitation were obviously inadequate. Even in London it was partly the existence of added amenities in the form of private latrines that made it necessary to consider culverting brooks and ditches. Careful collation of scattered information is likely to show that public latrines were both more numerous and more substantial in London than is usually assumed. The alternative was cesspools, some very large and others only the circumference of a barrel; the dangers of these to public health depended upon the surrounding soil.[37] In any event, the disinclination of Shakespeare's contemporaries to adopt Sir John Harington's valvular water closet at least meant that cesspits did not usually overflow or need constant emptying.[38]

Latrines and cesspools were often the site of accidents. Latrines tended to be built in alleys and to multiply at the riverside end of narrow lanes, which

33. Reynolds, *Cleanliness and Godliness*, pp. 57–8; C. Gill, *Plymouth: A New History*, vol. 1 (Newton Abbot, 1966), pp. 204–8.

34. Mayhew, *Tudor Rye*, is one example of this.

35. The infant and child mortality rates for Tudor and Stuart England were, however, relatively low: R. Schofield and E. A. Wrigley, 'Infant and Child Mortality in England in the Late Tudor and Early Stuart Period', in Webster, *H, M & M*, pp. 61–95.

36. Pelling, 'Contagion/Germ Theory/ Specificity', p. 327.

37. This subject was pioneered by E. L. Sabine: 'Latrines and Cesspools of Mediaeval London', *Speculum*, 9 (1934), 303–21. See Jenner, 'Early Modern English Conceptions', pp. 214ff, 372 and *passim*.

38. On privies and their socio-literary context, see Reynolds, *Cleanliness and Godliness*. That cesspools are not incompatible with civilisation is perhaps demonstrated by the fact that they remain the basic system of domestic sanitation in modern Florence.

were in any case likely to be used for 'easement'. Relieving oneself in the open street might be tolerated in children under twelve years old, but citizens could be rewarded for informing against older offenders, and fines were often levied on parents or on masters in the case of servants. Indoors, chamberpots were common, and closestools were becoming increasingly so in better-furnished households.[39] These were usually emptied either into cesspools or at night in the channel of the street outside. However, effective connections between private latrines, rainwater cisterns, and external drainage systems were not unusual even at an earlier period.

Obviously, habits and tolerance varied, between localities as well as nations. The connections between circumstantial evidence and contemporary views on the nature of man (for example, the notion that defaecation became necessary only after the Fall) are still a matter of conjecture.[40] It is worth stressing that Shakespeare's contemporaries, preoccupied with the threats posed by the rootless poor and by immigrants and rivals from continental Europe, inevitably expressed these fears in terms of environmental pollution or concern about personal habits or cleanliness. This can be seen most clearly in contemporary satire, and in the widespread apprehension over the growth of London's suburbs.[41]

The work of recent decades has done much to establish the importance of demographic factors in historical change, even though the mode of operation of these factors is often contested. A number of presumptions, many of them based on literary evidence, have been shown to be ill-founded, although it is worth noting, first, that even on such questions as age at marriage literary sources may reflect some important aspect of contemporary culture or experience, and, secondly, that local variation could be considerable.[42] In general, families in early modern England were rather more nuclear than extended; large numbers of (surviving) offspring were unusual; and marriage after the age of 20 was the rule, even among the aristocracy, and took place comparatively late in life, given the age's shorter life expectancy. Old people, especially women, were often found living alone, or not with their immediate families; and many people remained unmarried, though remarriage was common. As already indicated, the average life expectancy was affected primarily by the frequent loss of infant lives: a person surviving to the age of 30 could expect to live another 30 years. As for mortality rates in general, Shakespeare's blessed plot compared favourably with the rest of Europe and with modern non-western societies.[43] On the

39. T. Atkinson, *Elizabethan Winchester*, p. 208. For chamberpots, see Pelling, 'Nurses', p. 191. The impression given here is based on Norwich inventories. Closestools could be hired (for a feast, for example): Young, *Annals*, p. 453 (1638).

40. Reynolds, *Cleanliness and Godliness*, p. 196, ascribes this view to Boehme and Swedenborg. See B. J. Gibbons, *Gender in Mystical and Occult Thought: Behmenism and its Development in England* (Cambridge, 1996), p. 95; for an English reflection on this topic, see [Benjamin Buckler], *A Philosophical Dialogue Concerning Decency* (London, 1751), pp. 26–7 (I am grateful to Scott Mandelbrote for both these references).

41. See the essays in Beier and Finlay, *London 1500–1700*; Wear, 'Making Sense of Health'.

42. The latter point is demonstrated by R. Adair, *Courtship, Illegitimacy and Marriage in Early Modern England* (Manchester and New York, 1996).

43. Palliser, *Age of Elizabeth*, pp. 38–46. For a positive view of population growth 1540–1640, see idem, 'Tawney's Century: Brave New World or Malthusian Trap?', *Eco. Hist. Rev.*, 35 (1982), 339–53.

other hand, compared with the twentieth century's profound shift to an ageing society, the Elizabethan period was dominated by young people: over half the population was under 25. This can plausibly be given considerable sociological importance; for example, with respect to religious, political and social unrest, or to the period's increase in the provision of different forms of education.[44]

For reasons to do with sources, many demographic generalisations have been developed with reference to rural populations and are only now being extended to early modern towns. It has customarily been assumed that in crowded urban areas, and above all in London, family life was less stable, marriages took place earlier, and death and decay came sooner. Recent emphasis on regional differences and neighbourhood has tended to underline contrasts in the experiences of 'settled' as opposed to migratory populations. Most literature, especially satire and plays, was produced in London for London audiences and may faithfully mirror – or, equally faithfully, distort – perceptions of life in the capital without being true for the country as a whole. There are interesting examples of gaps between contemporary perceptions and the findings of modern demographers; how the former were acted upon to produce the results observed by the latter is a controversial issue which is often avoided.[45] Although the presence of an 'urban penalty' seems established for the largest towns, the importance of mortality as a factor in demographic change, and historical change generally, is beginning again to be an active area of debate.[46]

Famine was a real cause of death, particularly during the disastrous years 1557–59 and 1596–98, and 'starvation' (this term being used by contemporaries to include exposure as well as lack of food as a cause of death) was probably a factor for many of those recorded as found dead by the more detailed registers of London churches. A major proportion of these are likely to have been 'subsistence' migrants.[47] As with epidemics, the contest to determine when there were crises of national importance (which do not seem to have been frequent) should not be allowed to obscure the significance of devastation on

44. Palliser, *Age of Elizabeth*, pp. 45, 356–65; L. Stone, 'The Educational Revolution in England, 1560–1640', *P & P*, 28 (1964), 41–80; K. Thomas, *Rule and Misrule in the Schools of Early Modern England* (Reading, 1976); K. Thomas, *Age and Authority in Early Modern England*, Raleigh Lecture (London, 1976); I. Krausman Ben-Amos, *Adolescence and Youth in Early Modern England* (New Haven, CT, and London, 1994); P. Griffiths, *Youth and Authority: Formative Experiences in England 1560–1640* (Oxford, 1996), pp. 5–7.

45. See P. Criffiths, J. Landers, M. Pelling and R. Tyson, 'Population and Disease, Estrangement and Belonging', in Clark, *Urban History*.

46. Ibid.; P. J. P. Goldberg, *Women, Work, and Life Cycle in a Medieval Economy: Women in York and Yorkshire c. 1300–1520* (Oxford, 1992), p. 357; P. Razzell, *Essays in English Population History* (London, 1994); N. Goose, 'Urban Demography in Pre-Industrial England: What is to be Done?', *Urban History*, 21 (1994), 279–83; and esp. J. Landers, *Death and the Metropolis: Studies in the Demographic History of London 1670–1830* (Cambridge, 1993), pp. 7–39. Cf. C. Galley, 'A Model of Early Modern Urban Demography', *Eco. Hist. Rev.*, 48 (1995), 448–69.

47. A. B. Appleby, *Famine in Tudor and Stuart England* (Liverpool, 1978); idem, 'Diet in Sixteenth-century England: Sources, Problems, Possibilities', in Webster, *H, M & M*, pp. 97–116, esp. 112–16; T. R. Forbes, *Chronicle from Aldgate: Life and Death in Shakespeare's London* (New Haven, CT, and London, 1971), pp. 77–80; Barry, 'Introduction', pp. 15–16. As in nineteenth-century civil registration, few were actually recorded as starving to death: J. Graunt, *Natural and Political Observations ... upon the Bills of Mortality* (5th edn, 1676), in C. H. Hull (ed.), *The Economic Writings of Sir William Petty*, 2 vols (New York, 1963–64), vol. 1, pp. 352–3. Literary sources were similarly reticent: W. C. Carroll, *Fat King, Lean Beggar: Representations of Poverty in the Age of Shakespeare* (Ithaca, NY, and London, 1996), p. 213.

a local scale. The relationship between dearth and disease remains unclear. The still mysterious crisis of mortality in the 1550s was followed by a period of demographic recovery lasting into the 1580s; the ensuing decades were punctuated by urban epidemics of plague that exceeded in severity, if not in notoriety, the 'great plague' of 1665. There are considerable difficulties involved in identifying epidemic outbreaks, and even the term *plague* had, like *ague*, a generic as well as a specific meaning.[48]

Much attention has been paid to epidemic crises or peaks of mortality, partly because such incidents are more discrete than other demographic phenomena and partly because of the view, first systematically put forward by nineteenth-century medical historians, that great epidemics not only are characteristic of the age in which they occur but also bring major features of society into high relief.[49] In demographic terms, this emphasis implies a neglect of the environmental context of infant death, although the subject itself is far from neglected. Comparatively little attention has been paid, moreover, to endemic or chronic disease. Yet it is arguable that such conditions are likely to have had a greater effect on the *mentalité* of the time, and certainly a greater part in everyday experience for all classes, than did the sporadic outbreaks of plague during which 'normality' was suspended.[50] At the same time one must respect what the pioneers of 'political arithmetic' were quick to notice: the diseases people were most likely to die from, or suffered most frequently, were not necessarily those of which they were most afraid.[51]

More specific conditions, of great consequence but less visible as causes of death, include malaria; scurvy (which was seen most clearly among sailors on long voyages but which also affected urban populations); stone, or calculus (which had a wide incidence among small boys as well as mature men and affected both sexes); and venereal disease, notably syphilis (which was a major social phenomenon of the sixteenth and early seventeenth centuries). Of these conditions, the prolific metaphors, euphemisms and symptomology of venereal disease most directly affected the extremely physical language of the urban satirists and playwrights, the celebrated outburst of Shakespeare's Timon being only one example.[52] It is beginning to be recognised that many of the major diseases of the period were as important for their influence on morbidity as for their mortality levels, although venereal disease remains seriously underestimated as a factor in social change.[53]

48. A. Dyer, 'The English Sweating Sickness of 1551: an Epidemic Anatomized', *Medical History*, 41 (1997), 361–83; P. Slack, 'Mortality Crises and Epidemic Disease in England 1485–1610', in Webster, *H, M & M*, pp. 9–59.

49. Pelling, 'Medicine since 1500', in P. Corsi and P. J. Weindling (eds), *Information Sources in the History of Science and Medicine* (London, 1983), pp. 391–2. See for example T. Ranger and P. Slack (eds), *Epidemics and Ideas: Essays on the Historical Perception of Pestilence* (Cambridge, 1992).

50. This is explored with respect to the definitive diseases of a later period in M. Pelling, *Cholera, Fever and English Medicine 1825–1865* (Oxford, 1978).

51. Graunt, *Natural and Political Observations*, pp. 350–1.

52. *Timon of Athens*, IV. iii. Pelling, 'Appearance and Reality', pp. 91–105. See in general C. Quétel, *History of Syphilis*, trans. J. Braddock and B. Pike (Cambridge, 1990); J. Arrizabalaga, J. Henderson and R. French, *The Great Pox: The French Disease in Renaissance Europe* (New Haven, CT, and London, 1997).

53. Slack, *Impact of Plague*, pp. 106, 175–7.

A high incidence of serious disease did not induce a state of apathy towards everything but the immediate threat to life itself. Case records and personal papers show that people constantly monitored their own state of health and were profoundly concerned about the significance of apparently trivial symptoms. It is not surprising that skill in prognosis was sought for as well as ability to cure. The inexorable process of physical degeneration from small beginnings was as familiar in the body as it was in crops and foodstuffs. Physical incapacity could lead to immediate economic and social degradation. Contemporaries feared any threat to the senses, especially the eyesight.[54] Anxious attention was paid to the normal and abnormal functioning of the generative organs. As in later periods, maternal disability consequent upon childbirth was a hidden enormity; more women consulted physicians than men, although then as now there could be many reasons for this. There is increasing evidence that medical attention was sought even for babies. The relief of pain was an object; backache, headache and toothache were not suffered in silence.[55]

The most prestigious specialties of modern medicine pay little attention to the surface of the skin, but in earlier periods this was in both theory and practice a major area of concern, equivalent in cosmological terms to the surface, as opposed to the unknown interior, of the earth. The probable incidence of dietary deficiencies and the number of serious diseases (including plague) that resolved themselves on the surface of the body justify this stress on cutaneous appearances; but Elizabethans also sought remedies for pimples and boils, and made extensive use of cosmetic aids and disguises. (It is consequently perverse to ascribe Shakespeare's attention to apparently minor defects to his superior powers of observation.) Accidents (especially drownings) and violence caused many deaths; but burns, scalds, dog bites and fractures also had long-term consequences, as did strains caused by work, especially rupture.[56] Stoicism did not even extend to congenital or traumatic deformity: the treatment of harelip and wryneck was a recognised specialty.

To these physical causes of anxiety must be added the Elizabethan obsession with mood and state of mind. Melancholy was not only a traditional symptom but also a mental disorder regarded as particularly afflicting the English. Not surprisingly, anxiety about physical disease itself emerges as a cause of mental disturbance, especially among women. Insomnia was a commonly reported complaint. Among ordinary people, the importance of family life was reflected in the main causes of mental stress as reported by patients: troubled courtships, marital problems, bereavements and economic problems. The last factor

54. It is not surprising that eye problems were foremost among the conditions for which people sought cures at wells or springs: Bord and Bord, *Sacred Waters*, p. 35.

55. These responses are evident not only in the case records of astrological practitioners such as Richard Napier and Simon Forman, but also in the multifarious incidents of practice investigated by the London College of Physicians (CPL) and recorded in its Annals (to be analysed in my forthcoming monograph, *Strength of the Opposition*).

56. On accidental death, see Forbes, *Chronicle from Aldgate*, chap. 6; idem, 'By What Disease or Casualty: the Changing Face of Death in London', in Webster, *H, M & M*, pp. 117–39. Accidents at work in seventeenth-century London are currently under investigation by Craig Spence of Royal Holloway College, University of London. In general see B. Luckin, 'Accidents, Disasters and Cities', *Urban History*, 20 (1993), 177–90.

– significantly expressed as 'loss of estate' – is a measure of the contemporary sense of social and economic precariousness.[57]

These circumstances created a situation in which the demand for all kinds of medical attention was very high. To a considerable extent this demand was met in the first instance within the family circle. The tie of blood was cited as prompting practice as well as justifying it.[58] It was not uncommon for individuals to study medicine for years in order to deal with their own persistent complaints, or with those of close relatives. Servants and apprentices, while not wholly equivalent in the household hierarchy to the master's children, were owed a duty of care and were consequently as likely as the children to receive treatment at the hands of the master, his wife, or other servants.[59] Procedures carried out at home and now formally thought to be 'neutral' or merely hygienic, like bathing, changes of clothing, dietary variation, and avoidance of heat or cold, were then regarded as strongly medicinal, just as they could, if rashly followed, be highly prejudicial.[60] Traditional herbal remedies were widely used, but laypeople were also alert to novel remedies and constantly exchanged such information. Books of recipes and 'bills' enjoyed a steady circulation in manuscript and printed forms.[61]

Outside the household, demand was met by a wide variety of medical practitioners, who may have been present in a ratio to population as high as 1:200. This estimate is based on the adoption of a broad definition of *practitioner*, as justified by the practices of the time. Other criteria, such as effectiveness or level of formal education, are either impossible to apply historically or of limited relevance to actual practice.[62] Sick people chose freely from among the range of practitioners according to their own and their friends' judgement of the nature and seriousness of their condition, although the anxieties and sources of conflict involved in such 'freedom' should not be glossed over.[63] A scale of fees and of practitioners existed to meet the needs and expectations of different social classes, although some sought-after practitioners could charge low fees and the venality of others was bitterly resented. An unmeasured but probably important amount of medical services was provided for nothing, or was paid for in kind. The former practice had an official existence in statutes.[64] It

57. Much of the considerable literature on melancholy and similar conditions is concerned with the history of ideas. For the lived experience of early modern people, including the non-literate, see M. MacDonald, *Mystical Bedlam*, on which this paragraph is based.

58. As evidenced by a number of unlicensed London practitioners of variable status: see Pelling, *Strength of the Opposition*.

59. Pelling, 'Apprenticeship'.

60. See Smith, 'Cleanliness'; J. O'Hara May, *Elizabethan Dyetary of Health* (Lawrence, Kansas, 1977).

61. I hope to say more about bills, or prescriptions, in *Strength of the Opposition*. On medical recipes, see the thesis of Jennifer Stine: 'Opening Closets: the Discovery of Household Medicine in Early Modern England' (Stanford University PhD thesis, 1996).

62. Pelling and Webster, 'Medical Practitioners', esp. pp. 166–7, 235 (and below, p. 240). For confirmation of the higher ratio there suggested, see the present volume, p. 226.

63. The concept of 'hierarchy of resort', introduced by the anthropologist Lola Romanucci-Ross, has proved especially useful to early modernists; Sawyer also describes this (often desperate) process as 'shuttling': R. Sawyer, 'Patients, Healers, and Disease in the Southeast Midlands, 1597–1634' (University of Wisconsin-Madison PhD thesis, 1986), pp. 193–204.

64. See Furnivall, *Vicary*, p. 209.

survived into the twentieth century, but motives altered radically according to social changes; much more investigation is required to document its history with respect to the individual practitioner. The persistence of payment in kind has led to levels of practice being underestimated, and to some forms of practice (especially by women) being discounted.

The high level of lay expertise and involvement in medicine in the early modern period has often been explained in terms of medicine's being then more elementary and more dependent upon traditional shared knowledge.[65] This perhaps oversimplifies both the social structure of medicine and the variety of schools of thought available at the time. It is also possible to argue that the relations between doctor and patient could be more evenly balanced than is the case today, although this proposition depends upon a recognition of the variable status of practitioners as well as of wide differences in 'degree' in general. It is clear that patients bargained with practitioners as in a commercial transaction and settled on an agreed outcome or 'cure'. Contracts, which seem usually to have been verbal, were used in which a portion was paid on account and the rest reserved conditionally upon completion of the cure. Physicians and some surgeons were just beginning to resist this system, although some of their fees were so high that they were paid in stages during the cure or even in the form of annuities.[66]

The social status even of academically qualified practitioners was not particularly high, although at the same time gentry or nobility who practised medicine or surgery did not lose caste by so doing. Further consideration of the economic framework of medicine as an occupation in the early modern period reveals the inappropriateness of the modern ideal of the full-time dedicated member of the professional classes.[67] Large numbers of practitioners existed, but many if not most of them engaged in other activities of economic significance.[68] Physicians and apothecaries could also be merchants; landholders, their agents, and schoolmasters practised medicine; medicine was a frequent resort for clergy who were poor, unlikely to rise, or deprived of their livings. The versatility of Timothie Bright, physician, cleric, pioneer on the subject of melancholy as well as in the development of shorthand, reflected not only his personal abilities but also the contemporary social and economic climate, which was nothing if not competitive.[69] Quite prosperous, as well as poor, practitioners diversified into the food and drink trades. Barber-surgeons were regularly trained in netmaking or musicianship and were likely to become involved in the textile trades where these were dominant. The better-known side of this coin is the way in which other trades branched out into medicine. In rural areas, where 'by-employments' and seasonal working were the rule rather than the exception, medicine was

65. F. N. L. Poynter, 'Medicine and Public Health', in A. Nicoll (ed.), *Shakespeare in His Own Age* (Cambridge, 1964), pp. 152–3.

66. On the contractual system in early modern medicine, see this volume, pp. 87ff, 246ff; and Pelling, *Strength of the Opposition*.

67. For references and general discussion, see Pelling, 'Trade or Profession'. On issues of status and gender, see idem, 'Compromised by Gender'.

68. On what follows see Pelling, 'Occupational Diversity'.

69. Pelling, 'Medicine and Economic Incentives', p. 60.

equally likely to be a part-time occupation. Even in the context of the ecclesiastical licensing structure dating from 1512, medicine was a skill in which experience and good character were regarded as adequate and necessary qualifications. The English universities themselves granted licences in physic and in surgery on this basis.[70]

As in the case of other established occupations, medicine was traditionally subject to restrictive and regulatory practices, which suggest a tripartite division into physicians, surgeons or barber-surgeons, and apothecaries.[71] It follows from the competitive situation described above that this division of labour was observed only according to social and economic circumstances. The division existed more as a weapon in conflicts between practitioners than as an agreed framework. Different strategies were adopted, that of the academically qualified physician being closest to the modern definition of a professional, although enjoying only a limited success at the time. The College of Physicians of London, founded in 1518, insisted on a level of humanist culture available only to a very few, thus raising the level of mystique of their occupation. (The College did not, however, invariably attract those with a high level of academic accomplishment.) In essence this strategy was also that adopted by many empirics. The leaders of the London barber-surgeons at first imitated the College's strategy but then came to appeal directly to the laity and to lesser practitioners by contributing to the increasing body of medical literature being published in the vernacular. The tripartite division was explicitly rejected by Protestant critics who praised the empirical efficiency of primitive and Hippocratic medicine, in which all parts of practice were combined within a religious and moral framework.[72]

Anxiety about health and the high level of demand for medical services produced, simultaneously, a concern for standards, and a fixity of belief on the part of the sick person in the practitioner of his or her choice. To regard the patient of this period as especially gullible is rather to miss the point. Scepticism as to the morality and expertise of practitioners in general was equally widespread. The forms of medical regulation demanded by the College of Physicians had the undesirable implication of severely restricting the range and amount of medical assistance available to the public, and the College's claims were never wholeheartedly upheld by the state.[73] In the so-called Quacks' Charter of 1542–43, London surgeons were also criticised by the state for their venality and their attempts to restrict the public's access to effective remedies for important conditions such as venereal disease.[74]

Medical regulation was also integrally related to broader economic and religious factors. The London medical corporations that emerged in the sixteenth and early seventeenth centuries drew on continental models but were also part of a wider economic trend towards companies and corporations. The ecclesiast-

70. Pelling and Webster, 'Medical Practitioners', pp. 192–5, 215–16, 226–7.
71. On this paragraph, see ibid.
72. Webster, *Great Instauration*, pp. 247–64.
73. See C. Webster, 'William Harvey and the Crisis of Medicine in Jacobean England', in J. J. Bylebyl (ed.), *William Harvey and his Age* (Baltimore, MD, and London, 1979), pp. 1–27.
74. On the last point see Pelling, 'Appearance and Reality', pp. 96–7. Statutes and other regulations affecting London surgeons are conveniently collected as appendices to Furnivall, *Vicary*.

ical licensing system was at its most rigorous, particularly for midwives, during the regime of Archbishop Laud in the 1630s.[75] The College of Physicians encouraged the separation of the apothecaries from the Grocers' Company in 1617 in the hope of being able to supervise the monopolistic sale of drugs in London. Slightly later, two royal physicians, *ex officio* fellows of the College, were granted a monopoly in distilling strong waters and vinegars that subsequently evolved into the Distillers' Company. This interest related to the profitability of the drink trade but also to the role of distillation in chemical therapy. For their part, Puritans were increasingly accusing learned medicine, as well as the law and the church, of being a professional monopoly.[76]

Medicine during Shakespeare's lifetime was notable both for its eclecticism and for struggles between the exponents of different schools of thought.[77] These struggles were an integral and important part of a major shift at the end of the sixteenth century towards a Neoplatonic philosophy, consistent with reformed religious views and symptomatic of the increasing cultural assertiveness of northern Europe. This, rather than any simplicity of medical theory, explains the degree of knowledge found among the laity, poets, playwrights, and intellectuals. The rational and sceptical Galenism embodied by the humanist Thomas Linacre in the London College of Physicians remained entrenched in the medical faculties of the universities, but increasingly lost ground as a philosophical system. The revival of anatomy led by Andreas Vesalius (1514–64), while having little immediate relevance to medical practice, was associated with orthodox views; nonetheless, its tendency was to undermine the self-sufficiency of classical medicine. Therapeutic effectiveness became an important criterion and prepared the way for the favourable reception of the teachings of the religious and medical reformer Paracelsus (*c.* 1493–1541) and a revitalised alchemy. Academic physicians were seen as having become aloof from their patients and from therapeutics; their outlook was fatalistic, and they had little to say to either the diseases or the remedies of the modern age.

The initiative lay instead with those who had knowledge of the plants and minerals of the New World or who arrived at the quintessential secrets of nature by chemical means. Their practice, which included (but did not introduce or monopolise) the use of mercury in syphilis, explicitly revived the Hippocratic principle of extreme measures in extreme cases[78] and was compatible with Protestant diagnoses of the world's ills. For Protestants, physical degeneration was linked to spiritual corruption as a result of the Fall; but by painful endeavour man's original powers could be regained and his span of life extended. The

---

75. C. Webster, 'Thomas Linacre and the Foundation of the College of Physicians', in F. Maddison, M. Pelling and C. Webster (eds), *Linacre Studies* (Oxford, 1977), pp. 200–6; J. H. Bloom and R. R. James, *Medical Practitioners in the Diocese of London* (Cambridge, 1935), p. 7; Pelling and Webster, 'Medical Practitioners', pp. 226–7.

76. M. Berlin, *The Worshipful Company of Distillers: A Short History* (Chichester, 1996); Webster, *Great Instauration*, pp. 252–4, 268–70. On the role of political factors see also A. Wilson, 'The Politics of Medical Improvement in early Hanoverian London', in A. Cunningham and R. French (eds), *The Medical Enlightenment of the Eighteenth Century* (Cambridge, 1990), pp. 4–39.

77. For what follows, see Webster, *Great Instauration*, section 4, 'The Prolongation of Life'; also idem, 'Alchemical and Paracelsian Medicine', in *H, M & M*, pp. 301–34.

78. Poynter, 'Medicine and Public Health', pp. 152–3.

pace was forced by immigrant iatrochemists (many of whom were also involved in mining projects) and by empirics pressing the claims of a narrow range of chemical remedies. These innovations gained a sophisticated intellectual framework with the influence of Paracelsian medical philosophy, which began in England as early as 1560. Francis Bacon, John Donne and Ben Jonson all wrote for an audience that had fully assimilated Paracelsianism.[79] Unlike Galenism, Paracelsianism had something to offer all levels of practitioner; the London medical corporations were eventually forced to compromise with both its commercial and its intellectual success.

English medicine of the sixteenth century was not remarkable for major innovations or discoveries. The achievements of William Harvey and other English physiologists belong to the revolution in natural philosophy that occurred in the seventeenth century. Instead, the liveliness of English post-Reformation culture was dependent upon a new receptiveness to continental developments, fruitfully combined with an increasing sense of national identity. A large number of minor figures, working in close collaboration with printers and publishers, produced translations and paraphrases of continental works for the English market, often adding their own material or urging attention to the native tradition.[80] Thus, continental herbals were copied, but observations were also made of the local flora. As in other areas of economic life, the growth of imports was met by schemes to supply the desirable commodities from the colonies or to promote the native product.[81] Timothie Bright's treatise on the 'sufficiency of English medicines' (1580) urged the extraction of chemical essences from plants and an improved knowledge of local flora.[82]

Similar parallels could be drawn with respect to the response of English poets and dramatists to continental models, a process also involving minor figures and complex bibliographical problems, although the flowering of the native tradition arguably took place earlier in literature than in medicine. The emergence of a literature in the vernacular was a major feature of both developments, although it should be noted that the book trade is an imperfect summary of either, since many works circulated in manuscript.[83] However, it is not surprising that the intermingling of science, literature and medicine that characterised the intellectual life of the Tudor period should also be represented at the economic level, especially in bookmaking and bookselling.[84] Neither is it surprising that some literary figures, such as Robert Greene and Thomas Lodge, turned to medicine as a means of supporting a literary career. This is perhaps best interpreted as an example of the occupational diversification or economic

---

79. Webster, 'Alchemical and Paracelsian Medicine', p. 322; also demonstrated in a sophisticated and persuasive manner by S. C. Lorch, 'Medical Theory and Renaissance Tragedy' (University of Louisville PhD thesis, 1976), on which the only limitation is the then state of knowledge of English Paracelsianism.

80. See P. Slack, 'Mirrors of Health and Treasures of Poor Men: the Uses of the Vernacular Medical Literature of Tudor England', in Webster, *H, M & M*, pp. 237–73.

81. J. Thirsk, *Economic Policy and Projects* (Oxford, 1988).

82. Webster, 'Alchemical and Paracelsian Medicine', p. 329.

83. This point is made most tellingly by Webster, 'Alchemical and Paracelsian Medicine', pp. 308ff. See in general A. F. Marotti, *Manuscript, Print and the English Renaissance Lyric* (Ithaca, NY, and London, 1995).

84. See lately P. M. Jones, 'Book Ownership and the Lay Culture of Medicine in Tudor Cambridge', in Marland and Pelling, *Task of Healing*, pp. 49–68.

flexibility attributed to medicine earlier in this essay, but it has also been see on a more elevated plane as characteristic of 'Renaissance man', or, more parochially, as an example of the enduring humanist sympathies of educated physicians.

For most of the period since his death, Shakespeare has been seen by many as the defining figure of his age. Estimates of the intellectual and scientific content of his achievement have varied according to the historical context in which such estimates were made. The eighteenth century, rediscovering Shakespeare and admiring polymaths, tended to see him as especially learned. By the end of the nineteenth century, professionalisation and specialisation, in combination with the jealously preserved (and often conflicting) ideal of the humanist physician, had given a new and often ludicrous dimension to 'bardolatry'. While it was still possible to feel that a physician might be steeped in literature, by this time extensive lay knowledge of medicine had become an ideological, if not, a practical, impossibility. The Tudor age had receded and become primitive, albeit illumined by such selected intellectual giants as Shakespeare and Bacon, and the broadly based philosophical and religious preoccupations of the period were no longer understood. Hence, medical lovers of Shakespeare could not comprehend his erudition, given, as they saw it, the age in which he lived. They asserted that his degree of acquaintance with medical matters was such that he must himself have been a physician or at least an apothecary. More rationally, some of them proposed that Shakespeare must have depended upon (or alternatively, been intolerant of) his physician son-in-law, John Hall.[85] In their turn, representatives of emerging medical specialisms (in particular, perhaps, psychiatry) have predictably found in Shakespeare's writings clear evidence of particular knowledge of their specialty. Above all, links have been forged between the equally important and often opposite humanist and scientific ideals of modern medicine: it has even been found necessary that Shakespeare, somehow, must have known about the circulation of the blood, with or without the assistance of Harvey himself.[86]

While both medicine and Shakespeare remain in high esteem, it is likely that such claims will continue to be made, in spite of effective criticism.[87] Even in the 1950s it was asserted that 'the medical reference frequency' of Shakespeare's works could be used as a yardstick to determine authorship.[88] It is doubtful if any historian of English literature would agree with this judgement now. With

---

85. For John Hall, see most recently J. Lane (ed.), *John Hall and his Patients* (Stratford-upon-Avon, 1996).

86. These points are illustrated by, for example, F. Douce, *Illustrations of Shakspeare and of Ancient Manners*, 2 vols (London, 1807); J. C. Bucknill, *The Medical Knowledge of Shakespeare* (London, 1860); L. M. Griffiths, 'Shakespeare and the Practice of Medicine', *Annals of Medical History*, 3 (1921), 50–61; J. W. L. Crosfill, 'Classified Medical References in the Works of Shakespeare', *Journal of the Royal Naval Medical Service*, 38 (1952) to ibid., 44 (1958); D. S. Miller and E. H. Davis, 'Shakespeare and Orthopedics', *Surgery: Gynecology and Obstetrics*, 128 (1969), 358–66; C. E. McMahon, 'Psychosomatic Concepts in the Works of Shakespere', *Journal of the History of the Behavioral Sciences*, 12 (1976), 275–82; I. I. Edgar, *Shakespeare, Medicine and Psychiatry. An Historical Study in Criticism and Interpretation* (London, 1971), esp. pp. 26, 38–42. For some further examples from before 1919, see W. Osler, *Bibliotheca Osleriana* (Montreal and London, 1969), pp. 486–7 and *passim*.

87. For such criticism, and the history of 'medicated' reference to Shakespeare as given here, see I. I. Edgar, 'Amariah Brigham, Isaac Ray and Shakespeare', *Psychiatric Quarterly*, 35 (1961), 666–74; idem, *Shakespeare, Medicine and Psychiatry*.

88. Crosfill, 'Classified Medical References' (1952), p. 113.

respect to the body, the mind, health and disease, Shakespeare's language fully participates in the physicality that was characteristic of Elizabethan satire and is thus a confirmation of contemporary preoccupations. Although frequently misinterpreted, the relevant references have been constantly quoted. But even enthusiasts are obliged to admit that there are relatively few references to medical treatment in Shakespeare and that these lack detail. Practitioners of medicine, like practitioners of law, are not represented in his work according to their ubiquity in contemporary life. It is indicative of the lack of civic or 'citizen' content in Shakespeare's plays that they make no substantial reference to barbers or barber-surgeons, who can be identified as carrying the main burden of general practice in towns.[89] Similarly, the poor (Italian) apothecary who makes a brief appearance in *Romeo and Juliet* is unrepresentative of the often wealthy retailers, associates of merchants and goldsmiths, who were frequently to be found as members of Elizabethan urban elites.[90]

More physicians appear as characters in the plays than do representatives of any other kind of practice, but even these are for the most part fairly dim appendages of aristocratic or royal households. Shakespeare's nurses – children's nurses, not sicknurses – are similarly situated but more definite in character.[91] The physicians are appropriate to their context, especially the vigorous 'evangelical' Dr Butts (*Henry VIII*), but their comparative ineffectuality is perhaps a reflection of contemporary scepticism about these practitioners, whose skill was merely 'opinion'.[92]

Suspicion of poisoning as a result of the involvement of medical practitioners was another Elizabethan motif that is reflected in Shakespeare. Xenophobia and official paranoia found expression in the much-debated case of Roderigo Lopez, the Jewish physician to Elizabeth; he was executed in 1594 for allegedly plotting against the queen's life. But the reality may also be seen, in the murder of Sir Thomas Overbury in the Tower in 1613 at the instigation of Frances Howard, countess of Essex and Somerset.[93] Physicians and other

---

89. This point is hardly affected by recent claims for Shakespeare's sensitivity to contemporary socio-economic realities: A. Patterson, *Shakespeare and the Popular Voice* (Oxford and Cambridge, MA, 1989); G. K. Paster, *The Idea of the City in the Age of Shakespeare* (Athens, GA, 1985), chap. 7. Shakespeare's 'practitioners' are identified by Edgar, *Shakespeare, Medicine and Psychiatry*, pp. 98, 101.

90. This point was appreciated by Bucknill (*Medical Knowledge*, pp. 11–12), possibly because the Victorians had some admiration for Tudor commercial magnates such as Thomas Gresham. Except for the largely unpublished work of R. S. Roberts, early modern apothecaries are very much under-researched. See Pelling and Webster, 'Medical Practitioners', pp. 177–9, 220–2 and *passim*, and references there cited; T. D. Whittet, 'Shakespeare and his Apothecaries', *Proceedings of the Royal Society of Medicine (History of Medicine Section)*, 57 (1964), 899–905; M. Pelling, 'Apothecaries and other Medical Practitioners in Norwich around 1600', *Pharmaceutical Historian*, 13 (1983), 5–8. For the earlier period, see C. Rawcliffe, *Medicine and Society in Later Medieval England* (Stroud, 1995), chap. 7.

91. See B. Everett, '*Romeo and Juliet*: the Nurse's Story', *Critical Quarterly*, 14 (1972), 129–39; Paster, *The Body Embarrassed*, chaps 4 and 5.

92. T. N. Toomey, 'Sir William Buttes of Norfolk: the Physician of Henry VIII Mentioned by Shakespeare', *Annals of Medical History*, 6 (1924), 185–94; M. Dowling, *Humanism in the Age of Henry VIII* (London, 1986), pp. 3–4 and *passim*; Thomas Powell, *Tom of All Trades, or the Plaine Pathway to Preferment* (London, 1631), p. 28.

93. For Lopez, Overbury, and poisoning, see Pelling, 'Compromised by Gender', p. 105; the debate between William Meyers, David Katz and others in *Commentary* (April, 1996), 32–7 and (July, 1996), 3–8; D. Lindley, *The Trials of Frances Howard: Fact and Fiction at the Court of King James* (London and New York, 1993). I thank David Katz for helping me to the second of these references.

practitioners close to officers of state were used as spies or pawns in diplomatic manoeuvres, most overtly perhaps by Elizabeth and the Stuarts in respect of the Russian court.[94] Royalty and the nobility followed a notably independent line in their choice of practitioners or, as in the case of James I and consorts born outside England, brought their attendants with them. When their choice fell on foreigners or unorthodox practitioners, as it frequently did, this could undermine regulation and arouse resentment.[95]

The success of immigrant practitioners in establishing themselves in Shakespeare's society finds a mocking echo in Dr Caius (*Merry Wives of Windsor*), although it seems unlikely that this figure was intended to represent any individual immigrant practitioner. Dr Caius is the only reminder in Shakespeare that the medical practitioner was a stock figure in traditional comedy, reinforced in the sixteenth century by imitations of continental models, such as the Italian *dottore*.[96] Many lesser-known plays, as well as such playwrights as Massinger, Middleton, and Beaumont and Fletcher, made greater use of these conventions.[97]

Other regions of practice that Shakespeare chose to represent in far less depth than did some of his contemporaries are alchemy and astrological medicine. The obvious contrast is with Jonson, who portrayed the adept; Heywood and others used as characters the cunning men and women who practised in towns as well as rural areas. Shakespeare's allusions to these complex subjects are in general terms and demonstrate his comparative lack of interest in contemporary intellectual debates.

Literary sources are indispensable for the study of the society that produces them, even with respect to supposedly esoteric areas such as medicine, but it cannot be expected that their coverage will be comprehensive, or even that information will be conveyed directly.[98] Many of Shakespeare's contemporaries give a fuller and more literal account of medicine and disease than does Shakespeare himself. A balanced view of the role of medicine and health in society can be attained only by attention to the broader social and economic context, and it is within such a view that the contribution of any given writer can most safely be interpreted.

---

94. The role of foreign medical practitioners at the Russian courts in the early modern period is the subject of a forthcoming monograph and a prosopography by Maria Unkovskaya of Oxford, whom I wish to thank for advance copies of some of her material. See also the work of John Appleby of Norwich.

95. This is repeatedly demonstrated in CPL, Annals: see Pelling, *Strength of the Opposition*.

96. Lord McNair, 'Why is the Doctor in *The Merry Wives of Windsor* called Caius?', *Medical History*, 13 (1969), 311–39.

97. Edgar, *Shakespeare, Medicine and Psychiatry*, pp. 87–9. H. Silvette, *The Doctor on the Stage. Medicine and Medical Men in Seventeenth-Century England*, ed. F. Butler (Knoxville, TN, 1967), now has to be used with caution. See the Oxford DPhil thesis and published work of Natsu Hattori of the Wellcome Institute for the History of Medicine, London.

98. The latter point is well demonstrated by Lorch, 'Medical Theory and Renaissance Tragedy'.

CHAPTER TWO

Food, Status and Knowledge: Attitudes to Diet in Early Modern England

Dietary recommendations, like polypharmacy, seem to have been a staple resort of physicians until at least the late nineteenth century, after which there is apparently a profound change. This chapter seeks to explore the background to this change. It does not attempt to cover a period of centuries, or to assert unbroken continuities over that time. However, we can begin with the contrast supplied by the present century, when most practitioners seem to know little about diet, or to feel that such knowledge is necessary.[1] This situation is changing, as the foregrounding of the degenerative diseases gradually shifts explanatory models back to multifactorial forms of analysis.[2] However dietetics – which I would define as theory related to practice – currently has paramedical status at best, and the initiative lies with alternative medicine and the laity. In spite of the efforts of alternative medicine to bring food and medicine together, most people today are likely to feel able to draw a distinction between the two, in a way that was hardly possible in the early modern period; this disjunction is shown most crudely in the suggestion by recent governments that meals for in-patients are not a hospital's responsibility because they form no part of the entitlement to treatment.[3] Medical sociologists analyse both the medical consultation, including 'compliance', and (more rarely) transactions involving food, but, as far as I know, they do not bring the two together.[4]

The first version of this chapter was given at an Annual Conference of the Society for the Social History of Medicine in Sheffield in July, 1986 (summarised in *Bull. SSHM*, 40 (1987), 11–15). A revised version was given in Oxford in May 1991. I am grateful to Ruth Harris, John Walter and Charles Webster for comments on earlier versions, and to Sara Pennell for discussion and many valuable references.

1. The few 'regular' practitioners of nutritional medicine therefore tend to address themselves to the laity: see for example S. Davies and A. Stewart, *Nutritional Medicine*, ed. A. Stanway (London, 1987). See also P. Fieldhouse, *Food and Nutrition: Customs and Culture*, 2nd edn (London, 1995).

2. This kind of analysis is however notoriously difficult: 'Nutrition Research' [editorial], *BNF Nutrition Bulletin*, 15 (1990), 135–6. I owe this reference to Leslie Dunn.

3. For a recent affirmation (and extension) of this approach, see 'Why Parties must Face the Real Problems', *The Guardian*, 18 April 1997.

4. A significant exception is B. S. Turner, 'The Government of the Body: Medical Regimens and the Rationalization of Diet', *British Journal of Sociology*, 33 (1982), 254–69, not seen when this essay was first written; the following interpretation differs from Turner's historical account while agreeing with many of his premises. See in general S. Mennell, A. Murcott and A. H. van Otterloo, *The Sociology of Food: Eating, Diet and Culture* (London, 1992).

It is possible to offer explanations of this contrast between the present century and earlier periods in terms of changes located approximately in the last hundred years.[5] These might include: the growth of state welfare systems; strategies of professionalisation and specialisation; gender factors determining divisions of labour, both in medicine and within the domestic environment; the decline of holistic approaches within orthodox medicine; the commitment to single-factor, ontological explanations of disease; and the related faith in the 'magic bullet' model of treatment which is grounded on the effectiveness of antibiotics in treating infectious diseases. The single-factor approach was even helpful to the emergence of a 'scientific' approach to diet based on the discovery of vitamins. Without seeking to suggest that there is no basis to these explanations, this chapter will look more closely at the early modern period in order to determine whether all the stress is indeed to be placed on a modern transition, or whether, alternatively, the contrast between the earlier and the modern period is not as great in important respects as might be expected. By examining contemporary interest in, and knowledge of, food and food issues, we may arrive at reasons why the educated physician was driven to abandon one form of intellectual justification (Galenic dietetics) for another (physiology).

It could be objected that such an approach would ignore the most important contrast of all for the present and past of developed western societies: that between plenty and want. Any discussion of food and nutrition in the early modern period must show awareness of the existence of dearth, if not of famine, and the complex relationships between food supply and the incidence of increased mortality or epidemic disease. With a majority of the population at or below subsistence level, the overriding question tends to become that of the supply of staple foodstuffs such as grain. This can only be mentioned here as the essential background for the discussion. However, it will be borne in mind throughout that food habits must be related to class as well as regional differences, and that, as in the present, notions implying 'choice' must be deployed only with great caution. There is a consensus that early modern English populations suffered less nutritional deprivation than many countries in continental Europe; nonetheless, as Appleby has pointed out, the divergences in dietary experience between rich and poor seem to have widened in the sixteenth century, even though, as contemporaries often noted, there can be said to have been two kinds of malnutrition present, the malnutrition of plenty, and the malnutrition of want.[6]

Early modern commentators had a heightened awareness of the contrasting moral implications of the two forms of malnutrition, and it would be wrong to attempt to obscure what they saw so clearly. However, the issue of absolute standards in diet is as complicated historically as is any similar issue, such as effectiveness in medicine. Our own dietary standards continue to change. For example, the standard historical survey for England by Drummond and Wilbraham (which dates from 1939), together with the 'optimum standards' still used in

5. For a summary account see G. Rosen, *A History of Public Health* (1958; enlged edn, Baltimore, MD, and London, 1993), pp. 380–95.

6. A. B. Appleby, 'Diet in Sixteenth Century England: Sources, Problems, Possibilities', in Webster, *H, M & M*, pp. 115, 97.

much comparative work, let alone political discussion, are very meat-based; according to current trends, such standards are increasingly likely to require revision.[7] This adds further interesting complications to historical analysis. As an illustration, we can take Rice's account of the difference in diets offered to the private and pauper patients in the same Scottish asylums in the 1850s: the private patients were given hams, roasts, stews, fowls, wines, malt liquors and coffee, while the paupers 'had to make do' with porridge, broth, vegetables, potatoes, and a small amount of boiled beef daily. In contemporary terms, this contrast perfectly illustrates Rice's point about class-demarcation within the institution, and there can be little doubt that the patients' attitude to their diet was affected accordingly; but it is more difficult to decide how (or whether) to deal with the nature and effects of the contrast in modern nutritional terms. That is, it is possible (depending on quantity and quality) that the paupers had what we would currently regard as the healthier diet.[8] Moreover, as we shall see, attitudes to the kind of diet ascribed to poor populations might show considerable consistency over time but were by no means static. They show as many permutations as other aspects of difference between popular and elite cultures.[9]

With these provisos in mind, the first point to establish for present purposes is how marked it is in early modern sources that a concern with diet was *not* the exclusive preserve of the physician. Here, concern must be assumed to overlap with knowledge. In this regard, diet can be seen as paralleling medicine in general, in terms of lay engagement with its theory as well as its practice.[10] Related imperatives made diet as well as health a major preoccupation in early modern society. As we all need to eat to survive, some level of consciousness can be taken for granted, but the character of this awareness must vary according to period-specific conditions. Early modern English society was still overwhelmingly agricultural, and this proximity to the main sites of food production is reflected in the literary sources generated in towns, even though contemporaries saw, partly as an effect of classical models, a huge gulf of sensibility and sophistication between town and country.[11] The details of preoccupation with eating, like the details of preoccupation with health, are not easy to recover reliably from single sources. The 'meals and manners' tradition of historiography has flourished unchecked, while those concerned with standard-of-living debates have clung to such apparently dependable indicators as grain prices.[12] Until recently, relatively few economic historians have ventured into the area on other

7. J. C. Drummond and A. Wilbraham, *The Englishman's Food: Five Centuries of English Diet* (1939; revd edn 1957; London, 1991).

8. F. J. Rice, 'Scotland's "Museums of Madness": the Origins and Early Growth of an Organisation of Insanity in Nineteenth-century Scotland', *Bull. SSHM*, 38 (1986), 26.

9. See for example E. Meyer-Renschhausen, 'The Porridge Debate: Grain, Nutrition, and Forgotten Food Preservation Techniques', *Food and Foodways*, 5 (1991), 95–120.

10. See Pelling, 'Medicine and the Environment'.

11. See more recently, G. K. Paster, *The Idea of the City in the Age of Shakespeare* (Athens, GA, 1985); F. Heal, *Hospitality in Early Modern England* (Oxford, 1990), esp. chap. 3; M. Butler, *Theatre and Crisis 1632–1642* (Cambridge, 1987), chaps 7 and 9; K. Thomas, *Man and the Natural World: Changing Attitudes in England 1500–1800* (London, 1983), esp. chap. 6.

12. For comprehensive analysis of current historiographical debates centring on food, see S. Pennell, 'The Material Culture of Food in Early Modern England, c. 1650–1750' (University of Oxford DPhil thesis, 1997).

terms, partly because, as an aspect primarily of inland trade, there was not the same systematic recording as for imports and exports.[13] Nevertheless, as with health, indicators abound if a variety of sources is used, and this is as true of the economic significance of food, as it is of the socio-cultural aspects which are now attracting considerable attention.

Modern Britain is seen as wedded to a policy of cheap food, and one indicator of the predicament of the poor is that the proportion of their income spent on food tends to decrease.[14] For the early modern period, food, like clothing, was a dominant item of expenditure, and contemporaries saw it as feasible even for the richest to destroy their estates (and the poor) by over-indulgence at table.[15] In an economy in which transactions at all levels could still be in kind rather than cash, and individual income derived from a wide range of sources, items of food and drink played a large part, changing hands not only in exchange, but also in the form of gifts, bribes, and fines, at all levels. Robert Greene, for example, accused summoners – minor legal officials – of allowing themselves to be bribed with, as he put it, cheese, bacon, capons, and 'such od reversios', by wanton wives, to swear falsely that they were of good behaviour.[16] As we shall see later, the inclusion of ill-behaved women in this equation was not incidental. Food lent itself to bribery not just because it had value but also because it disappeared as it was enjoyed. Food gifts were however an overt item of legitimate expenditure, for corporations as well as individuals. Wine, (lump) sugar, and marchpane (marzipan) were regularly given to notables like judges and officers of the crown on their visits to towns. Such gifts constituted a graceful recognition of different orders of being, as well as reminding recipients of local interests.[17] Contemporary concern about the break-up – or swamping – of the social structure, and the loosening of the ties of social obligation, was most characteristically expressed in laments over the decline of hospitality in terms of food and drink directly given. These views could be idealised but concrete: Greene regretted that Westminster Hall was currently being used not for feasts but for settling controversies, and saw the good old order in terms of lavishness with chines of beef. Feasting was of course traditionally (and ideally) a way not only of settling controversies but of preventing them.[18] Contemporary opinion

13. One of the few was F. J. Fisher, on London (1935, repr. 1954): see idem, *London and the English Economy, 1500–1700*, ed. P. J. Corfield and N. B. Harte (London and Ronceverte, 1990), pp. 13–14, 61–79.

14. Cf. D. Piachaud and J. Webb, *The Price of Food* (London, 1996); C. Webster, 'Health, Welfare and Unemployment during the Depression', *P & P*, 109 (1985), 211–13; C. Shammas, 'Food Expenditures and Economic Well-being in Early Modern England', *Journal of Economic History*, 43 (1983), 89–100.

15. See for example John Caius, *A Boke or Counseill against the Disease called the Sweate* (1552; facs. edn, New York, 1937), fols 17recto, 23verso and *passim*. Caius condemned current English dietary habits as 'unwisely fine, and womanly delicate'.

16. L. Stone, *The Past and the Present Revisited* (London and New York, 1987), pp. 137, 139; Robert Greene, *A Quip for an Upstart Courtier* (1592) in A. B. Grosart (ed.), *Life and Complete Works of Robert Greene*, 15 vols (London, 1881–86), vol. 11, p. 256.

17. See Heal, *Hospitality*, esp. pp. 312–14. Thus Chester could offer large quantities of cheese (M. Braddick, personal communication, 1993) or York visitors receive a special type of bread (D. M. Palliser, 'Civic Mentality and the Environment in Tudor York', *Northern History*, 18 (1982), 89).

18. See in general Heal, *Hospitality*, esp. pp. 108ff. Greene, *Quip*, pp. 251, 230, 234. G. Rosser, 'Going to the Fraternity Feast: Commensality and Social Relations in Late Medieval England', *Journal of British Studies*, 33 (1994), 430–46.

was not convinced that other forms of lavish expenditure by people of rank filtered down to nourish the poor in the same way, so that it could in fact be a reproach to the new order that its followers did not eat enough: they 'pinch[ed] their bellies to polish their backs', and kept 'their mawes emptie, to fill their purses'.[19]

However, food, like health, was so universal a language that it could be spoken by either side. In some contexts, like Reformed funeral rites, food could compensate for what had been lost. There was also a newer, exclusive language of display within upper social groups, involving hypothetically edible items in private gardens and orchards. An example provided by Sir Hugh Plat, known as a practical author interested in food preservation and the prevention of famine, is his instructions for creating the equivalent of alfresco after-dinner mints by sugaring roses that were still alive in the garden. These the guests – highly select individuals – could then pluck for themselves while admiring the host's horticultural expertise.[20] By contrast, fasting was still an accepted mode of expression, even for Protestants. While the Huguenot physician Baldwin Hamey the elder, when visiting Russia in the 1590s, could see it as reprehensible that a sick person should abstain from meat for religious reasons, Francis Bacon could view (moderate) fasting as different from the superstitious ceremonies characteristic of popery, being a real and not merely figurative 'impression' imposed by the mind on the body.[21] Moreover, the secular motives for fasting which prescribed fish rather than meat had greatly increased, as encouraging the fishing fleet was seen as vital not only for the economy but also for defence, as the backbone of men and skills for the navy.[22] Fasting would later become suspect, because of the dislike of the prayer-and-fasting practices of non-conformists, though non-conformists were themselves critical of extremes of fasting.[23]

Most fundamental of all in terms of social obligations and contemporary consciousness was the responsibility of the authorities for regulating the quality, quantity, and price of staple foodstuffs, in particular corn. In terms of consensual governance this topic has been extensively investigated, revealing the social assumptions behind responses to dearth or high prices. It has been stressed that the responses of the lower orders to dearth were active, graduated, and

19. Greene, *Quip*, p. 236.

20. C. Gittings, 'Urban Funerals in Late Medieval and Reformation England', in S. Bassett (ed.), *Death in Towns: Urban Responses to the Dying and the Dead, 100–1600* (Leicester, 1992), p. 173. Hugh Plat, *The Garden of Eden* (1st edn as *Floraes Paradise*, 1608; London, 1653), pp. 42–4. On the significance of enclosed gardens, see J. Prest, *The Garden of Eden: The Botanic Garden and the Re-creation of Paradise* (New Haven, CT, and London, 1981), pp. 21–6.

21. J. J. Keevil, *Hamey the Stranger* (London, 1952), pp. 46–7; F. Bacon, *The Advancement of Learning*, Bk 2, IX, 3, Everyman edn (London, 1965), p. 108.

22. Drummond and Wilbraham, *Englishman's Food*, pp. 63–4; Webster, *Great Instauration*, p. 456.

23. On fasting in general, see the essay review by C. M. Counihan of works by Bell, Brumberg, and Bynum in *Food and Foodways*, 3 (1989), 357–75; J. O'Hara May, *Elizabethan Dyetary of Health* (Lawrence, Kansas, 1977), chap. 7; P. Collinson, *The Religion of Protestants* (Oxford, 1982), pp. 260–3; M. MacDonald (ed.), *Witchcraft and Hysteria in Elizabethan London: Edward Jorden and the Mary Glover Case* (London, 1991), p. xx. Thomas Browne included fasting in a sceptical discussion of whether any lower animals lived on immaterial substance: *Pseudodoxia Epidemica*, Bk 3, XXI, in *Works*, ed. C. Sayle, 3 vols (London and Edinburgh, 1904–7), vol. 2, pp. 61–2. See also S. Schaffer, 'Piety, Physic and Prodigious Abstinence', in O. P. Grell and A. Cunningham (eds), *Religio Medici: Medicine and Religion in Seventeenth-Century England* (Aldershot, 1996), pp. 171–203.

intelligent, rather than instinctive or hysterical. Contemporary awareness of such questions was particularly sharp not only because of difficult economic conditions, but because the structure of buying and selling was perceived as rapidly changing, with the decline of the regulated market and the increase in wholesaling and middlemen. In spite of this decline, such concepts as 'wholesomeness' and the just price for foodstuffs were still firmly established and provide a sharp contrast with later periods.[24] In the modern period probably only World War II could provide a comparable moral climate with respect to the means of subsistence.[25] Inhibitions on 'taxing the workman's pint' can be seen as a lingering vestige of this set of attitudes.

The discovery by historians that women were involved in food riots in particular draws attention to gender as an important factor in food as an aspect of social interaction. That women have some kind of primary role with respect to nourishment may well be a consistent feature of western societies, but the structure of this role, and the limits on the 'rights' or control which women were able to exercise as a result of it, need careful definition.[26] Again, health care provides a useful comparison. The ambivalences which ensue, especially from the fact that women had most control in infancy and childhood, are elusive but can be explored using a wide range of approaches and sources.

Issues of quantity rather than quality are more accessible to historians and it is perhaps too readily assumed that these were more important. Early modern regulation shows a sensitivity to both. A problem recognised then, and still current today, was that of collusion among suppliers to prevent poor consumers buying in the small quantities which were all they could afford. It was also realised that farmers who held corn back from market could eventually force the poor to buy bad corn even though they and everybody else were aware that its consumption could lead to disease and death.[27] The major economic phenomena relating to staple foods have been given more attention by historians than the minutiae of control routinely carried out by craft companies and municipal authorities.[28] This degree of supervision, still being exercised in the sixteenth century although seen as under threat, comes as a revelation after conventional

24. J. Walter and K. Wrightson, 'Dearth and the Social Order in Early Modern England', *P & P*, 71 (1976), 22–42.

25. Less often noticed is the postwar backlash of resentment against rationing, particularly on the part of the middle class. Exceptions are E. A. McCarty, 'Attitudes to Women and Domesticity in England, *c.* 1939–1955' (University of Oxford DPhil, 1995), esp. chap. 8, and the work of Ina Zweiniger-Bargielowska. I am grateful to Ross McKibbin for his help with these references. In general see J. Burnett and D. J. Oddy (eds), *The Origins and Development of Food Policies in Europe* (London and New York, 1994).

26. For different approaches to this theme, see N. Z. Davis, 'Women in the Crafts in Sixteenth-century Lyon', in B. A. Hanawalt (ed.), *Women and Work in Preindustrial Europe* (Bloomington, IN, 1986), p. 179; R. A. Houlbrooke, 'Women's Social Life and Common Action in England from the Fifteenth Century to the Eve of the Civil War', *Continuity and Change*, 1 (1986), 176–8; W. A. McIntosh and M. Zey, 'Women as Gatekeepers of Food Consumption: a Sociological Critique', *Food and Foodways*, 3 (1989), 317–32; J. Adelman, '"Anger's my Meat": Feeding, Dependency, and Aggression in *Coriolanus*', in *Representing Shakespeare*, ed. C. Kahn and M. M. Schwartz (Baltimore, MD, and London, 1982), pp. 129–49.

27. J. H. Thomas, *Town Government in the Sixteenth Century* (London, 1933), p. 83; H. T. Riley, *Memorials of London . . . 1276–1419* (London, 1868), pp. 90, 121; William Harrison, *Elizabethan England*, ed. F. J. Furnivall (London, n.d.), p. 38.

28. Thomas, *Town Government*, chaps 8 and 9, provides many such details.

histories of public health which portray the nineteenth-century medical officer of health or sanitary inspector battling against such abuses as if for the first time.[29] Tudor and Stuart administrations are usually portrayed as being unable to control the course of economic events and, occasionally, as misguided even to try, but this perspective is not normally related to issues of quality and actual consumption. A depth of experience of routine proceedings against those who tried to sell food where the light was too bad to see clearly what was being sold, bakers who filched pieces of their neighbours' dough brought to their ovens for baking, butchers who smeared fresh blood on stale meat, and fishermen who used nets of too small a mesh, could be expected to produce a broadly based moral consensus with respect to food supply issues.[30] As is now well known, the early modern period also demanded the control of other industries which directly affected food supply, of which the most important was brewing. A lesser-known, new industry giving cause for concern, especially as it appeared to cater only for idle luxury and was carried on chiefly by female immigrants, was starchmaking.[31] Both brewing and starchmaking were prohibited when corn was in short supply. In all such contexts, the role of food is better seen as 'transformative' than as symbolic, even though regulatory proceedings may have been exemplary rather than universal or universally effective.[32]

It should already be clear that, whatever the continuing importance of commensality — eating together, and eating the same things — in defining social and familial groupings, food was equally expressive of hierarchy. It would be highly misleading to stress the prominence of food in social obligations and exchange without also bringing out its fundamental role in power relations, enforcement of hierarchy, punishment, and the violation of bonds seen as natural.[33] This historical reality has been taken to an extreme by Camporesi, who sees the state of the poor, starved by lack of food or drugged as a result of its poor quality, as an indicator of total powerlessness and the absence of even lipservice to natural bonds.[34] The unwillingness of early modern Englishmen to believe in this degree of social dissolution, whatever their sense of crisis, is perhaps indicated by the tendency to think of vagrants as overfed rather than starving, and the reluctance of parish officials to register deaths as from starvation even if the dead were a stranger from outside the parish.[35] Most of the examples I wish

29. A partial exception is Rosen, *History of Public Health*, pp. 34–5, making brief reference to continental sources.

30. For examples of these misdemeanours over an extended period see Riley, *Memorials of London*, pp. 162ff; Greene, *Quip*, p. 274.

31. J. Thirsk, *Economic Policy and Projects* (Oxford, 1988), pp. 83–93.

32. This distinction is borrowed from anthropological analysis: see J. Fajans, 'The Transformative Value of Food: a Review Essay', *Food and Foodways*, 3 (1988), 143–66.

33. Interest in anorexia nervosa has led to extensive discussion of this topic. See for example the review by Counihan, note 23 above; L. S. Dixon, *Perilous Chastity: Women and Illness in Pre-Enlightenment Art and Medicine* (Ithaca, NY, and London, 1995); I. S. L. Loudon, 'The Diseases called Chlorosis', *Psychological Medicine*, 14 (1984), 27–36; K. Figlio, 'Chlorosis and Chronic Disease in Nineteenth-century Britain: the Social Construction of Somatic Illness in a Capitalistic Society', *Social History*, 3 (1978), 167–97; A. Murcott (ed.), *The Sociology of Food and Eating* (Aldershot, 1983).

34. See esp. P. Camporesi, *Bread of Dreams*, trans. D. Gentilcore (Chicago and Cambridge, 1989); Camporesi, *The Land of Hunger*, trans. T. Croft-Murray (Cambridge, 1996).

35. See for example Pound, *Census*, p. 7; Pelling, 'Medicine and the Environment', p. 78 (27).

to give suggest that something like a dialogue was still being maintained, however unequal the balance of power. Telling incidents include the leniency ultimately shown to a London couple imprisoned in the 1550s during Lent for eating a dead cock they had found on a dunghill.[36] Obvious policy examples are sumptuary legislation, food doles at funerals and parish festivals, and, on the negative side, minimal provision for prison inmates. Elizabethan Ipswich, for example, provided eggs, whiting, butter, bread, salt, mutton, chicken, sugar, milk, cakes, oysters, and other delicacies for plague victims – however notionally – but also withheld food from those poor inmates of their hospital (Christ's) who refused to work. A sense of hierarchy was constantly expressed in food terms in legal documents. Late medieval maintenance agreements, as analysed by Dyer, in which property was handed over in return for annual subsistence, specified not an optimum or even a minimum standard of nourishment, but a level commensurate with the expectations to which the person maintained was entitled according to his or her position in life.[37] In sixteenth and seventeenth-century apprenticeship indentures, food and drink was specifically mentioned, and failure to provide it was a common cause of breakdown in a form of contract which was, in theory at least, rather rigidly preserved. Again, the standard expected was that appropriate to the master's occupation and style of living. It is possible that the alleged failure to observe the obligation to provide suitable food and drink was used as a pretext for breaking an unsuccessful arrangement. Certainly a master who simply beat his apprentice in the hope of getting rid of him was likely to be disappointed.[38] Similarly, infanticide by violence was, Wrightson has concluded, an uncommon crime; far more common was causing the death of the unwanted child by withholding nourishment or 'infanticidal nursing'. All of these were matters in which laypeople set standards and arrived at judgements. In all of them, the food relationship was very much a transitive one, even though it was apparent that food had to be accepted as well as offered in an acceptable form, and equally apparent that the case of an infant presented obvious difficulties in determining intent on the part of the mother. Less clear, for post-Reformation England, is whether self-starvation became self-murder or retained its ambiguous status.[39]

An interesting aspect of contemporary sensibility, interconnected with both food and medicine and worthy of further investigation, is what seems to have been a generalised fear of poisoning. This is usually discussed as an aspect of paranoia, xenophobic stereotyping (of Italians in particular), and covert operations among the ruling elite, but it has wider social ramifications than this. Given that it was mostly women who stirred the pot, as well as suckling infants, it

36. S. Brigden, 'Religion and Social Obligation in Early Sixteenth-century London', *P & P*, 103 (1984), 107–8. See also Walter and Wrightson, 'Dearth and the Social Order', pp. 24–5.

37. J. Webb (ed.), *Poor Relief in Elizabethan Ipswich*, Suffolk Record Society IX (1966), pp. 110–14 (1579), 16; C. Dyer, 'English Diet in the Middle Ages', in T. H. Aston, P. R. Coss, C. Dyer and J. Thirsk (eds), *Social Relations and Ideas* (Cambridge, 1983), p. 198.

38. Pelling, 'Apprenticeship', pp. 44–5; idem, 'Child Health', pp. 161–2 (130–1).

39. K. Wrightson, 'Infanticide in Earlier Seventeenth-century England', *Local Population Studies*, 15 (1975), 10–22; M. MacDonald, '*The Fearefull Estate of Francis Spira*: Narrative, Identity, and Emotion in Early Modern England', *Journal of British Studies*, 31 (1992), 42–3, n. 34.

is perhaps not surprising that poisoning, like witchcraft, seems to have been regarded as a 'woman's crime' in the early modern period as in the modern.[40] However poisoning was an act which connected suspect loyalty, suspect gender, and suspect status, all in a context of intimacy betrayed. It was not only women who fitted the stereotype of the poisoner: so did physicians, and cooks.[41]

Some points already mentioned indicate the ubiquity of reference to food and drink in contemporary sources, but suggest at the same time factors likely to increase the difficulty of deciding exactly what people ate, on the basis of what they chose to record. Modern surveys find that respondents are rarely comprehensive, exact, or even 'honest' about food intake; instead, food emerges as an element of subjectivity. It should not be surprising that the early modern period provides a wide range of variations on the theme of food as an aspect of self-definition. The ideal intake for Englishmen was seen as wine and particularly as meat, a subject brilliantly treated some time ago by the critic Dover Wilson in his essay on Falstaff, the 'sweet beef' of Shakespeare's Prince Hal.[42] This ideal, although constantly subject to revivals in later periods, was already partly nostalgic, given contemporary economic conditions, and partly being undermined by the social aspirations of upwardly mobile urbanites such as Robert Greene's character 'queasie maister velvet breeches', who could not digest his meat without conserves, or end his meal without suckets. Urbanites retaliated by condemning their country cousins as 'beef-witted',[43] but classical dietary theory ensured that the principle of *variety* in diet, an unquestioned premise in the present century, was not yet established as desirable or even safe.[44] Man was omnivorous, which some saw as signifying his microcosmic nature, but this entailed a special liability to 'distemper'.[45]

A corollary of the meat-eating ideal was the positive dislike of the poor for foodstuffs, however nourishing, which were generally categorised as appropriate for lower animals. This categorisation may have had as much effect as the insignificance of some vegetables in cost terms, in keeping them out of seemingly objective records.[46] Harrison thought seed crops had fallen into neglect in the fifteenth and sixteenth centuries, except as animal food. Although the poor were regularly advised to subsist on one or another lower-caste vegetable foodstuff, the distaste for such expedients was by no means confined to the poor.

40. On women, food, poison, and witchcraft, see D. Purkiss, 'Women's Stories of Witchcraft in Early Modern England: the House, the Body, the Child', *Gender and History*, 7 (1995), 413–17; L. Roper, *Oedipus and the Devil: Witchcraft, Sexuality and Religion in Early Modern Europe* (London and New York, 1994), pp. 207–9.

41. Pelling, 'Compromised by Gender', p. 105.

42. J. Dover Wilson, *The Fortunes of Falstaff* (1943; Cambridge, 1979), esp. pp. 25–31. A female counterpart to Falstaff is Jonson's Ursla, the pig-woman in *Bartholomew Fair*. In general see N. Fiddes, *Meat, A Natural Symbol* (London and New York, 1991).

43. Greene, *Quip*, p. 249. For play on this, see *Twelfth Night*, I, iii, 83–5 (Arden edn, London, 1985), p. 15. On the humoral effects of beef, see R. Burton, *The Anatomy of Melancholy*, ed. T. C. Faulkner, N. K. Kiessling and R. L. Blair, 3 vols (Oxford, 1989–94), vol. 1, p. 212.

44. Burton, *Anatomy of Melancholy*, vol. 1, pp. 220–1; vol. 2, pp. 25–6; vol. 3, p. 63. Cf. Meyer-Renschhausen, 'The Porridge Debate'.

45. Bacon, *Advancement of Learning*, Bk 2, X, 2, pp. 109–10.

46. See A. J. Grieco, 'The Social Politics of Pre-Linnaean Botanical Classification', *I Tatti Studies*, 4 (1991), 131–49.

Some contemporary commentators almost go so far as to suggest that it was less of a national disgrace for the poor to starve, than it was for them to survive by eating food fit for beasts.[47]

It was not only broad social categorisation which could be construed in terms of food. The delineation of typical 'characters' according to occupation was a popular literary pursuit, linked with the literature on social abuses. These satirical portraits concentrated on appearance and personal habits, including dietary stereotypes. Thus the tailors, dainty and proud from associating with their betters and from the 'clean' nature of their occupation, could be depicted eating buttered peas one by one by picking the peas up with their needles, the fine tools of their trade; shoemakers by contrast, who had the reputation of being good company but improvident, sat down together to 'powdered' (salted) beef and 'brewesse' (slices of bread with fat broth poured over them). Shared assumptions meant that details could be meaningful: peas were 'daintier' than beans, because less 'windy', and salted foods were known to encourage drunkenness.[48]

The stereotypes which were created as an aspect of the emergent nationalism of the sixteenth century also made reference to food habits. The intrusive and often successful Dutch immigrants and traders were called butter-tubs (-bags, -boxes, -mouths) and abused as wassailing drunkards.[49] By contrast, Turks and Moors, in Robert Burton's view, offended moderation by their extreme fasting. The Scots, according to William Harrison – writing before James's accession – abused the canons of hospitality by consuming their nicest food first and the coarsest last, so that their leftovers were never worth having.[50] In a divorce case of 1669 involving an English wife and a French husband, part of the wife's allegation of cruelty was that she was often left meatless and very hungry, her husband being 'a Frenchman and useth much the diet of herbs and other slight eating'.[51] Also emerging however were the grounds for what might be called a relativist or ethnological approach. Montaigne, writing in the 1580s of the force of habit in mankind, cited the example of 'great nations' in the new world of the Indies who, in the face of instincts assumed to be universal, ate spiders. According to Burton, custom altered nature itself: mediterranean peoples could eat quantities of vegetables, milk, and raw herbs with impunity, the Welsh could eat white meats, and the Dutch, fish, roots, and butter, all because they were used to them. The heat of digestion of northerners and southerners varied because

47. Drummond and Wilbraham, *Englishman's Food*, pp. 98–102; Harrison, *Elizabethan England*, pp. 25–6, 96–7; Burton, *Anatomy of Melancholy*, vol. 1, p. 217; Appleby, 'Diet in Sixteenth Century England', pp. 105–15; M. Thick, 'Root Crops and the Feeding of London's Poor in the Late Sixteenth and Early Seventeenth Centuries', in J. Chartres and D. Hey (eds), *English Rural Society, 1500–1800* (Cambridge, 1990), pp. 279–96, esp. p. 288.

48. Greene, *Quip*, pp. 264–5; Henry Buttes, *Dyets Dry Dinner* (London, 1599), sig. E7; Harrison, *Elizabethan England*, pp. 95, 103.

49. See for example *OED*; Greene, *Quip*, p. 288; Overbury's 'Drunken Dutchman Resident in England', in H. Morley (ed.), *Character Writings of the Seventeenth Century* (London, 1891), pp. 72–3. See in general S. Schama, 'The Unruly Realm: Appetite and Restraint in Seventeenth Century Holland', *Daedalus*, 108 (1979), 103–23.

50. Burton, *Anatomy of Melancholy*, vol. 1, p. 225; see also Bacon, *Advancement of Learning*, Bk 2, IX, 3, pp. 107–8. Harrison, *Elizabethan England*, p. 106.

51. London, Court of Arches, Lambeth Palace Library, Houston no. 842 (1669): Elizabeth Foyster, personal communication. I am grateful to Dr Foyster for this extract.

of the differences in climate, and the people of these different regions had to be fed accordingly.[52] Each country had its indigenous climate, soil, edible plants and animals, and remedies for its own diseases, and the character of its people was similarly determined. These themes were traditional, but were receiving new emphases and interpretations.

To some extent, the links perceived between food and identity also allowed a fixed, two-nations approach to be taken to the different diets of the rich and the poor.[53] Digestibility was increasingly valued as writers gave prominence to work that took place indoors, whence, it has been supposed, the growing preference in the seventeenth century for white, that is wheaten, bread. The twentieth-century economic historian, Ashley, arguing for the neglected importance of rye in the diet of the poor in the early modern period, quoted contemporary opinion to imply that labourers preferred a mixture of grains called maslin because bread made of it was filling and stayed a long time in the stomach. However, these properties were also attributed to beef. Nicholas Culpeper, translating into the vernacular in the middle of the seventeenth century, assumed that in a popular book priority needed to be given to purges and other evacuants, because the poor, having an ill diet, produced more excrements than the rich.[54] There is a hint here (unintended by Culpeper) of the equation of crudities with fallen man: the greater the refinement (in all senses), the less the need for evacuation, and the closer the person came to a more spiritual condition.[55] There were many variations around the themes of diet, health, and social class. Hentzner, travelling in England in the late sixteenth century, made often-cited observations on the unhealthy over-consumption of sugar by the rich, including the Queen. Burton, in indicting almost every class of food as capable of causing mental ill-effects, came close to saying that the poor, whatever the disadvantages of their coarse and immutable diet, were at least likely to stay sane and continent, even if they were, according to another article of general belief, doomed to remain stupid as well.[56]

Although apparently based on practical experience or observation, much of this type of writing also drew on existing preconceptions. The consumption of food can be seen as humanity's most fundamental relation with the natural world; it is not surprising that lying behind most of the examples already given were different views of the nature of providence.[57] The sixteenth century saw an

52. M. de Montaigne, 'On Habit', in *Essays*, trans. and ed. M. A. Screech (London, 1991), p. 123. Burton, *Anatomy of Melancholy*, vol. 1, pp. 225–7.

53. See Grieco, 'Social Politics'; O'Hara May, *Elizabethan Dyetary*, pp. 90, 118–19, 202, 226, 243.

54. W. Ashley, *The Bread of our Forefathers* (Oxford, 1926), pp. 16ff, 164–5. Burton, *Anatomy of Melancholy*, vol. 1, pp. 212, 227. N. Culpeper, *Medicines for the Poor . . . [with] Health for the Rich and Poor by Dyet* (Edinburgh, 1665), p. 2.

55. On evacuation and the Fall, see Pelling, 'Medicine and the Environment', p. 78 (26).

56. O'Hara May, *Elizabethan Dyetary*, pp. 280–2; P. Hentzner, *Travels in England* (London, 1889), pp. 47, 83. Burton, *Anatomy of Melancholy*, vol. 1, pp. 211–28, 238–45, vol. 3, p. 63. For Burton on the ill-effects of (comparative) poverty, see ibid., vol. 1, pp. 344–55.

57. On the broad appeal of providentialism, see most recently A. Walsham, '"The Fatall Vesper": Providentialism and Anti-Popery in Late Jacobean London', *P & P*, 144 (1994), 37–87, and references on pp. 61–2. More specifically, see D. Harley, 'Spiritual Physic, Providence and English Medicine, 1560–1640', in O. P. Grell and A. Cunningham (eds), *Medicine and the Reformation* (London, 1993), pp. 101–17.

upsurge of systematic works exhaustively surveying different classes in the living world, minerals, plants, birds, fishes, and even dogs and insects. These could be variously inspired, but many authors were prompted by different shades of Christian humanism.[58] According to the Spanish humanist and visitor to England, Juan Luis Vives, writing early in the century, natural history was a study to be built on the firm foundations of faith. Plants and animals were to be listed for their virtues, for their love and hate to man, and as evidence of God's care. Such an approach was for Vives entirely compatible with a range of practical results – benefits to husbandry, the culture of palatable fruits, and the discovery of remedies – but he noted that in this he differed from the usual academic view. Observing that most people thought it far harder to make discoveries in dietetics than in medicine, Vives accepted that the very first such discoveries must have been made under a providential dispensation, since man and animals alike would otherwise have died out as a result of experiments that failed.[59]

By contrast, Harrison, writing later in the century, gloried in the superior gardens and orchards of the English nobility; for him the function of new discoveries was less utilitarian than contemplative – in a post-Reformation style. Thus the beauties of these exclusive estates had a significance for the whole of society almost in the same way that the prayers of the closed orders had been thought to redeem the whole world. With respect to introductions from the new worlds of America and the Indies, Harrison did not think these were intended to be eaten by Englishmen, because God had ordained sufficient food sources for man's necessity in each country. Instead, exotics were to be cherished for the delight of the senses, and for the glorification of God through his gifts. Harrison urged attention to the common things crushed heedlessly underfoot, because the things most needed would, in God's design, also be the most plentiful. In spite of his somewhat casuistical justifications of noble estates, Harrison also deplored the tendency of merchants and nobles actually to eat dangerous items like mushrooms and 'verangenes' (eggplants), 'as if nature had ordained all for the belly', or that all should be eaten for which God had provided remedies. That is, the offending members of the elite were tempting God's providence. Harrison did however envisage a time when the new plants, by acclimatising themselves in England under favour from God, would signify that they had transmuted into native commodities, and this is certainly what happened for at least some classes of society in the following century.[60]

Man's relation to the natural world was also very relevant to the state of fallen man. For writers of a more millenarian bent, imitating Adam by giving names to the 'new' natural creation might be a duty which, like the conversion

---

58. See Thomas, *Man and the Natural World*, esp. chap. 2; A. S. Pease, 'Things without Honour', *Classical Philology*, 21 (1926), 27–42; A. G. Debus, *Man and Nature in the Renaissance* (Cambridge, 1978), chap. 3.

59. W. E. Houghton, 'The History of Trades: Its Relation to Seventeenth-century Thought', *Journal of the History of Ideas*, 2 (1941), 33–4; J. L. Vives, *Vives on Education*, trans. F. Watson (Cambridge, 1913), pp. 215–16.

60. Harrison, *Elizabethan England*, pp. 24–33. On Harrison's commitment to the established social order, see G. Parry, *A Protestant Vision: William Harrison and the Reformation of Elizabethan England* (Cambridge, 1987), pp. 282ff.

of the Jews, would hasten the second coming.[61] Man was distinguished from the rest of the creation, but fallen man was also uniquely sinful, a condition which expressed itself in the distorted character of his relationships with his means of subsistence. It was noted that while only man cooked his food, only man ate without appetite and sought by decadent means to stimulate his appetite beyond his need.[62] One thing led to another on the downward path, just as sauces (liquefying) led to tobacco (drying). There was traditionally a direct link between food and sex – 'without Ceres and Bacchus, Venus would freeze' – and thus between over-eating and lust.[63] Biblicism meant that both asceticism and vegetarianism were current topics, if not current practices. Meat-eating – recognised as a form of killing – and evil, had been accepted together as part of the world after the Flood. Later in the seventeenth century, Thomas Browne, thoughtfully examining the likely or naturalistic reality behind the apple eaten by Adam (a topic of recurrent interest), the pulses and water meted out to Daniel, and the locusts and honey consumed by St John (a topic also discussed by Paracelsus), nonetheless saw no absolute necessity to eat any animal, since scriptural authority was against it.[64]

Longevity, virtue, and moderate diet were all connected because they were so connected in the Bible, as well as being recommended by the 'honorary Christians' among pagan authors. As Charles Webster has shown, the restoration to fallen man of the length of life recorded in the Bible was a deliberate aim of Puritan thinkers in particular, although by no means confined to them. A concrete example of these attitudes was the Protestant scholar, controversialist, and medical practitioner Gabriel Harvey, who thought a spare diet favoured both mental and physical activity, although for him this was also enforced by poverty. One of Harvey's few mundane rewards was the fact that he lived to about eighty, on, according to Nashe, a diet of buttered roots, 'porknells', and sheep's trotters.[65] It should be stressed that early modern writers, 'sweet beef' notwithstanding, did not regard being fat as desirable. Plethora was an unsafe condition; the capacity for restraint was also what distinguished man from the beasts.[66]

61. Webster, *Great Instauration*, pp. 8, 10, 16–17, 324–30, 380–1 and *passim*; Prest, *Garden of Eden*, chap. 4; D. S. Katz, *The Jews in the History of England 1485–1850* (Oxford, 1994), pp. 107–14.

62. Burton, *Anatomy of Melancholy*, vol. 1, pp. 223, 365; vol. 2, p. 24 (quoting Cardano). Those closer to the Edenic state had less depraved appetites: H. C. Porter, *The Inconstant Savage: England and the North American Indian 1500–1660* (London, 1979), pp. 142, 239–40.

63. Buttes, *Dyets Dry Dinner*, Ep. Ded. 'Partem Amici'. S. Slive, *Dutch Painting 1600–1800* (New Haven, CT, and London, 1995), p. 11; P. Crawford, 'Sexual Knowledge in England, 1500–1750', in R. Porter and M. Teich (eds), *Sexual Knowledge, Sexual Science* (Cambridge, 1994), p. 85.

64. Thomas, *Man and the Natural World*, pp. 287–90. See in general C. Spencer, *The Heretic's Feast. A History of Vegetarianism* (London, 1993). Browne, *Pseudodoxia Epidemica*, Bk 7, chaps 1, 9, 25, in *Works*, vol. 3, pp. 1–5, 27–9, 76–84; 'Plants in Scripture', in *Certain Miscellany Tracts*, ibid., pp. 226–30.

65. Webster, *Great Instauration*, section IV; G. Moore Smith (ed.), *Gabriel Harvey's Marginalia* (Stratford upon Avon, 1913), pp. 56, 69; R. B. McKerrow (ed.), *Works of Thomas Nashe*, 5 vols (Oxford, 1966), vol. 3, p. 94. 'Porknells' were a variety of sheep's offal (*OED*).

66. See for example the practitioner of physic and surgery Richard Banister, who recommended his purging ale as a means of reducing fat bodies: idem, *An Appendent Part of a Treatise of One Hundreth and Thirteene Diseases of the Eyes* (London, 1621), chap. 8. For one man's sense of himself in this respect, see R. Jütte, 'Aging and Body Image in the Sixteenth Century: Hermann Weinsberg's (1518–97) Perception of the Aging Body', *European History Quarterly*, 18 (1988), 262–4, 274, 278ff. On the theory of 'surfeit', see O'Hara May, *Elizabethan Dyetary*, pp. 127–9.

'Mischiefs', concluded Jonson's magistrate, stating the obvious, 'feed like beasts until they be fat, and then they bleed'. Moderation, constantly recommended by the ancients, was also the quality which seemed closest to God's dispensation; the image of man, being in the image of God, should be neither gross nor wasted. Wasting was of course one of the effects of witchcraft, although, as Walter and Wrightson have suggested, dearth, or the wasting of the many, could be satisfactorily interpreted as the judgement of God, at least for some.[67]

Even at the practical level aimed at by Culpeper, the rewards of temperance covered almost all aspects of man's life on earth. A temperate diet, he wrote, drawing heavily on traditional as well as current thought, frees from diseases, arms the body against accidents, resists epidemic diseases, makes men's bodies fit for any employment, makes men live long, makes men die without pain, maintains the senses in vigour, mitigates passions and affections, preserves the memory, quickens the understanding, and allays the heat of lust. In a similar vein Henry More reported the adverse effects of extremes: he became ill not only while fasting for Lent but also on breaking his fast. He hoped to restore himself by diet and exercise. The obverse of such transformative views was of course that it was open to the satirically minded to suggest that people who thought they saw demons were merely suffering from indigestion brought on by some form of excess.[68] Temperate courses, the ideal of the ancients (especially Hippocrates) as well as of classically trained physicians, were also designed to imitate a state of grace in which expensive physic was something unnecessary and even unnatural.[69] Physic under this interpretation became a despised expedient needed not only by fallen man but by man who had fallen out of a 'state of nature'. The unnaturalness of physic was suggested by Harrison, who, for all his enthusiasm for fine gardens and rare plants, found the interference of modern gardeners in the quality of fruits very strange, as if they thought they were physicians acting on diseased bodies. Furthermore, many of these rare plants could only be kept going by special feeding and watering, as if apothecaries' shops were needful for gardens.[70]

Physicians, in giving advice, deliberately distanced themselves from the practical procedures (bleeding, dosing, topical applications of all kinds) carried out by the lower orders of practitioner. In effect their most valuable services to the patient were often diagnosis and prognosis; these were of course vulnerable to disproof or intervention by other practitioners. Otherwise, the physician's relationship with a patient depended upon his taking a sustained interest in the individual constitution as affected by every day's experience, and upon his giving minute advice on how to vary that experience to good effect.[71] The chief

---

67. Jonson, *Volpone*, IV, 7, 150–1. Walter and Wrightson, 'Dearth and the Social Order', pp. 28–9.

68. Culpeper, *Health for the Rich and Poor*, To the Reader. More to Anne Conway, 5 April and 5 Aug. 1662, in S. Hutton and M. H. Nicolson (eds), *The Conway Letters: The Correspondence of Anne, Viscountess Conway, Henry More, and their Friends 1642–1684* (Oxford, 1992), pp. 200, 205; see also p. 92.

69. On the attraction of Hippocratic ideas for sectarians, see G. Smith, 'Thomas Tryon's Regimen for Women: Sectarian Health in the Seventeenth Century', in London Feminist History Group (ed.), *The Sexual Dynamics of History* (London, 1983), pp. 47–65.

70. Harrison, *Elizabethan England*, pp. 31–2. See also Montaigne, 'On the Cannibals', in *Essays*, pp. 231–2.

71. For background see N. Siraisi, *Medieval and Early Renaissance Medicine* (Chicago and London, 1990).

factors determining well-being were traditionally codified into the non-naturals – the naturals being the body's own systems, or what began, in the late sixteenth century, to be called physiology.[72] Of all the non-naturals, diet was seen as the mother of diseases in humanity, because it was, of necessity, most lengthily internalised in the human body. Hence, physicians were most numerous and active at elite levels of society, where dietary principles were most liable to abuse (and where, in theory at least, there was most scope for variation and therefore for the means of correction).[73] But, at the same time, diet provided the best means of avoiding physic altogether. As already suggested, there was every reason why views giving primacy to diet should not be confined merely to physicians. In addition, the vernacular literature of the sixteenth and seventeenth centuries did much not only to provide alternatives to Galenic physic, but to demystify Galenic physic itself. Increased access to humoral physiology and the link between diet and health was given by a range of writers, from herbalists like William Turner, reformers and iconoclasts like Culpeper, and university physicians seeking to amuse their upper-class Anglophone patrons, like Henry Buttes.[74] In her pioneering work on the Elizabethan dietary of health, Jane O'Hara May has drawn attention to the commingling of food and medicine in contemporary thought, but this in itself indicates the degree to which medicine as well as diet was a matter of lay rather than exclusively 'professional' concern and knowledge.[75] By the late seventeenth century, even William Petty, who had a vested interest in the natural history of trades, could say dismissively that 'Vulgar People make the Cause of every Mans Sickness to be what he did last eat'.[76]

Thus, in relation to one of their central areas of expertise, early modern physicians were increasingly the victims of a paradox: diet was becoming common knowledge, while at the same time physic was seen as subordinate to diet, rather than the other way round. That diet was prior to medicine in the way already suggested was given explicit epistemological status by Vives, whose views on the usefulness of natural history we have already glanced at. For Vives, the origin of physicians in the ancient world – which followed, rather than preceding, that of surgeons – certainly lay in the creation of dietetics by Hippocrates, but the principles of dietetics were more universal than those of medicine. Dietetics proceeded by precepts and formulae; medicine proceeded not by precept but by action, and was applicable not to all people at all times (as was

72. P. H. Niebyl, 'The Non-naturals', *Bull. Hist. Med.*, 45 (1971), 486–92; L. Demaitre, 'Nature and the Art of Medicine in the Later Middle Ages', *Mediaevalia*, 2 (1976), 23–47; *DSB*, art. 'Fernel, Jean'.

73. Burton, *Anatomy of Melancholy*, vol. 1, p. 211 (quoting Fernel); Browne, *Pseudodoxia Epidemica*, Bk 3, XXI, in *Works*, vol. 2, pp. 54–5; Harrison, *Elizabethan England*, p. 105.

74. This did not apply only to the vernacular: see P. M. Jones, 'Book Ownership and the Lay Culture of Medicine in Tudor Cambridge', in Marland and Pelling, *Task of Healing*, p. 58. See also P. Slack, 'Mirrors of Health and Treasures of Poor Men: the Uses of the Vernacular Medical Literature of Tudor England', in Webster, *H, M & M*, pp. 249–50.

75. O'Hara May, *Elizabethan Dyetary*; idem, 'Foods or Medicines? A Study in the Relationship between Foodstuffs and Materia Medica from the Sixteenth to the Nineteenth Century', *Transactions of the British Society for the History of Pharmacy*, 1 (1971), 61–97.

76. C. H. Hull (ed.), *The Economic Writings of William Petty*, 2 vols (New York, 1963–64), vol. 2, p. 469.

diet), but only to sick people and the particular time of sickness. That is, to use anachronistic terms, one defined the normal, and the other the lesser case of the abnormal. It is probably not irrelevant to Vives's underlying scepticism about the academically qualified physician that he himself suffered frequently from both illness and poverty.[77]

Vives's definitions show how much has been submerged in accounts of the rise of physiology as the science fundamental to medicine. His analysis demonstrates to what extent the 'commonness' of dietetics had already led physicians to distance themselves from the realities of this essential area of their expertise. Vives recommended as objects of study the art of cooking, as well as techniques to do with clothing, building, agriculture, and navigation, while noting that the main obstacle to this educational reform would be the disdain for vulgar knowledge. Consistently with this, Vives recommended that would-be physicians should be discouraged from time-consuming and distracting literary studies, and that students of natural history should similarly save time by gleaning knowledge from hunters and gardeners. In a classic article on the seventeenth-century concept of the natural history of trades, Houghton observed of humanism that, while virtuous action was still the primary end of learning, there was a strain of practical wisdom and an appeal to reason and experience implicit in humanism which was given greater emphasis by Vives and others in the second quarter of the sixteenth century.[78] Vives's programme was partly carried out for English plants, by the humanist, botanist, and physician William Turner, who found that English physicians at least were ignorant about native flora; Turner therefore wrote for apothecaries and the laity as well as questioning common people about plants in their locality.[79] In spite of the involvement of physicians like Turner, the initiative on herbals describing native flora, as well as the exploitation of plants from the new world, passed first to barber-surgeons and then to apothecaries. The ideal humanist of the London College of Physicians was not William Turner, but Thomas Linacre.[80]

The education and strategies of orthodox physicians continued to place them at a distance from the useful arts. For Francis Bacon, who gave systematic expression to the concept of the history of trades, cooking qualified with agriculture, chemistry, dyeing, and such processes as the manufacture of glass, sugar, and gunpowder, as the most important arts, because these exhibited, altered, and prepared natural bodies and materials, unlike the purely manual arts, such as carpentry and clockmaking. On this scale of values, cooks were 'philosophers by fire', working to alter material states and to discover the secrets of nature.[81] Traditionally, physicians had assumed responsibility for the supervision

77. *Vives on Education*, pp. 42, 216; *DSB*, art. 'Vives'.

78. *Vives on Education*, pp. cxiv, 166–71, 208ff; Houghton, 'History of Trades', pp. 33–4.

79. Turner did except some learned physicians, but complained that they failed to 'set forth' their knowledge: C. E. Raven, *English Naturalists from Neckam to Ray* (Cambridge, 1947), pp. 60ff, 69. *DSB*, art. 'Turner'; Webster, *Great Instauration*, p. 271.

80. See V. Nutton, 'John Caius and the Linacre Tradition', *Medical History*, 23 (1979), 373–91.

81. Houghton, 'History of Trades', p. 38. For Plat's techniques of food preservation by 'philosophical fire' (1607), see Webster, *H, M & M*, Plate 4.

of cooks, but this connection seems to have been valid in England only in the peculiar conditions of large elite households, or in the prescribed relations of the refounded London hospitals.[82] In 1540 the College of Physicians apparently found it desirable to reinforce their rights to practise 'diet' as well as pharmacy and surgery, but no connection was made with the Cooks' Company.[83] Apart from token interventions in plague time which included dietary prescriptions, and effectively consisted of generalised advice given to the individual, the public role of English physicians with respect to the regulation of diet and hygiene was increasingly confined to utopias.[84] This contrasts, as already indicated, with the involvement of laypeople in the context of municipal regulation of food trades. Moreover, while practice in elite households may have represented the sum of a physician's ambitions, such success carried a burden of adverse status implications.[85] Just as corruption for the reformers of religion consisted of patrons who gave benefices to their cooks and other servants, so the physicians came to be mocked and criticised for being in a corrupt relationship with bakers.[86] Similarly, alchemists were mocked by association with (incompetent) kitchen work,[87] and the experiments of natural philosophers were derided as 'cooking'. Far from according cooks status as philosophers, or even allowing them some form of subsidiary association, orthodox physicians saw the term 'cook' as an insult to be levelled at lesser practitioners and empirics. In depressing the claims of apothecaries, for example, William Bullein asserted that their office was only that of being the physician's cook.[88]

Whether cooks benefited at all, or were in any way involved, in the Baconian programme is an issue awaiting exploration. It would seem that in general the social status of cooks in England was low. They had long been organised into gilds or companies, but the citizen status of cooks appears to have contracted in the seventeenth century, while the occupation itself was under threat from feminisation within the household.[89] Cooking was perceived as a 'housewife's trade' and therefore for status reasons one better avoided by men. Developments in the upper levels of the trade did not help. Already in the sixteenth century, an elite was emerging of French immigrants in particular who cooked for wealthy households: Harrison referred to these as 'musical-headed

82. A. R. Myers (ed.), *The Household of Edward IV* (Manchester, 1959), p. 123; C. Daly, 'The Hospitals of London: Administration, Refoundation, and Benefaction, *c.* 1500–1572' (University of Oxford DPhil thesis, 1994), pp. 284, 289, 292, 304.

83. 32 Henry VIII c. 40 (no reference to diet); CPL, Annals, [1554], p. 3.

84. C. Webster, 'William Harvey and the Crisis of Medicine in Jacobean London', in J. J. Bylebyl (ed.), *William Harvey and his Age* (Baltimore, MD, and London, 1979), pp. 1–4; M. E. Feldon, *Realistic Utopias* (Oxford, 1982), pp. 31, 41, 43–5, 49, 55.

85. Pelling, 'Compromised by Gender', pp. 103–5.

86. Harrison, *Elizabethan England*, pp. 74, 80; Webster, *Great Instauration*, p. 257.

87. This seems evident especially in Dutch genre paintings of alchemists: Philadelphia Museum of Art, *Masters of Seventeenth-Century Dutch Genre Painting* (Philadelphia, 1984), catalogue no. 3.

88. Quoted (without reference) by A. Maclean, *Humanism and the Rise of Science in Tudor England* (London, 1972), p. 205.

89. This appears to be an under-researched topic, but see P. Clark, *The English Alehouse* (London and New York, 1983), pp. 132–4, 227–8; M. E. Wiesner, *Women and Gender in Early Modern Europe* (Cambridge, 1993), p. 61; J. Thirsk, 'Foreword', in M. Prior (ed.), *Women in English Society 1500–1800* (London, 1986), pp. 13–14; G. Markham, *The English Housewife*, ed. M. R. Best (Montreal, 1994), p. 121.

Frenchmen'. Such cooks were accused of unmerited social mobility by Robert Burton, along with other servants of luxury, like tailors. Tailors, cooks, and physicians who serviced the elite shared a compromised status in gender terms which tended to cancel out any gains involved in associating with higher-status clients.[90]

This is not to say that there was no operative occupational connection at this time between medicine and the food and drink trades. This was however, as I have tried to suggest elsewhere, a feature not of physic or physicians but of the middle and lower levels of medicine and surgery. This relation was both formal and informal. Besides the associations between grocers and apothecaries, barber-surgeons and cooks were organised together in provincial towns (Salisbury, for example), or grouped together for purposes of supervision (as at Oxford).[91] The Oxford case, which reflects the dominance of the town by the university, is redolent of the status of both cook and medical practitioner as body servants, as in the elite households just discussed; but the two groups also had a good deal in common with respect to raw materials and products. As explored elsewhere, there were many-faceted connections between medicine, alcohol, and food. Poor barbers, who could not afford (soft) soap, used alefroth as shaving cream.[92] Other barbers were experts in making nets designed to trap birds and fish. There was a relatively common association between chandlers and barber-surgeons, for which there could be a number of practical, medically related explanations, including the use of wax or tallow in plasters, salves, and in embalming. However tallowchandlers, who were of course linked to the butchery trade, also shared with barber-surgeons a tendency to be involved in the vending of food and alcoholic drink, and had an established corner in sauces and pickling.[93] Sauces, pickles, and 'sops' are now rather peripheral, at least in nutritional terms, but in the early modern period they had great importance as an alternative to cooking raw food, in giving quality, piquancy, and individual choice to a monotonous diet, and in softening foodstuffs which would otherwise have been hard. Pickling was important because relatively little food, including vegetables, was eaten raw, this being a matter of theory-induced choice as well as (or because of) necessity.[94] Alcoholic drink was regarded as nourishing, but food and drink were in any case difficult to distinguish from each other given the contemporary taste for soups, possets, caudles, wine mulled with dried

90. M. Roberts, '"Words they are Women, and Deeds they are Men": Images of Work and Gender in Early Modern England', in L. Charles and L. Duffin (eds), *Women and Work in Pre-Industrial England* (London, 1985), p. 141; Harrison, *Elizabethan England*, p. 88; Burton, *Anatomy of Melancholy*, vol. 1, pp. 220, 222 (co-opting classical complaints); Pelling, 'Compromised by Gender', p. 104.

91. Pelling, 'Occupational Diversity', pp. 504–6 (222–4).

92. Ibid., pp. 505–6, 509, 511 (223–4, 227, 229); 'Trade or Profession', p. 103 (242–3). H. E. Salter, 'The Ordinances of the Gild of Barbers', in idem (ed.), *Records of Medieval Oxford* (Oxford, 1912), pp. 70, 71.

93. R. H. Monier-Williams, *The Tallow-Chandlers of London, Vol. 2* (London, 1972), pp. 42, 46–7, 77–8; A. D. Dyer, *The City of Worcester in the Sixteenth Century* (Leicester, 1973), pp. 130–1, 138, 144–5; Pelling, 'Occupational Diversity', p. 504 (222); R. Ashton, 'Popular Entertainment and Social Control in Later Elizabethan and Early Stuart London', *London Journal*, 9 (1983), 12.

94. T. Scully, 'Tempering Medieval Food', in M. W. Adamson (ed.), *Food in the Middle Ages* (New York and London, 1995), pp. 3–23; O'Hara May, *Elizabethan Dietary*, pp. 275–80; F. Braudel, *The Structures of Everyday Life* (London, 1985), pp. 78, 136–7. Sauces were of course also seen as sophisticated or degenerate: see above, p. 50.

fruit, spices and sugar, and concoctions like buttered ale.[95] Less wholesomely, it is interesting to note that all the main ingredients of ersatz wine – identified by a cynical sixteenth-century writer as sugar, starch, vinegar, dyes, and blackberry juice – could have been provided on the quiet as by-products of the several occupations being followed by barber-surgeons in this period. This applies even to the dyes.[96]

As well as these formal and material congruities, there were resemblances in occupational structure between the food and drink trades taken as a whole, and the occupation of medicine taken as a whole, particularly in an urban context. Each included a mobile crowd of 'irregulars' lurking in the suburbs or even further afield, who were difficult if not impossible to police. Elements of both could be a public nuisance on the streets, particularly if there was in early modern London a trade in second-hand food like that described for nineteenth-century Paris by Aron.[97] Both occupations were noted for the involvement of strangers, a shared tendency which was recognised quite early by a statute of 1531 passed to exempt foreign surgeons, bakers, brewers, and scriveners from measures intended to control stranger handicraftsmen.[98] Thirdly, as much work in recent years has shown, both occupations provided important niches for women.[99] Brewing, dairying, and petty retail have perhaps received the most attention.[100] For Oxford, Mary Prior found that, even at a respectable level of society, and over a long period, the food and drink trades were the most common occupation for women, while on a comparable basis these trades were only the fourth most important for male apprenticeship. Harrison thought that the vices of purveyors or middlemen in foodselling were increased by their using their wives as agents.[101] The herbs (including fresh vegetables) bought for a multiplicity of overlapping culinary, medical, and aesthetic purposes were generally sold by herbwomen. 'Sowse wives' sold cheap pickled and similar messes, especially of vegetables.[102] As already indicated, women tended to be associated with starchmaking. As with medicine, few of these areas were free of the taint of sexual licence, or at least sexual accessibility. In London particularly, women, food, drink, tobacco, and barber-surgeons came together in the context of the common locations for prostitution.[103] From all these associations the academic

95. Drummond and Wilbraham, *Englishman's Food*, p. 51; J. K. Crellin, 'Possets', *Notes and Queries*, n.s. 14 (1967), 2–4; C. A. Wilson (ed.), *'Liquid Nourishment': Potable Foods and Stimulating Drinks* (Edinburgh, 1993). For buttered ale as enjoyed by London barber-surgeons, see Young, *Annals*, p. 457.

96. Drummond and Wilbraham, *Englishman's Food*, pp. 43–6; Pelling, 'Appearance and Reality', p. 84; Pelling, 'Occupational Diversity'.

97. J.-P. Aron, 'The Art of Using Left-overs: Paris, 1850–1900', in R. Forster and R. Ranum (eds), *Food and Drink in History* (Baltimore, MD, and London, 1979), pp. 98–108.

98. Furnivall, *Vicary*, pp. 200–1.

99. For overviews, see A. Laurence, *Women in England 1500–1760* (London, 1994), chap. 9; M. E. Wiesner, *Women and Gender in Early Modern Europe* (Cambridge, 1993), chap. 3.

100. See for example J. M. Bennett, 'Misogyny, Popular Culture, and Women's Work', *History Workshop Journal*, 31 (1991), 166–88.

101. M. Prior, 'Women and the Urban Economy: Oxford 1500–1800', in idem, *Women in English Society*, pp. 106–7; Harrison, *Elizabethan England*, p. 39.

102. Pelling, 'Older Women', pp. 168, 172; Greene, *Quip*, p. 284.

103. Ashton, 'Popular Entertainment', pp. 13–15; Pelling, 'Appearance and Reality'; I. Archer, *The Pursuit of Stability: Social Relations in Elizabethan London* (Cambridge, 1991), pp. 211–15.

physicians were concerned to distance themselves, not least because they had significant gender and status problems of their own.[104]

I have given elsewhere examples of the way in which, in both London and the provinces, medical practitioners and victuallers intruded into each other's trades. Most of these examples were also formal or structural. Individual instances can also be instructive. At one end of the spectrum we find Henry Davies, itinerant surgeon, toothdrawer, and poacher, who was caught in Staffordshire in the 1590s staying with alekeepers and making good money by stealing fish.[105] A later, more urban and settled example is that of an anonymous alehousekeeper of Southwark of the early eighteenth century who took to selling an ague cure in the form of small ale brewed with (cinchona) bark, rhubarb (a purge), 'serpentery' (an antidote and diuretic), and cochineal (a dye). He claimed to have got the recipe from an old medical practitioner in the King's Bench Prison who, one could speculate, sold it to him in order to be supplied while in prison with food and drink. It is worth noting that there was a regular trade in purging ales in London earlier in the century, in which many of the suppliers were women.[106] The Southwark alehousekeeper dispensed his ale to fasting customers in the early morning, sending them off each with a 'cordial grip of the hand'. By this means, he claimed, he got a good trade to his house, and a comfortable maintenance as well.[107] These longstanding inter-relationships make it unsurprising to find, as Rice did, that licences to run private madhouses were granted in the nineteenth century to victual dealers, unsuccessful bakers, gardeners, and publicans. Such a list can always be made to slide off into burlesque for polemical purposes, as writers like William Clowes did in the late sixteenth century; this device has been highly successful in concealing or discrediting the social realities – and rationalities – involved in the association of medicine with other trades, including the victualling trades.[108]

As well as intermingling with the food and drink trades in various ways, barber-surgeons brought diet into their practice. In the course of their increasing encroachment on the medical role, they took account of the state of the whole body, and certainly employed polypharmacy and dietary recommendations in the preparation of their patients and their aftercare.[109] However, so degenerate was the world perceived to be, that they won especial approval for their use of more drastic remedies, the full strength of which had been released, or harnessed, by chemical means.[110] For the more worldly man of affairs, a traditional

104. Pelling, 'Compromised by Gender'.
105. Pelling, 'Occupational Diversity'. S. A. H. Burne (ed.), *Staffordshire Quarter Sessions Rolls, Vol. II. 1590–93* (Kendal, 1932), pp. 134–5.
106. M. Pelling, 'Thoroughly Resented? Older Women and the Medical Role in Early Modern London', in L. Hunter and S. Hutton (eds), *Women, Science and Medicine 1500–1700* (Stroud, 1997).
107. C. Creighton, *A History of Epidemics in Britain*, 2 vols (London, 1965), vol. 2, p. 325, quoting Simon Mason (1745). 'Serpentery' was Virginian snake-root (*OED*); cinchona or 'Jesuits' bark' is the source of quinine, a specific against malaria.
108. Rice, 'Scotland's "Museums of Madness"', p. 26; Pelling and Webster, 'Medical Practitioners', pp. 185–6.
109. See for example D'A. Power, *The Elizabethan Revival of Surgery* [London, 1902], pp. 9–10.
110. C. Webster, 'Alchemical and Paracelsian Medicine', in idem, *H, M & M*, pp. 301–34; idem, *Great Instauration*, pp. 248–50.

dietary regime of cure which confined him to his rooms or restricted his behaviour for long periods became a less attractive option than a treatment which
promised to be sharp but short. Chamberlain, complaining in 1624 of an 'infirm-
itie of sharpenes of urine', said that for him 'strict rules and diet' were 'as bad
as the disease'.[111] It is interesting to note that, while the dietary means by which
the individual could preserve his or her health were endlessly elaborated, the
diet actually given to the sick tended to involve simpler items associated with
other 'weak' (albeit numerous) groups in society, such as women, children, old
people, rural folk, and the poor.[112] Harrison for example, in describing the strong
beer enjoyed from the early sixteenth century onwards by the English nation,
stated that ale, previously the main drink, was now served only to the old and
the sick; while English 'mead', as made by some country wives, was mere 'swish
swash' but good for coughs and those who wanted to be 'loose bodied at large'
(that is, purged, but mildly enough not to be restricted). Similar cases might be
made for both vegetables, and white meats or dairy produce, at one time regarded
as the food of the poor, and over a long period thought fit for women.[113] It
is possible that these associations of weakness, effeminacy, and poverty indicate
a growing impatience with dietary means as a cure for contemporary diseases.
The long-term sick of the early modern period could still obtain special dietary
privileges, for example a licence to eat meat on fasting days, but this does not
necessarily conflict with such an interpretation; moreover, as already indicated,
fasting of this kind had an important economic dimension and such licences
must also have been of advantage to butchers. What kind of socially acceptable
sick role was available to early modern people, and whether this was changing,
is a topic well worth further investigation than is possible here.

The physicians thus lay between the polarities of the preservation of health
by godly life on the one hand, and the drastic but effective means adopted by
the surgeons on the other, and appeared to be battening on the evils of degeneration and indulgence without curing them. In between there also lay, for
direct access by the decaying urbanite, the increasing number of apothecary's
shops.[114] In the 1590s Greene virtuously claimed that he looked into an apothecary's shop scarcely once in seven years, and then only for a pennyworth of
wormseed to make his child a drink, or a little 'triacle' to drive out the measles,
or some powders to make his sick horse a drench (children and animals being
notoriously frail as well as precious, and it being the duty of a head of household to preserve them). When he was sick himself, Greene averred, he took
kitchen physic, and made his wife his doctor, and his own garden his apothecary's

111. N. McClure (ed.), *Letters of John Chamberlain*, 2 vols (Philadelphia, 1939), vol. 2, p. 573. See also
Burton, *Anatomy of Melancholy*, vol. 2, p. 27.

112. On what was given the sick, see T. Scully, 'The Sickdish in Early French Recipe Collections', in
S. Campbell, B. Hall and D. Klausner (eds), *Health, Disease and Healing in Medieval Culture* (Houndmills, 1992),
pp. 132–40; O'Hara May, 'Foods or Medicines'.

113. Harrison, *Elizabethan England*, pp. 102–3. Drummond and Wilbraham, *Englishman's Food*, pp. 49, 194.
Such diets, and cooling regimens in general, were prescribed for groups seen as in most need of temperate
courses: Smith, 'Thomas Tryon's Regimen', esp. pp. 55ff, 60.

114. Pelling and Webster, 'Medical Practitioners', pp. 177–9 and *passim*. Significantly, apothecaries were
among the shopkeepers of London's first Royal Exchange: A. Saunders, *The Royal Exchange* (London, 1991),
p. 12.

shop. It will be noted that Greene's idea of the good old days, like John Evelyn's nearly fifty years later, excluded medical practitioners altogether in favour of resources and practices within the family. Greene's satirical character Master Velvet Breeches, on the other hand, whenever he had the least thing wrong, had to have his purging pills, and glisters, or to evacuate by electuaries; if the least spot of morphew came on his face he had to have his oil of tartar, his camphire dissolved in verjuice, 'to make', Greene concluded, 'the foole as faire forsooth, as if he were to playe Maidmarian in a May game'.[115] It was clear that indulging his vanity, his effeminacy, or his hypochondria was something which Velvet Breeches could do himself or at the barber's or apothecary's shop, rather than requiring the services of a physician. This stress on both potent medicinal action and self-administration helps to explain why substances new in the early modern period like tea, tobacco, coffee, liquorice, and even sugar which rapidly became items of luxury and then of everyday consumption, were first consumed in quantity for medicinal purposes, largely without benefit of prescription.[116] By the 1640s, John Cook could complain that 'there is more gotten by Drugs, Roots, Weeds, and Hearbs in this City [London] yearely, then the Bakers, Brewers, Butchers and many others get by their substantiall Commodities'.[117]

In conclusion, it is clear that the contemporary preoccupation with illness was exceeded only by the preoccupation with health and the means of preserving it, including diet. Preoccupation with the means of subsistence was, not surprisingly, a function of the human condition and the agents, human and divine, thought responsible for providing it. In the worsening state of the world, whether one's outlook was moral or cynical, the physician appeared to be playing a limited or parasitic role, and laypeople were given every incentive to take the state of body and soul into their own hands. Virtually all forms of social authority with respect to food were now in lay hands. Corresponding with lay interest in, and knowledge of, dietary principles, was lay control over such matters as the diet of hospitals and prisons, the food given to plague victims and as poor relief, and perhaps most importantly, the quality and quantity of food and drink offered for sale. It was laypeople who condemned measly pork, diseased carcasses, and rotten grain, and punished cheating and unhealthy practices, such as (claimed Greene) the technique butchers had of blowing their breath (assumed to be foul) into meat to make it look plumper and fresher than it was.[118]

As we have seen, satirical comment about food habits was rife, but radical plans for the reform of diet of all classes did not emerge until the Baconian

---

115. Greene, *Quip*, pp. 248–9; C. D. O'Malley, 'John Evelyn and Medicine', *Medical History*, 12 (1968), 223ff; W. G. Hiscock, *John Evelyn and his Family Circle* (London, 1955), p. 209; M. Hunter, 'John Evelyn in the 1650s: a Virtuoso in Quest of a Role', in idem, *Science and the Shape of Orthodoxy* (Woodbridge, 1995), pp. 72ff.

116. See P. Griffiths, J. Landers, M. Pelling and R. Tyson, 'Population and Disease, Estrangement and Belonging', in P. Clark (ed.), *The Urban History of Britain, Vol. 2* (Cambridge, forthcoming); Harrison, *Elizabethan England*, p. 92 (sugar); Thirsk, *Economic Policy and Projects*, pp. 13, 143 (liquorice); J. Chartres, 'Food Consumption and Internal Trade', in Beier and Finlay, *London 1500–1700*, pp. 168–96, esp. pp. 174, 178. On liquorice, see also O'Hara May, *Elizabethan Dyetary*, p. 275.

117. J. Cook, *Unum Necessarium: or, the Poore Mans Case* (London, 1648), p. 63.

118. Greene, *Quip*, pp. 273–4.

programme was taken further by the Hartlib circle in the context of the Puritan revolution. These plans concentrated on the improvement of husbandry, horticulture, and fisheries, and the reduction of the import burden by means of plantations in the English colonies. Gardening (for the benefit of the many) was to be the direct means of creating a new Eden. Techniques of food preservation were also sought.[119] Effective agriculture was seen as going a long way towards solving the problems of ill health by preventive means, so that (as with nineteenth-century sanitarianism) curative medicine could again be regarded as secondary. Reformed agriculture also had the invaluable corollary of providing high employment, as had been found with the market gardens which were now developing on a large scale around London. In the end, the impact of most of these schemes was delayed. Histories of trades proved difficult to execute, and tended to degenerate into virtuoso pieces like John Evelyn's monograph on French bread.[120] Some of the Hartlib circle's other schemes, notably policy with respect to the colonies as primary producers, were of considerable long-term importance.[121]

In terms of useful knowledge the initiative lay with the surgeons and the anti-Galenical chemists. The lower orders of practitioner were, as we have seen, well-integrated with the food and drink trades, and were also increasingly encroaching on the physician's role of dietary prescription. This interdigitation involved a wealth of associations which physicians could only view as prejudicial. We have seen also that the barber-surgeons took an early interest in botanical observation; they arguably also made the most important contemporary contribution to better food policy in the form of the naval surgeon John Woodall's espousal of the use of lemon juice in scurvy. Though not a Paracelsian, Woodall adopted Paracelsian remedies which gave prominence to the idea of the potency of single substances.[122] Physicians on the other hand saw a crucial area of their knowledge become common, especially among the educated, and also commonplace; this process was by no means new to the early modern period, but by then had gone (for them) unacceptably far. By tradition custodians of the theory of diet, they lost ground in contemporary estimation and saw their special knowledge either devalued, or leaking away to the laity and to other practitioners. In addition, dietary matters attracted a range of connotations – gendered, artisanal, utilitarian, religious, even luxurious – which were repellent for most physicians. These can be seen as additional to the disadvantages long perceived by physicians themselves in what was in essence an expectant or non-interventive

119. J. Thirsk, 'Plough and Pen: Agricultural Writers in the Seventeenth Century', in T. H. Aston *et al.* (eds), *Social Relations and Ideas* (Cambridge, 1983), pp. 295–318; Webster, *Great Instauration*, esp. pp. 465–83. Cf. J. D. Hunt, 'Hortulan Affairs', in M. Greengrass, M. Leslie and T. Raylor (eds), *Samuel Hartlib and Universal Reformation* (Cambridge, 1994), pp. 321–42; Prest, *Garden of Eden*.

120. Webster, *Great Instauration*, pp. 420–46, esp. p. 427; Houghton, 'History of Trades', p. 55; Hunter, 'John Evelyn'.

121. Thirsk, *Economic Policy and Projects*, pp. 139–41, 177; C. Webster, 'Benjamin Worsley: Engineering for Universal Reform from the Invisible College to the Navigation Act', in Greengrass *et al.*, *Samuel Hartlib*, pp. 213–35.

122. J. Woodall, *The Surgions Mate*, ed. J. Kirkup (Bath, 1978); Webster, 'Alchemical and Paracelsian Medicine', p. 319.

mode of treatment.[123] It could be suggested that after this crisis period, which included a massive (although not conclusive) assault on the Galenic basis of knowledge of the individual constitution, the physicians shifted their area of intellectual investment and exclusive knowledge away from what had been a recondite analysis of dietetics, to even more recondite forms of what is now called physiology. It is tempting to contrast Woodall's achievement with that of William Harvey's pupil, Francis Glisson, whose accomplishment in defining the disease of rickets in clinical and anatomical terms was initially unrelated either to diet or to practice.[124] The seventeenth century saw considerable interest in the process of digestion as a form of fermentation – which itself became a model for the disease process – but this reflected the influence of Paracelsianism, Helmontianism, and the anti-Galenic theories of the chemists.[125] The *practice* of physicians continued to be both traditional, humoral, and inclusive of dietary questions, but dietetics had come to appear a poor ground on which to establish professional identity and exclusive expertise. The extraordinary success of George Cheyne, physician to the rich, who reverted to a holistic and providential view of illness based on a reintegration of dietetics with current intellectual concerns such as Newtonianism, can perhaps be seen as a measure of how far most physicians had moved away from the kind of interest the laity still took in diet.[126]

Individual physicians continued to contribute to dietetics, but when the chronology of medical developments is condensed, diet and nutrition tend almost to disappear, until the belated 'scientising' of diet in the twentieth century. An illustration of this is Shryock's still-valuable *Development of Modern Medicine*, in which the index entry for 'diet' lacks page references but directs the reader first to 'malnutrition' and secondly to 'vitamins', while an entry for 'nutrition' refers simply to medical criticism of the feeding of babies, and to nineteenth-century physiological chemistry.[127] This is one reflection of the scale of the physician's

123. Demaitre, 'Nature and the Art of Medicine'; important background is also provided by L. Garcia-Ballester, 'Changes in the *Regimina sanitatis*. The Role of the Jewish Physicians', in Campbell *et al.*, *Health, Disease and Healing*, pp. 119–31.

124. *DSB*, art. 'Glisson'; Webster, *Great Instauration*, pp. 272, 317–18, 322–3. For a detailed attempt to show Harvey's physiology as integrally related to practice, see J. J. Bylebyl, 'The Medical Side of Harvey's Discovery: the Normal and the Abnormal', in idem, *William Harvey and his Age*, pp. 28–102. Note that Harvey himself may have seen his work as a form of 'living' anatomy.

125. See W. Pagel, *Joan Baptista van Helmont: Reformer of Science and Medicine* (Cambridge, 1982), pp. 79–87, 129–40 and *passim*; R. P. Multhauf, 'J. B. van Helmont's Reformation of the Galenic Doctrine of Digestion', *Bull. Hist. Med.*, 29 (1955), 154–63. See also E. H. Ackerknecht, 'The End of Greek Diet', *Bull. Hist. Med.*, 45 (1971), 242–9.

126. See O. Temkin, *Galenism: Rise and Decline of a Medical Philosophy* (Ithaca, NY, and London, 1973), pp. 112–13, 152–3, 154, 157, 166–7, 176–7. On Cheyne, see G. S. Rousseau, 'Mysticism and Millenarianism: "Immortal Dr Cheyne"', in I. Merkel and A. G. Debus (eds), *Hermeticism and the Renaissance* (Washington, DC, 1988), pp. 192–230. See also in general A. Wear, 'Medical Practice in Late Seventeenth- and Early Eighteenth-century England: Continuity and Union', in R. French and A. Wear (eds), *The Medical Revolution of the Seventeenth Century* (Cambridge, 1989), pp. 294–320.

127. R. H. Shryock, *The Development of Modern Medicine* (1936; London, 1948). On diet and physiological chemistry, see M. Pelling, *Cholera, Fever and English Medicine 1825–1865* (Oxford, 1978), chap. 4; H. Kamminga and A. Cunningham (eds), *The Science and Culture of Nutrition, 1840–1940* (Amsterdam and Atlanta, GA, 1995), p. 3.

abandonment of the broader interpretative aspects of nutrition, a process which left only the limited authority involved in knowledge of the individual constitution. This loss of moral as well as intellectual authority over broader issues can also be seen in the politicisation of diet. The reform or improvement of diet continued to be a major political as well as economic area in which medical practitioners were inevitably involved. As medicine and patients became institutionalised – or rather, as institutionalised medicine became increasingly influential – the distinction between medicine and diet became a political battleground related to the practitioner's or his employer's definition of his proper area of responsibility. Heroic examples from the nineteenth century include the army surgeon, James McGrigor, who as medical chief of staff challenged the authority of the Duke of Wellington over the provisioning of casualties; or the provincial physician William Budd, who as physician at the Bristol Royal Infirmary was singled out for prescribing for his poorer patients too many items of diet like chicken, fish, wine, and eggs, which the lay governors of the hospital regarded as expensive luxuries.[128] More troubling instances from the professional point of view include those medical officers of health of the 1930s who refused to issue dietary supplements in distressed areas because they felt their centres should not be turned into milk depots or 'relief stations'.[129] This is not of course to suggest that such incidents can be directly traced to events more than two hundred years earlier. Rather, this essay has sought to establish that the connections and estrangements between medicine, diet, and social policy have a longer and essentially more political and cultural history than current views might imply.

128. J. McGrigor, *Autobiography and Services* (London, 1861), pp. 301–3; G. Munro Smith, *A History of the Bristol Royal Infirmary* (Bristol and London, 1917), pp. 323–4, 328–30, 31–2.
129. Webster, 'Health, Welfare and Unemployment', pp. 214, 216–18, 222–3.

CHAPTER THREE

Illness among the Poor in Early Modern English Towns

Much attention has been given to the poor in early modern Europe, especially the urban poor. The poor have been much categorised, but the sick poor have received less attention, particularly when compared with the prominence given them by earlier English writers concerned with welfare like the Webbs and Hermann Levy.[1] Research on England has focused instead on the emergence of outdoor relief. Sickness as a cause of poverty has been overshadowed by a justifiable preoccupation with the concept of life-cycle poverty, with the demographic balance as it affects dependency, with the changing age structures of populations, and with lone mothers or widows. Even the refounded hospitals of London set up to deal with the problem of the sick poor (St Bartholomew's, St Thomas's) have been comparatively neglected.[2] However, the balance of interest in the sick poor cannot in any case be redressed for England simply by the focus upon institutions, as is possible for continental Europe, because England (aside from London) offered little in the way of major institutionalisation for the poor.

In the present context, the advantage of recent work is that historians have discarded the idea that early modern authorities thought in binary terms of the deserving and the undeserving poor: economic and social crises created a class of able-bodied poor who could not find work or earn enough when they did.

Closer attention to the sick poor can help to show the complexity of both attitudes and realities with respect to the poor. First, just as economic crisis expanded the catchment population of the poor well beyond the category of the impotent or the sturdy vagrant, so sickness or disability could reduce the

I am grateful to Richard Smith for commenting on an earlier draft of this chapter, and to Roger Schofield and Tony Wrigley for permission to reproduce Figure 3.1 from *Population History*. All mistakes remain my own.

1. H. Levy, 'The Economic History of Sickness and Medical Benefit before the Puritan Revolution', *Eco. Hist. Rev.*, 13 (1943), 42–57.

2. P. Slack, 'Social Policy and the Constraints of Government, 1547–58', in J. Loach and R. Tittler (eds), *The Mid-Tudor Polity c. 1540–1560* (London and Basingstoke, 1980), p. 109. See however C. Daly, 'The Hospitals of London: Administration, Refoundation, and Benefaction, *c.* 1500–1572' (University of Oxford DPhil thesis, 1994). Christ's Hospital, Bethlem and especially Bridewell have been better served by recent historians, including Jonathan Andrews, Ian Archer and Paul Griffiths.

more prosperous to poverty. As the humanist Vives put it, 'there are many kinds of diseases, and, in fine, countless chances which bring distress on worthy homes'. The Italian Monte di Pietà were designed partly as an early form of sickness insurance.[3] Records of craft companies reveal substantial numbers of ex-masters and others of previously important estate sunk into permanent decay.[4] In the statements of the cost of living presented by London bakers, savings in case of sickness were placed on a par with provision for the education of children.[5] The cost of literally years of medical treatment, as well as protracted sickness itself, could lead to financial disaster. The pauperising effect of sickness on those already poor is, of course, recognised in the ubiquitous provision of outdoor relief in the form of financial support during periods of sickness. Even with respect to plague, 'it was morbidity rather than mortality which aggravated the problem of the poor'.[6] The category of the sick poor who deserved relief was enlarged by a roughly, but generally, applied principle of disapproval for extreme 'means testing', as voiced by Arth: 'for touching the sicke poore, (though they have some goods, gotten by sore labour in their health) yet I see no reason, that they should sell the Cowe that gives the children milke, nor the tooles they worke with . . . all which things in compassion are to be spared as the lawes of Moses provided in that case'.[7]

Secondly, there was an appreciation of the principle, reasserted by the humanists, that the decay of its citizens affected a city no less than the decay of the city walls.[8] Indeed, English municipal authorities believed in medical intervention to remove men, women, and children out of the category of the impotent poor. While there is more evidence for England from the sixteenth century, there is nothing to suggest that this change represents a shift by Protestants from the indiscriminate doling out of sickness benefits. As Natalie Davis points out, from the later middle ages the provision of free medical services had served as a means of redistributing wealth, and is commonplace in cities of different religious persuasions in the sixteenth century.[9]

Thirdly, English towns followed continental practice and humanist precept in assuming that some form of work could and should be found even for the most disabled members of society. There was even the suggestion of an institution akin to a sheltered workshop in London in the 1550s, but, apart from the tendency to require inmates of hospitals to work, the proposal came to

3. J.-L. Vives, *De Subventione Pauperum* (1526), translated in part in F. R. Salter, *Some Early Tracts on Poor Relief* (London, 1926), p. 26; B. Pullan, 'Catholics and the Poor in Early Modern Europe', *Transactions of the Royal Historical Society*, 26 (1976), 22.

4. See for example the returns as to members' estate made by London companies in 1641: T. C. Dale (transcriber), 'The Members of City Companies in 1641', 2 vols (bound typescript, Society of Genealogists, 1934) in the Guildhall Library, London.

5. See for example London, Guildhall Library, MS 5196 (Bakers' Memorandum Book), fol. 13recto (1632).

6. P. Slack, 'Poverty and Politics in Salisbury 1597–1666', in P. Clark and P. Slack (eds), *Crisis and Order in English Towns 1500–1700* (London, 1972), p. 170.

7. Henry Arth (1597) in R. H. Tawney and E. Power (eds), *Tudor Economic Documents*, 2nd edn, 3 vols (London, 1953), vol. 3, pp. 445–6.

8. Vives in Salter, *Early Tracts*, p. 9.

9. N. Z. Davis, 'Poor Relief, Humanism, and Heresy', in idem, *Society and Culture in Early Modern France* (London, 1975), esp. p. 36. See also Pullan, 'Catholics and the Poor', pp. 24–5.

nothing. On an individual basis, occupations like alehousekeeping, or portering, were explicitly regarded as suitable for aged or disabled poor.[10]

Fourthly, there was the belief that the undeserving poor should not only be examined for malingering, but, if actually disabled, also remodelled physically as well as morally, so that they could be put to work. This line of argument did not exclude the actual practice of compulsory medical treatment. The interplay of the physical and the moral was extremely intimate, and, as Slack has noted, both attitudes and behaviour are reflected in the language used. Thus Fleetwood of London noted that some notorious beggars might be blind, but were also great usurers and very rich; such beggars were described as having their eyes 'blinded by malice'.[11]

Lastly, the sick poor were also the importunate or professional poor who endangered other citizens as well as civic self-respect by congregating together, concentrating infection, and forcing themselves on the senses of others. This longstanding aspect of urban life was made particularly acute in the sixteenth century by the prevalence of plague and the French pox. In dispassionate terms, the principle was that no body of citizens should be useless or positively harmful; but the terms more often used were those expressing considerable fear and revulsion.[12]

Elsewhere I have argued that, in order to meet these different aims and demands, the English city by the early seventeenth century was capable of developing a complex but informal medical poor-relief system which both operated largely outside institutions, and also showed considerable continuity up to the era of the New Poor Law.[13] The system was under municipal control, but adapted rather than changed practices characteristic of the private sector. In one important respect, however, there seems to have been a difference. Medical practice, like many pensioning arrangements and judicial proceedings, took account of the estate or accustomed way of life of the recipient in its scales of charges and treatments. Medical poor relief, on the other hand, seems to have drawn on all classes of practitioner, not just the lower grades, in order to treat the poor.

In this chapter, I wish to pay further attention to the problem of morbidity. To some extent the sensitiveness of morbidity as a social indicator must be defined in contrast with mortality, which is a much more straightforward index. Morbidity is an elusive adjunct of life-events such as birth and death, but is (naturally) a more frequent experience and source of crisis, and may also be lifelong. A simple or direct relationship between morbidity and mortality cannot be assumed.[14] Although virtually impossible to quantify in the same way as

10. Levy, 'Economic History of Sickness', pp. 52–3. See also Pelling, 'Child Health', p. 161 (130); 'Old Age, Poverty and Disability'; 'Older Women'.

11. William Fleetwood, quoted by P. Slack, 'Poverty and Social Regulation in Elizabethan England', in C. Haigh (ed.), *The Reign of Elizabeth I* (London, 1984), p. 229; William Marshall's version of the Ypres *Forma Subventionis* in Salter, *Early Tracts*, p. 43.

12. See for example Vives in Salter, *Early Tracts*, p. 8.

13. Pelling, 'Healing the Sick Poor'.

14. See the interesting and controversial work by J. C. Riley, for example his 'Disease without Death: New Sources for a History of Sickness', *Journal of Interdisciplinary History*, 17 (1987), 537–63; 'Ill Health during the English Mortality Decline: the Friendly Societies' Experience', *Bull. Hist. Med.*, 61 (1987), 563–88; *Sickness,*

mortality, contemporaries showed their awareness of the importance of sickness by attempting to measure it, even in financial calculations and most notably in censuses of the poor. Such censuses, as well as population listings, were carried out in a large number of English and continental towns in the sixteenth century, and the motives behind them have been well described by Natalie Davis.[15] The English censuses are variable, the compilers having used, as Slack has noted, different definitions of poverty and having been prompted by different local circumstances.[16] I shall be using mainly the Norwich census of 1570, a uniquely comprehensive listing.[17] Although it described a population selected for poverty, the Norwich census has the advantages of having been confined to a delimited urban centre, and based upon house-to-house visitation. In spite of its declared aims, the census records not vagrant, but resident, poor, many of whom were in some kind of employment. Entire households are recorded, not simply individuals who worked. The census, therefore, has some of the same advantages that nineteenth-century dispensary records have over the records of hospitals of the same date, but with the added advantage of not being dependent upon the initiative of the poor themselves.[18] Before analysing the census, I should like to consider its strengths as a source by contrasting it with present-day estimates of morbidity.[19]

Even in the modern context, the usual indicators, maternal and infant mortality, are less sensitive than rates of morbidity, and the extent and social distribution of morbidity are best demonstrated by local sources. No systematic base for morbidity studies was available in England before the sickness surveys of World War II; before the war, the most 'attractive and accessible' sources, like those generated by Medical Officers of Health and School Medical Officers, are in fact not reliable.[20] That this should be so with respect to major but ill-defined conditions such as malnutrition is perhaps not surprising; but even in the case of specific (albeit protean) diseases like tuberculosis and cancer, for which registration was required, the historian must estimate the degree of inaccuracy likely to be caused by social factors. As late as 1952, the level of registration of cancer cases was probably about 50 per cent of actual cases.[21] Under-recording, caused by the social stigma attached to tuberculosis in the twentieth century,

Recovery and Death: A History and Forecast of Ill Health (Basingstoke and London, 1989). On the modern picture, see for example L. Verbrugge, 'Longer Life but Worsening Health? Trends in the Health and Mortality of Middle-aged and Older Persons', *Milbank Quarterly*, 62 (1984), 475–519.

15. Davis, 'Poor Relief', esp. pp. 39–41.

16. Slack, 'Poverty and Social Regulation', pp. 230–1. On English listings and censuses see also Phythian-Adams, *Desolation of a City*, esp. Appendix 2.

17. Pound, *Census*. Although I have made my own calculations, what follows is based on Pound's valuable transcript.

18. See I. S. L. Loudon, 'The Origin and Growth of the Dispensary Movement', *Bull. Hist. Med.*, 55 (1981), 323–42; R. Kilpatrick, ' "Living in the Light": Dispensaries, Philanthropy and Medical Reform in Late Eighteenth-century London', in A. Cunningham and R. French (eds), *The Medical Enlightenment of the Eighteenth Century* (Cambridge, 1990), pp. 254–80. Although far less selective than hospitals, dispensaries still recorded on the basis of 'use of service' rather than actual incidence of sickness.

19. The following paragraph is based on C. Webster, *Health: Historical Issues*, CEPR Discussion Paper V (London, 1984).

20. Webster, *Health: Historical Issues*, p. 7. On this see also idem, 'Health, Welfare and Unemployment during the Depression', *P & P*, 109 (1985), 204–30.

21. Webster, *Health: Historical Issues*, p. 13.

can be paralleled by the widespread disguise of syphilis in the sixteenth and seventeenth centuries as a recorded cause of death.[22] In each case, exposure to infection is likely to have been almost universal. Even in the present day, most data arise not from the experience of illness, but from the use of services, and it is agreed that use of services is a highly inadequate measure of the extent, nature, and social distribution of illness. From 1971 this deficiency was underlined by the *General Household Survey*, hereafter *GHS*, which for a selected population gave figures for self-reported acute and chronic illness, as well as for recourse to general practitioners and hospitals.[23]

The *GHS* did not record the nature or degree of severity of sickness or disablement, but used duration, and simple limitation of activity. As in the Norwich census, stress was placed on function or ability rather than symptoms. The population observed was around 26,000. Information was self-reported only to the extent of being obtained by an interviewer using a questionnaire.[24] Information about children was obtained from those caring for them, usually their mothers. In essence, selection apart, the technique used by the Norwich censustakers was little different.

Nevertheless, the *GHS* illustrates both the disparity in scale between health problems as perceived by the population and as resulting in the use of services, and the difficulties inherent in making direct quantitative comparisons between the past and the present day. For example, the figure for self-reported chronic illness among all females in all classes in 1983 was 33 per cent; limiting longstanding illness was 20 per cent. For males the comparable figures were 31 per cent and 18 per cent. For acute illness (restricted activity within fourteen days of interview) the figures were 14 per cent for females, and 11 per cent for males. With respect to services, 16 per cent of females and 12 per cent of males had consulted their general practitioner; 16 per cent of females and 19 per cent of males had attended as outpatients. To take a group which might be thought equivalent to the poor of the Norwich census, 44 per cent of male unskilled manual workers between the ages of 45 and 64 reported chronic sickness in 1983; the figure for 65 and older was 65 per cent. For females the comparable figures were 52 per cent and 68 per cent. The professional classes in the same agegroups had lower rates: males 35 per cent and 46 per cent, females 39 per cent with the elder group negligible in number. For all agegroups among the unskilled, chronic illness was reported by 34 per cent of males and 45 per cent

22. See Webster, *Health: Historical Issues*, pp. 10–14; L. Bryder, *Below the Magic Mountain: A Social History of Tuberculosis in Twentieth-Century Britain* (Oxford, 1988), pp. 103–9. On syphilis, see John Graunt, *Natural and Political Observations . . . made upon the Bills of Mortality*, in *Economic Writings of Sir William Petty*, ed. C. H. Hull, 2 vols (New York, 1963–64), vol. 2, p. 356; G. Williams, 'An Elizabethan Disease', *Trivium*, 6 (1971), 43–4.

23. See Office of Population Censuses and Surveys [now Office of National Statistics], *General Household Survey 1983* (London, 1985), chap. 9. The work of the ONS has been placed in doubt under recent governments. The *GHS* for 1995 has been published (1996); that for 1996 is due to appear. Field work for 1997 has been suspended at least until 1998. These reports continue to analyse morbidity.

24. See *General Household Survey 1983*, chap. 3. A designed sample of addresses was used, reduced in 1982 by *c.* 14% to a maximum of 12,480. See also S. Curtis, *Intra-Urban Variations in Health and Health Care: The Comparative Need for Health Care Survey of Tower Hamlets and Redbridge, Vol. 1: Adult Morbidity and Service Use*, Health Research Group, Department of Geography and Earth Science, Queen Mary College, London, 2nd edn (London, 1984), pp. 45, 49.

of females, compared with 25 per cent for both sexes among professionals. The *GHS*'s unskilled category (10 per cent) is a lower proportion (by more than half) of the total sample population than is represented in the Norwich census. The category of unskilled worker used by the *GHS* is, of course, as socially relative as the selection of poor in the Norwich census. It should be noted that the *GHS* figures for longstanding illness have tended to fluctuate upwards more than ten percentage points even between the early 1970s and the early 1980s; this was not then reported as significant. These extremely high self-reported levels of morbidity in a post-industrial society are not simply a function of an ageing population. The greatest increase in longstanding illness from 1972 occurred in the agegroup 45–64.[25]

One criticism of the *GHS* is that its class categories make primary reference to the occupations of men; this creates difficulties in estimating the income differentials affecting women's health. The value of local studies has been reasserted by some critics of the *GHS*. Like the *GHS*, and like the Norwich census, such studies use lay rather than professional reporting. To require a high specificity of diagnosis is seen as double-edged.[26]

After looking at the *GHS*, the limitations of the Norwich census seem less troublesome. It is a local survey, based upon detailed local knowledge. Like the *GHS*, though rather more so, it is a snapshot as far as the individual is concerned. The total population (2,359 men, women and children) is of considerable size, comprising approximately 790 households.[27] Internal evidence confirms that information was gathered by interview and personal observation. There may have been considerable social distance between the censustakers and those interviewed; contact between more prosperous citizens and the homes of the poor was prescribed in the literature on poor relief as a means of strengthening social bonds.[28] Social distance is however also a factor in modern surveys. On the other hand, acquaintance between censustaker and householder was more likely in sixteenth-century Norwich, than in twentieth-century Britain. Although selected for poverty by the Norwich authorities, the census population more closely resembles a natural population than some other groupings, usually workplaces, which generate useful records of morbidity.[29] Moreover, the Norwich

25. *General Household Survey 1983*, pp. 151, 158, 160.

26. S. Payne, *Women, Health and Poverty: An Introduction* (Hemel Hempstead, 1991), pp. 108–12 (note here also Arber's work which corrects the *GHS* for age differences in class structure). See D. Bucquet and S. Curtis, 'Socio-demographic Variation in Perceived Illness and the Use of Primary Care: the Value of Community Survey Data for Primary Care Service Planning', *Social Science and Medicine*, 23 (1986), 737–8. See also Curtis, *Intra-Urban Variations*.

27. For an analysis of households, see Pound, *Census*, p. 101.

28. See for example Marshall in Salter, *Early Tracts*, p. 70.

29. For example, emigrant vessels, in which a delimited population also creates its own special conditions. For an analysis of the advantages of early sick fund records, see Riley, 'Disease without Death', esp. p. 540. Other valuable early sources, the casebooks of Richard Napier and of Simon Forman, were generated on a 'use of service' basis. See R. Sawyer, 'Patients, Healers and Disease in the Southeast Midlands, 1597–1634' (University of Wisconsin PhD thesis, 1986), and (on Forman) the thesis nearing completion by Lauren Kassell (University of Oxford). The results of inspection of military recruits had considerable effects on social policy at later periods, but early musters lack details of infirmity and of course all such records are concerned only with men of certain agegroups: see A. Kussmaul, *Servants in Husbandry in Early Modern England* (Cambridge, 1981), p. 18.

census is perhaps the most detailed contemporary estimate of sickness, including other censuses of the poor.[30]

The Norwich census is also useful because it was made in the 1570s, during a period when it is estimated that 'mortality was lower than it was again to be until after 1815' and when English populations had high life expectancy relative to the rest of western Europe. Lower mortality, however, did not imply an absence of morbidity.[31] Similarly, the Norwich authorities of 1570 were explicitly concerned about the level of disease among the poor.[32] With respect to Norwich's population as a whole, the census was taken just before the great losses occasioned by the plague, and just after the onset of Dutch and Walloon immigration. The census only covered the English population, of which it may represent approximately a quarter (22.2 per cent),[33] comprising about 16 per cent of the total population.[34] There are more women identified as poor than men (see Table 3.1) and the proportion of those 60 and over, at 14.8 per cent, is closer to the 1950s (with about 15.7 per cent of the total population[35]) than the 7.3 per cent estimated for the 1571 population structure by Wrigley and Schofield (see Table 3.2 and Figure 3.1).[36] The ability of some poor to survive well into old age is striking (the census shows few signs of gullibility on the subject of greater ages[37]). In spite of the high proportion of elderly, the census population was also nearly 40 per cent made up of children under 15, and included substantial numbers of parents in the middle decades of life (see Tables 3.1 and 3.2).[38]

30. Space has not allowed further comparisons. The censuses nearest in value to Norwich's, with respect to sickness as well as poverty, relate to Salisbury (c. 1635), Ipswich (1597) and Warwick (1586).

31. D. Palliser, *The Age of Elizabeth* (London and New York, 1983), pp. 45–6.

32. Pelling, 'Healing the Sick Poor', p. 118 (82).

33. Pound estimates the English population of Norwich in 1570 as 10,625 (*Census*, p. 10).

34. Estimated stranger immigration into Norwich had reached 4,000 by 1571, making a total population of approx. 14,500 at that date (Slack, *Impact of Plague*, p. 128, and see note 33 above). Total population before the plague is estimated at less than 17,000 (Slack, *Impact of Plague*, p. 130). The stranger community included its own proportion of poor.

35. For the UK the figure for 1951, at 15.7% for those 60 and over, is closest to the Norwich figure. By 1971 this agegroup had risen to nearly 19%, as calculated from Central Statistical Office, *Annual Abstract of Statistics* (London, 1987), p. 8. Figures for 1981 are not strictly comparable.

36. See Wrigley and Schofield, *Population History*, Appendix 3, p. 528. I am grateful to Roger Schofield for providing me with five-year breakdowns of the published 1571 figures. The basis for the *PHE* population estimates is least urban for the sixteenth century. However, in the absence of complete urban listings the age structure of large English towns in this period must remain conjectural. On social factors affecting urban age structure, see Phythian-Adams, *Desolation of a City*, esp. pp. 80–98. Norwich's population underwent violent fluctuations between 1560 and 1600 (see note 34 above). Like London, Norwich attracted large numbers of apprentices, and immigration of this kind seems to have increased towards the end of the sixteenth century, but 'wastage' also increased (see Pelling, 'Child Health', pp. 147–8, 151–2 (116–17, 120–1)). Far less is known about emigration. Norwich is an example of 'subsistence migration' in that, of the 30% of the census population for whom such information is recorded, more than half were not born in Norwich (Pound, *Census*, p. 12 and Appendix VII). Norwich probably suffered a higher infant mortality rate than smaller centres, although Pound sees Norwich's poor as long-lived owing to comparative cleanliness and lack of overcrowding (ibid., p. 13).

37. The tendency towards rounding at ages 40, 50, 60 and 80 means that for some purposes, analysis in decadal age groups is more desirable than using five-year agegroups (see Table 3.2). Other evidence also suggests that contemporary age-recording, while not always exact to the year, was likely to be correct to within five years: R. Finlay, *Population and Metropolis: The Demography of London 1580–1650* (Cambridge, 1981), pp. 124–6. See also Pelling, 'Old Age, Poverty and Disability', p. 76 (135–6).

38. To the 30% of children under 15 whose ages were stated may be added the 8.2% of children of unstated age (see Table 3.2), as the latter were almost invariably indicated as being less than 10 years old, and consequently not expected to work – hence the lack of detail.

TABLE 3.1 *Norwich poor and sick poor by age and gender*

Age	00–09	10–19	20–29	30–39	40–49	50–59	60–69	70–79	80–89	90–99	100+	'Child'[a]	Adult[b]	Ambiguous[c]	Totals
Poor, by gender															
Unstated	456	146	19	2	0	0	0	0	0	0	0	166	0	10	799
Male	53	24	64	118	128	83	72	17	23	2	0	12	10	0	606
Female	32	71	84	153	217	120	133	37	41	3	2	15	37	9	954
Total	541	241	167	273	345	203	205	54	64	5	2	193	47	19	2,359
Sick poor, by gender															
Unstated	4	0	0	0	0	0	0	0	0	0	0	3	0	0	7
Male	1	0	6	5	11	14	14	4	11	2	0	0	0	0	68
Female	0	2	1	6	18	8	16	12	15	3	1	0	6	4	92
Total	5	2	7	11	29	22	30	16	26	5	1	3	6	4	167

[a] See note 38. [b] Comprises married persons. [c] Includes 'maid', servant, etc.
Source: Pound, *Census*.

TABLE 3.2 *Age structure of Norwich poor and* PHE *populations*

Age	00–04	05–09	10–14	15–19	20–24	25–29	30–34	35–39	40–44	45–49	50–54	55–59	60–64	65–69	70–74	75–79	80–84	85–89	90–94	95–99	100–04	'Child'	Adult	Ambiguous
Poor	229	312	168	73	68	99	175	98	270	75	158	45	169	36	40	14	57	7	3	2	2	193	47	19
Percentage	9.7	13.2	7.1	3.1	2.9	4.2	7.4	4.1	11.4	3.2	6.7	1.9	7.7	1.5	1.7	0.6	2.4	0.3	0.1	0.1	0.1	8.2	2.0	0.8
PHE 1571	13.3	11.8	7.7	9.7	10.1	8.6	7.2	6.3	5.7	4.9	4.1	3.4	2.8	2.1	1.4	0.7	0.3	0.1	0.01	0	0	0	0	0

Age	00–09	10–19	20–29	30–39	40–49	50–59	60–69	70–79	80–89	90–99	100–04	'Child'	Adult	Ambiguous
Poor	541	241	167	273	345	203	205	54	64	5	2	193	47	19
Percentage	22.9*	10.2	7.1	11.5	14.6	8.6	9.2	2.3	2.7	0.2	0.1	8.2	2.0	0.8
PHE 1571	28.1	17.4	18.7	13.5	10.5	7.5	4.8	2.1	0.4	0.01	0	0	0	0

* 31% if 'children' are included.

Sources: Pound, *Census*; Wrigley and Schofield, *Population History* and personal communication, R. S. Schofield (see note 36).

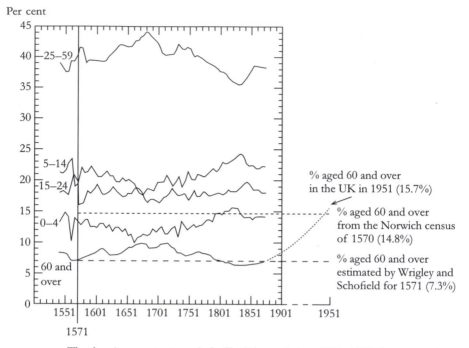

FIGURE 3.1 *The changing age structure of the English population, 1541–1871 (percentages in five age groupings). The percentage of the population aged 60 and over from the Norwich census of 1570 is closer to figures for the 1950s than to those estimated by Wrigley and Schofield for 1571*
Source: Wrigley and Schofield, *Population History* (see note 36).

The chief abnormality of the census in contemporary terms is that it shows a small proportion of young people between the ages of 15 and 24, that is, 5.7 per cent compared with just under 20 per cent in the Wrigley and Schofield estimate.[39] Presumably adolescent offspring of poor families were living in other, better-off households as servants and apprentices; if ill or injured, they would be the responsibility of their masters.[40]

Having discussed the value of the census, we may now observe its findings with respect to the actual condition of the sick poor. Norwich used the same generic terms as other censuses, but gave far more detail. To some extent the censustakers were observing the distinction, traditional but still used in the *GHS*, between acute and chronic conditions. Thus, the term most commonly used was 'lame', often with further specification, not just of legs but of other limbs and

39. Fewer boys (30) were present than girls (61), but 50 in this agegroup were unspecified as to gender. One of the defects of the twentieth-century decennial census is a 'loss' in urban environments of young mobile adults aged between 25 and 44: Curtis, *Intra-Urban Variations*, p. 12. On problems of estimating the presence of children and servants in sixteenth-century urban populations, see Phythian-Adams, *Desolation of a City*, esp. pp. 221–37.
40. See Pelling, 'Child Health'; 'Aprenticeship'.

even of the body as a whole. The next most common term was 'sick' or 'very sick' and, as in other censuses, this was applied across a wide age range. The term 'sickly' was applied to a smaller number; the word 'ill' was not used at all. The duration of some sickness was indicated by such formulae as 'longtime', 'many days' or 'since Christmas', showing reasonable knowledge or level of enquiry on the part of the censustakers. Such precision was part of poor-relief practice; in 1625 the Salisbury authorities deplored the fact that the state of half of the population was such that 'they must be relyeved by the City if they happen to be sick but one week'.[41] The last of the generic terms used in Norwich were 'past work' and 'diseased'. The latter could be further specified, but when used alone was probably most often applied to conditions approximating to syphilis, and apparent on the surface of the body. Not surprisingly, these terms were not mutually exclusive.

Of more specific conditions, those affecting the senses were the most numerous, with twice as many identified as suffering degrees of blindness as deafness. Present, or rather identified, in small numbers (but on other evidence representing only the tip of the iceberg) were broken legs and ribs, sore legs, sores, gout, one-handedness, one-leggedness (or the loss of use of one hand, or one leg), crookedness, the stone, dumbness, mouth disease, lunacy and distraction, fistula, French pox, and being 'brusten' or ruptured.[42] These conditions represent severe sickness or disability, but most of them, except dumbness, deafness, limb-loss and perhaps lunacy, are conditions for which the Norwich authorities arranged, or enforced, medical intervention, at considerable cost.[43] Major preoccupations missing from the census, but recurrent in other poor-relief sources, were scrofula or the king's evil, scurvy, and scaldhead, the last being possibly related to venereal disease and a particular problem and expense in children. Falling sickness was a very commonly used term, and, as a condition or conditions, was the subject of licences to beg for the cost of treatment by the sufferer or his or her friends; but it was not a condition for which poor-relief authorities paid the cost of treatment.[44]

The proportion of sick and disabled in the census population is lower than the well-known mid-century London estimate, around 7 per cent. But, as in Ipswich, little is recorded of the state of children (see Table 3.3). If only those 20 and over are considered, the Norwich figure of 11 per cent sick and disabled among the poor approximates to that found for London. While the younger end of the age structure of the sick population might be dubious, the proportions shown in Table 3.3 for the middle decades of life indicate the importance of sickness in the 'economically active' sectors of the population. This finding in the Norwich census contrasts with the false impression given by some less comprehensive censuses that sickness was officially a function only of aged

41. Quoted by Slack, 'Poverty and Politics', p. 171.

42. Cf. for the eighteenth century I. S. L. Loudon, *Medical Care and the General Practitioner 1750–1850* (Oxford, 1986), pp. 54–9, 74–5, showing considerable similarities.

43. Cf. Marshall's Ypres list of conditions requiring cure among the poor, which, besides those 'roughe and scourvy and ronnynge with matter', included especially the 'brasten such as have the stone such as ar diseased in their faces', in Salter, *Early Tracts*, p. 70.

44. See Pelling, 'Healing the Sick Poor'.

TABLE 3.3 *Norwich poor and sick poor by age and percentage*

Age	00–09	10–19	20–29	30–39	40–49	50–59	60–69	70–79	80–89	90–99	100–09	'Child'	Adult	Ambiguous	Totals
Total poor	541	241	167	273	345	203	205	54	64	5	2	193	47	19	2,359
Sick poor	5	2	7	11	29	22	30	16	26	5	1	3	6	4	167
Total poor as %	22.9	10.2	7.1	11.6	14.6	8.6	8.7	2.3	2.7	0.2	0.1	8.2	2.0	0.8	
Sick poor as %	3.0	1.2	4.2	6.6	17.4	13.2	18.0	9.6	15.5	3.0	0.6	1.8	3.6	2.4	
Sick poor as % of poor	0.9	0.8	4.2	4.0	8.4	10.8	14.6	30.0	40.6	100.0	50.0	1.5	12.8	21.0	7.08

Source: Pound, *Census*.

impotence. It should not be thought, however, that the Norwich authorities targeted the breadwinner in the prime of life, as did the nineteenth-century New Poor Law. Ability to work was the primary concern, but, having a different view of economic activity, the Norwich authorities expected such activity to continue in some form until death, even in the presence of severe disability.[45] Thus the censustakers sometimes startle a modern reader by recording severe disability and then rating the person as 'able'.[46] This suggests that the use of the term 'able' alone in censuses is no measure of the health status of the population concerned.

It should also be noted that the censustakers were as concerned with the condition of women as of men, reflecting the economic importance of work by women among the poor.[47] I have not counted pregnant or nursing women as among the sick, even though the censustakers clearly regarded both these conditions as worth noting; their inclusion would increase the proportion of those disabled for work in the middle decades of life.

Finally, one aspect of both policy and action inadequately represented in the census is the treatment and care of sick children. Although the level of observation of the condition of children in the census is low, the degeneration of children was a matter of concern in the 1570s, and children later absorbed a high proportion of the medical care provided by the municipality for the poor.[48]

The last set of calculations in Table 3.3, and the broken line of Figure 3.2, represent the sick poor as a proportion of the poor in any given agegroup. The most striking effect is at the 'elderly' end of the graph, but here the numbers concerned are very small. However, once the effects of distortion are taken into account, there is a consistent level of disability among the poor throughout adult life. As already noted, the proportion of age 60 and over in the census population is close to the 1950s figure for the total population, just under 16 per cent. If the age structure derived from *The Population History of England* (*PHE*) is used (and the proportion of 'strangers' in the Norwich population eliminated) then the Norwich over-60s suffered between a one-in-three and one-in-two chance of poverty – or of being defined as poor – at some point at, or after, 60. It seems fair to say that their actual chances were probably rather worse. Further, the aged poor stood about a one-in-four chance of also being severely disabled. For the elderly English population of Norwich as a whole, the chance of sickness or disability was at least one in ten (see Table 3.4). For adults between 25 and 59 (again using *PHE* figures), the chances of poverty were approximately one in five; once poor, about one in thirteen could expect

45. For London, see John Howes's 'Discourse' (1582), in Tawney and Power, *Tudor Economic Documents*, vol. 3, pp. 418, 424–5. Given the Norwich authorities' assumption that a person would continue to work, however aged, I have equated expressions such as 'past work' with major debility (see on this Pelling, 'Old Age, Poverty and Disability'). 'Laborer work not for age' is applied to a man of 60, but does not imply 'retirement' for persons this age or older (Pound, *Census*, p. 36). Persons described as 'miserable' or 'desolate' have not been included, although it is likely that they were sick or disabled in some way. See for example 'Maude House of 60 yere, a wedowe that is a desolete thinge & beggethe . . . Veri pore' (Pound, *Census*, p. 50).

46. Thus Elizabeth Mason, a widow of 80, lame and one-handed, is rated able: Pound, *Census*, p. 28.

47. As Pound notes (*Census*, p. 16), fewer than 14% of poor women lacked employment, compared with 34% of men. For development of this point, see Pelling, 'Older Women'.

48. On this see Pelling, 'Healing the Sick Poor'; 'Child Health'.

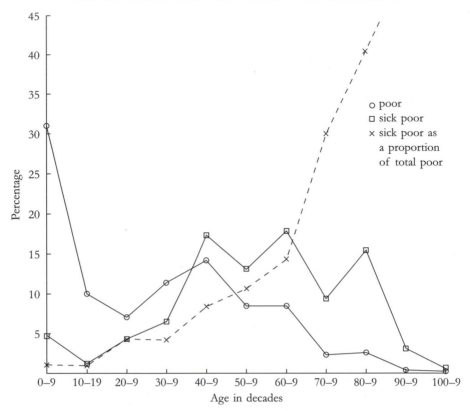

FIGURE 3.2 *Norwich poor and sick poor by age and percentage, 1570*

TABLE 3.4 *Poor and sick poor by agegroup as a proportion of Norwich (English) population*

Agegroup	00–04	05–14	15–24	25–59	60+	Ambiguous	Totals
PHE 1571 (%)	13.3	19.5	19.8	40.2	7.3	0.0	–
Estimated population 1570	1,413	2,071	2,103	4,271	775	0.0	10,625
Poor	325	576	141	967	330	19	2,359
Poor as % of population	23.0	27.8	6.7	22.6	42.6	0.0	–
Sick poor	2	7	3	73	78	4	167
Sick poor as % of population	0.1	0.3	0.1	1.7	10.1	0.0	–

Note: 'Children' of unknown age have been divided equally between the first two agegroups; 'adults' have been added to agegroup 25–59.
Sources: Pound, *Census*; Wrigley and Schofield, *Population History*. See also note 34.

to be sick or disabled. For English middle-aged adults as a whole in Norwich, the chances were at least one in fifty.

Although the purposes served by the census might be seen retrospectively as narrow and selfish, the census itself is nonetheless revealing. The extreme vulnerability of the poor to the threat of sickness is shown in the congruity between the conditions identified by the censustakers, and those conditions which created a demand for lower levels of practitioner, including itinerant specialists. Examples include oculists, bonesetters, truss-makers, and lithotomists or cutters for the stone. Their activity is partly a reflection of the prevalence of certain conditions, but must also be a reflection of the effects of inability to work. The effectiveness of treatment by any practitioner in the past is a vexed question, but it should be noted here that one London hospital, St Bartholomew's, was claiming a mortality rate of 10 per cent and a discharged/cured rate of nearly 70 per cent in 1645 for a range of similar cases (though including maimed soldiers).[49] Popular healers obviously had other specialties apparently more trivial, like corncutting and toothdrawing. The Norwich authorities allowed such practitioners to practise in Norwich for restricted periods. Popular remedies were also sought for the ague, catarrh, colic, coughs, consumption, 'wry-neck' (a twisting of the neck which could follow from severe scarring), dropsy, harelip, worms, inflammation, and diseases of women. While some of these maladies could be included among those simply called 'sickness' by the censustakers, others belong to the wider fields of illness, approximating to self-reported illness, which Paul Slack has identified as attracting the greatest number of remedies in the vernacular medical literature of the sixteenth century.[50] Even greater variety can be found in the antidotaries and similar sources intended for the practitioner or the lay reader, and which stressed symptomology.

The congruity in the sixteenth century between the concerns of municipal authorities and those of the poor themselves is perhaps paralleled by the stress placed by modern working-class respondents on their own ability to earn a living and to carry out domestic work. Disability not affecting work tends to be disregarded by these classes, while it is likely to be registered by more privileged social groups.[51] Even self-reported sickness or disability, therefore, is minimised by social circumstances; modern local studies attempt to circumvent this by a variety of stresses on general rather than particular symptomology, or on 'ill-ness' rather than disease.[52]

The Norwich census obviously offers no more than the most tentative basis for calculation. However, in addition to its qualitative interest, it is probably uniquely systematic, and also reflects contemporary attitudes to sickness within the context of the life of the poor. As already stressed, the problems of estimating morbidity at all periods are as great as its importance as a measure of social conditions. Common themes emerge in these wider comparisons, as for example the tendency of social conditions to affect the diagnosis of disease,

49. D'A. Power, 'Some Early Hospital Statistics', *Proceedings of the Royal Society of Medicine (History of Medicine Section)*, 14 (1921), 21–2.

50. P. Slack, 'Mirrors of Health and Treasures of Poor Men: the Uses of the Vernacular Medical Literature of Tudor England', in Webster, *H, M & M*, pp. 237–73.

51. Curtis, *Intra-Urban Variations*, pp. 61–2.

52. Bucquet and Curtis, 'Socio-demographic Variation', pp. 737–8. The Nottingham Health Profile, for example, which is based on a self-completion questionnaire, uses such measures as lack of energy, pain, emotional distress, sleep disturbance, social isolation, and physical immobility. See in general S. M. Hunt, J. McEwen and S. P. McKenna, *Measuring Health Status* (London, 1986).

and the tendency for officials to report only the degree and kind of disease that can be managed politically. Similarly, it is likely to be as true of early as of later periods that anything approaching self-reported morbidity would be a phenomenon different in scale from any estimate related to the provision or use of services. Although adjusted to the latter aim, the house-to-house visitation basis of the Norwich census remains a point of superiority. Nonetheless, in present-day even more than in early modern situations, it is almost axiomatic that there will be major discrepancies between social action and the scale of health problems present in major sectors of the population.

The importance of the sick as a group complicating definitions of the poor seems to me undoubted. This is as true for action as it is of attitudes. Finally, it seems necessary to take into account in a variety of contexts that an absolute minimum of 7 per cent of the urban population at any time might be grossly infectious, repulsive, confined within doors, immobilised, bedridden, or unable to see. Such calculations, and the implications that follow from them for a wide range of social, political, and economic issues, may be necessary not only in respect of those defined as poor, but for all classes in early modern society.

CHAPTER FOUR

Healing the Sick Poor: Social Policy and Disability in Norwich, 1550–1640

In the history of social policy in Britain, state medicine is not seen as the natural state of affairs. Rather, it seems that medical services have been provided by the state in the twentieth century only after a process of painful evolution in the nineteenth, which even now is not complete. Only the inexorable effects of industrialisation, it appears, were able to force upon policy-makers an awareness of the social and economic cost of ill health and early death. Before this point of crisis, health care was primarily delivered by voluntary agencies. Medical poor relief began to be organised on a parochial basis in the eighteenth century, but this remained a meagre and makeshift version of what was evolving on the voluntary level in hospitals and dispensaries. The workings of private philanthropy continued to be the main support of the less fortunate members of society.

This perspective has been supported by assumptions about the growth of medicine as a profession. Medical historians, although increasingly aware of the sophistication of public medical provision in continental Europe, incline to the view that medical poor relief began in England towards the end of the seventeenth century, because they also assume that the medical profession was insufficiently developed before this date. If the poor were treated at all previously, it was by barbers and old women. It is inferred that authorities of the earlier period either had no faith in the effectiveness of medical practitioners – a view which leads inevitably to anachronism – or practitioners were too few, or too expensive, to have any relevance to the poor.[1]

I should like to thank Ludmilla Jordanova, Mary Hilton, and especially Charles Webster for their comments. I am also grateful for comments made on versions given in Cambridge, Lancaster, and Melbourne.

1. Prevailing assumptions on medical poor relief are exemplified by G. W. Oxley, *Poor Relief in England and Wales 1601–1834* (Newton Abbot, 1974); P. Rushton, 'The Poor Law, the Parish and the Community in North-East England, 1600–1800', *Northern History*, 25 (1989), 146. Still to be recommended are E. M. Leonard, *The Early History of English Poor Relief* (Cambridge, 1900); A. Clark, *Working Life of Women in the Seventeenth Century*, 2nd edn (London, 1982); H. Levy, 'The Economic History of Sickness and Medical Benefit before the Puritan Revolution', *Eco. Hist. Rev.*, 13 (1943), 42–57; F. G. Emmison, 'Poor Relief Accounts for Two Rural Parishes in Bedfordshire, 1563–1598', *Eco. Hist. Rev.*, 3 (1931), 102–16; F. G. Emmison, 'The Relief of the Poor at Eaton Socon, 1706–1834 . . .', *Publications of the Bedfordshire Historical Records Society*, 15 (1933), 1–98; F. G. Emmison, 'The Care of the Poor in Elizabethan Essex. Recently Discovered Records', *Essex Review*, 62 (1953), 7–28. See also J. Webb (ed.), *Poor Relief in Elizabethan*

This set of assumptions could be attacked in a number of different ways. It has been remarked that, with respect to the early modern period, attitudes to social policy are better known than their application.[2] An intensive study of the scattered evidence relating to the practices of one early modern town, Norwich, has shown that attention to applications can be unexpectedly rewarding. This evidence shows considerable municipal provision of medical services, existing independently of any major institutionalisation, and calling on a remarkably high proportion of the numerous medical practitioners active in the town. Norwich can be shown to have had a well-developed awareness of the social and economic importance of illness, and to have been prepared to invest not only in prevention but also in medical intervention. Although Norwich seems to have acted primarily to avert public danger and public expense, it could be suggested that the town's authorities were showing a collective alertness to the manifestations of disease which paralleled the individual's concern for health matters at this time.[3] A high incidence of disease does not seem to have bred indifference at any level.

Much excellent writing on the subject of poor relief in general in the early modern period has been concerned with definitions of the poor connected with the principles of Catholicism, humanism, or Protestantism. Stress has been placed on the fragmentation of 'God's poor' – a holistic attitude supposedly characteristic of the pre-Reformation period – into the deserving and the undeserving, the able and the impotent. It has often been stated that sixteenth-century authorities, in their obsession with putting down vagrancy, were slow to evolve even relatively crude categories of 'approved' poor. However, Paul Slack has suggested in relation to Salisbury that these binary distinctions could become modified, as well as sharpened, as a result of economic crisis leading to massive unemployment.[4] The Norwich evidence confirms that towns of this period were capable of more discrimination as to the causes of poverty than binary categories imply. I should like to suggest further that this degree of insight, although made more evident by economic crisis, was also based on traditional practices and the adaptation of existing institutions.

A strong faith in the results that could be expected from a system of medical intervention is not unknown as a feature of some ambitious plans for improving the condition of the poor in the early modern period. During the Puritan Revolution, the economic reformer Henry Robinson, for example, recommended that physicians and surgeons should be appointed in every county at the public expense, to visit and administer on request, for no consideration other than

Ipswich, Suffolk Records Society IX (1966); Slack, *Impact of Plague*; P. Slack, *Poverty in Early Stuart Salisbury*, Wiltshire Records Society XXXII (1976); Webster, *Great Instauration*, Section IV; Pelling and Webster, 'Medical Practitioners', esp. pp. 217–23. For London evidence supporting the conclusions of this chapter, see A. Wear, 'Caring for the Sick Poor in St Bartholomew Exchange: 1580–1676', *Medical History*, Supplement no. 11 (1991), 41–60.

2. P. Slack, 'Social Policy and the Constraints of Government 1547–58', in J. Loach and R. Tittler (eds), *The Mid-Tudor Polity* c. *1540–1560* (London and Basingstoke, 1980), p. 107.

3. C. Webster, 'Medicine as Social History: Changing Ideas on Doctors and Patients in the Age of Shakespeare', in L. G. Stevenson (ed.), *A Celebration of Medical History* (Baltimore, MD, 1982), pp. 115–16.

4. P. Slack, 'Poverty and Politics in Salisbury 1597–1666', in P. Clark and P. Slack (eds), *Crisis and Order in English Towns 1500–1700* (London, 1972), pp. 164–203.

that allowed them by the state. Similar ideas had also been put forward in the sixteenth century by utopian writers and humanist reformers. Henry Brinklow, in the context of the use of the profits of the Dissolution, had advocated physicians, surgeons, and houses for the sick in every city, town, and hundred. The practitioners, again, were to live on their stipends alone, on pain of mutilation.[5] The religious reformer William Marshall has been credited with a poor-law scheme which had great influence on the poor law legislation of 1536. This scheme included the following provisions:

It is also enacted by thauctorite aforeseid that if any such vacabunde and idle persones be sicke, which of likeliod myght well labour if they were hoole, that then theseid deputies shall assigne certeyn Phisicians and Surgeons to loke vnto and remedie ther diseases; And that thesame Phisicians and Surgeons shalbe paied for ther labour and paynes in and about the curyng and helpyng of the sicke and sore vacabundes and idle persones, as is aboueseid, of theseid moneye and of thother charite of the people; And when such sicke and sore persones ben cured and heled, then they to be put to labour in theseid workes vnder the paynes before expressed.

The possible application of such schemes has hardly been considered by historians. Marshall's scheme is regarded as beyond the capacity of Tudor or even of later administrations.[6] Nonetheless, the system in use in Norwich can be shown to have had some of the essential characteristics of Marshall's plan. The most important of these was the attention paid to those who 'myght well labour if they were hoole'. It is significant that those too old, weak, or sick to work again were dealt with separately in a later part of Marshall's scheme. Similarly, this chapter will not be particularly concerned with almshouses or the impotent poor. Norwich's approach to the sick poor lacked the broader vision of Robinson's proposals, in particular the state-salaried element, but was suited to the climate of the time. Tempering this outlook was a well-developed conviction of the role of sickness in creating poverty. Marshall himself, writing in the 1530s, placed sickness first among the 'casualties' affecting people who were poor through no fault of their own.

Norwich is of course famous for its initiatives in respect of poor relief and regulation, particularly in the 1570s.[7] Marshall's national scheme, which predated the Dissolution, depended heavily on voluntary almsgiving; by contrast, Norwich introduced a compulsory poor rate only 14 years later, in 1549, and was apparently the first provincial town to enforce such a measure. Some of its medical poor-relief practices seem to be associated with its major poor scheme of the 1570s; nonetheless, in many respects these practices reached their greatest

5. Webster, *Great Instauration*, p. 291; see also the schemes of 'Dr Turnbull', ibid., p. 300; D. Harley, 'Pious Physic for the Poor: the Lost Durham County Medical Scheme of 1655', *Medical History*, 37 (1993), 148–66. Henry Brinklow, *Complaynt of Roderyck Mors* [c. 1542], ed. J. M. Cowper, Early English Text Society Extra Ser. XXII (1874), p. 52.

6. G. R. Elton, 'An Early Tudor Poor Law', *Eco. Hist. Rev.*, 6 (1953), 143, 154, 140.

7. See Leonard, *English Poor Relief*, pp. 101–7; J. F. Pound, 'An Elizabethan Census of the Poor: the Treatment of Vagrancy in Norwich, 1570–1580', *University of Birmingham Historical Journal*, 8 (1961–62), 135–62, esp. 136.

development some decades later, in the early seventeenth century. An apparent decline in the 1630s, particularly in the institutional side of the system, raises questions connected with poor-relief policy in general in the Laudian period, but the evidence is insufficient for clear answers to these questions. More striking is the continuity of Norwich's *ad hoc* provision of medical care, which in terms of its funding was centralised and largely independent of the poor rate, and which seems to have persisted to some degree into the eighteenth century.

The operation of Norwich's system is best dealt with by first considering sickness as an aspect of poor-relief problems and practices in the town before 1600. I shall then go on to examine the role of individual practitioners employed to treat the poor. Later sections will establish that, while no major part was played by any single institution, short-term institutional care was provided for the sick by the keepers of lazarhouses, the importance of which increased after 1600.

The scheme of the 1570s involved custodial care, discipline, training, some education, and work for all ages according to their capacities. It was intended to make the poor entirely self-supporting or even profitable. Less attention has been paid to the fact that it also laid considerable stress on the prevention of disease. The lives of the poor were so ill-regulated, according to Norwich's interpretation of the rules of health, that if allowed to beg they suffered from excess as well as privation. Indiscriminate private philanthropy had led directly to ill health. And:

So cared they not for apparel though the cold struck so deep into them, that what with diseases and want of shifting their flesh was eaten with vermin and corrupt diseases grew on them so fast and so grievously that they were past remedy... for want of exercise of body and shift of apparel both the old and the young fall (by extreme poverty) into such incurable diseases and filthiness of body as one so corrupteth another that the charge to heal them is very great.[8]

The reference to 'old and young' was not simply proverbial. As we shall see, the elderly were required to work, and therefore to be 'able'. Children living shiftless lives became physically disqualified from being apprenticed. Prosperous parishioners obliged to take on a parish apprentice could reject the child on such grounds as its lameness, sickliness, or scald head; one such apprentice had a 'scald and scurvy head which is infectious', another developed a 'thistell upon his body and limes'. As always at this period, the perceived link between morality, behaviour and disease was very close. In one incident, an apprentice who ran away was recorded as contracting diseases from sleeping in ditches; in a more extreme case of absconding involving theft, the apprentice's legs rotted off.[9] The emphasis on clothing complements the dominance, evident in

---

8. Quoted from R. H. Tawney and E. E. Power (eds), *Tudor Economic Documents*, 3 vols (London, 1953), vol. 2, pp. 317–18.

9. Ibid.; D. E. H. James, *Norfolk Quarter Sessions Order Book 1650–1657*, Norfolk Record Society XXVI (1955), pp. 19, 39, 46, 47, 50, 84–5. For an earlier reference to sickness and parish apprenticeship, see 27 Henry VIII c. 25.

the records, of diseases showing themselves on exposed parts of the body, and helps to explain the considerable expenditure on clothing for the poor at this time.

The stress in the 1570s on prevention stemmed directly from the fact that the community was already providing substantial sums for the cure of disease. It was claimed at the end of the first year of operation of the Norwich poor scheme that supervising the poor and putting them on work had saved the cost of an annual burden, arising directly from cases of disease, of 200 'licences to collect', each licence involving at least 26s., giving a total of over £260 per annum.[10] These licences were specifically for raising money to finance expensive cures. Different forms of licences to collect, also called protections, were widely used in the sixteenth century to sanction traditional although increasingly suspected forms of begging, for example the financing of their studies by poor university students, and the support of poor parishes or hospitals.[11] At this time, such licences were issued by all levels of authority, ecclesiastical and lay, and were taken from door to door, as well as from church to church. The text of the licence to gather in respect of sickness could include the testimony of a practitioner as to the necessity, feasibility, and cost of treatment, as well as a statement of the licensee's inability to raise the cost by his or her own efforts. Parish officials and the clergy were required to assist or at least not to hinder the licensee both in the collection and in his or her travelling either to seek treatment, or to contact friends and relatives who might be able to help.

Norwich's hope of permanently superseding this type of licensed begging by the systematic preventive measures of its poor scheme was not fulfilled, although the volume of licensing may have been greatly reduced as a matter of policy. Nine such licences to collect for medical reasons were recorded as being issued by Norwich's mayor's court during the lean years 1596–98, for periods of six weeks to three months, to persons unable to pay for treatment of such conditions as fistula, falling sickness, and broken legs. In respect of a case of calculus or stone in the bladder, which could involve very high fees, the licence was renewed for a second period of three months. The use of these licences may explain the mobility of some patients and suggests a less restricted capacity in the market to pay high fees, as well as a broader class range of recipients of medical 'poor relief'. Licences were probably most used where they have been least noticed, that is, at the local level as dictated by the municipal authority. In such cases, the area of collection was restricted to the city boundaries or even limited to a particular ward. These licences also allowed the poor of the suburbs some access to the greater affluence of the town. Similar licences were still being used in respect of costly medical services in the late seventeenth century. In thus linking over time the pre-Reformation stress on almsgiving with the voluntaryist principles evident in the early-eighteenth-century founding of the infirmaries,

10. Quoted in Tawney and Power, *Tudor Economic Documents*, vol. 2, p. 318.
11. T. N. Brushfield, 'Devonshire Briefs', *Transactions of the Devonshire etc. Association*, 27 (1895), 311–57 and ibid., 28 (1896), 606–711; W. A. Bewes, *Church Briefs; or Royal Warrants for Collections for Charitable Objects* (London, 1896); B. Clarke, 'Norfolk Licences to Beg: an Unpublished Collection', *Norfolk Archaeology*, 35 (1970–73), 327–34.

they are a reminder of the persistence of the connections between medicine and religious grounds for social action.[12] It is equally characteristic of the 1570s that Norwich should have wished to supersede these licences. They may have been revived in the 1590s as an emergency measure for more expensive cases, with the hope that their use could be avoided in future by directly employing bonesetters, lithotomists, and lazarhouse-keepers.

The use of licences was not systematic, and depended on individual application and individual generosity. That Norwich saw sickness as a vital element in any thorough effort connected with the poor is shown by the inclusion of details of state of health in the famous and unusually comprehensive 'Census of the Poor' conducted at the outset of the poor scheme in 1570. The census thus provides an opportunity of estimating morbidity which may be unique.[13] A total of 2,359 men, women, and children were described in the census, being perhaps a quarter of the whole native-born population.[14] Although the preamble to the census complained of vagrancy, the poor counted in the census, as in earlier continental instances, were not vagrants, but resident poor. Some were in their own houses; a majority were the tenants of prominent citizens or aldermen. About 9 per cent of the adult poor (that is, over the age of 16), were described at that time as being in some way sick or disabled, although many did some work nonetheless. A further 1.5 per cent of adults, all of them aged, were described simply as past work. These included many of the very few women who did no work.[15] Rather more women than men were affected by sickness or disablement, but this was merely in proportion to the greater number of poor women overall (i.e. 860:525). A few ill children were mentioned. Among adults, the greatest numbers suffering illness or defect combined with poverty were between the ages of 41 and 60; in early adulthood, sickness was more noticed among men, but sick women were more numerous in old age. Clearly, in adulthood, sickness was a function of increasing, rather than old age, being a problem from the age of 40 onwards.

The census population is artificial in lacking the major part of the agegroup 15–24, which has been estimated as 19.8 per cent of the English population in 1571, as compared with only 5.7 per cent of the census population. The extent to which sickness affected the middle-aged becomes more striking when account is taken of the unsurprising tendency of a population selected for poverty to include many old people, who might have been expected to dominate any picture of morbidity. Those aged 60 and over formed an estimated 7.3 per cent of the total English population of 1571, compared with twice that percentage

12. NRO, Press D, Case 16, shelf a, Mayor's Court Proceedings no. 13, pp. 106, 115, 119, 123, 145, 167, 175, 177, 182. For late seventeenth-century examples, see C. Williams, 'Extracts from the Court Rolls [sic] of . . . Norwich Relating Chiefly to . . . Stone', *The Lancet*, ii (1898), 1181–2.

13. For a comparison of the Norwich estimate with others, see Pelling, 'Illness among the Poor'. The substantial introduction to Pound, *Census*, does not analyse morbidity.

14. Hudson and Tingey, *Records*, vol. 2, pp. cxxvii–cxxviii.

15. Pound, *Census*, pp. 13–15, 66, Appendix I, 15–17, Appendix III. Unemployment of males, by contrast, stood at one-third: ibid., p. 16. For further discussion, see Pelling, 'Old Age, Poverty and Disability'; 'Older Women'.

(14.8 per cent) of the census population (or 13 per cent if the 'missing' adolescents are added).[16]

About one-third of the sick poor of the census were simply described as sick, sickly, or very sick. Others were called weak, diseased, bed-ridden, lame, crooked, or suffering from stone, gout, dumbness, deafness, broken legs, diseases of the mouth, broken ribs, thigfola (?fistula), or were one-legged or one-handed. One woman aged 36 lay 'in the pokes [pox] as she sayth by Tomson'; three men and women were 'somewhat lunatic' or 'beside themselves' and unable to work, though all three were apparently living independently. One sick woman aged 60 (with a husband aged 37) nonetheless 'spins white warp and teaches youth'. A lame but able woman in her fifties did not work but had alms of 1d a week, distilled aqua vitae, and 'lived off her friends'. Of ten blind or 'almost' blind men and women, one still worked as a baker, and a woman of 80 managed to knit; the others could do nothing, and one blind man of 50 was, in addition, married to an 'unable' woman of 96. Such discrepancies of age between partners point to marriage as a strategy for survival. Another blind man in his fifties had a fatherless child of 12 to lead him about, and there were other 'symbiotic' relationships of this kind.[17]

Although generically described in many cases, the sick poor of the census obviously suffered from conditions appreciable by inspection. The information was evidently gathered by house-to-house visitation. Many conditions based primarily on individuals' perceptions of themselves (for example, colic) did not apparently threaten either their neighbours or their own capacity to work and were ignored by the city's inspectors. No great differentiation in diagnosis was required. The Norwich census is particularly valuable, however, in indicating a range of acute and chronic conditions, many of which, on the basis both of the annotations to the census and of their actual proceedings, the Norwich authorities would have regarded as amenable to treatment or to improvement (however temporary) in the necessaries of life, such as diet.[18] Blindness is a case in point; although to be blind was virtually to be 'unable', the city authorities were at the same time ready to support the extensive (and apparently successful) activities of such peripatetic oculists as Richard Banister.[19] Similarly, the possibility of medical poor relief was extended by Norwich to all ages from four to 80, a reflection of the wider age range of those thought capable of contributing directly to their own support.

The sick poor identified in 1570 were not, therefore, regarded fatalistically, or abandoned to any mere rhetoric of prevention. The 1570s scheme provided that the proctors or keepers of the city's lazarhouses, as well as poor women,

16. The English population estimates derive from Wrigley and Schofield, *Population History*, p. 528.

17. Pound, *Census*, pp. 60, 62, 70, 73, 79, 33, 29, 66, and *passim*. For more on these themes, see Pelling, 'Old Age, Poverty and Disability'; 'Child Health'.

18. Although it cannot be dealt with here, it is important to note the part played in poor relief in Norwich and elsewhere by extra or temporary payments made to the poor in time of sickness, i.e. 'sickness' as opposed to 'medical' benefit: see Levy, 'Economic History of Sickness', pp. 45–50.

19. See *DNB*; R. Banister, *Treatise of One Hundred and Thirteene Diseases of the Eyes* (London, 1622), sigs [d7verso–d8recto]; NRO, Mayor's Court Proceedings no. 15, 1615–24, fol. 303.

should receive into their houses 'the diseased, including the leprous'; and from this time onwards, the city employed significant numbers of practitioners to treat the poor.[20] A few people mentioned in the census can be identified with those subsequently provided with medical relief. Among those treated at city expense after 1570 there were, as the census details would lead one to expect, as many women as men, but, by contrast, a much higher proportion of children or young people. This more accurately reflects the age structure of the population as a whole, as well as the poor scheme's concern for the physical and moral degeneration of children, a concern which parallels that expressed in London's policies, and in humanist attitudes to the poor. Even very young children were able to help their parents (or the people with whom they lived); sick children could neither learn nor become apprentices; it was therefore worthwhile for the city to pay for them to be treated. The census provides clear evidence that children worked and contributed significantly to the support of the household.

At this time, Norwich had a ratio of practitioners to population of around 1:200.[21] Of this large and disparate group no less than one-eighth, at a minimum, were employed at some time by the city. More than one-third of these were women, including a woman surgeon and women keepers of the lazarhouses or poorhouses who are known to have taken on cures.[22] The remaining two-thirds were chiefly barber-surgeons, surgeons, and bonesetters, with a sprinkling of apothecaries, physician-surgeons, and recruits to medicine from other trades. Although the proportion of women is high, the city effectively chose representatives of the full range of available practitioners, roughly in the proportions in which they were present, from the more to the less formally qualified.

The city's choice was not affected by any of the factors conventionally regarded as restricting or regulating medical practice in this period, such as being free of the city, native-born, or licensed to practise. Some of those chosen were freemen, some were not, although this might have varied in other towns where the freedom was more important for all trades. Similarly, from Norwich's point of view, standing in the barber-surgeons' company made no difference, and the city also felt able to employ strangers, in particular 'Dutchmen'. Since weakness of restriction on English-born immigrants to Norwich was a feature of the economic life of the town, it would be surprising if the city had favoured indigenous practitioners in particular.[23] Of the whole group of 34 practitioners employed by the city, only five show any signs of contact with the ecclesiastical licensing system, and there is no evidence that this affected their employment. This also is hardly surprising, since ecclesiastical licensing had little impact on Norwich medical practitioners as a whole.

20. The chief sources are the 'Mayor's Book of the Poor', I and II, and the Mayor's Court Proceedings (NRO). Transcripts of the former and associated documents by J. M. Dixon were deposited in the Local History section of the Central Library, Norwich (destroyed by fire in 1994). See also J. M. Dixon, 'Poor Relief in Norwich' (University of Leeds MA thesis, 1927).

21. See Pelling and Webster, 'Medical Practitioners', pp. 207–26, esp. pp. 225–6; see p. 208, n. 83 for sources. Revised totals are given in Pelling, 'Occupational Diversity', p. 508 (226).

22. Midwives have been excluded from this calculation.

23. This point is developed in Pelling, 'Occupational Diversity'.

That the city did not more often choose the same practitioner from the wide range of available personnel was a reflection, circumstances apart, partly of a mode of practice in which fewer patients were taken on for longer periods of time, and partly of the commercial system under which practitioners were employed. With a few important exceptions, Norwich did not pay stipends to practitioners who treated the poor, but instead came to a separate agreement for each case. Like the individual, the city exercised consumer choice, being one party in a conditional contract in which the practitioner was usually first paid something on account, and then a balance when the contract was fulfilled. Conditional contracts were the rule, rather than the exception as is usually suggested; they are not peculiar to Norwich, and continued well into the seventeenth century. The advantage to practitioners of this style of agreement was that they took only those cases where they estimated they stood a definite chance of success, or at least of an agreed level of success. This principle was enshrined in barber-surgeons' ordinances, which prohibited the taking-on of dangerous cures until the case had been seen by those best able to assess the risks of the contract, to the practitioner as well as to the patient.[24] The Elizabethan class of incurables thus has some contact with the contemporary systems of medicine and law, rather than being a vague or merely fatalistic description. A main charge of deceit by practitioners could consequently lie in their taking in hand diseases which they knew to be incurable, as well as in their not attending their failures.[25] In certain cases a charge of witchcraft could arise from a claim to cure an incurable disease.[26] Most proceedings against practitioners fit much more readily into the framework of breakdown of agreed contracts, than into the modern category of malpractice suits.

Regardless of formal provisions, however, the number, diversity, and competitiveness of practitioners ensured that risks continued to be taken. With respect to poor patients at least, there was often an element in the contract guaranteeing that the practitioner would 'keep the patient whole' for the rest of his or her life. This is best seen as referring not to drastically different life expectancies as between rich and poor, or to an exaggerated faith on the part of the practitioners in their own powers, but rather to a kind of speculation involving a transfer of responsibility. Should the patient in question be found again in the same condition, the city would regard the practitioner as liable to treat him or her under the terms of the original agreement.

The city authorities may therefore be regarded as in a sense putting out to tender, and it should not be supposed, because practitioners were sometimes imported from Yarmouth, or cases sent to Coventry, that there must have been no practitioners close by. The prevalence of this type of contractual agreement helps to explain why the few practitioners whom the city attempted to employ

24. For ordinances see sources given in ibid., notes 28 and 29. For further discussion of contracts, see Pelling, *Strength of the Opposition*.

25. See Banister's criticisms of Henry Blackburne: A. Sorsby, 'Richard Banister and the Beginnings of English Ophthalmology', in E. A. Underwood (ed.), *Science, Medicine and History: Essays . . . in Honour of Charles Singer*, 2 vols (London, 1953), vol. 2, p. 52.

26. P. Richards, *The Medieval Leper and his Northern Heirs* (Cambridge and Totowa, NJ, 1977), pp. 71–2.

on a retainer basis were specialists. The special skills of the latter gave them a bargaining advantage. In the eighteenth century, 'contracts' appear more like retainers, and are seen as peculiar to the poor-law context; expensive or ubiquitous conditions such as bonesetting or midwifery continued to require special arrangements.[27] 'Tendering' continued to be a feature of medical life into the twentieth century, but was increasingly excluded from 'private' practice for the better-established practitioner.

More investigation is required before it can be decided whether the town physicians and surgeons employed at Chester in 1574, Ipswich in about 1585, Newcastle from 1599, and Barnstaple in 1629, were of this type or were closer to the continental model of the medical and public health officer salaried by the city-state. Certainly, in all these English towns there is evidence of the presence of a large number of other practitioners. In the Chester example, there was reference to ulcers and wounds, but also to sicknesses and diseases in general; Barnstaple, characteristically of a period in which more was being expected of the professions, described its physician as 'learned'. These towns paid higher fees than Norwich; Ipswich in allowing £30 per annum, and Newcastle in rising to £40 per annum in 1632, came closest to Brinklow's idea of stipend. It may be noted that money had been bequeathed from before 1550 to pay stipends to physicians to treat the poor of specified parishes, although such charity was principally confined to London.[28]

Norwich's most successful arrangement of the regular kind was with bonesetters. Richard Durrant, the best-known example, was probably an immigrant to Norwich, and first came to the city's notice during the poor scheme of the 1570s. Paid at first on the usual contractual basis, Durrant impressed by his skill and for about ten years was paid quarterly first £4 and then £8 per annum, as well being allowed a house in the city rent-free. Durrant's connection with the city outlasted the main provisions of the poor scheme. By 1589, just after his period of employment by the city, Durrant was a householder, warden of the barber-surgeons' company, and engaged in an activity common among prosperous barber-surgeons, that of standing surety to licences relating to the retailing of drink. While on the city's payroll, Durrant was subject to one restriction, that of residing in Norwich (facilitated by his rent-free accommodation). In addition to being skilful, Durrant was not grasping: he was rewarded in 1574 for healing poor people without asking for payment. After his death, the city retained the services of Phineas Reve on the same terms. This type of commitment, like so many other aspects of Norwich's medical relief system, had

27. E. Melling (ed.), *Kentish Sources: IV. The Poor* (Maidstone, 1964), p. 135. Emmison, 'Poor Relief Accounts', p. 76, thus finds that contracts with medical practitioners appear at an earlier date than contracts with workhouse-keepers.

28. R. H. Morris, *Chester in the Plantagenet and Tudor Reigns* (Chester, [1895]), p. 357; Pelling and Webster, 'Medical Practitioners', p. 228; Leonard, *English Poor Relief*, pp. 201–2; C. H. Mayo (ed.), *The Municipal Records of the Borough of Dorchester, Dorset* (Exeter, 1908), p. 518. Cf. C. M. Cipolla, *Public Health and the Medical Profession in the Renaissance* (Cambridge, 1976); Webster, *Great Instauration*, pp. 256–64; W. K. Jordan, *Philanthropy in England 1480–1660* (London, 1959), p. 272. Norwich's fees to specialists were comparable with those paid to bonesetters and others by London hospitals; the stipends paid by other towns were higher than the salaries of St Bartholomew's surgeons: G. Whitteridge and V. Stokes, *A Brief History of the Hospital of Saint Bartholomew* (London, 1961), p. 23.

diminished by the mid-1630s: the city's employment of bonesetters continued, but on the old contract basis, and it was on the same basis that one of Durrant's bonesetter descendants was paid in the 1660s.[29]

After their successful experience with Durrant, the city attempted a similar arrangement in respect of another specialty, lithotomy, particularly important because of the high incidence of bladder stone in East Anglia. These patients were most often small boys, as young as four years; it was at this age that the operation stood the best chance of success, but the acuteness of their suffering was perhaps another reason why sums as high as £10 were paid for them to be operated upon.[30] Lithotomists' contracts were unusual in often including a clause guaranteeing the whole contract even if the child died. Sometimes the operator was required to produce the stone in evidence. As is more familiar from later periods of poor-law administration, the city's retention of Miles Mayhew, surgeon, freeman, and officebearer in the barber-surgeons' company, at an annual fee, was an attempt to reduce the high overall costs of these cases. A search for less drastic and therefore cheaper methods of surgical treatment probably lies behind the interest taken in the achievement of the Norwich surgeon John Hobart, who, in 1593, was reported as having removed a very large stone from a woman without cutting.[31] Some indication of the city's motives may be gathered from a reference by Kent authorities in 1598 to a boy of eleven 'so grevously torment with the stone that he ys not able to work but needeth dayly relief'.[32]

Initially, the city arranged a contract with Mayhew for one patient for £3, subject to his being granted an annual fee of £10 at the next Assembly, in which case the contract was to be absorbed. Mayhew was so retained, but he continued to be paid totals of £3 and £4 for separate cases. By 1618, the city was making these additional contracts dependent upon the patient's survival; it was then put in writing that Mayhew was to take for them what the court decided; and finally, Mayhew's fee was reduced to £5 a year. By 1621, matters had reached breaking point and it was resolved not to pay Mayhew his stipend because he refused to do anything for the poor and had demanded £10 for a single cure of a child.[33] This, if the child achieved adulthood, would, according to one estimate, be enough for him to live on for four to five years.[34] Mayhew's original agreement with the city clearly resembled the Chester arrangement in which the surgeon was to treat those living on alms for nothing (in which case they would not be recorded), and to cure others among the poor 'for such reasonable sum and sums of money and other considerations as shalbe appointed

29. Pelling and Webster, 'Medical Practitioners', p. 217; NRO, Case 18, shelf d, Clavers' [Hamper] Accounts 1550–1601, see years 1574–87; Case 17, shelf d, Book of innkeepers and tipplers 1580–90, fol. 11.

30. Pelling and Webster, 'Medical Practitioners', p. 219 and note 92.

31. Williams, 'Extracts from the Court Rolls', p. 1181. This case may mark a shift from the Celsian to the Marian operation, which was based on observations on women, but which was, however, more elaborate: H. S. Shelley, 'Cutting for the Stone', *Journal of the History of Medicine*, 13 (1958), 52–4.

32. Melling, *Kentish Sources: IV*, p. 13.

33. NRO, Mayor's Court Proceedings no. 15, 1615–24, fols 76verso, 77verso, 186verso, 211verso, 364recto, 384verso; Press E, Case 18, shelf a, Chamberlain's Accounts, 1603–25, *passim* 1617–22. Mayhew first came to the city's notice as a medical practitioner in 1610: Mayor's Court Proceedings no. 14, 1603–15, fol. 276verso.

34. W. K. Jordan, *The Charities of Rural England 1480–1660* (London, 1961), p. 11.

by the mayor'. The Chester surgeon would receive for the almspeople some payment in kind, referred to as 'the stuff being ordinary'. The 'other considerations' at the disposal of Chester's mayor included the freedom. Dispensation from rents, fees, or taxes was a convenient (and often invisible) method of paying for such services: Norwich lazarhouse-keepers were excused part of their rent, and there is evidence that in Norwich a practitioner who took responsibility for one of the sick poor, which included an undertaking that the patient would not thereafter be chargeable to the city, would be exempted from paying the poor rate, at least for a time.[35] It is important to stress that financial records do not necessarily give the whole picture. Payment, even by municipalities, was often invisible, or in kind, as is better known in the context of rural practice.

With respect to the cost of an individual contract, that proportion which the Norwich parish did not pay (from the poor rate, or by special collection) usually came from a special account called the hanaper or hamper. Money went into this account from regular city sources of income, from fines relating to guild misdemeanours, trades offences, keeping alehouses, playing illegal games, putting on plays, and ill rule generally. By this time, guild finances and organisation in Norwich probably allowed little scope for support of members of an occupation, although such sources were occasionally tapped: Tailors' Hall was asked in 1620 to contribute towards the cure of a tailor's widow being treated at some expense at St Bennet's gates lazarhouse.[36]

The stipend of Richard Durrant, however, derived from the revenues of Norwich's main 'hospital', known as St Giles's, or the Great Hospital, or God's House. This institution, substantially endowed and physically enduring, is of the kind often placed in the foreground of the historical picture.[37] In the present context, however, it has no great importance. When badly run, it catered for the pensioners of aldermen; when well run, for those past work. During a reform period around 1620, better provision was made for those inmates who fell ill; but not long after, inmates were being expelled specifically because they were 'grievously diseased' or infirm. One man, terminally ill, was sent home, although he continued to receive the 'allowance of the House' for his relief; another sick inmate, significantly, was sent to St Bennet's lazarhouse.[38] God's House, like the voluntary hospitals of the eighteenth century, undoubtedly rejected 'infectious' cases. A 'place of ministering physic and surgery to the poor in the Hospital' persisted into the 1630s, and tended to be held by aldermanic apothecaries.[39] This office, at £4 per annum, was worth rather less (allowing for inflation) than the fee paid to Durrant when he was first appointed.

35. Morris, *Chester*, pp. 201–2; NRO, Mayor's Court Proceedings no. 15, 1615–24, fol. 62.

36. Hudson and Tingey, *Records*, vol. 2, pp. xcviii, ci; NRO, Mayor's Court Proceedings no. 15, 1615–24, fols 320recto, 324recto. Expenditure on medical relief from the Hamper (including Durrant's annual payments) was also continuous over the period when the Bridewell Accounts and the Mayor's Books of the Poor record some similar outlays. Some expensive *ad hoc* cases were part paid for out of the revenues of the Great Hospital.

37. C. B. Jewson, *History of the Great Hospital, Norwich*, 2nd edn (Norwich, 1966); Jordan, *Charities of Rural England*, pp. 115–16; C. Rawcliffe, *The Hospitals of Medieval Norwich* (Norwich, 1995), chap. 3.

38. NRO, Mayor's Court Proceedings no. 15, 1615–24, fols 263verso, 272recto, 387recto; W. L. Sachse (ed.), *Minutes of the Norwich Court of Mayoralty 1630–1631*, Norfolk Record Society XV (1942), pp. 143, 172.

39. Pelling and Webster, 'Medical Practitioners', p. 221.

Norwich did not require a single institutional framework for the provision of medical care. With respect to the poor in institutions, care was, in practice, provided where it was needed, whether for inmates of the gaol, Bridewell, or the old 'Normanspitel', which was for women. Although even the Great Hospital was to some extent (largely in the negative sense, by expulsion, or the threat of it) used to control unruliness, it was in the lazarhouses that the regulation of health was positively and effectively combined with the regulation of behaviour. Like Sir Thomas More's utopian hospitals, and for similar reasons, lazarhouses were on the outskirts of the city, at the main points of entry. The best-known and longest-lived of these comparatively fragile medieval and late medieval institutions was the Lock in Southwark. The last of London's ten lazarhouses was founded as late as 1473. After 1547, when St Bartholomew's Hospital was granted by the crown to the city of London, five or six of these houses took on a more visible life. Their proper inmates were described by William Harvey in 1633 as the incurable, the infectious, and the scandalous. St Bartholomew's surgeons operated there, and dismemberments or dissections were carried out in the later sixteenth century, apparently by the keepers. Claims were made by some keepers as to a high turnover of patients and cures of difficult cases, but the houses also had an explicit role in suppressing begging and idleness, and, more covertly, served as a repository for decayed servants of patrons or of the supervising institutions.[40]

The officer in charge of a lazarhouse was expected to be resident and to attend the poor in his own person. He was called variously the governor, keeper, or guider of the poor or of the hospital, and his grant was normally for life.[41] Although not of the same magnitude or dignity as masterships of hospitals or almshouses, the keeperships of lazarhouses could represent a modest sinecure or speculation. Families established interests in them, and a husband could transfer his part in them to his widow; the guidership could also be disposed of as an asset for short periods. In London, the keeper was usually paid a stipend and expenses for his inmates, although in difficult times the stipend could disappear. A keepership could also be given to buy off a petitioner who was poor or disabled himself, especially through war service. As we shall see, the Norwich keepers ranged from the poor to the prosperous. Even lazarhouses unendowed with land, being just outside the city and on main roads entering it, were well

40. London's lazarhouses are extensively surveyed by M. B. Honeybourne, 'The Leper Hospitals of the London Area: with an Appendix on some other Medieval Hospitals of Middlesex', *Transactions of the London & Middlesex Archaeological Society*, 21 (1963), 1–61. See also Thomas More, 'Utopia', in *Famous Utopias* (New York, [n.d.]), p. 175. On lazarhouses in general, see J. Y. Simpson, 'Antiquarian Notices of Leprosy and Leper Hospitals in Scotland and England', *Edinburgh Medical and Surgical Journal*, 56 (1841), 301–30; ibid., 57 (1842), 121–56, 394–429; C. Creighton, *A History of Epidemics in Britain*, 2nd edn, 2 vols (London, 1965), vol. 1, chap. II; Richards, *Medieval Leper*. Thorough revision of the medieval history of leperhouses is currently being carried out by Carole Rawcliffe (University of East Anglia), and Max Satchell (University of Oxford).

41. Traditionally, funds were collected for lazarhouses in the outside world by travelling proctors or foregoers, who were often elected or selected from among the house's inmates. As the functions of proctors were eroded or discredited, the distinctions between guiders, proctors, and keepers increasingly disappeared. 'Keeper' was most commonly used by the Norwich authorities. See F. Cohen, 'On the Word Proctor . . .', *Archaeologia*, 18 (1817), 9–11; Hudson and Tingey, *Records*, vol. 2, p. 169; NRO, Mayor's Court Proceedings no. 13, 1595–1603, pp. 29*, 299.

placed for an activity much favoured by medical practitioners at all levels, the sale of food and especially of drink. London and Norwich lazarhouse-keepers were prohibited from keeping alehouses and fined for unlicensed tippling.[42]

The Norwich lazarhouses differed from the London examples in not being directly connected, even administratively, with the city's refounded hospital. Although essentially independent, their activities were increasingly supervised by the magistracy of the mayor's court, a more direct method of centralised control. A more important difference is that it is easier to suppose a significant role for such places in the care and treatment of the poor at this period in the case of King's Lynn, which had five houses, or Great Yarmouth, which had two, or Norwich, which had at least five, than it is in the case of London, which then had the same number or fewer than Norwich for a population more than ten times as large.[43] This is not to say that the houses were imposing structures, like Thomas More's hospitals, which were envisaged as large enough to be taken for small towns. Norwich's lazarhouses probably followed one of the common patterns for leper hospitals in consisting of one solid structure at most combined with a number of small cottages. They were conveniently placed on the north-west boundaries of the city, close to the parishes which, in the late sixteenth century, were both densely populated and poor.[44]

Another difference between London and Norwich was that in Norwich it was the rule rather than the exception for a husband and wife to act as joint keepers. In 1618, when part of an aldermanic legacy was distributed to the keepers, three of the five recipients were women.[45] The role of the women increased as the houses were more extensively used by the city, and very often it was the wife rather than the husband who was employed by the city to cure the sick poor. On the deaths of their husbands, the women often carried on alone as keepers. No distinction was made between men and women as to the type of cure, the fee paid, or the sex and age of their patients.

The role of women, and other aspects of the activities of Norwich keepers, can be illustrated by specific examples. Lawrence Wright is designated a physician in Raach's directory of provincial practitioners on the strength of his undertaking cases for the city, including one of 'thistely' (?fistula), the contract being priced, appropriately to the difficulty of the condition, at £3. Wright was, in fact, a barber or barber-surgeon, a freeman, and an officebearer in the barber-surgeons' company.[46] During the 1590s, he had indentured the unusually large

42. Honeybourne, 'Leper Hospitals', p. 33; NRO, [Hamper] Accounts 1550–1601, fol. 132; W. L. Sachse (ed.), *Minutes of the Norwich Court of Mayoralty 1632–1635*, Norfolk Record Society XXXVI (1967), p. 53. For the connections between medical practitioners and the food and drink trades, see Pelling, 'Occupational Diversity'; 'Food, Status and Knowledge'.

43. *Victoria History of the Counties of England: Norfolk*, ed. W. Page, Vol. 2 (London, 1906), pp. 453, 442.

44. Pound, *Census*, pp. 10–11.

45. NRO, Mayor's Court Proceedings no. 15, 1615–24, fols 186verso–190recto.

46. J. H. Raach, *A Directory of English Country Physicians 1603–1643* (London, 1962), p. 95. For the main sources used in compiling Wright's biography, see Pelling and Webster, 'Medical Practitioners', p. 208, note 83. In the Mayor's Court Proceedings, Wright is often called Leonard rather than Lawrence, but the two are identical. Full details are obtainable from the Biographical Index of Medical Practitioners, *c.* 1500–1720, covering especially London and East Anglia, at the Wellcome Unit for the History of Medicine, University of Oxford.

number of six apprentices, one of them in conjunction with his first wife Margaret, herself the daughter of a barber, William Pickering, who also employed large numbers of apprentices. Wright and his father-in-law are typical of barber-surgeons who may have been engaged in manufacture as well as barbering.[47] A second phase of Wright's life began when he married as his second wife Alice Edwards, whose first husband, William Edwards, had rented St Bennet's gates lazarhouse and taken charge of poor diseased people for at least 25 years up to 1614.[48] On their marriage, Alice and Lawrence Wright became joint keepers and were paid individually by the city for undertaking cures. Between June 1615 and June 1616, Lawrence was entrusted with a new medical case almost every month, his contracts ranging between £3 and 4s., for conditions including lameness of both legs and a sore on the back. Wright's contracts varied in amount with the length of time for which he was to keep the patient, but also according to the severity of the condition, since the cost of keeping was low compared with the cost of some treatments.[49]

That Wright had some reputation as a practitioner, and also took on patients on his own account, is indicated by such cases as Margaret Betts, who was sent to him for cure by her brother from Elsing, about ten miles from Norwich. The city was only concerned that, having been cured, she should now return to her work on a farm near Elsing. In his will, Wright specified bequests totalling in the long term over £350, rather more than the bonesetter Durrant.[50] His widow Alice continued to act as keeper of St Bennet's, dealing over the two years following Lawrence's death with a range of serious medical cases, including two of the French pox, one of them involving a whole family. Her contracts were priced similarly to Lawrence's at sums between 15s. and £3. At the same time, Alice took custodial cases and set them on work. She was succeeded by a couple called Stephenson, of whom the husband paid the rent of the lazarhouse, while the wife, Rose, took on Alice's responsibilities. Rose's cases included scurvy and scald head, the latter being, as already indicated, a very common cause of concern, something of a woman's specialty, and one for which the London hospitals made at first female and then male appointments.[51] There is evidence to suggest that scald head was (or was thought to be) related to venereal infection.[52]

47. See Pelling, 'Occupational Diversity', pp. 498–501 (217–19).

48. The sources for Edwards are the Mayor's Court Proceedings, the Chamberlain's Accounts, and especially the [Hamper] Accounts (NRO). It was probably he who obtained a 'protection to gather' from the Privy Council as one of the proctors of St Giles's gates lazarhouse in March 1579/80: Historical Manuscripts Commission, *Calendar of the Manuscripts of . . . the Marquis of Salisbury*, Pt II (London, 1888), p. 246. For Alice Edwards/Wright, besides NRO, Mayor's Court Proceedings no. 15, 1615–24, see Lawrence Wright's will, PCC 95 Weldon (1617).

49. For examples of Lawrence's contracts see NRO, Mayor's Court Proceedings no. 15, 1615–24, fols 17, 35, 38, 46, 51, 62.

50. Ibid., fol. 19verso (July, 1615); PCC 95 Weldon (1617).

51. For Alice's contracts, see for example NRO, Mayor's Court Proceedings no. 15, 1615–24, fols 94verso, 110verso, 122recto, 144verso, 177recto. For the Stephensons, see ibid., e.g. fols 253verso, 257verso, 295recto; NRO, Press E, Case 18, shelf a, Chamberlain's Accounts 1603–25, e.g. fol. 351; N. Moore, *The History of St Bartholomew's Hospital*, 2 vols (London, 1918), vol. 2, pp. 732–3; K. F. Russell, 'John Browne, 1642–1702: a Seventeenth-century Surgeon, Anatomist and Plagiarist', *Bull. Hist. Med.*, 33 (1959), 395, n. 5.

52. This possibility is taken further in Pelling, 'Appearance and Reality'.

To the full life history of the prosperous barber and keeper Wright may be contrasted that of William Roberts, keeper of St Stephen's gates lazarhouse. The sum of Roberts's inventory at his death in 1601 was just under £6. In addition, however, to keeping a poor woman at the rate of 2s. 6d. a week, seemingly a low sum but still 150 per cent above what charitable bequests of the time thought sufficient for maintenance, Roberts was involved in contracts with the city for up to £3 for keeping the sick poor, including a woman and four children with the French disease. Roberts's chief moveable assets at his death included a cow worth 20s., wood worth 12s. 4d., and 'certain instruments to draw a tooth with' valued at 12d.[53]

Just as conventional practitioners dealt in the future liability to illness of their poor patients, so the lazarhouse-keepers accepted as part of a bargain the responsibility for future maintenance or keeping of a poor person in the event of their not being able to effect a lasting cure. The keepers also speculated on their own behalf in the future liability represented by a poor person. Thus the amount agreed on between the keeper and a parish or individual for 'keeping for life' was not necessarily a realistic estimate of the cost of a person's subsistence over an indefinite period, but a more actuarial speculation involving an estimate of risks. The subjects of these speculations could be illegitimate infants, young children, and apprentices, as well as the adult poor.

All such transactions, involving as they did a transfer of responsibility, brought a kind of commercial flexibility to practices generally thought fairly rigid, like apprenticeship and settlement. This rigidity tended to reassert itself when an arrangement broke down, which was usually revealed when the poor person concerned was found begging at large by other authorities. Thus when, in 1630, Elizabeth Carter was punished for begging in Norwich and sent back to Cley in Norfolk, the inhabitants of Cley complained that they had made a bond as long as eleven years previously with Heath, the keeper of St Augustine's gates lazarhouse in Norwich, for him to keep Elizabeth for her life for the sum of £4 13s. 4d. Even in the stricter climate of the 1630s, the justices of assize did not question the parish's right to transfer its responsibility, but dealt with the agreement as a private transaction: Cley's inhabitants might take remedy against Heath, but in the meantime the Norwich authorities had acted lawfully in expecting Cley to provide for Elizabeth.[54]

The lazarhouses thus performed a number of functions for their keepers and for the city. In particular, the city used them for the treatment of conditions that threatened the working capacity of the patient or, in the case of infectious conditions, of other poor as well. This latter quarantine function extended to any appearance of the person indicating communicable disease, by which could be meant an extensible corruption, as much as something more specific. Thus Thomas Gyles, keeper of Magdalen gates lazarhouse, was paid in 1598/99 for

53. NRO, [Hamper] Accounts 1550–1601, fol. 137recto; Mayor's Court Proceedings no. 13, 1595–1603, e.g. p. 358; NCC Inv. 17/91 (1601).

54. Sachse, *Minutes of the Norwich Court of Mayoralty 1630–1631*, p. 66; cf. idem, *Minutes of the Norwich Court of Mayoralty 1632–1635*, pp. 32, 59–60, for a similar case, not so easily settled, involving the keepers of St Stephen's gates lazarhouse.

receiving from Bridewell a 'loathsome boy', who had been sent to Norwich on a passport because he had been born in Berstreet.[55] As a massive corruption of the humours, showing itself very visibly on the surface of the body and especially the face, leprosy, which was declining, was seen as closely related to the newer disease, the French pox or syphilis, and also to scurvy, leprosy being sometimes known as inveterate scurvy.[56] In humoral pathology, the distinction between one disease and another was of degree rather than of kind. This did not mean that practitioners or even laypeople failed to recognise specific conditions when strongly marked, but merely that they accepted the existence of intermediate states.[57] Hence Susan Goose, a poor fatherless child, could be described as late as 1651 as 'always sick, now leprous, and probably incurable'.[58] Attention to any putrefactive condition in its early stages could thus prevent much worse forms of infectious decay.

The Norwich authorities were plainly more concerned about the 'French disease' than about any other. This was seen as affecting whole families, and constituted sufficient grounds for breaking indentures – something normally done only with great reluctance – and removing the apprentice if the master's family was known to have the disease. In 1600, the Norwich overseers and churchwardens were instructed, as part of a detailed programme for confining the city's charges for the poor to its statutory responsibilities, to enquire in their parishes if there were any persons who were sick and diseased and could do no work, what their infirmity was, 'whether the French pox or some other contagious disease'.[59] Such instructions are reminiscent of the census of 1570, but with a more specific emphasis. They are a significant indication of the importance of venereal disease in contemporary public as well as private life. Attention has rightly been drawn to plague as the most influential manifestation of disease in the late sixteenth and early seventeenth centuries, but it is arguable that the effects of syphilis were also a major – and more continuous – preoccupation over the same period. The incidence of venereal disease may have been extremely high, and each case could cast a shadow over the life of the individual for 20 years or more. Both economic and social relations were affected. Unlike plague, the French disease could repeatedly impose the burden both of moral misdemeanour and disqualification from active employment.[60]

Public danger of different kinds was thus a major criterion influencing the treatment of the sick poor, so that in many cases such treatment would be imposed rather than sought. Vagrants ran the risk of quarantine, confinement, or cure by local authorities. Literary sources also indicate that such risks, combined

---

55. NRO, Case 19, shelf c, Bridewell Accounts 1585–1686, 1598–99 [not foliated].

56. The connection between syphilis and leprosy was still being debated in the nineteenth century: G. Newman, 'On the History of the Decline . . . of Leprosy . . . in the British Islands', *Leprosy Prize Essays*, New Sydenham Society CLVII (1895), pp. 64–5.

57. Paracelsus also held this view of syphilis: W. Pagel, *Joan Baptista Van Helmont: Reformer of Science and Medicine* (Cambridge, 1982), p. 153.

58. James, *Norfolk Quarter Sessions Order Book 1650–1657*, p. 33.

59. NRO, Mayor's Court Proceedings no. 13, 1595–1603, p. 325; Press D, Case 16, shelf c, Assembly Minute Book no. 5, 1585–1613, fol. 244verso.

60. Pelling, 'Appearance and Reality'.

with that of forced labour, may have existed at an early date. To quote Crowley, 'such as be sore, and will not be healed / Ought not in any case to be cherishèd'. Terms such as 'eligibility' or 'entitlement' must therefore be used with caution. Nonetheless, Norwich's medical relief practices could attract: in 1617 they drew Simon Bushe, aged 12, from ten miles away. He had been brought to Norwich on a cart by someone from his home village of Scottow who told him that he should have 'meat enough in Norwich and a surgeon to heal him'. The eligibility of a sick person for relief was usually sorted out at parish level, before the case was raised at the mayor's court. As might be expected, length of residence was the most important criterion, apart from public danger: at the time of the census, when systematic forced working was in contemplation, residence of more than two or three years was sufficient, but by the 1630s, the criterion of place of birth was more often applied.[61]

At the same time, the city was more concerned about consequential than immediate expenditure, and medical relief often came into the latter category. The lazarhouses, lying outside the city walls and to some extent independent of the city, provided an especially convenient transit station for disabled people whose place of origin was in dispute, such as the blind cripple Mary Ambree, who was kept at the Magdalen gates house for several weeks before being sent back to Newcastle.[62] A lazarhouse was also an ideal compromise solution for people like maimed and diseased soldiers, to whom the city might hope to avoid paying a pension.[63] In such cases, the city could pass on the problem by paying the lazarhouse-keeper a lump sum. However, for other kinds of disabled poor, who were allegedly 'settled' elsewhere and whose disability – dumbness, falling sickness – affected only themselves, without immobilising them, Norwich often did nothing, and did not withhold the usual punishments either. 'Distracted' and 'mad' people not settled in Norwich were told to leave under threat of punishment, or carried out of town, a city employee being paid to effect this; some mad people, presumably out of their own control, were carried as far as their place of origin. Norwich's practices reveal why some 'sturdy' vagrants might have chosen particularly to counterfeit as 'dummerers', 'bedlams', cripples, or sufferers from falling sickness. These intractable conditions aroused a response from passers-by without involving the same risks of quarantine, confinement, and cure, even though such disabilities would not necessarily inhibit authorities from using the whip.[64]

61. Robert Crowley, quoted in Tawney and Power, *Tudor Economic Documents*, vol. 3, p. 406; NRO, Mayor's Court Proceedings no. 15, 1615–24, fol. 117recto.

62. NRO, Mayor's Court Proceedings no. 13, 1595–1603, p. 345; [Hamper] Accounts 1550–1601, fol. 134. For a similar policy towards sick poor in transit, see Webb, *Poor Relief in Elizabethan Ipswich*, pp. 75, 80, 85, 86.

63. See, for example, the case of Robert Wyatt: NRO, Mayor's Court Proceedings no. 13, 1595–1603, pp. 128, 155.

64. Ibid., no. 15, 1615–24, fols 369recto, 310recto. Thomas Harman, *Caveat for Common Cursitors vulgarely called Vagabones* [1567], ed. E. Viles and F. J. Furnivall, Early English Text Society Extra Ser. IX (1869), pp. 47–8, 51–9. The authorities in Salisbury refrained from punishing some, but not all, poor people who were sick, lunatic, weak, pregnant, crippled, or lame: see Slack, *Poverty in Early Stuart Salisbury*, pp. 21, 24, 30, 32, 35–7.

The treatment of the insane tends to be taken as a sure test of contemporary attitudes. Norwich's disposition of its own lunatics varied. It maintained, at least after the setting up of the new Bridewell in 1585, a house for mad people supervised by the keeper of Bridewell. One of the inmates was a lunatic minister, Mr Kirby, who was in and out of gaol and Bridewell for two years in the 1590s at an average cost of three to four shillings weekly, before the city managed to arrange with the diocese a levy on the county ministers of 12*d*. a week to match the city's contribution.[65] There is no evidence that Kirby or any other lunatic in Bridewell was ever treated medically at the city's expense, so that it might seem as if Norwich's attitude to lunacy was purely supervisory. Lunatics were placed in bridewells in other towns from an early period, and are found in a house of correction (also, however, used as a sickhouse) in rural Norfolk in the 1650s.[66] In the light of this institutionalisation of some lunatics, and the overlap of regulatory functions of the institutions involved, the later history of the poor insane becomes less remarkable. It was to some extent traditional for lepers and lunatics (as well as epileptics) to share an asylum, as all three were often excluded from other medieval foundations. Leperhouses sometimes evolved into lunatic asylums at a later date, when leprosy had all but vanished; the presence of lunatics in what were once leperhouses has suggested a similar static and isolated role in society for confirmed lunatics as for confirmed lepers, but the traditional association should be borne in mind. Moreover, the presence of lunatics in the Norwich lazarhouses may even suggest some hope of cure; and it seems unlikely that Norwich either failed to discriminate among lunatics or entirely lacked such practitioners as Widow Mercer of Chester, who, on the grounds of her experience of such diseases, was given charge of a poor woman who had fallen into a frenzy.[67]

By the early seventeenth century, then, Norwich's authorities had evolved a range of expedients and institutions to deal with the sick poor. How were these experienced by a poor person? Only sequences of events can be reconstructed. In October 1615, for example, two boys, Daniel Stephenson and Philip Emes, were both ordered to be healed and kept by Lawrence Wright for a year, for which Wright was to have 10s. with 10s. to follow. By the end of December, Stephenson had got on to the streets again, was punished, and sent back to Wright at St Bennet's gates. Wright's regime again proved inadequate, and Stephenson was this time subjected to the stricter conditions of Bridewell. By early 1617, he had been discharged, and placed, according to the best intentions of the Statute of Artificers, as an apprentice in husbandry. Events for his

65. NRO, [Hamper] Accounts 1550–1601, fols 104, 105, 108; Mayor's Court Proceedings no. 13, 1595–1603, pp. 239, 250.

66. J. R. Chanter and T. Wainwright, *Reprint of the Barnstaple Records*, 2 vols (Barnstaple, 1900), vol. 1, p. 42; James, *Norfolk Quarter Sessions Order Book 1650–1657*, p. 29.

67. R. M. Clay, *The Medieval Hospitals of England* (London, 1909), p. 32; Simpson, 'Antiquarian Notices of Leprosy', p. 308; Morris, *Chester*, pp. 370–1; M. Foucault, *Madness and Civilisation*, trans. R. Howard (London, 1971), pp. 3–7, 45. Further evidence for the conclusions here, dating mainly after the mid-seventeenth century, has been provided by P. Rushton, 'Lunatics and Idiots: Mental Disability, the Community, and the Poor Law in North-East England, 1600–1800', *Medical History*, 32 (1988), 34–50.

co-sufferer Emes were more summary. At about the end of the year he spent with Wright, he was taken vagrant in the city, whipped, and sent back to the city parish where he claimed to have been born.[68] A third poor child, Thomas Hemblinge, was only five or six when the city and his parish paid for him to go to Rose Stephenson of St Bennet's to be cured of a scald head. In early 1621, about eighteen months after first coming to the city's notice, Thomas was among the first to be admitted to the new Children's Hospital, another example of the re-institutionalisation characteristic of the early seventeenth century. When old enough, he, too, would have been apprenticed.[69]

Similarly, the example of John Blackborne and his daughter shows both the combination of medical with other forms of relief, and the recurrent nature of the city's responsibilities. In 1595, Blackborne's daughter's eye was treated at a cost of 7s. 8d. by John Hobart, surgeon, freeman, householder, and officebearer in the barber-surgeons' company. Five years later, Hobart was paid a total of £3 for attending to John Blackborne's leg. A little later, William Edwards, the then keeper of St Bennet's, and a woman were paid 6s. for clothing Blackborne and his daughter, and Edwards was paid further for keeping the daughter.[70]

To what extent were these practices an innovation? Norwich's interest in the lazarhouses became more pronounced in the sixteenth century, but was not new to the post-Reformation period. Municipal participation was not alien to medieval foundations, and institutions depending partly on the municipality often had a better chance of surviving over the Dissolution period than entirely ecclesiastical or even private foundations. St Giles's gates lazarhouse in Norwich was known variously as a 'poor house' and 'sickhouse' from around 1540, but the city had had some stake in it since the early fourteenth century. Attempts by the city to control all the lazarhouses were made as early as the 1540s, when St Stephen's and St Bennet's, as well as St Giles's, were referred to as 'sickhouses', but such attempts were hampered by the crown's appropriation of keeperships and the continuance of church ownership of the land of the houses, which in some cases persisted well into the seventeenth century. Nonetheless, the city was using St Stephen's gates lazarhouse and its proctor for the custody of lame beggars as early as 1562, that is, before Norwich's main effort of poor-law organisation in the 1570s. St Bennet's gates house, also called the spital-cotes or cottages, was city property from 1584; its keepers paid rent to the city from the 1580s, sometimes, as already mentioned, obtaining remission for taking in the city's poor. Of the five active houses, St Bennet's was most extensively used by the city for the care of the sick.[71]

68. NRO, Mayor's Court Proceedings no. 15, 1615–24, fols 38, 48, 114verso, 89recto.

69. Ibid., fols 253verso, 272verso, 315recto, 328verso.

70. NRO, [Hamper] Accounts 1550–1601, fols 103, 135–7, 139.

71. F. Blomefield, *An Essay Towards a Topographical History of the County of Norfolk*, 11 vols (London, 1805–10), vol. 4, pp. 166–8, 245, 408–9, 438, 460–1, 509; Clay, *Medieval Hospitals*, pp. 235–6; NRO, Society of Genealogists' transcript of parish register of St Giles, Norwich, PD 192/142; Hudson and Tingey, *Records*, vol. 2, pp. xcix, 169–70. Apart from Blomefield, the main sources for the Norwich lazarhouses are the Mayor's Court Proceedings and the Chamberlain's and [Hamper] Accounts (NRO). The Magdalen gates house is to be distinguished from the Magdalen Hospital or lazarhouse at Sprowston, of which part survives: R. Taylor, *Index Monasticus* (London, 1821), pp. 56–8; G. A. Stephen, 'A Norman Relic: the Lazarhouse, Norwich', *The Millgate Monthly*, November (1921), 102–7; Rawcliffe, *Hospitals*, chap. 1.

The city's increased use of the houses after 1600, very evident in the activity of the Wrights and others in the 1610s, was matched by increasing investment. Repairs were made and the houses benefited from aldermanic bequests. In 1623, three prominent aldermanic benefactors settled St Stephen's on the city, and this was shortly followed by the proxy acquisition of St Augustine's. St Augustine's is an example of a lazarhouse gradually coming under local control. Under the perhaps unusual circumstances of his being brother to Matthew Parker, who, as Archbishop of Canterbury, had already taken a conscientious interest in hospitals and almshouses, Thomas Parker, Mayor of Norwich, had joined with the Bishop of Norwich in 1568 in removing an unsatisfactory keeper of this lazarhouse. Although St Augustine's was used as a kind of quarantine station by the city as early as 1580, its chief proctor was then still acting for the settled inmates on the basis of a licence issued not locally but nationally. By 1591, the proctor was too poor to pay the fee for this kind of licence, and the bishop and local magistrates stepped in with a substitute permission to enable one of the inmates to travel and beg on behalf of the sixteen people then living in the house. Twenty years later, Norwich's aldermen took over the lease.[72]

This increased investment, as well as the continuing need to prevent the poor of other areas taking up residence in the town in a period of economic slump, inspired a covenant drawn up in 1623/24 between the city and the keepers of the houses, which reserved the houses to the city's control, even with respect to the 'settled inmates'. Although not salaried, the keepers were not to take any poor into their houses without the consent of the mayor's court, and they were to 'keep their bellgate' according to the rules prescribed by the court. The second article seems to refer to the means by which keepers or their agents were entitled to extract money from members of the public, a practice which continued on a local level long after more wide-ranging collection was restricted. Thus Rose Stephenson, keeper of St Bennet's, in return for keeping during his life and attempting the cure of Thomas Gurney of the outlying district of Trowse, was to have £3 in two stages, Gurney's bedding, and also to 'have her bellwalk in the said town': that is, to collect money in a locality previously closed to her.[73]

The city's commitment to the houses in the 1620s probably included the intention of finding a regular means of support alternative to the small annual 'country benevolence' which each of the houses had received since before 1600. This contribution from the county rates may have been jeopardised as a result of the determination of the city to have the final word on all admissions. The financing of the houses was always problematic. Like many lazarhouses, the Norwich examples were largely without settled revenues, and money left them by will, as by the barber Thomas Fulke in 1593, was for immediate use. The 'country benevolence' was similarly divided up and placed in the hands of

72. Blomefield, *Norfolk*, vol. 4, p. 408; John Strype, *The Life and Acts of Matthew Parker* (London, 1711), p. 272; Clarke, 'Norfolk Licences to Beg', pp. 332–3; NRO, Mayor's Court Proceedings no. 15, 1615–24, fol. 511recto.
73. NRO, Mayor's Court Proceedings no. 15, 1615–24, fols 511recto, 246verso.

the keepers, who, even after the covenant of 1623/24, persisted in making independent agreements with parishes outside Norwich.[74]

Norwich's activity in the field of medical poor relief in the 1620s seemed to presage a commitment to wholehearted municipal provision. Even the strong line taken with Mayhew, the lithotomist, in the early 1620s, may be seen as part of a determination to bypass market conditions in favour of municipal control. The city seemed prepared to abandon the marginal advantages of being able to transfer responsibility to the lazarhouse-keepers as independent agents. Over the next ten years, however, this trend, which was never completed, went into reverse, a process which may have begun with the plague of 1625 and the consequent escalation of the poor rate. By the early 1630s, there was evident disillusionment with the lazarhouses themselves, their lack of revenues, and the frequency with which their inmates were found begging in the streets. The city began to grudge expenditure on repairs, and went so far as to withhold from the keepers the regular contribution from the county outside Norwich, in the hope of forcing the keepers to pay off arrears of rent. During 1634, the city's 'evidences' for all the lazarhouses were examined to see if any of them could be 'otherwise employed'; and, by the end of that year, St Stephen's, the house settled on the city in 1623, was voted to be disposed of out of city ownership.[75]

Even institutionally, however, there was a degree of long-term continuity in Norwich's medical relief system. In the early eighteenth century, St Augustine's was an 'infirmary' for aged poor people past work, who were unfit for common workhouses. In 1814, the buildings were being used for the same purpose, the land being leased from the bishop, the buildings owned by the city, and the enterprise supported by the poor rates, a structure not dissimilar to that of the early seventeenth century, except in the last respect. Blomefield, the early historian of Norfolk, was under the impression that most of the lazarhouses, even St Stephen's, continued as sickhouses until around 1700. By the early nineteenth century, the Magdalen gates lazarhouse had changed from leperhouse to 'almshouse', to workhouse, and finally to alehouse, the last being, as we have seen, not so far from the first as might be imagined.[76]

The 1570s will rightly continue to be regarded as the most notable decade in the history of Norwich's attempts to deal with the problem of the poor. It has been assumed that little of this effort, which is seen by Pound as having been prompted by political events, survived beyond 1590, owing to a combination of immigration leading to plague and decimation of the poor population concerned.[77] Moreover, even in Norwich, as in Salisbury, systematic schemes for providing the poor with work proved difficult to sustain. It does not seem plausible, however, to assume that either the need or Norwich's initiatives to meet it were confined to the period before 1600. The elements of Norwich's

74. Thomas Fulke or Hooke, NRO, NCC 138 Clearke (1593). For a distribution of the 'country benevolence' in 1599, see NRO, Mayor's Court Proceedings no. 13, 1595–1603, p. 367.

75. Sachse, *Minutes of the Norwich Court of Mayoralty 1632–1635*, pp. 13, 120, 183, 184.

76. P. Browne, *The History of Norwich* (Norwich, [1814]), pp. 159, 228, 237; Blomefield, *Norfolk*, vol. 4, p. 168.

77. Pound, *An Elizabethan Census*, pp. 149–50.

approach that related to medical services show a remarkable persistence from before 1570 and a development into the 1620s and beyond. The lazarhouses later assumed on a minor level some of the functions of work promotion and regulation which the poor scheme had originally intended for other institutions, and, like the latter, were notable for the role played by women. The great plague epidemics between 1580 and 1625 may have encouraged the increased use of scattered institutions which would prevent the concentration of contagious putrefaction, but, at the same time, the lazarhouses were never used as pesthouses and had 'ordinary' rather than extraordinary functions, as they did in London.

As in Salisbury, the Norwich initiatives of the 1620s and their decline in the 1630s coincided with a period of economic crisis. The chronology of 'challenge and collapse' described by Slack for Salisbury in these decades is very similar to that in Norwich. Some support is provided for the view of Slack and of Davis that the context for welfare reform is urban crisis, a 'conjuncture of older problems of poverty with population growth and economic expansion'. As in Salisbury, however, decline or collapse occurred just when the need was greatest.[78] It is not possible, by contrast with Salisbury, to say much about the influence of religious and political factors on short-term events in Norwich. The aldermen most involved in the lazarhouses, for example, belonged to both Puritan and royalist persuasions. The overall phenomenon of municipal interest in medical poor relief is probably of greater importance than any observable short-term fluctuations. Medical aid continued, even if only to prevent greater expenditure, public danger, or increase in the numbers of the impotent poor. Strong reactions continued to be aroused by individual cases. In spite of the events of the 1630s, aspects of Norwich's system, in particular the element of the *ad hoc* service by 'general' medical practitioners, remained as stable as other aspects of administration.

The Norwich methods show that the presence of town physicians or officials on the continental model is not the only measure of public investment in medical care. Considerable expenditure was involved in the Norwich system, and a surprisingly high proportion of the city's substantial complement of practitioners was employed in treating the poor over an extended period. Norwich was not, like Marshall, primarily concerned with curing vagabonds of their diseases so that they could be employed on major public works like fortifications and harbours. The city was, however, acting on the local level on behalf of its own residents to limit the extent and expense of incapacity. Specialised medical services were attracted to the city for the poor's benefit. The lazarhouses represent an attempt to provide cost-effective short-term medical treatment and supervision for the potentially able poor, on a joint basis with the parishes (and, in a sense, with the keepers) but with the main responsibility resting on the city magistrates. For the city, there were obvious advantages of flexibility in the connections of the houses with the functions of the parishes, bridewell, and

78. Slack, 'Poverty and Politics', p. 192; N. Z. Davis, 'Poor Relief, Humanism and Heresy', in idem, *Society and Culture in Early Modern France* (London, 1975), p. 59.

other city institutions, and with other relevant practices supervised by the mayor's court such as apprenticeship. Equally flexible was the combination of *ad hoc* or piecework medical service which needed no institutional basis, and the diverse, unpretentious institutionalisation represented by the lazarhouses.

This chapter has been concerned to approach an important area of social policy from the viewpoint of practice rather than statements of intent. The case of Norwich shows that in practice the poor were not divided simply into 'the impudent and the impotent'. Categories other than the traditionally impotent could be included in those eligible for relief, and such relief involved a flexible attitude to institutionalisation. City authorities could indeed seek to 'remodel' the poor themselves, to borrow Slack's phrase, in a highly literal and physical sense.[79] This task was too important to be left to private philanthropy or even to the parishes. London was not alone among English urban centres in seeing the connections between different kinds of decay, and London was not the only city to centralise its response to these problems.

79. Slack, 'Poverty and Politics', p. 183.

PART II

AGEGROUPS AND GENDER

CHAPTER FIVE

Child Health as a Social Value in Early Modern England

The history of childhood is now a going concern. In 1981 Hendrick referred feelingly to the long-term neglect of childhood as a historical topic, attributing it to the child's lack of status and political significance.[1] He saw this neglect as having been alleviated chiefly by historians of the family and of *mentalité*, as indeed it has been since Hendrick's time of writing. To a considerable extent, however, especially for the early modern period, the child has been treated as a passive element within the family, a hostage to conflicting interpretations of relationships between children and parents. The 'rediscovery' of the persistence of the affectionate nuclear family has reinforced this trend, as well as tending to discredit the hypothesis of major change in notions of 'public' and 'private' spheres of activity. Another effect of this 'rediscovery' has been a continued concentration on child-rearing, with a particular emphasis on infants. In pointing to this bias Hendrick rightly instanced a lack of interest in such topics as child labour, especially for the period before 1760.[2] In spite of the important role given by Ariès to apprenticeship and particularly to the school, little attention was paid until recently to the complex of structures connecting the family with society at large and involving the child.[3] The child's experience within the

This chapter is an expanded and revised version of a paper given first to 'The Child in History' conference in London in April 1986, and subsequently at seminars at Oxford. I am grateful for comments made by then editors of *Social History of Medicine*, by audiences at London and Oxford, and especially for information from Jonathan Barry, Mark Burnett, Robert Dingwall, Mark Jenner, Richard Smith, and Keith Thomas.

1. H. Hendrick, *The History of Childhood and Youth. A Guide to the Literature*, Oxford Polytechnic Faculty of Modern Studies Occasional Papers I (Oxford, [1981]), p. 5. See also idem, 'The History of Childhood and Youth', *Social History*, 9 (1984), 87–96.

2. Hendrick, *History of Childhood*, p. 4. For a more recent overview, see H. Cunningham, *Children and Childhood in Western Society since 1500* (London and New York, 1995). For the period after 1760, see recent monographs by H. Hendrick, *Child Welfare: England 1872–1989* (London and New York, 1994); idem, *Children, Childhood and English Society 1880–1990* (Cambridge, 1997); P. Horn, *Children's Work and Welfare, 1780–1890* (Cambridge, 1995); E. Hopkins, *Childhood Transformed: Working-Class Children in Nineteenth-Century England* (Manchester and New York, 1994); J. Neubauer, *The fin-de-siècle Culture of Adolescence* (Bloomington and Indianapolis, 1990); L. Rose, *The Erosion of Childhood: Child Oppression in Britain 1860–1918* (London and New York, 1991); C. Nardinelli, *Child Labor and the Industrial Revolution* (Bloomington and Indianapolis, 1990).

3. A. Wilson, 'The Infancy of the History of Childhood: an Appraisal of Philippe Ariès', *History and Theory*, 19 (1980), 141; R. T. Vann, 'The Youth of Centuries of Childhood', ibid., 21 (1982), 289. Two important studies of adolescence have since appeared, each of which considers apprenticeship and service as 'different

early modern family has thus been given a more positive cast, but outside the family the prospect still seems defined largely by negatives.[4] Similarly, concentration on the movement or otherwise of resources between generations of the same family has tended to absorb attention at the expense both of such transfers within social structures other than the immediate family or kin group, and of forms of interdependency not involving relatives.[5]

Debates over the history of childhood are undoubtedly sharpened by current anxieties about the neglect and exploitation of children. It tends to be a feature of such discussion that the family and 'the state' are simplified into a confrontation of opposites. The 'state' may be represented as a recent development, with obvious implications for the history of responsibility for the child; or transferred back on to earlier periods in the centrist terms derived from nineteenth- and twentieth-century welfare provision. In the case of the latter perspective, the intentions of extra-familial agencies before 1800 are at least recognised, but the scope of activity on behalf of the child is made to appear limited both in conception and execution.[6]

This chapter will suggest that the subject of child health in the early modern period offers a chance of examining the child outside the circumscribed context of the family and family relationships. As a consequence, it is possible to glimpse the child as an individual in his or her own right, and also to bring out the significance of children in relation to wider social and economic questions. Specifically, this chapter seeks to show that these wider questions entail consideration of the health and ill health of children, and of provisions which reveal something of mechanisms of interdependence outside the family group.

The high mortality of infants and children has of course received attention as a major feature of western populations before the twentieth century. Policies towards foundlings have also attracted interest. For reasons already suggested, there have been protracted debates about infant care and child-rearing within the family context, and the effect on other family members of the deaths of children.[7] The care of children during illness and their own experience of illness are, by contrast, issues relating to the majority of the population that have rarely been given more than anecdotal notice by historians.[8] This is true even for more

---

ways of growing up': I. Krausman Ben-Amos, *Adolescence and Youth in Early Modern England* (New Haven, CT, and London, 1994); P. Griffiths, *Youth and Authority: Formative Experiences in England 1560–1640* (Oxford, 1996).

4. See for example T. R. Murphy, '"Woful Childe of Parents Rage": Suicide of Children and Adolescents in Early Modern England, 1507–1710', *Sixteenth-Century Journal*, 17 (1986), 259–70.

5. For a critique, see R. M. Smith, 'Welfare and the Management of Demographic Uncertainty', in M. Keynes and D. Coleman (eds), *The Political Economy of Health and Welfare* (London, 1988), pp. 108–35.

6. See for example P. Meyer, *The Child and the State*, trans. J. Ennew and J. Lloyd (Cambridge, 1983); R. Dingwall, J. M. Eekelaar and T. Murray, 'Childhood as a Social Problem: a Survey of the History of Legal Regulation', *Journal of Law and Society*, 11 (1984), 207–32.

7. For example D. Hunt, *Parents and Children in History. The Psychology of Family Life in Early Modern France* (New York and London, 1970); V. Fildes, *Breasts, Bottles and Babies: A History of Infant Feeding* (Edinburgh, 1986); P. Crawford, '"The Sucking Child": Adult Attitudes to Child Care in the First Year of Life in Seventeenth-century England', *Continuity and Change*, 1 (1986), 23–51; A. G. Carmichael, *Plague and the Poor in Renaissance Florence* (Cambridge, 1986), pp. 41–54.

8. Evidence is not lacking, although much detailed comment is in the form of adult recollection. Such sources show that childhood illnesses and accidents were regarded as significant if not portentous experiences:

recent periods, and is explicable by the higher visibility of institutions as objects of research, compared with the problems of investigating domiciliary and informal provision of health care.[9] For example, the voluntary hospital movement of the eighteenth century largely ignored younger children, and it is not without significance for the present discussion that the refounded London hospitals of the sixteenth century did not. They did take in children, and were especially concerned with such problems as scurvy and scald head, accidents including dog bite, broken limbs, and with providing artificial limbs. This provision was, of course, additional to that of Christ's Hospital which was specifically for children and had a sick ward of its own, while sending its serious cases elsewhere.[10] As we shall see, the London institutions were imitated in major provincial towns, notably Norwich. The present discussion will, however, be less concerned with these institutions than with the related social practices of poor relief and apprenticeship, both of which illustrate the perceived social value of the health of children. Neither of these practices can be divorced from the norms of parenthood, especially given the need to assess the alleged paternalism of Tudor administrations – not exceeded, in Pinchbeck and Hewitt's view, until the twentieth century.[11] This will involve reference not to the 'state', but to relatively autonomous local authorities and their dependencies such as the parish and the craft company.

Inevitably, there are problems of definition. As with other more or less 'invisible' groups in history, the nature of the sources dictates that we are forced, to a large extent at least, into discussing attitudes *to* the child and events happening *to* the child, rather than the child's own point of view. The difficulties of defining childhood itself are particularly acute in the period under consideration, one which is designated as 'transitional' in much of the secondary literature. Even if this historiography is set aside as problematic, the sixteenth century, in particular, saw so much debate on religious, moral, social, and economic issues affecting the status and nature of childhood that questions of definition are unavoidable.[12] Some variation is caused by overlapping frameworks (for example, the legal, or the religious), some by changing, and less codified, social circumstances.

A surprising number of the records used in this chapter do give ages at least on occasion, but this is not in general true at this time, and the agegroup implied

for a merchant's son, see D. Palliser, 'Civic Mentality and the Environment in Tudor York', *Northern History*, 18 (1982), 104; for childhood illness as part of the horoscope of Johannes Kepler, see A. Koestler, *The Sleepwalkers* (Harmondsworth, 1973), pp. 233–4.

9. Even so, it is only recently that the specialist children's hospitals of the nineteenth century have begun to attract serious historical attention. See in general R. Cooter (ed.), *In the Name of the Child: Health and Welfare 1880–1940* (London, 1992), esp. the chapter by Paul Weindling.

10. See N. Moore, *The History of St Bartholomew's Hospital*, 2 vols (London, 1918), vol. 2, p. 219; London, St Bartholomew's Hospital, Hb/1/1, Ledger 1547–61, for example fols 15, 23, 26; John Howes's manuscripts of 1582 and 1587, extracted in R. H. Tawney and E. Power (eds), *Tudor Economic Documents*, 3 vols (London, 1924; repr. 1953), vol. 3, esp. pp. 416, 430, 432ff; [G. A. T. Allan] (ed.), *Christ's Hospital Admissions Vol. I, 1554–1599* (London, 1937), esp. pp. 10, 12, 133, 257; E. H. Pearce, *Annals of Christ's Hospital*, 2nd edn (London, 1908). Children were also sent to the London lazarhouses.

11. I. Pinchbeck and M. Hewitt, *Children in English Society*, 2 vols (London and Toronto, 1973), vol. 1, pp. 1–2.

12. Relevant and important aspects of this debate are covered by R. DeMolen, 'Childhood and the Sacraments in the Sixteenth Century', *Archiv für Reformationsgeschichte*, 66 (1975), 49–71; K. Thomas, *Age and Authority in Early Modern England* (London, 1976).

by such terms as 'child', 'infant', 'maid', and 'boy' may vary greatly according to context. Identifications and categorisations are most difficult between the approximate ages of 15 and 30.[13] In what follows, the term 'child' will be used in a broad sense without trying to distinguish adolescents as a particular group. This is justified by contemporary usage, in spite of the fact that contemporaries readily recognised forms of behaviour and even stages of pre-adult life which would now be called adolescent.[14] Initially, I will be referring mainly to agegroups around the ages of 'reason' and 'discretion', that is between about seven and 14.[15] There is a risk that some of these, in the absence of more specific information, may have been older. However, most of the apprentices mentioned seem to have been well under 20. Some 'apprentices' were indeed of mature age, but this was probably much less common in urban areas. It will be necessary to return to the difficulties of distinguishing between apprentices and servants, but it should be said here that one of the advantages of dealing with apprentices is that one can be more confident of their age range. In the main, the chapter will be referring to children who were to be taught a particular trade. Where possible, contemporary usage has been followed in taking 'children' to refer to both sexes, but the balance of evidence inevitably causes boys to predominate, especially in the context of apprenticeship.

As already suggested, a consensus has been reached suggesting that we can take the concern of medieval and early modern parents for their children for granted. The realisation is also emerging that this concern might be appropriately reflected in motives, expressions, and advice unfamiliar to modern sensibilities. Much the same should be said of evidence of the health care of children.[16] There is little information to date on the treatment of English children by physicians, but many reasons can be found for this, including the position of physicians as a small elite minority, and the probability that they were relied upon more for prognosis than for cure.[17] It is a sidelight on the importance of diagnosis and prognosis that examples can be found, for continental Europe at least, of parents demanding postmortems on their children.[18] Contemporaries dreaded

13. Phythian-Adams, *Desolation of a City*, pp. 228–9, 273–4; R. W. Beales, 'In Search of the Historical Child: Miniature Adulthood and Youth in Colonial New England', *American Quarterly*, 27 (1975), 388. See also P. Laslett, *Family Life and Illicit Love in Earlier Generations* (Cambridge, 1978), pp. 163–4.

14. Literature on this topic is conveniently located by R. Thompson, 'Adolescent Culture in Colonial Massachusetts', *Journal of Family History*, 9 (1984), 127–44, but see esp. N. Z. Davis, 'The Reasons of Misrule: Youth Groups and Charivaris in Sixteenth-century France', *P & P*, 50 (1971), 41–75.

15. On these stages of spiritual maturity, see DeMolen, 'Childhood and the Sacraments'.

16. In particular see M. MacDonald, *Mystical Bedlam: Madness, Anxiety and Healing in Seventeenth-Century England* (Cambridge, 1981); B. A. Hanawalt, 'Childrearing among the Lower Classes of Late Medieval England', *Journal of Interdisciplinary History*, 8 (1977), 1–22; M. M. McLaughlin, 'Survivors and Surrogates: Children and Parents from the Ninth to the Thirteenth Centuries', in L. DeMause (ed.), *The History of Childhood* (New York, 1974), pp. 101–81; J. Simon, 'Childhood in Earlier Seventeenth-century England', in K. Dent (ed.), *Informal Agencies of Education* (Leicester, 1979), pp. 1–27; K. Wrightson, 'Infanticide in Earlier Seventeenth Century England', *Local Population Studies*, 15 (1975), 10–22; L. Pollock, *Forgotten Children* (Cambridge, 1985); Crawford, 'The Sucking Child'; R. A. Houlbrooke, *The English Family 1450–1700* (London and New York, 1984).

17. On the relative position of physicians, see Pelling and Webster, 'Medical Practitioners', esp. pp. 167–73, 188–206, 208–11; Pelling, 'Trade or Profession'; 'Compromised by Gender'.

18. Hunt, *Parents and Children*, p. 121; S. Ozment, *When Fathers Ruled. Family Life in Reformation Europe* (Cambridge, MA, and London, 1983), p. 169.

childhood diseases, but they seem to have had reservations on the advisability of calling in outside assistance.

Surgeons, women, and both male and female specialists in the treatment of women and children were much more active than university-trained physicians in this context, but concern was also sometimes expressed in terms of dislike of drastic intervention in childhood illnesses. However, certain conditions such as falling sickness, the stone, ruptures, accidents, or limb-threatening sores and injuries regularly induced parents and friends to pay large fees to practitioners, or to seek means to do so.[19] It is notable that the relatively few cases of children brought to the astrological physician Richard Napier were those which were found to be so sudden or inexplicable that witchcraft was suspected.[20] It could be suggested that Napier was also the kind of practitioner to whom parents might resort if they feared that parental cursing or rejection, said to have great potency at this period, had led to physical or psychological damage to the child.[21] In any case, when the question of choice of practitioner at this time is considered, it has to be remembered that the contemporary consumer of medical care was critical and assertive as well as avid, so that the apparent absence of some recognisable practitioner is not the same as an absence of medical care, and certainly not the same as an absence of concern.[22]

The physical nature of children was something on which a range of values could be placed, just as attitudes to children had as wide a range of complexity and ambiguity as can be found today. For example, great interest was attached to monstrous births and freaks which had a range of functions from fairground entertainment to religious and political portentousness.[23] Just as wholesome food was perceived as a blessing and rotten food as a threat, so unhealthy children at large could be seen as menacing. Even healthy children in the wrong hands could threaten the social order by their physical virtues becoming vices, although the full-blown rhetoric which either condemns, or finds a use for, the nimbleness, quick-wittedness, and quick-footedness of children belongs to later periods. Tudor and Stuart authorities acted to keep children out of the hands of beggars, vagrants, and fortunetellers even if the persons concerned were the natural parents.[24] The free movements and actions of children were similar to those of animals and could require comparable controls.[25] In Elizabethan

---

19. MacDonald, *Mystical Bedlam*, p. 42; Webster, *H, M & M*, pp. 187, 267, 295; P. Crawford, 'Printed Advertisements for Women Medical Practitioners in London, 1670–1710', *Bull. SSHM*, 35 (1984), 67. Children's conditions were the motive for many 'licences to collect': Pelling, 'Healing the Sick Poor', pp. 118–19 (83–4). Cf. Phaer's list of the chief problems of children, reproduced by G. F. Still, *The History of Paediatrics* (London, 1931; repr. 1965), p. 111. For a father's claim to impoverishment as a result of eight years' surgical treatment of his elder child, see G. G. Harris (ed.), *Trinity House of Deptford Transactions, 1609–35*, London Record Society XIX (1983), p. 46.

20. MacDonald, *Mystical Bedlam*, p. 42.

21. A. Macfarlane, *The Family Life of Ralph Josselin* (Cambridge, 1970), p. 110.

22. Pelling and Webster, 'Medical Practitioners', pp. 232–5.

23. For a particular interpretation see K. Park and L. J. Daston, 'Unnatural Conceptions: the Study of Monsters in Sixteenth and Seventeenth-century France and England', *P & P*, 92 (1981), 20–54.

24. For an instance involving the child of a woman fortuneteller, see W. L. Sachse (ed.), *Minutes of the Norwich Court of Mayoralty 1630–1631*, Norfolk Record Society XV (1942), p. 162.

25. For some aspects of parallels between children and animals, see MacDonald, *Mystical Bedlam*, p. 43; Hunt, *Parents and Children*, pp. 122ff; G. K. Behlmer, *Child Abuse and Moral Reform in England, 1870–1908*

Winchester children under 12 were allowed to relieve themselves out of doors; parents or masters were held responsible if older children or servants did so with the assent of their elders.[26] The later sixteenth-century concern with children vagrant, begging, or simply 'abroad' reflects a negative response to children out of doors arising out of altered social conditions. Paul Slack has further noted that children playing in the streets could be seen as a portent of plague, which particularly affected younger agegroups. Slightly later, in the seventeenth century, children at large were seen as a possible source of contagion, just as were rabbits, pigeons, and dogs.[27] Such ambivalences need to be borne in mind in assessing action taken in respect of children.

Not surprisingly, evidence relevant to the concerns of this chapter tends to be scattered. It is relatively concentrated in the rich records of Norwich, second city after London, and provincial capital of the populous region of East Anglia. These latter are attributes which justify extensive use of Norwich data in this discussion. In the scale and range of its municipal activity Norwich may well have been unique among provincial centres, a distinction perhaps epitomised by the Norwich census of the poor of 1570.[28] At the same time, there is reason to suppose that similar aims in relation to children would have been pursued elsewhere according to local circumstances. For the period around 1600 in particular, the importance of child labour to household economies can be assumed to have had general currency as both an ideal and a practice.[29] The proceedings of the Norwich authorities nonetheless support the view that economic *independence* was thought neither possible nor desirable for younger children.[30] Part of the perceived function of work obviously lay in training children in good habits, in preventing them from begging, and in keeping them out of trouble and off the streets – even, in Norwich's view, in improving their health. Very young Norwich children knitted and span or were in the process of acquiring these skills, and the city authorities tried various means of training those who had not yet learned them.[31] The Norwich census described poor children as young as six as 'idle', implying a more desirable alternative, and noted the occupations of working children of both sexes of around that age. The actual economic value

(Stanford, CA, 1982), pp. 65, 67–8 and *passim*; Dingwall *et al.*, 'Childhood as a Social Problem', pp. 217–18. On animals and plague, see M. Jenner, 'The Great Dog Massacre', in W. Naphy and P. Roberts (eds), *Fear in Early Modern Society* (Manchester, 1997), pp. 44–61. On neighbourhood and street life, see Phythian-Adams, *Desolation of a City*, pp. 158–69.

26. T. Atkinson, *Elizabethan Winchester* (London, 1963), pp. 207–8. This ruling was directed at girls as well as boys.

27. Slack, *Impact of Plague*, pp. 34, 183, 204–5, 296; Sachse, *Minutes of the Norwich Court of Mayoralty 1630–1631*, p. 45.

28. For the Norwich census, see Pound, *Census*. For details and further analysis, see Pelling, 'Healing the Sick Poor'; 'Illness among the Poor'; 'Old Age, Poverty and Disability'. Norwich sources are also used by Griffiths, *Youth and Authority*. See also his 'Masterless Young People in Norwich, 1560–1645', in Griffiths, A. Fox and S. Hindle (eds), *The Experience of Authority in Early Modern England* (Basingstoke, 1996), pp. 146–86.

29. Pinchbeck and Hewitt, *Children in English Society*, vol. 1, p. 98.

30. Pound, *Census*, pp. 16–17, 55; Thomas, *Age and Authority*, p. 14.

31. J. F. Pound, 'An Elizabethan Census of the Poor. The Treatment of Vagrancy in Norwich 1570–1580', *University of Birmingham Historical Journal*, 8 (1961–62), 146–7; Pelling, 'Healing the Sick Poor', pp. 118, 121 (82, 86). Defoe's pleased observations of industrious children in eighteenth-century Halifax could have been duplicated in the older textile centre of Norwich a century earlier; cf. A. Macfarlane, *Marriage and Love in England: Modes of Reproduction 1300–1840* (Oxford, 1987), p. 76.

of a child's more formal employment would obviously depend on the availability of suitable work, the pressure of population, the number of children at home, and the space available for them.[32] Occasionally the census noted explicitly that a household was dependent mainly on the work of a child, as in the case of an unnamed and unsexed child of 14 whose knitting of great hose was the 'chief living' of a couple in their forties.[33] If such a child fell ill or was injured, not only his or her own future independence but the marginal economy of the household could be affected, and the evidence suggests that both the Norwich authorities and the child's own connections saw the point of putting his or her case forward for a cure at public expense.

The potential value of the labour or activity of a child is, at the least, an indication of the burden to a poor household of a child who was chronically ill and who could not be moved on, either into apprenticeship or another poor household or into service. The Norwich census duly noted the presence in some households of children who were sickly or 'long time sick'.[34] The importance of ill health or disability in the assessment can be illustrated from a range of sources besides the Norwich census. These examples further confirm that the value of child labour was very much dependent upon circumstances. In a case from the records of the Norwich court of mayoralty, a John Roote had hurt the eye of a child: the mayor's court ordered 18*d*. weekly to be paid out of Roote's wages to the child's mother, until the boy was again able to work. This seems a substantial amount and may have included the cost of medical treatment and nursing. It is interesting to note that the money was to be paid to the mother although the father was apparently still living. Examples from other locations also show that a sick child could become a drain on public resources if unable to work.[35]

It is clear enough that sixteenth-century authorities saw mental or spiritual and physical concerns as a continuum, but it is more difficult to trace the articulation of these ideas in practice. In the case of such institutions as the Children's Hospital of Norwich, opened in 1621, the whole environment of the young inmate was to be changed and regulated, a step beyond enforced employment or training under approved agencies.[36] Physical and spiritual concerns were certainly blended in this initiative, which is likely to have been a belated copy of much earlier continental provision for orphan children and of the example

32. This point is made for the later period by E. A. Hammel, S. R. Johansson and C. A. Ginsberg, 'The Value of Children during Industrialization: Sex Ratios in Childhood in Nineteenth-century America', *Journal of Family History*, 8 (1983), 340–66. On very young working children, see also M. Spufford, 'First Steps in Literacy: the Reading and Writing Experiences of the Humblest Seventeenth-century Spiritual Autobiographers', *Social History*, 4 (1979), 413–16.

33. Pound, *Census*, p. 55. The wife in this couple was employed in spinning white warp. For a similarly supported couple (husband unemployed, wife disabled), see ibid.

34. For example, ibid., p. 37.

35. W. L. Sachse (ed.), *Minutes of the Norwich Court of Mayoralty 1632–1635*, Norfolk Record Society XXXVI (1967), p. 65; Pelling, 'Healing the Sick Poor', p. 124 (89).

36. On the hospital, see F. Blomefield, *An Essay Towards a Topographical History of the County of Norfolk*, 11 vols (London, 1805–10), vol. 2, pp. 407–14; Sachse, *Minutes of the Norwich Court of Mayoralty 1630–1631*, p. 34; Hudson and Tingey, *Records*, vol. 2, pp. cx–cxiv; W. K. Jordan, *The Charities of Rural England 1480–1660* (London, 1961), pp. 131–7.

set in mid-sixteenth-century London by Christ's Hospital. This process of influence was explicit in another East Anglian centre, Ipswich. The accommodation provided by Norwich's Children's Hospital did not supersede individual 'keeping' arrangements, and, as in the case of more specifically medical care, it is likely that extra-institutional provision remained the more important. As with Norwich's Great Hospital and lazarhouses, however, the Children's Hospital does show that institutionalisation was experimented with at this time by local (rather than 'state') authorities, albeit on a scale incommensurate with the problems involved.[37]

The Norwich Children's Hospital had echoes of the arrangements for selected children made as part of the influential Norwich poor scheme nearly 50 years before. According to the hospital's first founder, the ex-mayor Thomas Anguish, such a project had been in mind on and off for many years. He referred to the need for a convenient place for the 'keeping, bringing up, and teaching of young and very poor children' born in Norwich, especially 'such as for want, lie in the streets, vaults, doors, and windows, whereby', as he said, 'many of them fall into great and grievous diseases and lamenesses, as that they are fit for no profession, ever after'. Anguish gave his own motives for forwarding this scheme as compassion and pity, and regretted that he could not establish the hospital single-handed, being 'weak in ability', having many children himself. Anguish's view of the importance of health care of children was further expressed in his provision that, if sufficient funds for a hospital were still unforthcoming ten years after his death, income from his estate should be used to pay for surgical treatment in cases of accident, and especially for the cure of diseased children.[38] However, it should be noted, first, that the Children's Hospital was not solely or even primarily a medical institution in the modern sense, being in any case concerned with prevention rather than cure; and, secondly, that the numbers involved were minute, the original idea of 40 inmates dwindling in practice to 12.

This kind of incongruity between level of provision and the dimension of social problems is, of course, characteristic of much philanthropic institutionalisation. The Norwich poor scheme of the 1570s reported itself as having successfully converted from begging to useful work in one year, a total of 950 children (c. 9 per cent of the estimated total English population of Norwich and a hypothetical 22 per cent of the agegroup 5–24), and this figure, even if exaggerated and likely to have been reduced by the shocking plague epidemics of the intervening decades, does indicate the limits of the hospital as a solution to Norwich's difficulties.[39] As in Ipswich, the record of poor relief in Norwich from the late sixteenth century into the seventeenth shows an increasing concern with children. It is significant that both the Norwich poor scheme and

---

37. P. Slack, 'Social Policy and the Constraints of Government, 1547–58', in J. Loach and R. Tittler (eds), *The Mid-Tudor Polity c. 1540–1560* (London and Basingstoke, 1980), pp. 108–14; J. Webb (ed.), *Poor Relief in Elizabethan Ipswich*, Suffolk Records Society IX (1966), pp. 14–15. On Norwich's lazarhouses see Pelling, 'Healing the Sick Poor', pp. 126–35 (91–100). Norwich had also attempted to institutionalise children in the 1570s: Pound, 'Elizabethan Census', p. 146.

38. Blomefield, *Norfolk*, vol. 4, p. 407; Hudson and Tingey, *Records*, vol. 2, p. cx. Spelling has been modernised throughout.

39. Pound, 'Elizabethan Census', p. 148.

later the hospital were concerned with children between the ages of about five and 12: that is, to put it at its most unvarnished, surviving, mobile, articulate, and potentially handy children, old enough to learn how to be idle or to be a trouble if out of their parents' control in the streets, but still economically dependent and not old enough for most forms of apprenticeship. The perceived nuisance-value of boys, as well as their potential as heads of household, is perhaps indicated by the fact that the hospital, at first intended for both sexes (an interesting point in itself), took in boys almost exclusively. Girls were not specifically provided for until the Commonwealth period.[40]

It may already be evident that, in principle and practice, medical treatment in this period was difficult to separate from the benefits expected from improved clothing, feeding, housing, and general care, including washing. Later economic and professional developments have worked to create distinctions such as that between medical benefit and sickness benefit; this contrasts with, for example, the explicit intention with respect to the refounded St Thomas's Hospital in London, that people taken in out of the streets should have (in that order) meat, drink, lodging, and surgeons provided for them. While not wanting to perpetuate any distinction between medical poor relief and poor relief in general, the present chapter is particularly concerned with the uses to which resources were put specifically to maintain health. Clearly it was important both to the health of Norwich children and as an expression of the value placed by society on the child, that municipal authorities attempted to extract 10 to 14 years of financial support for bastard children from their fathers, gave extra support to the parents of large families, and obliged parishes to finance even the support by families of fairly close relatives. But it is also of significance that a child of 12 could be lured to Norwich by the combined prospect of 'meat' and a surgeon to heal his condition. By both theory and practice contemporaries knew that there was little point in investing in expensive medical treatment unless provision was also made for what was called keeping, including nursing and nutrition. So potent were the conditions of life thought to be, that children were sometimes assumed to have died simply from the change from bad to good conditions – a lingering idea, and one with an approximate physiological basis – and beggars were seen as suffering from excessive eating and drinking and want of exercise as well as privation.[41]

Treatment and keeping were commonly combined in the attempts made by Norwich to restore the health of children. In a typical contract with one of their regular woman keeper-practitioners, the city of Norwich agreed in 1630 with Rose Wright, first, that she should try for a month to heal the head of Tye's child, and then, the cure having partly succeeded, that she should keep

40. Pelling, 'Healing the Sick Poor', p. 118 (82); Webb, *Poor Relief*, p. 17; Hudson and Tingey, *Records*, vol. 2, p. cxii; Jordan, *Charities of Rural England*, pp. 136–7.

41. H. Levy, 'The Economic History of Sickness and Medical Benefit before the Puritan Revolution', *Eco. Hist. Rev.*, 13 (1943), 42–57, esp. p. 51; T. Wales, 'Poverty, Poor Relief and the Life-cycle: Some Evidence from Seventeenth-century Norfolk', in R. M. Smith (ed.), *Land, Kinship and Life-Cycle* (Cambridge, 1984), pp. 351–404; Pinchbeck and Hewitt, *Children in English Society*, vol. 1, p. 130; Pelling, 'Healing the Sick Poor', pp. 118, 131 (82, 96). For a Norwich woman paid at the direction of the city to keep her nephew (aged under five), see Sachse, *Minutes of the Norwich Court of Mayoralty 1630–1631*, p. 165.

him until he turned 16 in return for 20*s*. for his keeping and 20*s*. more if she managed to cure him entirely. She was to get the second 20*s*. anyway after six months if the Tye boy lived that long. Rose Wright was not herself dependent upon poor relief, although Norwich, as was common, regularly killed two birds with one stone by paying very poor women for keeping patients and even for providing certain forms of medical treatment. Contracts for medical treatment also often involved, as in the Tye case, an element of transfer of responsibility for the future keeping and/or healing of children. As described elsewhere, under this speculative form of 'insurance' a practitioner, in return for a lump sum, became liable for the cost of future treatment if the child was later found in a similar diseased condition. With respect to practitioners who also went in for keeping on what might be called a commercial basis, their contracts also involved liability if their charge was later found vagrant on the streets. Thus in 1599 William Roberts, one of the practising keepers or guiders of the Norwich lazar-houses, was paid 20*s*. and promised £3 for healing four children of the widow Williamson, to keep them until their healing, he 'doing his goodwill thereto', and thirdly to keep the widow 'during her life', this being the formula conventionally used. In a similar way the guider of another lazarhouse, acting on his own behalf, took a lump sum from a Norfolk parish to relieve it of responsibility for the future of a poor lame boy aged four. Such bargains in respect of children do not make much sense unless (as in the case of Tye) the child was likely to die; alternatively, if he or she survived, expense could be avoided by the child's labour, or responsibility terminated by service or apprenticeship.[42]

It is very difficult to arrive at any aggregate picture of the extent of investment in medical and medically related poor relief for children. In 1570 Norwich cited an annual total of over £260 as the cost of licences to collect for cures for all agegroups, but this was only one form of expenditure. It was a disfavoured kind, being a form of begging, and involving only the most expensive cures. Using records of poor-relief expenditure it is often impossible to know the exact age of the person being treated, although it seems clear, as already suggested, that the proportion of children being treated in Norwich became greater rather than smaller in the decades after 1570. Apart from defects in the records, practitioners were often paid in kind by such means as rent rebates and exemption from poor rates. Another problem hindering aggregated analysis is the lack of any standard unit of payment. A wide variety of practitioners were contracted to carry out treatment; the payments to them, ranging in the early seventeenth century from about 4*s*. to £3, keeping included, seem to have varied with the condition as much as the practitioner, and to have been similar to fees paid by private individuals, a situation which apparently persisted up to the end of the Old Poor Law in 1834. Unit expenditure on keeping was low compared with the cost of many treatments. The upper limit for the Norwich authorities is perhaps illustrated by their decision in the 1620s to sack a lithotomist whom they had paid by retainer in the hope of reducing the overall cost of his operations.

42. Sachse, *Minutes of the Norwich Court of Mayoralty 1630–1631*, pp. 95–102; NRO, Clavers' [Hamper] Accounts, 1550–1601, fol. 134; Blomefield, *Norfolk*, vol. 4, p. 168. See also Pelling, 'Healing the Sick Poor', pp. 129–30 (94).

The lithotomist provoked dismissal by refusing to do anything for the poor and trying to charge £10 for the cure of a child.[43] The city's dealings with this lithotomist do not indicate an unwillingness to pay for expensive treatment for children, but rather the reverse: those of his patients paid for at public expense seem most often to have been children.

Such contracts were peculiar neither to municipal authorities nor to poor-relief administration. Private contracts for the keeping and the more long-term transfer of children past weaning age are an underexplored area and might have been quite common even between poor people.[44] A few of the scattering of children among the households of the Norwich poor, who are described as fatherless, but not identified as parish children, could be present as a result of such arrangements.

As I have tried to suggest elsewhere using the Norwich census, children below the age of apprenticeship and sexual maturity but above the age of physical dependency can be found distributed among the narrow households of the poor to alleviate the disadvantages of old age, deformity, or infirmities such as blindness, while at the same time relieving pressure on the household of origin.[45] It seems reasonable to suggest that a child between the ages of, say, seven and 12 was found active, useful, and even companionable under the right conditions, which could be said to include the absence in the household of other children of similar age.[46] The census mentions a number of children as helping in the home, but also notices such specific examples as Richard Sandlyng, a blind man of 54, whose household included a working wife and 'child' aged 21, but also a fatherless child of 12 who led Sandlyng about.[47] Arrangements of this kind seem not to have depended on blood relationships.

The poor households of Norwich including older adults and a child not of the immediate family were often headed by or composed of women, partly because, as analysis of the Norwich census indicates, even very aged poor men tended to solve their difficulties by remarriage, often to women much younger than themselves. These 'symbiotic' marriages often led to the presence of young children, either because the woman's prior disadvantage was that she had been left with very young children, or as a result of the marriage itself.[48] Such children could, of course, be later either a burden or a help to the new household. One such example, in which the woman's liability in respect of more equal marriage included physical disability, was the Wytherly family, comprising John aged

---

43. Pelling, 'Healing the Sick Poor', pp. 118–19, 124–5 (83–4, 89–90), and *passim*.

44. See E. Clark, 'The Custody of Children in English Manor Courts', *Law and History Review*, 3 (1985), 338–9, for the medieval practice among the poor of reassigning orphans.

45. Pelling, 'Old Age, Poverty and Disability'.

46. That children of this agegroup were found helpful, and particularly so in cases where the adult was disabled, is not of course confined to the early modern period, but continues up to living memory. For a nine-year-old boy assisting the career of his brother, a general practitioner, in the late nineteenth century, see M. J. Peterson, *The Medical Profession in Mid-Victorian London* (Berkeley, CA, 1978), p. 96. In Manchester in the 1930s, unemployment forced the parents of the playwright Trevor Griffiths to send him at the age of three to his grandmother. She had gangrenous legs and failing eyesight, and immediately taught Griffiths to read so that he could read to her: *Observer*, February 1985.

47. Pound, *Census*, p. 66.

48. For examples, see ibid., pp. 47ff. On marriage, see also Pelling, 'Old Age, Poverty and Disability'.

80 who was still in work, Elizabeth his wife aged 40 who was lame but did sewing, and three children between seven and under one year.[49]

In the female-headed households, an older woman can be found living with a daughter's child, or sister's children. The disadvantage to a lone young adult woman of even an older child could be such that a grandparent would often be called upon to take the child over, but this arrangement should also be seen as of benefit to the older person, or as a means of assisting an elderly, disabled person without having to admit her to the household of her son or daughter.[50] For example, Eme Stowe, a widow aged 80 who was lame in her arm, lived with her daughter's bastard, a boy of 11. Another household, in which the child was apparently unrelated, was headed by Elizabeth Tidemunde, aged 80, a widow, who spun white warp and lived with a 'girl' of 14 who also did spinning. A more complicated calculus of disadvantage involving a disabled child was the Barthlett family, who had come to Norwich from the north seven years before the census. The father was 50, had lost a hand (or the use of it), and was out of work. His wife, about that age, went abroad outside the house peddling; there were three children of eight, six, and three, and an apparently unrelated girl or young woman described as a 'deaf wench that beg'.

It is not suggested that these arrangements made a great deal of difference in real economic or cash terms. Rather, any difference could be important to the large proportion of households or people on the edge of survival, and the possibility of such a difference would provide the motivation for such arrangements to come about. These instances, which are indicative of the transfer of resources between related generations, also provide evidence of the need to look outside family and even kin for the means of survival. It is clear that much of the assistance given by children in such situations would have been in kind rather than cash, and this may constitute a valid reason for doubting, at least among the poor, the thoroughness and permanence of the English transition to a cash economy.[51]

In general demographic terms, the late sixteenth-century population was relatively youthful, resembling that of the mid-nineteenth century, and contrasting with that of the late seventeenth. Also according to current estimates, the relative size of younger agegroups fluctuated more than the proportion of those between 15 and 24, which was comparatively stable.[52] It is not easy, however, to match these generalisations, based largely on estimates of national populations, with urban conditions in which demographic circumstances would be influenced by high mortality and migration. Children under 15 comprised about 38 per cent of Norwich's poor (English-born) population as measured by the census, compared with Wrigley and Schofield's estimate, for England in 1571, of about 33 per cent. By contrast, this poor population lacked a high

49. Pound, *Census*, p. 66.

50. The census implies that while poor households were small, contact over more than two generations was not so uncommon. Cf. Phythian-Adams, *Desolation of a City*, p. 156. See also Pelling, 'Old Age, Poverty and Disability'.

51. Pound, *Census*, pp. 36, 92, 55. Cf. Macfarlane, *Marriage and Love*, p. 68.

52. Wrigley and Schofield, *Population History*, pp. 215–19, 528. The proportion of the agegroup 15–24 is estimated to have fluctuated between 16 per cent and 21 per cent over the period 1551–1651.

proportion of the estimated group of apprentice or servant age, that is, 5.7 per cent of the poor were aged between 15 and 24, as opposed to a 'predicted' 19.8 per cent in the population at large.[53] The Norwich censustakers found few servants or apprentices in the households identified as poor, but the implication is that most of this agegroup were in service elsewhere or in better-off Norwich households. That 6 per cent still remained perhaps confirms Wall's view of the wide variation in age of leaving home, but Norwich's economic difficulties should be taken into account. It may also be that in a population enumerated on account of its poverty, in which very few households were able to take in an apprentice or a servant, the ideal and expectation from the point of view of the city authorities and perhaps even of the households themselves, would be a proportion of that age still at home even lower than 6 per cent.[54] Some allowance should probably be made here for the effects of disability.

As the Norwich authorities were especially concerned to sort out family groups, children not of the family can usually be identified as such. One would expect such children, if able-bodied, to be below the age of service or apprenticeship. Upward mobility for children transferred to another household has been given much emphasis by historians, as well as the tendency to exploitation of the poor inherent in this practice, but *downward* mobility as a result of a bargain struck with a poorer family in the case of a less-wanted child is also a real possibility, as is a bargain between families of roughly equal status. Such arrangements usually become visible to the historian only when they break down in some way and it is often difficult to determine the standing of the different parties. Sometimes the bare fact is recorded for future reference. In 1591, for example, the parish register of St Olave's, London, recorded that a boy of '5 years and better' had been given away after a trial of one year, the parents agreeing not to have any more to do with him during the life of his 'master' John Callock, other than as petitioners to God for the health of their son and for the prosperity of Callock.[55] In a more complicated Norwich example of 1630, a married woman, Margaret Grove, was rebuked by the city authorities for being familiar with Robert French. She was forbidden to meddle any more with her son, who was apprenticed to another man, and a little later a child was taken from her and returned to its mother. Whether the unnamed child was with her by private arrangement or as a result of a decision of the city is not clear.[56]

It can be deduced from such cases that the city, as might be expected, was not indifferent to the moral character of childkeepers, however poor they might be, although Norwich could also have been sharing in the general tendency towards greater strictness characteristic of the 1630s. Often these keepers were

53. Detailed analysis of the census population by agegroup is given in Pelling, 'Illness among the Poor'.
54. R. Wall, 'The Age at Leaving Home', *Journal of Family History*, 3 (1978), 181–202.
55. T. F. Thiselton-Dyer, *Old English Social Life as told by the Parish Registers* (London, 1898), pp. 174–5. Such cases of more or less permanent transfer are of particular interest given the very recent development of formal adoption law in England: J. Goody, 'Adoption in Cross-cultural Perspective', *Comparative Studies in Society and History*, 11 (1969), 58. For a less formal 'adoption', see Allan, *Christ's Hospital Admissions*, p. 2.
56. Sachse, *Minutes of the Norwich Court of Mayoralty 1630–1631*, pp. 76, 77.

bridging the dangerous gap already mentioned, before the child was old enough to go into service or apprenticeship.

A child's welfare also became the concern of city authorities if a complaint was made to them as justices of the peace. Thus in 1608 a complaint was made by the mother of a child of seven, Ann Love, described as 'dwelling' with a grocer John Jaxon. The child Ann was with Jaxon as a result of an arrangement, nature unspecified, between Jaxon and Ann's father. The father did not appear in the case, which casts an interesting light on the perceived and actual roles of both parents. The city did not dissolve the father's agreement but put it on probation for the next six months, and also ordered that Ann Love should only be reasonably corrected and never by Jaxon but always by his wife. For her part, Ann Love's mother was to be whipped if she violated the agreement made by her husband, by using 'extraordinary' or 'unlawful' means to entice her child away from Jaxon. Norwich's mayor and aldermen, like other justices, had a statutory role in adjudicating between masters and servants, but it is not apparent that Ann Love was in service, although at seven years she was 'reasonable' if not 'discreet' and, as we have already seen, children of this age certainly worked. However, Ann Love may have been with Jaxon as a result of the kind of private agreement already described.[57]

Other cases of a similar kind showed that the city felt few inhibitions about interfering in matters to do with the welfare of children whether of age to be servants or not. Local authorities were, of course, given greater powers in respect of children regardless of their parents by sixteenth-century poor-law legislation, but the paternalism of such authorities could also be described as spontaneous rather than legalistic.[58] The comparative lack of distinction between public and private responsibility was such that cases could, to a considerable extent, be judged on their merits. Thus around 1622 a Norwich mother had her child, whom she was beating, taken away and was made to pay for the child to be maintained by someone else. It was also possible for parents (and masters or mistresses) to ask the city to chastise children whom they could not control themselves. Although contemporaries could themselves be oppressed by the size of the problems they faced, it may be said that the scale of events even in a large city like Norwich still allowed flexibility of ideology and especially of practice. It should be stressed that Norwich was not unique.[59] A willingness to intervene on the part of local authorities was a corollary of the existence of social structures that provided for the child outside the family.

The interaction of urban practices and institutions in relation to younger children can be summed up in the person of Thomas Hemblinge, a Norwich child and one of a number whose early life can be pieced together at least as they came to the attention of the local authorities. Thomas can have been only

57. NRO, Mayor's Court Proceedings No. 14, 1603–15, Jan. 1607/8. On the powers of justices and the activities of the Norwich mayor's court in particular, see O. J. Dunlop and R. D. Denman, *English Apprenticeship and Child Labour* (London, 1912); Sachse, *Minutes of the Norwich Court of Mayoralty 1630–1631*, pp. 14ff.
58. Pinchbeck and Hewitt, *Children in English Society*, vol. 1, pp. 94–8.
59. NRO, Mayor's Court Proceedings No. 15, 1615–24, fol. 410; Webb, *Poor Relief*, esp. p. 16 (n.); Pinchbeck and Hewitt, *Children in English Society*, vol. 1, p. 134.

five or six when the city and his parish together paid 20*s.* for him to be kept and cured of a scald head by a female practitioner. Four months later Thomas's father was being ordered not to endanger the city's investment by allowing Thomas, now cured, to wander abroad. Thomas or his father was threatened with Bridewell if this happened again, but when it did, ten months later, the boy was simply sent home to his father. Three months later, Thomas, then described as aged over seven years, was admitted with others to the new Children's Hospital. The next event designed for Thomas would have been apprenticeship.[60] The age of apprenticeship is known to have varied considerably depending on context, but in general boys were indentured earlier than girls, and parish apprentices, apprentices in husbandry, and apprentices in the poorer crafts tended to be indentured younger and for longer periods. In spite of their poverty, however, it was intended that hospital children would not be 'employed' until they were 15, testimony as to their age being required of their parishes.[61]

So far we have looked at the usefulness of younger children and noted a variety of expedients adopted by municipal authorities aimed at maintaining the child in a fit state for the next stage of life – that is, service or apprenticeship. It is one aim of this chapter to suggest the value of reviving interest in apprenticeship as an enduring institution profoundly influencing the lives of a high proportion of early modern children. The main purpose will be to stress the importance of apprenticeship with respect to the mental and physical health of children. As it was so widely used, apprenticeship can be given no single character, good or bad, but it can at least be noted that much historiography, including that of the professions, has tended to devalue its content and importance. In particular, it is seen in economic terms as conservative and inefficient, whatever its value in socialising the young.[62] Ariès suggested a significant shift from apprenticeship to schools, but his treatment of the former was cursory and these aspects of his thesis have had, by comparison, very little critical attention. One of the exceptions to the general trend, Joan Simon, has drawn attention to the overriding importance for children of socio-economic conditions affecting their employment, a perspective which places apprenticeship on a proper level of significance.[63] A contrasting approach to apprenticeship suggests that it was a peculiar practice, confined to a few societies in northern Europe – even, perhaps, peculiarly English.[64] It would be more accurate to describe apprenticeship as an enduring and widespread institution which was practised in different forms, and more or less extensively, according to policy and socio-economic circumstances. It may be noted, however, that English villages were seen as unusual

60. NRO, Mayor's Court Proceedings No. 15, 1615–24, fols 253verso, 272verso, 315, 328verso.

61. Houlbrooke, *English Family*, p. 173; Wall, 'Age at Leaving Home'; Sachse, *Minutes of the Norwich Court of Mayoralty 1630–1631*, p. 160. See also W. Newman Brown, 'The Receipt of Poor Relief and Family Situation: Aldenham, Hertfordshire 1630–90' in Smith, *Land, Kinship and Life-Cycle*, esp. pp. 417–19. For changes in the eighteenth and nineteenth centuries for male and female servants and apprentices, see K. D. M. Snell, *Annals of the Labouring Poor: Social Change and Agrarian England 1660–1900* (Cambridge, 1987), esp. pp. 323–34.

62. I have tried to take these questions further in Pelling, 'Trade or Profession'.

63. M. H. Curtis, 'Education and Apprenticeship', in *Shakespeare Survey*, XVII, ed. A. Nicoll (Cambridge, 1964), p. 62; Simon, 'Childhood', p. 23. See also I. Q. Brown, 'Philippe Ariès on Education and Society in Seventeenth and Eighteenth Century France', *History of Education Quarterly*, 7 (1967), 357–68, esp. p. 366.

64. Macfarlane, *Marriage and Love*, pp. 82–5.

for the number of their craftsmen, one indication that apprentices were not confined to towns.[65] At present English apprenticeship is still seen broadly in terms of a long post-medieval decline, ending in discredit in the eighteenth century. Such an interpretation is distorted partly by its failure to dissociate craft (primarily urban) from parish (both urban and rural) apprenticeship.[66]

As is well known, apprenticeship was widely viewed in the sixteenth century as a source of solutions to social and economic problems, including those of the poor.[67] The compulsory allocation of poor apprentices to better-off parishioners was a predictable extension, in a period of population expansion, of the aims expressed in charitable provision for the apprenticing of poor or orphan children. It may be that apprentices were in fact particularly numerous around 1600, but precise calculation is problematic, the consensus being that it is 'impossible' at present to say what proportions of the population were in service as opposed to apprenticeship at any one time.[68] One of the main difficulties is that of determining the extent of, and reasons for, the heavy 'wastage' of apprentices after the stage of indenturing.[69] Another is the major difficulty of distinguishing apprentices from young or 'life-cycle' servants.[70] Contemporaries often used the terms apprentice and servant interchangeably, even in indentures, 'servant' being the more common term in most other records. Moreover, it was possible for a child beginning as a servant to be taken on later as an apprentice; a male servant (especially after his master's death) could subsequently be in a position to follow his master's calling; and it was common for craftsmen and tradesmen, even in towns, to follow more than one occupation at the same time. This is not to deny either that contemporaries saw a difference between the two conditions, or that indentures often attempted to enforce the distinction. For some demographic historians the distinction has been of little moment, the main stress being on life-cycle service as restricting nuptiality; for others, especially urban historians, the problem can hardly be avoided.[71] For England, the institution of service (tacitly including apprenticeship) is indisputably of

65. Laslett, *Family Life*, p. 64; J. Patten, 'Village and Town: an Occupational Study', *Agricultural History Review*, 20–1 (1972–73), 1–16. The growth at this period of forms of apprenticeship in the newer industries outside towns should also be noted: Simon, 'Childhood', p. 14. For a particular agreement allowing spurriers and bitters and their apprentices to participate in harvesting, see S. A. H. Burne (ed.), *The Staffordshire Quarter Sessions Rolls, Vol. IV, 1598–1602* (Kendal, 1936), p. 232.

66. Snell, *Annals of Labouring Poor*, chap. 5, summarises conflicting views as to timing and suggests a resolution. Recent work has concentrated on the socio-political status of apprenticeship, rather than its economic history, but on urban apprenticeship in the eighteenth and nineteenth centuries, see the detailed study of Joan Lane: *Apprenticeship in England 1600–1914* (London, 1996).

67. See in general Dunlop and Denman, *English Apprenticeship*; M. G. Davies, *The Enforcement of English Apprenticeship, a Study in Applied Mercantilism* (Cambridge, MA, 1956).

68. L. Schwarz, 'London Apprentices in the Seventeenth Century', *Local Population Studies*, 38 (1987), 18-22; Houlbrooke, *English Family*, p. 173.

69. On the minorities of apprentices becoming freemen, and the difficulty of locating them by other means, see Curtis, 'Education and Apprenticeship', pp. 67–8; P. E. Jones, *The Butchers of London* (London, 1976), p. 20; Pelling, 'Occupational Diversity', p. 497 (215–16); I. Krausman Ben-Amos, 'Failure to Become Freemen: Urban Apprentices in Early Modern England', *Social History*, 16 (1991), 155–72. On 'dropping out', see also Ben-Amos, *Adolescence and Youth*, pp. 129–31; Griffiths, *Youth and Authority*, pp. 324–34.

70. The adjective is Laslett's: *Family Life*, p. 34.

71. Cf. for example ibid.; M. K. McIntosh, 'Servants and the Household Unit in an Elizabethan English Community', *Journal of Family History*, 9 (1984), 3–23, esp. p. 13; Phythian-Adams, *Desolation of a City*.

major significance, summarised in Laslett's dictum that this was the largest single occupational group until within living memory. There are estimates of those in service at any one time ranging from 60 to 30 per cent of those aged between 15 and 24, depending on period and whether the setting was rural or urban.[72] Given the limited range of alternatives for children, an impressionistic view would suggest that the higher estimates are more realistic for the period in question. The discussion that follows concentrates on apprentices, partly to achieve greater certainty as to age, but, as we shall see, the two conditions of service and apprenticeship raise similar questions with respect to health care. In apprenticeship, however, the obligations between child and adult were the greater.

For the connections between apprenticeship and child health, we were until very lately dependent upon older work such as that of Dunlop and Denman, or the positivistic treatment of Pinchbeck and Hewitt. The demographic importance of the patterns of migration of apprentices has, of course, been recognised, as has the potential of 'adolescent' apprentices in respect of disorder and political unrest. In re-establishing the existence of adolescence in the early modern period, the emphasis has been on a post-Eriksonian view of the apprentice as a member of a peer group at odds with authority.[73] For economic historians, the interest has long lain more in the relations between masters and journeymen, than between masters and apprentices, as the journeyman increasingly broke out of the domestic system and also found his way upwards blocked. The prominent position of the apprentice in contemporary literature is difficult to ignore, and has led to reflections on social mobility, gentility, and life course, but somewhat in isolation.[74] Phythian-Adams, however, in his classic book on pre-Reformation Coventry, has gone so far as to suggest that the craft fellowships of this period overshadowed the household in the importance of their social functions. Phythian-Adams summed up the craft as 'the transforming agency in a continuous process whereby the life-style of the citizen was related to the working of the urban social system as a whole'. In the post-Reformation period the crafts were declining as independent entities, but in a number of towns at least, their functions were revived or enforced by the municipality at the same time as apprenticeship was deployed centrally for a number of economic and social aims.[75]

72. Laslett, *Family Life*, pp. 34, 35; Phythian-Adams, *Desolation of a City*, p. 204; A. Kussmaul, *Servants in Husbandry in Early Modern England* (Cambridge, 1981), pp. 3, 11–22; Griffiths, *Youth and Authority*, p. 7. See also R. Wall, 'Regional and Temporal Variations in English Household Structure from 1650', in J. Hobcraft and P. Rees (eds), *Regional Demographic Development* (London, 1977), pp. 95, 96, 98, 106–8.

73. See notes 4 and 14, above; for example, S. R. Smith, 'The Social and Geographical Origins of the London Apprentices, 1630–1660', *Guildhall Miscellany*, 4 (1973), 195–206; idem, 'The London Apprentices as Seventeenth-century Adolescents', *P & P*, 61 (1973), 149–61; P. Rushton, '"The Matter in Variance": Adolescents and Domestic Conflict in the Pre-Industrial Economy of Northeast England, 1600–1800', *Journal of Social History*, 25 (1991), 89–107; J. Patten, 'Patterns of Migration and Movement of Labour to Three Pre-Industrial East Anglian Towns', *Journal of Historical Geography*, 2 (1976), 111–29. See, most comprehensively, Ben-Amos, *Adolescence and Youth*; Griffiths, *Youth and Authority*.

74. C. W. Camp, *The Artisan in Elizabethan Literature* (New York, 1924), esp. pp. 6–7, 115–20; Smith, 'London Apprentices', p. 160.

75. Phythian-Adams, *Desolation of a City*, pp. 97–8, 104–17, esp. p. 117. See also, on life-course, the companies, and social conditions in the special case of London, the work of Ian Archer, Steve Rappaport and Vivien Brodsky Elliott.

Although very suggestive about the craft and the household, even Phythian-Adams was unable to say much about apprentices as such. As Camp and Smith have pointed out, the domestic guidebook literature of the sixteenth and seventeenth centuries stresses the patriarchal character of the *ideal* master–apprentice relationship. This was not exclusive of a major role for wives of masters or widows, and as Phythian-Adams implies, in practice the relationship between mistress and apprentice continued to have some importance.[76] This is not to suggest that these relations were as between parents and children, or intended to be such. Here again emphasis on the family has been somewhat distracting. We have been left with conflicting interpretations of apprenticeship as, on the one hand, indicating the premature thrusting of children into the adult world and, on the other, as delaying that entry. This inconsistency perhaps suggests that apprenticeship is better taken out of the straitjacket of the family and instead considered more flexibly, as Phythian-Adams suggests, as one of the structures creating intimate connections between the family and society in general. The two most important recent studies, by Ben-Amos and Griffiths, have pursued this approach, and provided a far more comprehensive picture of the content of apprenticeship.[77]

Certain realities of existence of the period in question heavily underline the importance of apprenticeship compared with parental relations, especially for the poorer family. It should be noted first that in general at this time the proportion of masters related to their apprentices was apparently very low, and that, similarly, it was not common for servants to work for their own kin.[78] Leaving aside such possible effects for the apprentice as role experimentation or social mobility, it would appear, for example, that poorer children left home earlier; and that, before this event, there was a good chance of the natural father's being either dead or almost equally at a remove from the child because at work. Fatherlessness could itself be a reason for a child's being apprenticed at a young age. The proportion of apprentice-age fatherless children in later pre-industrial urban contexts has been put by Holman at about 30 per cent; this is substantially above estimates based more on rural data, but for certain towns, notably ports, the proportion may have been even higher.[79] Presumably

76. Camp, *Artisan*, p. 4; Smith, 'London Apprentices', p. 151; S. R. Smith, 'The Ideal and Reality: Apprentice-Master Relationships in Seventeenth Century London', *History of Education Quarterly*, 21 (1981), 449–59; Phythian-Adams, *Desolation of a City*, pp. 87–92, 95–6. See also Ben-Amos, *Adolescence and Youth*, pp. 106–7. The use of 'master' in this chapter is not intended as excluding 'mistress'. Snell, among others, has argued forcefully for the place of women in craft and trade organisation (*Annals of Labouring Poor*, chap. 6, 'The Apprenticeship of Women') and further investigation is required, but in numerical terms women must have been in a minority in the better-known occupations in the period before 1640. For further references see Pelling, 'Older Women'; 'Nurses'.

77. Ben-Amos, *Adolescence and Youth*; Griffiths, *Youth and Authority*; I. Krausman Ben-Amos, 'Service and the Coming of Age of Young Men in Seventeenth-century England', *Continuity and Change*, 3 (1988), 41–64.

78. See for example Phythian-Adams, *Desolation of a City*, p. 96; A. Yarbrough, 'Apprentices as Adolescents in Sixteenth-century Bristol', *Journal of Social History*, 13 (1979), 68; Wall, 'Age at Leaving Home', p. 182; Ben-Amos, *Adolescence and Youth*, pp. 100–2, 165–6.

79. Smith, 'London Apprentices', p. 158; Houlbrooke, *English Family*, p. 173; Spufford, 'First Steps in Literacy', pp. 420–1; Wall, 'Age at Leaving Home', p. 197; Phythian-Adams, *Desolation of a City*, pp. 95–7; J. R. Holman, 'Orphans in Pre-Industrial Towns – The Case of Bristol in the Late Seventeenth Century', *Local Population Studies*, 15 (1975), 44; Ben-Amos, *Adolescence and Youth*, p. 48. Cf. Laslett, *Family Life*, p. 37. For

for poor children the proportion might be higher still. In such circumstances the connection between apprentice and master and/or mistress assumes considerable importance, even with respect to emotional life. In many trades, it was unusual for a household head to have more than one apprentice at a time, except for brief overlapping periods; households with more than one or two servants were also relatively uncommon.[80] Apprentices and servants consorted together and even slept together, but work and living patterns, as well as the efforts of authority, were against their isolation as a group from adult influence. Although different roles are also in contention, the absence of natural fathers is perhaps confirmed by the fact that in cases involving apprentices communicating with a parent and especially being 'enticed' away for a number of reasons including ill-treatment by the master, the parent concerned tends to be the mother rather than the father.[81] Such cases incidentally cast some light on the strength of the bond between mother and son at this period.[82] Although very different in other respects, the renunciation of family ties in favour of a strong but different relationship which is made explicit in apprenticeship indentures, has some affinity with the marriage contract.

As is well established, the responsibilities incurred in taking on an apprentice included manners and morals as well as relevant skills and education. Training (physical and mental) for a creditable role in the wider society was not confined to noble households. Unless special arrangements were made, licitly or illicitly, apprentices were entirely dependent upon their masters or mistresses not only for the wherewithal to pass themselves off with credit in society, but for very survival. Food, drink, clothing, shoes, bedding, and washing were explicitly mentioned in indentures, and even their quality specified. Defects in the provision of these essentials were often grounds for serious complaint, and give some idea of what was necessary before an apprentice could break his or her indentures. Complaints about lousiness and lack of change of clothing were upheld by craft, municipal, and judicial authorities.[83] In the case in 1608 of Mary Duffin, aged '12 or thereabouts', who was allegedly very ill-used by her master and 'kept very unclean and full of lice', the Norwich mayor's court broke her indentures and set her out instead to Ann Barber, singlewoman.[84] The adequacy

the effects of fatherlessness on girls of somewhat more prosperous families, see V. Brodsky Elliott, 'Single Women in the London Marriage Market: Age, Status, and Mobility, 1598–1619', in R. B. Outhwaite (ed.), *Marriage and Society* (London, 1981), pp. 90–1.

80. Pelling, 'Occupational Diversity', pp. 498–501 (217–19); Phythian-Adams, *Desolation of a City*, pp. 204–11. As Phythian-Adams makes clear, variation occurred according not only to changes in the trade but to levels of prosperity. For servants see Wall, 'Regional and Temporal Variations', pp. 95, 98, 106–7.

81. For a counter-example involving the father, see Davies, *English Apprenticeship*, p. 210 (n.). For suggestions as to sleeping arrangements, see S. A. H. Burne (ed.), *The Staffordshire Quarter Sessions Rolls, Vol. V. 1603–1606*, Staffordshire Record Society (1940), pp. 85–6; Griffiths, *Youth and Authority*, pp. 269–71.

82. Cf. Macfarlane, *Ralph Josselin*, p. 118.

83. Excellent examples of indentures for all trades are to be found in Norwich enrolments: see NRO, Enrolments of Apprenticeship Indentures, 1548–1581, 1583–1625. For examples among London barber-surgeons of complaints as well as specification in indentures, see Young, *Annals*, pp. 264–8. That the cost of washing was considerable is indicated by its making the difference between £5 and £6 per annum in a servant's wages: E. M. Symonds, 'The Diary of John Greene (1635–57)', *English Historical Review*, 44 (1929), 103.

84. NRO, Mayor's Court Proceedings No. 14, 1603–15, fol. 205recto.

of the economic position of the master or mistress was obviously important, and sometimes had explicitly to be guaranteed in advance. With respect to meat and drink, it may be that the withholding (or even rejection) of proper nourishment, as in the case of infanticide, was a more frequent expression of breakdown of relationship between master or mistress and apprentice than were the more spectacular forms of violence. An interesting contest on these grounds was that between a Cheshire apprentice of the 1630s, Thomas Hardinge, and his master, a shoemaker of Nantwich called William Crewe. Crewe alleged that after three years Hardinge had become skilled and was making unjust claims in order to break his indenture and set up for himself. Hardinge's allegation was that he had not been given sufficient meat and drink. The justices referred the dispute to the mediation of neighbours, who were presumably in a position to know the truth of the matter. It was eventually agreed that Hardinge should serve out his term, but that he should be fed not by his master but by his mother, the master paying the mother cash in lieu and continuing to clothe the apprentice.[85]

Responsibility for the apprentice's well-being was specific as well as generic. Of great significance in the present context is the legal obligation on the master to support the apprentice 'in sickness and in health', even if the apprentice continued to be unable to work. The phrase itself is a feature of some sixteenth-century indentures.[86] Chaloner's 1543 translation of Cousin, in urging the reciprocity of the master–servant relationship, asserted that it resembled that between Christ and man. In addition to guiding the youthful rashness of the servant, who but the master would defend him against violence and slander done upon him, and 'if he fall into any grievous malady, what thought (trow ye) will a loving master conceive for his recovery?' This obligation supplies a further example of major benefit bestowed outside the family and still to some extent not given a monetary value as part of the cash economy. It seems to have become increasingly codified as it came under threat.[87] In seventeenth-century indentures, in which premiums were more and more being paid not by the master but to him by the connections of the apprentice, the obligation to provide clothing and medical care was apparently also being forced back on to the parents and friends. In the eighteenth century, indentures were used which explicitly relieved the master or mistress of the obligation to pay for medical treatment and, in particular, for any expenses relating to smallpox. In spite of

85. Wrightson, 'Infanticide', p. 16; J. H. E. Bennett and J. C. Dewhurst (eds), *Quarter Sessions Records ... for the County Palatine of Chester 1559–1760*, Record Society of Lancashire and Cheshire XCIV (1940), pp. 88–9. For indentures broken on the ground of economic default of two successive masters, see ibid., p. 129. On food and social obligation, see Pelling, 'Food, Status and Knowledge'.

86. For example NRO, Enrolments of Apprenticeship Indentures, 1548–1581, fol. 24verso (Thomas Bretton, 1553); ibid. 1583–1625, fol. 93verso (Francis Beales, 1599). Each of the masters in question indentured more than the usual number of apprentices, which may explain more careful specification.

87. Gilbertus Cognatus [Gilbert Cousin], *Of the Office of Servants*, trans. T. Chaloner (London, 1543), sig. Ciii verso. G. Jacob, *The Compleat Parish Officer*, 5th edn (London, 1729), p. 113; cf. p. 125 (sick maidservants). The growth of the obligation also requires investigation. For some background see E. Clark, 'Medieval Labor Law and English Local Courts', *American Journal of Legal History*, 27 (1983), 330–53, esp. pp. 339–40, 346; R. H. Hilton, *The English Peasantry in the Later Middle Ages* (Oxford, 1975), pp. 51–2.

these changes, it was still thought even in the early nineteenth century that the master took his apprentice for better or for worse, in sickness and in health.[88] Kussmaul has shown that even servants employed by the year on verbal contracts were entitled to wages if sick or disabled by act of God or on the master's business. This obligation was, of course, often ignored, but the records of quarter sessions also show that it was enforceable, and it could be suggested that this was one reason for the decline of the system of living-in service in husbandry.[89] Since service could establish settlement and thereby entitlement to relief, and medical poor relief was an accepted practice, there could also be social pressure on masters and mistresses to fulfil their traditional obligation, so that the burden would not fall on the parish. A Warwickshire example of 1635 shows how a solution might be sought in terms of cure. Thomas Greene of 'Brayles', a labourer, had been blind for two years when he petitioned the justices. He had gone blind in service at Brayles, and it was decided that this parish should substantially increase his weekly allowance of relief, and that in addition the Treasurer of Kings Bench and Marshalsea should pay 6s. 8d. for his immediate needs and more for the recovery of his sight.[90]

It may be possible to provide only anecdotal evidence of what was likely to occur if an apprentice was ill or injured. Information tends to derive chiefly from cases of dereliction of duty, or from the downgraded version of the relationship involved in parish apprenticeship. If, however, the obligation was met to any significant degree, then this is of considerable importance for the health care of a particular agegroup at this period. This agegroup was not that most at risk, but did suffer from mental perturbation, accidents, some major epidemic diseases such as plague, typhus, smallpox, and tuberculosis, and from occupational diseases. As already seen, this group constitutes a significant proportion of early modern populations, especially around 1600 and in urban contexts. Measuring mortality in this group by family reconstitution is very difficult because of the problems of pinning individuals down for a long enough period of observation.[91]

Little information can be gained by reference to brick-and-mortar institutions, although it is possible to speculate that the rise of the voluntary hospitals in the early eighteenth century had something to do with the decline of apprenticeship and what might be called an increased assertion of distaste for the commingling of classes and sexes at the domestic level. Attempts to restrict entry to trades in the later seventeenth century, especially in the old corporate towns which also saw the first voluntary hospitals, show that it was increasingly

---

88. Dunlop and Denman, *English Apprenticeship*, pp. 179, 195–6; J. Chitty, *A Practical Treatise on the Law Relative to Apprentices* (London, 1812), p. 75.

89. Kussmaul, *Servants in Husbandry*, pp. 32–3 and 129.

90. S. C. Ratcliff and H. C. Johnson (eds), *Warwick County Records, Vol. I: Quarter Sessions Order Book Easter 1625 to Trinity 1637* (Warwick, 1935), p. 228. For a clear assertion of settlement in the case (1605) of an injured servant, see H. W. Saunders (ed.), *The Official Papers of Sir Nathaniel Bacon of Stiffkey*, Camden Society 3rd Ser. XXVI (1915), p. 58.

91. Wrigley and Schofield, *Population History*, pp. 110–11, 248–50. Issues raised in these and the following paragraphs have been further explored in Pelling, 'Apprenticeship'.

common even in the older crafts for the apprentice not to live in his master's house.[92]

The role of the master's household in the health care of the apprentice in the earlier period points to an added dimension for those cases in which an apprentice was bound to master and mistress jointly, and, even where this was not the case, suggests another important and more or less invisible function for women in health care. This is not to imply, however, that the health care function was not also exercised by the master. The close proximity in which the apprentice or servant and the master's household were expected to live had obvious health implications. To take a Norwich example, in 1599 the mayor's court ruled that Katherine Vardine, aged 18, should be discharged of her four-year contract of service and given permission to travel either to her friends or to her father in Norfolk. The reason for this decision was that both her master and her mistress were infected with venereal disease, 'whereby the said maid may in the like take hurt'. Additionally, the master was not of ability to maintain and keep Katherine 'as a servant ought to be kept'. This instance helps to balance the more generally expressed contemporary fear that servants and apprentices, as a result of ill behaviour, would infect their masters with venereal disease.[93] Characteristically, Katherine Vardine did not come from Norwich but from the surrounding countryside. She needed permission to travel to her father, but even though he lived in Norfolk, the option was allowed her that she might rather go to friends who presumably lived nearer. As is well known, many apprentices and servants served their time a considerable distance away from their place of origin. This migratory tendency presumably both allowed, and was allowed by, the convention of responsibility on the part of the master or mistress. In many cases, it would be impossible for a sick apprentice to return to his or her family to be nursed or treated. The household of the clergyman Ralph Josselin, who lived near Colchester in Essex, provides concrete examples of sickness among indentured offspring in the middle and late seventeenth century, a period which might be regarded as transitional for the practices under consideration.[94] It seems reasonable to assume, from their level of prosperity and mobility in other circumstances, that the Josselin parents would not have been deterred from bringing home their sick children by the expense involved.

Anne Josselin was bound servant for eight years in London in 1668, at the age of 14. About ten weeks after her arrival she suffered the common fate of the unacclimatised immigrant and caught smallpox. She did not return home,

---

92. For the location of voluntary hospitals, see C. Webster (ed.), *Caring for Health: History and Diversity*, Open University Course Book (Milton Keynes, 1993), pp. 52–3. Admissions policies with respect to servants varied, as did practice: see J. Woodward, *To Do the Sick No Harm: A Study of the British Voluntary Hospital System to 1875* (London and Boston, MA, 1974), pp. 40–2. The hope was expressed that 'domestic' or 'menial' servants would be cared for by masters rather than by the hospital.

93. NRO, Mayor's Court Proceedings No. 13, 1595–1603, p. 325; Cognatus, *Office of Servants*, sig. B[v]; McIntosh, 'Servants and the Household Unit', p. 21.

94. On the health of the Josselin family in general, see L. M. Beier, 'In Sickness and in Health: a Seventeenth Century Family's Experience', in R. Porter (ed.), *Patients and Practitioners* (Cambridge, 1985), pp. 101–28.

but was visited by her father a month and a half later when he went to London on other business. There is every indication that Josselin was concerned about his daughter. About a year later Anne did return home for a period, apparently to recuperate from a more protracted illness. Between these bouts she seemingly had other illnesses, particularly affecting her eyes, and also quarrelled with her mistress. Three years later, five years after her indenturing and three years before the end of her term, Anne returned home to die.[95] Another daughter in service, Rebecca, was ill for as long as four months in London at the age of 16 with what was feared to be smallpox and was later found to be measles; her worried father noted that she 'had a mother to nurse her', apparently not her own mother. On the other hand, Rebecca seems to have returned home from London to be nursed during a previous serious illness.[96] Josselin's eldest and favourite son Thomas, catching smallpox only two weeks after going to London as an apprentice, returned home for several months, but the cause of his return during the customary 'trial period' at first appeared to be his dislike of his apprenticeship. Smallpox declared itself the day after he arrived home.[97] The shifting obligations in service and apprenticeship are indicated by the premium paid by Josselin to Thomas's master, of £100, as well as the cost to him (£50) of Anne's setting out. Thomas was to return home for six months later in his apprenticeship during the great plague of London. Under less extraordinary circumstances, although chronically ill, he remained where he was.[98] Josselin's second surviving son John, also apprenticed in London, had an unsatisfactory career which can be summarised in Josselin's comment on him at the age of 15: 'sadness in my family, John returned'. In effect John refused to leave home or, later, to live independently, and was clearly unwilling to find a substitute father-figure in either of his two London masters. John also caught smallpox in London, but in spite of his dislike of being away, did not return home on that occasion.[99]

The histories of Josselin's children show the ubiquity of smallpox in the urban environment at that period, and also the disabling consequences of the disease. Anne Josselin suffered from a degree of blindness as well as deafness.[100] Such histories illustrate why, for urban apprentices at least, exclusion clauses relating to the master's obligations in the event of smallpox in particular were intruded into apprenticeship indentures. The Josselins also provide concrete examples of the role of London as a kind of black hole for apprentices.[101] Other urban centres, even though comparatively minor as foci of epidemic disease, may nonetheless have followed precedent in adopting the 'custom of London' in limiting the master's responsibility for the apprentice during serious illness,

95. Macfarlane, *Ralph Josselin*, pp. 49, 112–13.
96. Ibid., p. 113; A. Macfarlane (ed.), *The Diary of Ralph Josselin 1616–1683* (London, 1976), pp. 623–4.
97. Macfarlane, *Diary*, p. 447.
98. Macfarlane, *Ralph Josselin*, pp. 48–9, 118–20.
99. Ibid., p. 120; Macfarlane, *Diary*, pp. 546–7, 534.
100. C. W. Dixon, *Smallpox* (London, 1962), pp. 94–6; Macfarlane, *Diary*, pp. 547, 567.
101. This point is confirmed, with particular reference to smallpox, by J. Landers, 'Mortality and Metropolis: the Case of London 1675–1825', *Population Studies*, 41 (1987), 59–76. See also idem, *Death and the Metropolis: Studies in the Demographic History of London 1670–1830* (Cambridge, 1993).

at least in respect of financial expenses, if not of the duty to see that the apprentice was properly cared for.

A glimpse of how a master might deal with his servant in this situation is provided by the lawyer John Greene. Greene took on his 'man' Francis Vere in 1645; in December the following year Vere fell ill with smallpox. He recovered rapidly, being well and able to go abroad two weeks after the disease declared itself. Greene noted that he 'removed [Vere] into the alley and paid 5s. a week for his chamber and looking to' – an outlay which may be compared with Vere's wages of £5 a year.[102]

Even if apprenticeship did contain within it some means of health care for older children, there is an obvious point of reservation which is that masters would take good care not to be saddled with a sick or disabled apprentice in the first place. That this was the case is confirmed by Norwich's anxiety to maintain its children in good health up to the age of service or apprenticeship. Many of the crafts with regulations dating back to the fifteenth century excluded candidates for apprenticeship on the grounds of deformity as well as bastardy and alien birth. The ordinances of 1530 for the London Barber-Surgeons' Company ratified by Sir Thomas More included the provision that all prospective apprentices were to be inspected to see that they were 'clean without continual diseases or grievous infirmities whereby the king's liege people might take hurt', on pain of a fine. Other crafts with public health responsibilities, such as bakers, also attempted to exclude apprentices with venereal and other diseases.[103]

Where a craft or parish apprentice was revealed to be ill, the master might seek to be rid of him or her by establishing that the condition was chronic, and that it was concealed from him at the time of indenture. Where a sick parish apprentice was concerned, the master was much more likely to be relieved of the child, responsibility for whom would then fall back on the parish.

In the first of three examples of the 1650s from Norfolk, Robert Burges of Tilney petitioned to be discharged of Vallenger Mason, put out to him by the justices as an apprentice three years previously. Burges alleged that Mason had had a scald head 'ever since' which could not be healed. The discharge was granted unless the Tilney overseers could show cause; and the justices also directed, regardless of Burges's claim as to incurability, that 'the best means' were to be used to cure Mason's head. In the second example, it is not clear that the apprentice had been disabled from the outset, but the authorities show the same concern that the apprentice's condition be improved if possible. Thomas Rysing of Colby petitioned against the allocation to him by the justices of an apprentice, 'the widow Starling's son', alleging that the boy was lame. The justices actually viewed Starling, and agreed that he was lame and 'not fit to serve as an apprentice'. Rysing was discharged of the boy and Colby parish was made to provide for him as 'an impotent creature', until he was cured. These cases contrast with a third of the same place and period (Norfolk, 1655), in which a master, Lionel Hargrave, was bound over to sessions on the complaint

---

102. Symonds, 'Diary', p. 108. On nursing and infectious diseases, see Pelling, 'Nurses'.
103. Dunlop and Denman, *English Apprenticeship*, pp. 44, 136; Young, *Annals*, p. 582.

of his apprentice (evidently not a parish apprentice), Charles Spendlove. The justices agreed that Spendlove was to be discharged from his master, and that Hargrave was to pay Spendlove's father 40s. for the keeping of Charles during his sickness.[104]

Sick or disabled children who could not be indentured were not a problem only for local authorities. A wide range of evidence, including wills, attests to the ubiquity of apprenticeship as a means of providing for children. Hence, private individuals who as executors or in other capacities were left with the responsibility of other men's children, could equally find themselves in difficulties. One Norfolk parishioner claimed to be in the position of having inherited from his uncle responsibility for a fatherless deaf and dumb boy as well as a poor boy. He stressed the weight of these obligations in order to be relieved of the prospect of taking on another parish apprentice. In a Warwickshire instance of 1637, George Gaydon sought to repudiate an apprentice he had taken for seven years at the special instance of William Glover, gentleman, and Richard Baseley, yeoman; Gaydon testified that he had kept the apprentice for six months but the boy was found to have 'this infirmity that he cannot lie dry in bed and voids his excrements in clothes and bed, whereby he becomes troublesome and loathsome to the whole family where he lieth' – that is, the boy for whatever reason was doubly incontinent. Gaydon further testified that this fact had been kept from him by Glover and Baseley, neither of whom was the father of the apprentice. Gaydon's case was allowed and the indenture unravelled, an interesting result in view of Lawrence Stone's rather sweeping remarks about the unimportance of toilet training to a population which 'lived in its own excrement, hardly ever washed, and whose women and children wore no underwear'.[105] This instance also underlines the point about physical proximity between the apprentice and the master's family within the one household.

Glover and Baseley's subterfuge is a measure of the liability with which they were burdened, but in other contexts it is evident that some version of apprenticeship according to ability was acceptable. It was conventional in indentures for it to be provided that the apprentice be taught 'according to his capacity'. The Norfolk authorities, faced with a repudiated parish apprentice who had contracted diseases from running away and sleeping in ditches, set themselves to consider what trade might be suitable in view of the particular infirmity. (It later emerged that the master was lying about the lameness and the apprentice was thrust back on to his responsibility.)[106] In a Norwich case, a deaf and dumb child was apprenticed; in London, a Christ's Hospital child sent back by his master, a glover in Ipswich, because of his poor sight, was re-apprenticed to a packthreadmaker a year later. Christ's Hospital also managed to apprentice an 'innocent' of 18, but he had to be taken back after two and a half years

104. D. E. Howell James (ed.), *Norfolk Quarter Sessions Order Book 1650–1657*, Norfolk Record Society XXVI (1955), pp. 84–5, 47, 49, 81.

105. Ibid., p. 46; Ratcliff and Johnson, *Warwick County Records Vol. I*, p. 257; L. Stone, 'Children and the Family', in idem, *The Past and the Present* (Boston, MA, 1981), p. 217.

106. See for example NRO, Enrolments of Apprenticeship Indentures, 1583–1625, fols 89verso, 93verso (both 1590s); James, *Norfolk Quarter Sessions*, pp. 39, 47, 57.

and died aged about 23 in the Lock Hospital, one of London's ten lazarhouses. Most arrangements involving a disabled apprentice are likely to have been hard bargains between the relevant authorities and the master in question. In general, disabled people were expected to work to the degree that they could, but there seems to have been no systematic attempt to provide what was suggested in 1552 for Bridewell, that is, a house of occupations for those who were lame of legs but whole of hands. The occupations thought suitable included making featherbed ticks, spinning, carding, knitting, and winding of silk – a London version of the occupations followed by many of Norwich's children and disabled poor on their own initiative.[107]

A second point of reservation about apprenticeship and service which should be mentioned is that it could itself involve new dangers to the health of the child, especially through exposure to 'new' diseases, accidents at work and in the streets, and through excessive 'correction' by the master. An interesting case of occupational accident is that of a Norfolk apprentice called Mann, scalded *c.* 1605 while 'trying oil'. Mann's master, Thomas Wildblond of Wells, 'being more greedy of his work than forward to get him remedied', as the witnesses put it, obliged Mann to work in spite of his injury. Master and apprentice then agreed to break the indentures and the boy Mann sought official witnesses to this. The latter, on confronting Wildblond, were told by him that if they wanted the boy better tended they could do it themselves. Wildblond clearly thought he could defend himself by claiming that he had cared for the boy well enough and that the local officers would not relish having the obligation transferred.[108] Abuse by masters involved a range from the brutal to the bizarre, from head injuries to poison in the apprentice's food. 'Lawful correction' was either explicitly or implicitly part of an apprentice's contract, as an obligation on the master; the law had less hold over the master and an offending master was often simply put on probation not to misuse the apprentice again.[109] The practice of the crafts was probably more flexible, especially in London. Physical injury was not necessarily pre-eminent in the minds of contemporaries among the wrongs done to early modern apprentices. The results had to be fairly severe and, more importantly, likely to be permanent, before indentures were broken on that ground alone, although both craft elders and justices seem to have been willing enough to check a heavy-handed master if they could, and there is evidence of strong reaction on the part of parents to the treatment of their children. As Yarbrough has pointed out, some sixteenth-century writers stated that the master's right was to the body and not the soul of the apprentice. Behind such views may lie sources of conflict which ultimately led to such complaints as that of an older Cheshire apprentice in carpentry, who in 1640 gave as his greatest grievance

107. NRO, St Helen's Parish, Society of Genealogists Transcript, Overseers' Accounts 1617–1727, year 1618/19; Allan, *Christ's Hospital Admissions*, pp. 43, 39; Levy, 'Economic History of Sickness', pp. 52–3.

108. F. W. Brooks (ed.), *Supplementary Stiffkey Papers*, Camden Miscellany XVI (1936), p. 19.

109. For some examples of abuse, see Smith, 'London Apprentices', p. 152; S. C. Ratcliff and H. C. Johnson (eds), *Warwick County Records Vol. II: Quarter Sessions Order Book Michaelmas 1637 to Epiphany 1650* (Warwick, 1936), p. 94; Ratcliff and Johnson, *Warwick County Records Vol. I*, p. 212. For accounts stressing the weakness of the apprentice's position, see Murphy, 'Woful Childe', and D. Simon, 'Master and Servant', in J. Saville (ed.), *Democracy and the Labour Movement* (London, 1954), pp. 160–200.

against his master that the latter was a 'most fearful curser and a most grievous blasphemer of God's most holy name upon every slight occasion'.[110]

Tudor and Stuart authorities who freely invoked parental responsibility for younger children, were usually reluctant to bring in the parents once the child had become apprenticed. As we have already seen, mothers could be enjoined not to interfere, and it seems plausible to suggest that the authorities were echoing the line taken by fathers, rather than adopting a new hard line of their own. Considerable difficulties must have arisen when the major threat to the apprentice came from the master himself, and this awareness must have lent some weight to the pressure of censure exerted by fellow masters. The presence in the locality of 'friends of the family' must have made an important difference. In London there was some institutional support or refuge provided, although it should be noticed that this was (like Norwich's Children's Hospital) limited. Thus Jeoffrey Cooke, apprentice to a Newington combmaker in the 1660s, was so beaten and wounded by his master that by the time the case came up in quarter sessions, he had been for ten weeks in St Thomas's Hospital and was not yet cured. Even so, Cooke was only to be discharged from his apprenticeship if his master failed to show cause to the contrary; in the meantime it was decided, probably on the grounds of expense, that Cooke could go and stay with his mother.[111]

The longer-term consequences to an apprentice of injury are illustrated by the petition in 1634 of a gentlewoman who was raised by an uncle after the death of her father. The uncle, by way of dealing with this added responsibility, had followed the predictable course of putting her to service: unfortunately, with a mistress who 'by a blow struck on my nose dejected my fortunes in marriage'. The woman had married, but the deformity had forced her down the social ladder, so that she and her husband had both to take 'hard pains for [our] living'.[112]

In the above discussion, the effects of mortality among apprentices have been neglected in order to concentrate on aspects of morbidity, for which the evidence is inevitably more impressionistic. It can be claimed, however, that the study of morbidity, however difficult, can bring us close to conditions of life and daily experience, and even to the point of view of the object of study, in this case the child. Perceived and anticipated morbidity was also a major factor in social policy, promoting urban systems of poor relief in which the health and viability of children were essential aims. In terms of policy, even in an overcrowded urban environment, such as London, the authorities were not disposed to allow children to go to waste, and were, as well, fully aware of the ways in

---

110. Bennett and Dewhurst, *Cheshire Quarter Sessions Records*, pp. 112, 98; Yarbrough, 'Apprentices as Adolescents', p. 72. I know of no detailed work on the effect of religious divisions on apprenticeship and whether a more latitudinarian attitude was encouraged for economic reasons, or what effect this might have had on attitudes to chastisement. In general, Ben-Amos and Griffiths both cast some doubt on a 'youth culture' of spirituality and stress inter-generational influences: *Adolescence and Youth*, pp. 184–91; *Youth and Authority*, pp. 178ff, 81ff (anti-popery may have been a factor: pp. 190, 193, 329).

111. D. L. Powell and H. Jenkinson (eds), *Surrey Quarter Sessions Records. The Order Books and the Sessions Rolls Easter 1663–Epiphany 1666*, Surrey Record Society XXXIX (1938), p. 14.

112. Thiselton-Dyer, *Old English Social Life*, pp. 172–3.

which neglect could redound to their disadvantage. It would not be right however to suggest that care for children was motivated entirely by self-interest. Even
the bald language of the mayor's court and quarter sessions suggests otherwise.
Rather, the aim of the present chapter is to redress the balance by considering
the child outside the family or at least the home, and to establish a minimum
case. The evidence also suggests that the strategies and concerns of the authorities were not always very different from those employed among the poor
themselves. Here I have stressed the idea of survival expedients, and a 'calculus
of disadvantage', both of which might involve a value being placed on children
such as to lead to differently constructed households, and the movement of
individuals between households. In such circumstances, intergenerational dependency becomes a more complex question, involving networks that transcend
the immediate family. Similarly, the conventional 'dependent' roles of younger
and older people can be drastically modified by economic and physical disability.

Solutions to the problem of the poor, like other socio-economic policy areas,
made considerable use of the traditional system of apprenticeship, although,
as has been suggested, apprenticeship and its conditions affected the futures
of a wide range of social groups. Especially where medical poor relief was less
elaborate than in cities such as Norwich, the temptation for authorities, as for
individuals, was to apprentice the child at a younger age in order to shorten the
dangerous, mobile period between about four and 14. Where the child was
more strenuously supervised, as in Norwich's Children's Hospital, the age of
apprenticeship could be later. The assumption was that, once apprenticed, the
child was provided for in sickness as in health and could become a useful member of society. The liability having been transferred, whose duty it was to care
for a sick parish apprentice became a contest between the master and his parish.
In such a situation there was every inducement to look to medical care for a
solution.

Although personal, the bond between apprentice and master also created links
between the child and the wider society. The relationship between apprentice and
master in general can be seen as one test of the vision of England as an 'orderly'
society. In such a society there must necessarily be strong bonds bridging the
gap between the citizen and 'the state'. The practice of apprenticeship is a subject meriting consideration in its own right, rather than as a negative or ancillary
factor in family relationships. To be apprenticed was not simply to be expelled
from the family; similarly, the presence of apprentices meant more than family
extension. What happened when an apprentice was ill or disabled is one effective test of a changing or traditional social institution involving children, which
was affected by disease patterns as well as economic conditions. The relation of
health and disease to apprenticeship is an area which could be explored further.
It is desirable, for example, to test the hypothesis that the convention of support during sickness eroded the practice of apprenticeship over the long term,
together with other social changes, driving a wedge between apprentices and
the family of the master or mistress. Dunlop and Denman praised the 'eugenic'
value of apprenticeship and the nature of the contract between apprentice and
master, which in their view combined with the supervisory activities of the

crafts to mitigate the ill-effects of child labour on the national health.[113] These authors were, of course, motivated by a highly critical attitude to post-industrial child labour, which they saw as a dead-end for the child in its lack of education, training, and welfare. Whether apprenticeship in the early modern period had all the virtues Dunlop and Denman ascribed to it in practice as well as intention seems a question well worth further investigation.[114]

113. Dunlop and Denman, *English Apprenticeship*, p. 21.
114. These issues are taken further in Pelling, 'Apprenticeship'.

CHAPTER SIX

Old Age, Poverty and Disability in Early Modern Norwich: Work, Remarriage and Other Expedients

This chapter will be considering the older members of a major section of early modern urban society. For the period in question, the later sixteenth century, the poor could by various criteria be defined as a quarter, a third, or an even larger proportion of the population, and so cannot be regarded as insignificant.[1] Demographically, the elderly among the poor could be seen as marginal, especially given their comparatively small numbers, and their lack of relevance to the engine of fertility. Of this group, the disabled elderly poor constitute a smaller group still. Nonetheless, in historical terms there is every justification for analysing the social conditions of these smaller groups in society, even if it is possible to use only very simple methods. The interest and ubiquity of concepts and social practices to do with age was demonstrated some time ago by Thomas.[2] However, the elderly themselves, and especially the elderly poor, are still a neglected topic for the early modern period, even though their situation, and even more that of the disabled, constitutes a kind of acid test for any society. My main concern in this chapter will be with the imperatives of survival among the elderly poor, the essential place of work and perhaps migration in their lives, and the strong possibility that household structure among the poor was influenced by the need to balance, or compensate for, extreme forms of disability.

There is an increasing awareness among historians of the mutability of early modern households. Stress has been placed on regional and temporal differences, or differences related to passing phases in the lifecycle of households, which are 'normal', but which deviate from the overall picture. The developmental cycle of the family has also been emphasised in the context of explaining structural poverty, which for the majority of the poor is seen not as lifelong but as age-specific and crisis-related. Increasingly it is the poor family that is

---

I am grateful to Jonathan Barry, Richard Smith, and Charles Webster for comments and bibliographical advice on this chapter, the first version of which was given at the Society for the Social History of Medicine conference on Old Age held in Oxford in May 1984, and summarised in *Bull. SSHM*, 34 (1984), 42–7.

1. P. Slack, *Poverty and Policy in Tudor and Stuart England* (London, 1988), pp. 2–4 and chap. 4. See also T. Arkell, 'The Incidence of Poverty in England in the Later Seventeenth Century', *Social History*, 12 (1987), 23–47; J. Boulton, *Neighbourhood and Society: A London Suburb in the Seventeenth Century* (Cambridge, 1987), pp. 104–19.

2. K. Thomas, *Age and Authority in Early Modern England* (London, 1976).

seen as small and nuclear, although whether this promotes or threatens survival is less clear. Either way, it seems to be generally accepted that for the English poor even close kin were not a primary source of support, although this is still too often measured simply in terms of co-residence. Co-residence is in any case an awkward criterion to apply to the urban poor, who were often crowded together in subdivided houses, or in parts of buildings difficult to define as houses in the normal sense.

In what follows I wish to reflect on some of these generalisations, using a late-sixteenth-century source which provides access to a substantial group of the elderly urban poor. The group is large enough to claim some representativeness, yet at the same time there is sufficient detail given to allow close examination of particular circumstances. This examination reveals rather striking facts about marriage and remarriage among the elderly poor which may be seen as bearing out Wrightson's point that English marital practice reflected less a uniform code of behaviour, than the varying needs and opportunities of people of differing social position.[3] I shall also be discussing the position of children, though without entering into the highly developed debate as to the economic incentives for or against having children and the implications of this for fertility levels in early modern society.[4] The main tendency of the evidence to be examined here adds support to the growing body of discussion which implies the lesser importance of kinship in organising social relations in early modern England – unless marriage itself can be regarded as a kinship connection.[5] The expedients to which I shall be referring could also be adopted by people unrelated to each other, even though co-residence was the result – a description which could also be applied to marriage, if undertaken for expedient purposes. These expedients may even have involved monetary or material exchanges, and were closely related to ability to work. They seem also (although here marriage was an important exception, at least at this date) to have been freely adapted and absorbed by local authorities in their schemes for poor relief, thereby adding further proof to the case of those who would argue that the growth of poor relief took place through the co-option of traditional practices.

Identification is the first of the main problems with respect to the elderly in the early modern period. Age-listings are not common in English records of early date, and family reconstitution is difficult in major towns affected by a high rate of migration. With respect to individuals, it is recognised that, while there was a sharp awareness of the different phases of life, including old age, and the legal definition of an idiot was one who could not tell his own age, there is little hope of people knowing their age *precisely* until the eighteenth century or even later.[6] There is some sense, backed partly by conventional wisdom and partly by contemporary records, that the elderly are particularly elusive because that

3. K. Wrightson, *English Society 1580–1680* (London, 1982), p. 67.

4. See for example (for England), A. Macfarlane, *Marriage and Love in England. Modes of Reproduction 1300–1840* (Oxford, 1986), section II.

5. R. M. Smith, 'Fertility, Economy, and Household Formation in England over Three Centuries', *Population and Development Review*, 7 (1981), 606.

6. Thomas, *Age and Authority*, p. 5; D. Thomson, 'Age Reporting by the Elderly and the Nineteenth Century Census', *Local Population Studies*, 25 (1980), 13–25.

stage of life lacks the great legal, administrative, and developmental milestones which marked childhood and early adulthood. It is possible, however, that this is an anachronistic view, stemming from our own concentration on youth, and from the persistent feeling that high levels of mortality must have robbed the later decades of life of any social or structural differentiation.[7]

The group that might be supposed to illustrate these assumptions most thoroughly is the poor. It has, however, been suggested that, even for a much later period, literacy was less important for knowledge of age than community habits and social pressures. Leaving aside autonomous knowledge of age, there were many ways in which the poor of sixteenth-century England were taught to know their age, or at least had an estimate of age thrust upon them. The passports which the travelling poor were obliged to carry and present wherever they went in order to avoid punishment for vagrancy, identified an individual by age as well as by sex, hair colour, and other characteristics. By definition the poor (except for the flamboyant and most threatening few) lacked distinctiveness based on clothing and material possessions, yet the need to identify them precisely was felt to be acute.[8] In seventeenth-century urban environments, age could be combined with occupation, marital status, and residence to identify people such as servants for legal purposes; such people could also be asked to estimate in years how long they had known other individuals.[9] A more collective process involving the poor in which age was recorded was the census, and it is one of the best of these, that taken in Norwich in 1570, which will be analysed in more detail here.[10]

The census was taken at a relatively calm moment demographically, before either the plagues or the major immigrations which altered Norwich's population at the end of the century. There was, however, an increasing sense of economic crisis, which is likely to have influenced migration. The census is an extremely thorough document, giving details of 2,359 men, women, and children in Norwich, about a quarter of the English-born population of the city at that time. This large proportion is a telling reminder that 'the poor' then comprised a much larger and more elastic category than was covered at a later date by the term 'pauper', which was confined to those who had lost all hope of independent existence, and which tended to erase all other social and occupational designations. More women were listed in the Norwich census than men, and more children than women (men _c._ 22 per cent, women 36 per cent, children – those under 16 – nearly 40 per cent).[11] Selection for poverty by local officials had apparently skewed the census population in two important ways: first, a major proportion was missing of the agegroup 15–24 which should have been present according to current estimates – the 'hole in the middle'

7. D. H. Fischer, _Growing Old in America_ (New York, 1977), p. 12. Specific later ages (e.g., 60 for men, 40 for women) were formalised in such contexts as labour laws, ecclesiastical duties, and military service: Thomas, _Age and Authority_, pp. 33, 35.

8. Thomson, 'Age Reporting', p. 23; Slack, _Poverty and Policy_, chap. 2, and pp. 98–9.

9. CLRO, Mayor's Court Interrogatories, MC6 (apprenticeship).

10. Pound, _Census_.

11. Ibid., Appendices I and II; 48 persons aged 16 and over were unspecified as to sex, nearly all of them under 30.

characteristic of poor populations.[12] It is therefore all the more striking that young children were present in about two-thirds even of households with elderly adults (one or more aged 50 and over). Secondly, the proportion of those over 60 should have been about 7 per cent at this date according to the 'national' age structure, instead of about 15 per cent as in the census. Comparable age-specific estimates are not available; it remains debatable whether in poor populations (as compared with early modern populations in general) women were disproportionately represented among adults because of an (adult) mortality differential more markedly in their favour as compared with men. Another hypothesis would be that women are likely to be disproportionately represented in *any* population selected for poverty. A related unresolved issue is the tendency for women to be present in greater numbers than men at certain periods in many early modern towns; this aspect of English sex ratios seems however not to have been true of the largest towns and cities, at least with respect to the period around 1600.[13]

For all those listed in the census, details are given of name, age, sex, marital status, occupation both past and present, and, for women and children as well as men, length of stay in Norwich, place of residence, and an indication as to ownership of the property in which they lived. Information was also gathered on state of health, including pregnancy, suckling, and disability.[14] In its combination of these categories of data, the Norwich census is probably unique among surviving examples; the detail of state of health is almost certainly unique; and it is even unusual to be given both nominal and real, past and present occupations for men, and systematic detail about the occupations of women and children. With respect to men at least, some indication is given of occupational 'downward mobility'. The census was taken with a view to putting the poor to work, so that estimates are also given of degree of poverty of the household and its 'ability' to work. This last, as we shall see, was not at all the same as health or even absence of disability.

For present purposes my discussion considers all individuals aged 50 and over – 50 rather than 60, largely because contemporaries seem to have regarded the age of 50 as a milestone, the end of adult maturity and the start of old age, though not necessarily the start of decrepitude, and certainly not, as we shall see, the end of work; and also to cover the point that poor people of this age

---

12. The estimates referred to are those of Wrigley and Schofield, *Population History*, bearing in mind that the data used were chiefly (outside London) from rural parishes. For the 'hole in the middle' see A. L. Beier, 'The Social Problems of an Elizabethan Country Town: Warwick, 1580–90', in P. Clark (ed.), *Country Towns in Pre-Industrial England* (Leicester, 1981), pp. 60–3; Smith, 'Fertility, Economy and Household Formation', pp. 602–6; also Pelling, 'Child Health', pp. 147–8 (84). For the nineteenth-century equivalent, see M. Anderson, 'Households, Families and Individuals: Some Preliminary Results from the National Sample from the 1851 Census of Great Britain', *Continuity and Change*, 3 (1988), 433.

13. My calculation. For an analysis of family size according to the age of the father, see Pound, *Census*, p. 17. There is some correlation between elderly fathers and the really large (young) families (p. 18), possibly as a result of remarriage; see below. On sex ratios in towns, see P. Griffiths, J. Landers, M. Pelling and R. Tyson, 'Population and Disease, Estrangement and Belonging', in P. Clark (ed.), *Urban History of Britain, Vol. 2* (Cambridge University Press, forthcoming). See Pelling, 'Older Women', p. 162.

14. Pound, *Census*, includes breakdowns for household and family structure, length of stay, and occupation for the census population as a whole. See also Pelling, 'Illness among the Poor'.

in the early modern period might legitimately be regarded as old in real terms, prematurely worn out.[15] 'Premature ageing' might be supposed to affect women in particular, with respect to appearance and as an effect of child-bearing, but with some degree of reservation. For women of the early modern period, the age of 50, the end of the reproductive years, signalled not simply a loss of function, but also to some extent a gain in qualification for certain social purposes. It should not be assumed that the end of reproductive life was perceived as purely negative in its effects, either by society or by the individual.

The question of the reliability of the census details obviously arises. An important point is that those concerned were nearly all resident, and 'labouring', rather than vagrant, poor. The information was apparently obtained by house-to-house visitation.[16] Occasionally it is reported what the poor themselves actually said, and other details show a fairly intimate knowledge, for example the details about pregnancy or suckling children, or the family's place of origin even when they are reported as having come to Norwich as long as 20 years previously, or the fact that a woman normally worked at spinning for a living but was not doing so at that moment because of sickness.[17]

Rather than dealing with individuals, the censustakers were concerned with dependency and the extent of Norwich's liability for its poor. Their aim was the assessment of the condition and relations of the household as a whole, so that it is not surprising that they occasionally described as children, people given ages of 20 or even 30. Family groups, or groups imitating families, are entered separately even if resident in the same house. In a major urban centre such as Norwich, crowded conditions and large and indistinctly divided buildings meant that the term 'houseful' as currently used is of limited application. Exact relationships and even ages were important because of the residence requirement defining Norwich's responsibility. Adolescents who had left their service, or grandparents recently arrived, could be sent away. It followed from this that the responsibility of one family member for another was also defined within very narrow limits. Because they were assessing households and familial relationships as a whole, the result is also a measure of what the censustakers thought was credible, whether biologically or in relation to the poor in particular. Whatever their liability to belief in exceptions, it seems unlikely that Norwich's officials would, on a mass scale, have been inclined to accept glaring biological improbabilities – to take a hypothetical example, an old woman's claim to be the natural mother of very young children. Nonetheless, the influence of official or elite preconceptions about the poor cannot be entirely ruled out, even in respect of very broadly defined groups of poor probably belonging to the same neighbourhood as the recordtaker, as was the case with the Norwich census population.

15. P. N. Stearns, *Old Age in European Society: The Case of France* (London, 1977), p. 16; Phythian-Adams, *Desolation of a City*, p. 93; Thomas, *Age and Authority*, pp. 33, 38. The first proposed old-age pensions were to be payable from age 50: Thomas, *Age and Authority*, p. 38. See also the thoughtful discussion in C. Gilbert, 'When did a Man in the Renaissance Grow Old?', *Studies in the Renaissance*, 14 (1967), 7–32, esp. p. 9.

16. Slack, *Poverty and Policy*, p. 73. See also F. R. Salter, *Some Early Tracts on Poor Relief* (London, 1926), p. 11.

17. See for example Pound, *Census*, pp. 69, 23.

With respect to ages, the census may be accurate without being absolutely precise. Of the total of 533 people aged 50 and over, about 60 per cent were given an age in round figures, confirming the tendency to rounding found in other records where ages are given. Sometimes a husband was given an age and his wife was simply described as 'of that age', which certainly implies approximation. However, as already suggested, the censustakers were not uncritical, and their subjects not necessarily ill-informed about their own stage of life. Sometimes a round figure was given by the tellers specifically in the format of '60 and odd', and there are no extravagant claims for an undue number of centenarians. That the poor themselves gave their ages is indicated by the doubt cast by the teller on the claim of one widow to be 100.[18] Less than 5 per cent of adults were *not* given an age, nearly half of them married women, and only one of them described as a widow.[19] This may suggest that old age was not in fact seen simply as an amorphous decline without need of differentiation. It should also be noted, as a general point, that a precise link between a particular age and some legal or social milestone may in itself have been an incitement to distortion of the record, especially where there were tax implications.[20] Other records where discrepancies have been noted in the ages attributed to individuals at different times within a short period, seem to indicate that such discrepancies were usually of the order of within five to ten years, and it may be that many of the ages of the Norwich census are imprecise within this comparatively narrow range.[21] I should like to argue that, even if this is the case, a lack of absolute precision does not stand in the way of the following enquiry, which accepts as a broad principle the reliability of contemporary perceptions of age, state of health, and family structure.

In Norwich's discovery of the extent of the city's obligations to its poor, one issue of importance, as already noted, was the length of residence in the city. The right to poor relief as a function of settlement – defined by place of birth, service, or length of stay – had been established in labour law by the fourteenth century. When vagrancy and population increase among the poor again became a pre-occupation in the first half of the sixteenth century, attempts were made to control landlords, occupiers, and poor 'inmates' which inevitably reinforced criteria of residence. This trend was probably led by London, a three-year qualification for residence having been first introduced in a statute of 1504. It is notable that Great Yarmouth's town assembly had laid down a precise three-year criterion for establishing the settlement (and consequently the rights to relief) of 'honest', non-indentured labour by 1553. Because of the scope of its poor relief schemes, and the undoubted fact that these schemes were put into practice, Norwich's application in the 1570s of the same three-year settlement

---

18. Ibid., p. 49. The only other centenarian, also a woman, was entered without comment, p. 69.

19. Ibid., Appendix I.

20. D. Herlihy and C. Klapisch-Zuber, *Tuscans and Their Families: A Study of the Florentine Catasto of 1427* (New Haven, CT, and London, 1985), pp. 138–43; for rounding according to social context, see pp. 169–79. The same is suggested for both the professional classes and the elderly poor under the different conditions of the nineteenth century: Thomson, 'Age Reporting', pp. 21–2.

21. R. Finlay, *Population and Metropolis: The Demography of London 1580–1650* (Cambridge, 1981), pp. 124–6. See also Thomson, 'Age Reporting', pp. 18–22.

rule stands out as particularly rigorous. Here again the question arises of the accuracy of the information gathered and presented by the censustakers. Only those arriving within the last two or three years were noted as having to depart, and in at least one ward there is a suspicious uniformity of people who had 'lived there ever'; on the other hand, arrivals as long before as 40 years or more were also recorded, with places of origin, besides shorter periods of residence. The usual form used by the censustakers was 'ever' or a specified number of years, although a very few people were given as having been born in Norwich, or apprenticed there. Information is lacking in about 10 per cent of cases. Leaving these out, a little over half of the elderly had, so far as the censustakers were concerned, always lived in Norwich. The proportion is roughly the same as for the census population taken as a whole. It should be stressed that Norwich was a considerable centre of attraction for immigrants, having a comparatively open policy even with respect to adults wanting to enter the town to pursue a particular occupation.[22] Against this must be set anxiety about economic decline, and unwillingness to provide for any other than Norwich's own – that is, settled – poor.

Of more interest in the present context is how many of the group being considered had moved to Norwich when already 50 or older. Again, the data recorded are also significant as a measure of contemporary experience, of what the censustakers found credible. Nearly a quarter of the elderly known to have come, at some time in their lives, from outside Norwich, had migrated in old age, of whom most had apparently been in their fifties at the time. A handful of these elderly immigrants – 14 people, or 5 per cent – had come in their sixties and a mere eight, or just under 3 per cent, in their seventies or eighties. Of these oldest immigrants three came with, or came to join, the households of grown-up children, and one of these, who had come very lately as a widow of 80 to join a married son of 30 who had arrived six years before, was to be forced to go away again by the city authorities.[23]

It is notable that nearly all of the elderly immigrants had come not as a grandparent to join the household of a grown-up child, but as the partner of a much younger spouse. This is only one aspect of the expedient which I will call for the moment 'unequal marriage'. From another point of view such marriages could equally be seen as symbiotic, and I shall be returning to this later. It is possible of course that in the case of men the marriage took place after arrival; similarly, the few immigrant widows, and the only immigrant unmarried old man, might have arrived as married people and then lost their spouses. Because length of residence was taken from head of household (male or female), no information is given as to the origins of wives still with their husbands. The movements of women are therefore to a significant extent obscured, making

22. E. M. Leonard, *The Early History of English Poor Relief* (Cambridge, 1900), pp. 3–5, 107–9; Slack, *Poverty and Policy*, p. 118; Great Yarmouth Town Hall, Great Yarmouth Assembly Book, Y/C19/1, fol. 103verso (26 December 1553). I am grateful to Mr Paul Rutledge of the Norfolk Record Office for drawing my attention to the Yarmouth reference. Pound, *Census*, Appendix VII; idem, *Tudor and Stuart Norwich* (Chichester, 1988), p. 50.
23. Pound, *Census*, p. 85; see also the similar case of Agnes Barnarde (p. 73).

the above proportion of migrant elderly a minimum figure. It can nonetheless be concluded that, however limited its extent, migration was a real experience for some old people. This reality can be exemplified by John and Agnes Silie, who had come to Norwich from 'Ryson chace' seven years before the census, when he was 81 and she was 69. By 1570 he was 'sykly' and she was 'lame handad' and neither was regarded as able to work, in spite of which Agnes, characteristically, continued to work at spinning and carding.[24] The Silies did not live with anyone else and there was no-one of the same name among the poor, although this precludes neither the existence of a married daughter in the census population nor the presence of better-off relatives in Norwich. If, as seems to be the case, employment – of some kind – went on to as late an age as possible, then subsistence migration among the elderly cannot be ruled out.[25] The greater diversity of occupations and institutions in larger towns is likely to have offered the best chance of minor employments for the elderly, although this remains a presumption except for such clear examples as portering, a job often needing to be done in ordinary shops as well as more obvious establishments.

The continuance and necessity of work in the lives of the elderly poor is heavily underlined by the census. Pensions among household servants, institutional employees, and others cannot be ruled out as a possibility, but only for the few. The desire of the Norwich authorities that the elderly should work was not restrained by the probable deficiency of 'realistic' employment opportunities in the town. As well as being prepared to create work, and to promote new trades, the Norwich authorities, in common with their contemporaries, could see employment and subsistence in piecemeal terms. Those regarded as totally *unable* to work were nearly all elderly, as even severe disablement in younger people was not enough for the Norwich authorities to dismiss all possibility of employment. However, the proportion of those unable to work at all was very small, about 1.5 per cent of all those over 16. The general expectation or attitude on this point is shown in, for example, the description of three widows, aged 74, 79, and 82 respectively, as 'almost past work', just as others, with respect to disablement, were described as almost lame, or almost blind.[26] Each of these three widows was recorded as working by spinning white warp, the most common occupation among poor women in Norwich. Among poor men, there is confirmation of the supposition of Thomas and others that by the time they reached old age many men had shifted, if they could, into more minor employments, although they were still often identified by the occupation of their prime years.[27] This was not always a case of seeking or being forced into physically less arduous work. A goldsmith and a worsted weaver, for example, had had to become labourers. These two men could have been affected by economic misfortune, or by some condition affecting the hands and disabling

---

24. Ibid., p. 92. In spite of their condition, the Silies were also noted as 'hable'.

25. On migration in general see P. Clark and D. Souden (eds), *Migration and Society in Early Modern England* (London, 1988). On migration among the elderly at a later period, see J. Robin, 'Family Care of the Elderly in a Nineteenth-century Devonshire Parish', *Ageing and Society*, 4 (1984), 514–15.

26. Pound, *Census*, pp. 62, 64, 65.

27. Thomas, *Age and Authority*, p. 38; Boulton, *Neighbourhood and Society*, pp. 83, 155 (esp. note 78).

them for finer work. Another weaver had turned to pipefilling (to do with textiles, not tobacco), one of the few occupations followed by elderly women as well as elderly men. Although no elderly man is recorded as spinning even on the 'industrial' level, some older men did drift into jobs which could similarly be regarded as roughly equivalent to domestic work, like caretaking, sweeping, portering, keeping prisoners, 'keeping kitchen', and turning spits. Many men, however, on becoming unemployed, simply remained so: one carpenter had been out of work for 14 years. He may have had casual work over that period, and the attitudes of the censustakers may have led them to record this less thoroughly than in the case of women, but in general the census is dominated by the aim of recording all sources of subsistence. On this basis, and as a corollary of the expectation that old people would continue working, it does not seem that older men were radically more likely to become unemployed than younger men. Unemployment among all men over 21 in the census population was about 33 per cent; among those aged 50 and over, including those totally unable to work, it was about 40 per cent.[28]

With elderly women the situation was rather different. Almost none was unemployed in the sense of lacking any occupation outside the domestic sphere. This contrasts with the position of women taken as a whole: women of childbearing age were more likely to be 'unemployed' outside the home than elderly women, even among the poor, who would be less able to allow 'time off' for child-rearing.[29] Older women seem therefore to have returned as far as possible to the labour market, rather than becoming home- and childminders for younger families. It is clear that the censustakers were not recording merely the work a woman did for her family's needs, because it was sometimes noted when a woman worked only at home, or for herself. Margaret Baxter, for instance, a widow of 70 living with her daughter who was a deserted wife, 'spyn hir owne work in woollen & worketh not'. A certain moral disapproval was reserved for women regarded as able who made their presence felt outside the home but who did not work; for example Margaret Fen, an 'unruly' lame widow of 60. On the other hand it was also routinely (and often feelingly) noted when a woman's husband had left her and failed to provide her with help or comfort.[30]

Women in their seventies who were blind, weak or lamehanded continued to knit, card, and spin. The occupations of women of all ages were dominated by spinning, especially the spinning of white warp. Many of the miscellaneous employments found among the women in the census, as opposed to the major categories of occupations in the textile, clothing, and victualling trades, are in fact attributable to the elderly women. It was common for these women to have more than one occupation, because such employment was the most contingent and sporadic. Nonetheless, even given the effects of disability, employment

28. Pound, *Census*, p. 16; my recalculation.

29. For the occupations of women taken as a whole, see ibid., Appendix IV. Lynn Botelho has found Suffolk parishes more likely to find work for older men than older women (L. Botelho, 'Provisions for the Elderly in Two Early Modern Suffolk Communities' (University of Cambridge PhD thesis, 1995), pp. 342–3); this may reflect the fact that older women were readier to find employment than older men. I wish to thank Dr Botelho for providing information from her thesis.

30. Pound, *Census*, pp. 28, 29, 62.

among older women was actually *less* diversified – and, by inference, perhaps less contingent – than among the younger agegroup.[31] Employment was likely to have been even more diverse than the census suggests, in spite of the relatively searching nature of its enquiry into subsistence occupations. Some older women were among those chosen by the Norwich authorities – called the select women – to run schools in each parish for teaching poor children to knit and spin, but this role was not confined to the elderly.[32] The elderly women also provided many of the hidden army of those who washed, scoured, helped neighbours at need (a common formula, the meaning of which is unclear), dressed meat and drink, and, intriguingly in the present context, 'kept wives' or 'kept women'. The implication is that these more domestic functions were not being undertaken for their own families.[33] Also hidden among the by-employments of these women were the roles more explicitly concerned with the sick, such as 'keeping sick persons' and 'tending almspeople'. Older women serving these functions were to be extensively deployed by the Norwich authorities over the following decades.[34] In such contexts post-menopausal women appear to have been seen as having a positive value in society which men over 50 would have lacked. The refounded hospital in Norwich, for example, re-iterated the traditional ecclesiastical stipulation that the women keepers were to be 50 years of age or older.[35] It will be recalled that searchers for the bills of mortality were to be 'ancient' women, a specification originally intended to carry positive connotations but rapidly devalued in the chaos of plague experience.[36] Recent work on the eighteenth century suggests the possibility that later

31. The census gives details of employment for 294 elderly women; of the total of 332 aged 50 and over, only 29 were unable to work or were unstated as to occupation. For almost all of the latter category, sickness or disability was also noted. Nine more were regarded as doing no work, but three of these nonetheless did something to support themselves (these details exclude prostitution, which the Norwich authorities were also concerned to identify). For more extensive analysis of the situation and occupations of older women, see Pelling, 'Older Women'.

32. J. F. Pound, 'An Elizabethan Census of the Poor: the Treatment of Vagrancy in Norwich, 1570–1580', *University of Birmingham Historical Journal*, 8 (1961–62), 146; D. Willen, 'Women in the Public Sphere in Early Modern England: the Case of the Urban Working Poor', *Sixteenth Century Journal*, 19 (1988), 567; Pound, *Census*, p. 29.

33. In general see esp. S. Wright, '"Churmaids, Huswyfes and Hucksters": the Employment of Women in Tudor and Stuart Salisbury', in L. Charles and L. Duffin (eds), *Women and Work in Pre-Industrial England* (London, 1985), pp. 100–21; M. Kowaleski, 'Women's Work in a Market Town: Exeter in the Late Fourteenth Century', in B. Hanawalt (ed.), *Women and Work in Preindustrial Europe* (Bloomington, IN, 1986), esp. pp. 155–8; M. Prior, 'Women and the Urban Economy: Oxford 1500–1800', in idem (ed.), *Women in English Society 1500–1800* (London and New York, 1985), pp. 93–117. On older women, see P. Earle, 'The Female Labour Market in London in the Late Seventeenth and Early Eighteenth Centuries', *Eco. Hist. Rev.*, 42 (1989), 345–6.

34. Pelling, 'Healing the Sick Poor', pp. 122, 127–8 (86, 92–3) and *passim*; also Willen, 'Women in the Public Sphere', esp. pp. 570–1; Botelho, 'Provisions for the Elderly', pp. 342–3; A. Wear, 'Caring for the Sick Poor in St Bartholomew's Exchange: 1580–1676', *Medical History*, Supplement no. 11 (1991), 46ff. On nursekeepers, see Pelling, 'Nurses'.

35. See O. Hufton, 'Women without Men: Widows and Spinsters in Britain and France in the Eighteenth Century', *Journal of Family History*, 9 (1984), 360. Menstruating women could be seen as threatening contamination of both the sick, and of religious ceremonial: C. Rawcliffe, *The Hospitals of Medieval Norwich* (Norwich, 1995), p. 102. For age-restrictions on entry to almshouses, see Hudson and Tingey, *Records*, vol. 2, p. cxv.

36. F. P. Wilson, *The Plague in Shakespeare's London* (Oxford, 1927), pp. 65–6; T. R. Forbes, 'The Searchers', *Bulletin of the New York Academy of Medicine*, 50 (1974), 1032, 1034. For 'ancient' linked with 'eminent' and 'able' in respect of a master of apprentices, see 'Mr Clay', druggist, in CLRO, MC6/152B. See also Thomas, *Age and Authority*, pp. 7–8, 32; Pelling, 'Nurses'.

poor-relief authorities tended to employ younger, unmarried mothers for some of these tasks, a change with moral as well as economic implications, which needs to be explained.[37]

The census very much implies – and sometimes states – that women, and children doing similar work, like knitting and spinning, were the only means of support for many poor households. It does not affect this point that, even with the addition of a small weekly alms, this work often could not raise the household above subsistence level. The importance of women and children for (attempted) survival if not for prosperity appears to be reflected in the structure of the households of the poor. The pattern for English households in the pre-industrial period continues to be seen as simple, with rarely more than two generations under one roof. As already noted, it is increasingly allowed that, within this pattern, variety and flux can be found according to social and economic circumstances.[38] Disablement (mental and physical, all agegroups) is however very much a neglected factor in this context.[39] The elderly poor of Norwich conform to pattern in that, as indicated above, they are very rarely found living with their married children and grandchildren, even given a wide age range representing different stages in the life course. (Clearly, also, as previously indicated, Norwich's policies on settlement would discourage this.) However, it is possible that more complicated households were commoner in an urban population selected for poverty.[40] This is not to say that such households would be anything but small. Instead, the variations are lateral rather than generational, and the household usually retains the appearance of being nuclear, if not the reality.[41] It is perhaps not surprising to find apparently unrelated widows living together,

---

37. Mary Fissell, personal communication; see also her *Patients, Power, and the Poor in Eighteenth-Century Bristol* (Cambridge, 1991), pp. 67–8. I am grateful to Dr Fissell for allowing me to consult her as yet unpublished evidence on this point, which is also being investigated by Richard Smith and Samantha Williams (University of Cambridge): see R. M. Smith, 'Ageing and Well-being in Early Modern England: Pension Trends and Gender Preferences under the English Old Poor Law *c.* 1650–1800', in P. Johnson and P. Thane (eds), *History of Old Age and Ageing* (forthcoming).

38. See for example L. K. Berkner, 'The Stem Family and the Developmental Cycle of the Peasant Household: an Eighteenth-century Austrian Example', *American Historical Review*, 77 (1972), 398–418, esp. pp. 405–8; R. Wall, 'Regional and Temporal Variations in English Household Structure from 1650', in J. Hobcraft and P. Rees (eds), *Regional Demographic Development* (London, [1980]), pp. 89–113; R. M. Smith, 'Kin and Neighbours in a Thirteenth-century Suffolk Community', *Journal of Family History*, 4 (1979), 219–56; M. Chaytor, 'Household and Kinship: Ryton in the Late 16th and Early 17th Centuries', *History Workshop*, 10 (1980), 25–60; M. Anderson, *Approaches to the History of the Western Family, 1500–1914* (London, 1980); P. Laslett, 'Family, Kinship and Collectivity as Systems of Support in Preindustrial Europe: a Consideration of the "Nuclear Hardship" Hypothesis', *Continuity and Change*, 3 (1988), 153–75, esp. p. 154.

39. One exception is P. Rushton, 'Lunatics and Idiots: Mental Disability, the Community, and the Poor Law in North-east England, 1600–1800', *Medical History*, 32 (1988), 34–50, esp. pp. 39ff. Modern figures can be assumed to be minima in comparison with the early modern period. For morbidity comparisons including shorter- and long-term sickness using the *General Household Survey*, see Pelling, 'Illness among the Poor', pp. 277–8, 286 (67–8, 77).

40. Slack, *Poverty and Policy*, pp. 76–7, 84–5.

41. The challenging findings of T. Sokoll, 'The Pauper Household Poor and Simple? The Evidence from Listings of Inhabitants and Pauper Lists in Early Modern England Reassessed', *Ethnologia Europaea*, 17 (1987), 25–42, derive principally from late eighteenth-century data and appear incidentally to underestimate the information on family and housing given in the Norwich census (ibid., p. 30). I am grateful to Dr Sokoll for a copy of his article. See also his thesis, 'Household and Family among the Poor: the Case of Two Essex Communities in the Late Eighteenth and Early Nineteenth Centuries' (University of Cambridge PhD thesis, 1988), of which I have been unable to consult the published version (Bodium, 1993).

or older widows living with unmarried or deserted daughters and sometimes with the illegitimate children of these daughters.[42] (It perhaps needs stressing that disability could prevent offspring from leaving home, or possibly enforce their return.[43])

Rather more unexpected are the households consisting of a grandparent and a grandchild, both of them usually but not always female, and with the child of reasonable age, that is around ten or older. This does not suggest that the child was with the grandparent simply in order to be brought up, or to relieve pressure on the household of origin. Rather, it is hard to resist the impression that children of an age to be useful were distributed among those most in need of them, not merely for companionship but as a survival measure.[44] One such example is that of a couple called Trace, a man aged 80 and his wife aged 60. He was past work and deaf, she span white warp, and, aside from her work, their main advantage was that they had a life tenancy of their house. They had no alms, and were poor. With them lived a son's child aged ten, who also span.[45] This small household, of three people belonging to two generations, was thus more complicated than it would appear if fewer details were available about it. There would presumably be benefit to the child in learning the skills of the grandparents, especially the grandmother, unimpeded by the demands of other children. As well as his work, and services within the home, the Traces' grandchild would have the eyes, ears, and agility to act as their proxy in the outside world. It should be noted that the sex of such children was often unspecified; the census further records that (in contrast to male adults) male children were occupied in spinning and knitting as well as female. This suggests that in terms of the usefulness of children of this age, gender was a matter of indifference. A more striking example from the survival point of view is Alice Cotes, a widow of 92 unable to work, who had living with her a 'childes daughter' of 18 who knitted hose.[46]

It is important to stress that this sharing out of the able-bodied could extend to others apparently not members of the family. Elizabeth Cowes, a younger widow of 50 who span white warp, had one child, a daughter of 14 who lived not with her but with another widow called Haryson. The Cowes daughter cannot be identified, but another possible 'recipient' of such an arrangement is Elizabeth Tidemunde, a widow of 80, who lived with 'a gerle of 14 yere'; both span white warp. Of the Rudlandes, the husband had no occupation and did no work, and the wife (60) sold fish at the staithe and span; they lived with a 'mayd of 13 yer that work gyrth webe'. The poor condition of John Rudlande

---

42. Hufton, 'Women without Men'.

43. For example, Alice Waterday: Pound, *Census*, p. 57, and below, p. 162.

44. For further consideration of this point, see Pelling, 'Child Health'.

45. Pound, *Census*, p. 88. The Traces had been in Norwich for six years, having come from 'Walsam' (it is not clear when the child joined them). There are no others of the name in the census.

46. Ibid., p. 59. For other grandparents and grandchildren, see the Harvi couple (M aged 60, F the same: ibid., p. 81), who lived with an 'idle' daughter's child of ten; widow Helen Curson (66) and the Fakeners (M 80, F 60), who lived with 'a mayd' (26) surnamed Santri as well as a daughter's child of eight who then went to school (p. 78). For a household (M 40, F 64) probably formed by an 'unequal' remarriage and including a daughter's child of eight, see the Kyg couple (p. 74).

is perhaps indicated by the censustaker having first given him an age of 80, later altered to 60.[47] In some cases of disablement, the picture is even clearer: that of the blind Richard Sandlyng, for example, aged 54, whose household included a fatherless child of 12 who led him about. There are other examples of fatherless children in the households of the elderly poor, and it is probable that children like these might explain the apparent anomaly of so-called servants being present even in very poor households. Another good example involving disablement was a couple called Hales, both in their eighties and both 'not hable to worke', who had with them a 'mayd' of 18 who span and 'loke to them'. This couple was receiving a comparatively high level of alms relief – 12*d.* a week – and was still in extreme poverty, but the reason for the arrangement with the girl is nonetheless self-evident.

Older women could of course act in the same capacity. Elizabeth Petis, aged 68, 'very syk & feble', lived with a deserted wife, called Newman, of 40, who span and sewed and 'help women'.[48] Where poor households included a parish child or an almschild,[49] it is easy to imagine that a mutually beneficial arrangement had been made with the parish or the city authorities, but it is important to stress the possibility that the poor made arrangements with other poor people for the support of elderly people, as well as children, on what might be described as an exchange basis; and that the other parties might be from outside as well as inside the family. Where more property was involved, such arrangements sometimes surface in legal proceedings. An example from a rather later period, the 1650s, is Margaret Cully of Norfolk, a blind and aged widow who made over her estate of £40 in exchange for a guarantee of being 'kept' for the rest of her life. The beneficiary, apparently unrelated to her, first persuaded Timothy Cully to take her in and keep her, and then refused to pay him any proceeds of the estate.[50] Without knowledge of the initial transaction, this example might appear as a kind of kinship support. Such agreements emerge as a secularised version of the way in which widows used to make over their property to the church in exchange for maintenance, or as resembling maintenance agreements in general. Similar agreements relating to the poor were made between parishes, individuals, and the keepers of secularised lazarhouses, sickhouses, and houses of correction, involving the payment of lump sums.[51] Agreements of this essentially commercial kind were certainly made between individuals with respect to children, even the children of relatively poor families, and they may have been quite common with respect to the elderly as well.

47. Ibid., pp. 92, 81. For other possibilities, see the Skott and Barny couples, pp. 80, 81.

48. Ibid., pp. 70, 66, 47.

49. For examples see the widow Gaunte (60); the Cullingtons (M 56, F 50), a couple otherwise alone; and the widow Rowland (52), living with her daughter (17) and 'hir ward', Jone Esing: ibid., pp. 64, 39, 34.

50. D. E. Howell James (ed.), *Norfolk Quarter Sessions Order Book 1650–1657*, Norfolk Record Society XXVI (1955), p. 25.

51. On corrodies, see B. Harvey, *Living and Dying in England 1100–1540: The Monastic Experience* (Oxford, 1995); on maintenance agreements, see R. M. Smith, 'The Manorial Court and the Elderly Tenant in Late Medieval England', in M. Pelling and Smith (eds), *Life, Death and the Elderly: Historical Perspectives* (London, 1991), pp. 39–61. See also Pelling, 'Healing the Sick Poor', pp. 129–30 (94). For interesting variants, including 'pensions' negotiated by servants, see I. Chabot, 'Widowhood and Poverty in Late Medieval Florence', *Continuity and Change*, 3 (1988), 291–311.

In dealing with the complicated households that may have arisen as a result of poverty among the elderly, we have been dealing chiefly with women. The obvious reason for this is that men comprised only 37 per cent of the elderly population here being considered. However, it is interesting to look at the men in the light of Laslett's comment that older men were likely to live as lodgers or in institutions if they had no wives.[52] The number of elderly men without women among Norwich's poor was extremely small, being ten in all, or 5 per cent of the elderly men. Of these, three were living as single parents with children under 16. Another, a working cobbler aged 78, lived with another cobbler, his servant, whom he had taken on only four years before, that is when he, the cobbler, was 74. Of the men who were entirely alone, one was described as beside himself a little, that is mentally ill, and another as an evil husband, which presumably meant that he was a wastrel and improvident. Both characteristics could be regarded as substantial disqualifications for marriage, or remarriage. It is noticeable that the term widower is used only once in the census, in describing John Bacon, 'of 67 yeris, almost blynd, and doth nothinge, widower, and lyveth of his son that kepe a skole'. This situation of the older men among the poor suggests first, a studied avoidance of being left alone, and second, that this was mainly achieved by marriage or remarriage, often late in life.[53] Such an expedient would be facilitated by the strongly unequal sex ratio among those over 50. However, the evidence of the census suggests that even among the poor, older men tended to marry women very much younger than themselves, and that, more unexpectedly according to conventional assumptions, older women also made unequal marriages in terms of age, although to a much lesser extent. I should now like to look in more detail at the phenomenon of 'unequal' marriage as illustrated among the elderly of the census taken as a whole.

In the population of 533 old poor people identified in Norwich, there was a total of 130 marriages where one spouse was ten or more years older than the other (see Table 6.1). This constitutes a high proportion of the marriages, given the presence, among the group of 533, of 127 widows and of 58 other women without spouses. In many cases the age difference was so great that the younger spouse falls well outside the older agegroups, and would, if detached, seem to belong to a different phase of life altogether, of middle or even early middle age. In 71 per cent of the 130 marriages, it was the man who was the elder, and in these cases the age discrepancy tended to be greater. Over half of the older women were between 10 and 20 years older than their spouses, but with men, in spite of the effects of mortality, the majority were 20, 30 or even 40 years older than their wives. Even if the attributed ages were exaggerated in some cases, the perceived discrepancy asserts something about what contemporaries thought probable, especially given the assumption already mentioned,

52. P. Laslett, *Family Life and Illicit Love in Earlier Generations* (Cambridge, 1977), p. 200 (although institutions divided couples as well as taking in solitaries, see below, p. 153). See also Smith, 'Fertility, Economy and Household Formation', p. 608; R. Wall, 'The Residential Isolation of the Elderly: a Comparison over Time', *Ageing and Society*, 4 (1984), 483–503.

53. Pound, *Census*, p. 68. I hope to look further at the behaviour of widowers in an essay for a volume on widowhood to be edited by Sandra Cavallo and Lyndan Warner.

TABLE 6.1 *Unequal marriages and disability among the Norwich poor, 1570*

Spouse	10–19 yrs younger	20–29 yrs younger	30–39 yrs younger	40–49 yrs younger
Old men	40	39	7	6
Old women	21	15	1	1
Totals	61	54	8	7
Older spouse disabled	14	11	3	3
Younger spouse disabled	6	1	1	1
Both disabled	1	–	–	1
Totals	21	12	4	5

Source: Pound, *Census*.

that poor women must have aged in appearance earlier than men.[54] It is not possible to tell whether these unions among the poor were the result of marriage or remarriage, but remarriage is strongly suggested in some instances by the particular attribution of children, or the coincidence of young children and very aged wives. An example is the Coks, where the husband was 34, the child two, and the wife 62 years of age.[55] That the union might be comparatively recent, that is, during the later years of the elder spouse, is suggested by the age of the wife or the frequent presence in the household of very young children: for example, the Lekes, of whom the husband Valentine was 70, his wife Curstance (?Constance) 26, and the single child 'veri yonge'.[56]

Sometimes an incentive is suggested by the fact that the elderly spouse might have owned his or her own house. Twenty-five couples, of whom 33 individuals fall into the category of the elderly poor, were in their own homes. Another nine without spouses were similarly situated and tended to be older, including one very old man and several aged widows. Thus a total of 8 per cent of the elderly poor were owner-occupiers, although this conclusion must be heavily qualified by the fact that many of the houses were mortgaged or 'in purchase'. Age was not obviously compensated for by accumulation, since the proportion of owner-occupiers was the same as among the poor in general.[57]

54. The scope for very unequal marriages among adults younger than 50 is naturally limited, but analysis of the census population below this age gives a total of only 51 'unequal' marriages, nearly all of which (46) involved partners with 10–19 years between them. In 26 of the latter cases the man was the elder. In the few cases (five) where the age difference was over 20 years, the woman was the elder in all but one union, and remarriage is suggested in all five cases by the ages of the children. The censustakers' expectations in respect to the middle-aged as opposed to the elderly are perhaps indicated by the 'rounding' which resulted in 22 of the 46 couples being exactly ten years apart in age.

55. Another poor couple of the same name were apparently living in the same house, which was in purchase by the first couple. No relationship is stated. Pound, *Census*, p. 70.

56. Ibid., p. 30.

57. Ibid., p. 15.

It is noticeable that 'owner-occupiers' among the poor also tended to be those few who had elderly grandparents included in the household. Also suggestive is that only five of the 25 couples were 'equal' (having an age difference between them of less than 10 years). Over half of the 'house-owning' couples were unequal in age by 20 years or more. An interesting example is the Mordewes: William Mordewe was aged 70, blind, but still working as a baker. His wife Helen was 46 and there were two children aged ten and four. The family lived not in 'their' (as used elsewhere in the census) but in '*his* own house'.[58]

In general, however, the impression is one of a balance of abilities and disabilities with a view to common survival, the main property of the poor being the attributes of their own bodies – their ability to work – rather than material, for example house-ownership. The house-owners were very much in the minority. Disability or sickness, on the other hand, was a feature of one in three of the 'unequal' marriages, a rather higher proportion than among the elderly poor as a whole.[59] The problems and limited means of survival of the poor are succinctly suggested by the Wytherlys: John Wytherly was 80 but 'in worke', his wife Elizabeth was 40 and 'a lame woman', and there were three children aged between seven and three months. They had 3*d*. in alms a week and were 'veri pore'.[60]

The census upon which this chapter is based is not of course a moving picture but a snapshot taken at a particular time. Nonetheless, the cross-section it offers is unusual in yielding considerable information on the past history of the individuals it lists. Given the difficulties of finding out about poor households, this information is worthy of investigation. Three main conclusions are suggested. The first relates to the situation of children and old people and hence to the structure of the small, poor household of this date. As has been shown elsewhere, the census took it for granted that even very young children could be employed, or at least productive while they were being taught a skill.[61] More importantly in the present context, there are many respects in which the alertness, mobility, and dexterity of children of pre-apprentice age would have added greatly to the viability of a poor household, especially an elderly household with disabled members. The presence of such a person might mean the difference which would have made it possible for an aged person to remain in his or her own home. The sharing out of children among older households has been noticed in the post-industrial period, and oral evidence can be found for it in the present day.[62] This phenomenon may have a great many different causes, but in the particular circumstances we are now considering, some of its functions at least seem clear.

The second conclusion relates to the role of work in the lives of old people in towns, and the third, like the first, to the structure of poor households, and

---

58. Ibid., p. 83. My italics.
59. Pelling, 'Illness among the Poor', pp. 282–3 (75–6).
60. Pound, *Census*, p. 66.
61. See also Pelling, 'Child Health', p. 141 (110) and *passim*.
62. See ibid., p. 146 (115), n. 46; M. Anderson, *Family Structure in Nineteenth-Century Lancashire* (Cambridge, 1971), pp. 149, 165; G. Belfiore, 'Family Strategies in Essex Textile Towns, 1860–1895: the Challenge of Compulsory Elementary Schooling' (University of Oxford DPhil thesis, 1986), chaps 3 and 4.

in particular unequal marriage. Both work in old age, and unequal marriage, can be seen as means to an end – survival – and they are closely connected in that one could be a reason for the other. Given the necessity for both men and women to continue working, work and marriage or remarriage should certainly not be seen as alternative choices, even though women and children can be found supporting unemployed men. When historians and others have considered marriage and remarriage in an economic context, the emphasis has usually been on younger agegroups, rural societies, or, more frequently, motives to do with the presence of property, not its comparative absence.[63] However, Steve Hindle has recently considered attitudes among parish elites tending to inhibit marriage among the poor in the first half of the seventeenth century; these, I would argue, tend to relate to the desire to prevent settlement, as well as to housing scarcity and the likelihood of dependent children (possibly as a result of remarriage). Hindle's study perhaps confirms the suggestion made earlier, that marriage was one exception to the adoption by poor-law authorities of expedients used by the poor themselves. Janet Griffith has found for rural Hertfordshire that, contrary to expectation, remarriage was more rapid among landless men than among the propertied. She also concluded that rapid remarriage, especially among poor, older, widowed men, was more common between 1560 and 1699 than during the eighteenth century. She was, however, considering remarriage as conforming to the accepted English pre-industrial norm in which the couple were similar in age, or the woman a little older. Thus she suggested that the possibility of poor relief might reduce the incidence of remarriage, because the disadvantage of remarriage was that the new partner would also be old and as likely to become ill or disabled.[64] Similarly, it has been assumed that marriage between elderly partners was likely to take place to some extent because of the desire for companionship. This would seem to imply that marriage or remarriage between poor people of disparate ages would be unlikely – because disparate ages would rule out companionship, and poverty would rule out property gain. However, these assumptions leave out the likely high incidence and disastrous consequences of disability for the isolated individual, and the poor's dependence upon forms of work by some member of the household, even if young or very old.

63. In general see J. Dupâquier, E. Hélin, P. Laslett, M. Livi-Bacci and S. Sogner (eds), *Marriage and Remarriage in Populations of the Past* (London, 1981). V. Brodsky, 'Widows in Late Elizabethan London: Remarriage, Economic Opportunity and Family Orientations', in L. Bonfield, R. Smith and K. Wrightson (eds), *The World We Have Gained* (Oxford, 1986), pp. 122–54, effectively stresses opportunities for some (more prosperous) urban women and suggests that very poor widows rarely remarried (p. 128). Cf. S. Grigg, 'Toward a Theory of Remarriage: a Case Study of Newburyport at the Beginning of the Nineteenth Century', *Journal of Interdisciplinary History*, 8 (1977), 183–220, esp. p. 193. See also B. J. Todd, 'The Remarrying Widow: a Stereotype Reconsidered', in Prior, *Women in English Society*, pp. 54–92. Jeremy Boulton's 'London Widowhood Revisited: the Decline of Female Remarriage in the Seventeenth and Early Eighteenth Centuries', *Continuity and Change*, 5 (1990), 323–55, presents findings for London populations poorer than Brodsky's, but see the reply by B. Todd, 'Demographic Determinism and Female Agency: the Remarrying Widow Reconsidered . . . Again', *Continuity and Change*, 9 (1994), 421–50. See also S. J. Wright, 'The Elderly and the Bereaved in Eighteenth-century Ludlow', in Pelling and Smith, *Life, Death and the Elderly*, pp. 102–33.

64. See above, p. 135; S. Hindle, 'The Problem of Pauper Marriage in Seventeenth-century England', *Transactions of the Royal Historical Society* (forthcoming); J. D. Griffith, 'Economy, Family and Remarriage: Theory of Remarriage and Application to Preindustrial England', *Journal of Family Issues*, 1 (1980), 479–96. I am grateful to Steve Hindle for an advance copy of his essay, and to Roger Schofield for access to the last reference.

The high incidence of unequal marriage among the poor in Norwich, and the scarcity of old men on their own compared with women, suggests more than just unequal demographic survival between the sexes. Taking Thomas's figure[65] of a total of 454 marriages among those given an age in the census, the 130 and 51 unequal marriages among those 50 and over and the under-fifties respectively gives a proportion of nearly 40 per cent unequal marriages among the poor as a whole, with nearly 72 per cent of these unequal marriages occurring among the elderly poor. At this point it may be reiterated that the census represents about a quarter of Norwich's estimated native-born population. Conditions in large towns may have created both greater opportunities, and greater incentives, for these unions, among the former being the possible surplus of younger women. However, it must not be forgotten that older women were apparently able to marry younger men.[66] Among the poor, motives to do with entry to a craft are not likely to have been important, house-ownership is likely to have been minimal, and a younger man would not have established settlement by such a marriage. Marriages between elderly spouses of similar ages undoubtedly also occurred, but there are clearly advantages, in the context of survival, in matching an older with a younger spouse. The younger spouse could also be facing problems of survival (including the possibility of making an 'equal' marriage) because of disablement, young children, or lack of work. It would therefore be more appropriate to suggest that such marriages be called complementary, or symbiotic, rather than unequal. This argument would be compatible with the general finding that remarriage was more common in towns than in rural areas – bearing in mind that all unions were more likely to be broken in towns by a higher level of mortality. Remarriage, like the sharing-out of children (related and unrelated), complicates poor households without necessarily making them larger. (Households transferring children of course become smaller.) These expedients add a modification to the idea of life-cycle poverty, which sees support as required by age-related crises in the standard course of family development. It is usually assumed that disparate marriages of this kind were disliked by church and state and subject to popular disapproval. It is possible, however, that during the period in question, the late sixteenth and early seventeenth centuries, they were tolerated among the poor, both by the poor themselves and by authority; and that the association of such unions with the poorer classes and their circumstances might be one reason why they came to be so disliked at the end of the seventeenth century. At the same time remarriage itself declined in incidence, which may have been related to this effect. As the condition of the poor of the census shows, such marriages must be regarded as a partial expedient rather than as a solution to the problems of the poor, and for a significant proportion of elderly women even this expedient was not available.

65. Thomas, *Age and Authority*, p. 42.

66. This point is stressed, in respect of the census, by Thomas, ibid. Wall has found 'a significant number' of marriages characterised by major age differences in early modern listings; Goldberg, while placing emphasis on companionate marriage, finds a similar phenomenon for the medieval period, with somewhat greater age differences in rural areas: P. J. P. Goldberg, *Women, Work, and Life Cycle in a Medieval Economy: Women in York and Yorkshire c. 1300–1520* (Oxford, 1992), pp. 226–7, 328. See also, with reference to the Norwich census, p. 273.

In this discussion the term 'strategies' has been avoided: following Hufton and others, 'expedient' has been used instead, in order to reduce the connotation of deliberate (and free) choice.[67] The census hints at causes but it cannot, of course, convey inside information on the motivation and decisions of the poor themselves. These remain a matter of inference. In many respects the expedients discussed here may have been common, rather than lasting, solutions. The census only looks like a still picture: quite apart from any interference by the authorities, its population is in reality depicted in a continual state of movement and change. Helpful young children became older and presumably sought employment in service, leaving the older person alone again; the older spouse of a symbiotic marriage died, or became bedridden and incapable of work; younger spouses had more children, became disabled, or lost their employment. Few expedients could last for long or be relied upon, as indeed is indicated by the census itself, with its depressing repetition of 'pore' and 'veri pore'.

As a major urban centre with innovative social policies, Norwich offers a possibly unique opportunity of investigating the circumstances of the elderly poor of this period. However, there must be limitations to the representativeness of Norwich's elderly poor, imposed by the particular socio-economic context. As the second city after London, a long-standing focus of the textile industry, and a developing centre of consumption, Norwich may have presented particular features with respect to employment, in particular that of women and children. Although 'in decline' in the 1570s, Norwich could be seen as already having characteristics which were to develop in lesser centres at a later date.[68] Nonetheless, it is worth underlining the role of work in the lives of older women in Norwich. Even though many of them may have worked from home, there is little conformity to the pattern observed in some industrial urban contexts, in which the older woman or widow joined a son or daughter's family out of necessity and earned her place by minding house and children while the younger woman (or widower with children) went out to work. Similarly, disability did not mean the end of work for elderly women; and while profound disability may have led to changes in the composition of households, these did not usually include the older woman's joining the son or daughter's household. Norwich poor-law practice mirrored this situation in the stress it laid on putting even the elderly poor to work. At the same time, the patchwork nature of employment among the elderly was compatible with poor-law practices in which employment and relief were not mutually exclusive.

In what the poor tried to do for themselves to meet the constantly changing circumstances threatening their survival, and in the schemes which the Norwich authorities attempted to impose on them, institutions played a relatively minor role. Except for a select few, there was no institutional solution available when all else had failed. Instead, institutions provide another example of the way in which it was the resources of the community itself which were drawn

---

67. Hufton, 'Women without Men', p. 363. See also the criticism of T. Fox, '"Traditional Marriage": an Image or a Reality? A Look at Some Recent Works', *Journal of Family History*, 10 (1985), 206–11.
68. Cf. Anderson, *Family Structure*; Belfiore, 'Family Strategies'.

upon – particularly, as already indicated, the poor themselves. In Norwich, as elsewhere at this period, there seems to have been a striking discrepancy between the number of elderly poor in need of help, and the amount of institutional provision for them. Norwich's Great Hospital, for example, refounded under municipal control after the Dissolution, was not reserved for the elderly infirm but took in poor of all ages who were 'unable to live', even children; the numbers involved grew only very slowly from 40 to around 90 after 1630. The work principle was reinforced both within the hospital and outside it: hospital inmates were expected to do what they could, and it was city policy usually to admit either husband or wife of a poor couple, not both. A much smaller hospital, the Normans, functioned for much of the sixteenth century as a refuge and source of outrelief for old women, but lost this specific role in the 1560s. It was eventually appropriated for regulating the able-bodied rather than relieving the aged.[69] *All* expedients being discussed here still failed to provide for many older widows and spinsters, some of them disabled, who were left stranded and alone.[70]

More attention should perhaps be given to different forms of subsidy practised by municipal authorities, in the form of housing in city property, or minor forms of employment. The census locates a significant number of the poor already in *ad hoc*, subsidised city or parish housing.[71] The Norwich poor-relief schemes in general followed the lines thrown up by the census itself – that is, the main stress was on putting the poor to work, whatever their age. There was no question of an age of retirement, and the elderly disabled were also expected to work according to their capacity. The kinds of work and work-training involved were closer to the work of women than to the work usually done by adult men, although allowance should be made for the predominance in Norwich of the textile trades. Even in institutions, the number of poor who were expected to be able to do nothing at all was very small. In all areas of poor relief Norwich followed the practice of employing the poor to help the poor. Thus even in the hospital many of the inmates were expected to do work such as cobbling, sewing, and washing for the institution. Similarly, poor women, many of them elderly, were extensively used in medical poor relief both to treat and nurse the sick poor. There was therefore a certain consistency between Norwich's poor schemes and the expedients followed by the poor, in that the problem of the elderly was one of employment rather than relief.

How adequate this approach was is another matter. On the theoretical level, it has been noted that policy at this period was aimed not so much at independent economic viability for the individual as at eliminating idleness.[72] This was

69. W. K. Jordan, *The Charities of Rural England 1480–1660* (London, 1961), pp. 116–20; W. L. Sachse (ed.), *Minutes of the Norwich Court of Mayoralty 1630–1631*, Norfolk Record Society XV (1942), p. 162. The census appears to list women (not all aged) and a few children as 'in the Normans', but the listing is slightly ambiguous: Pound, *Census*, pp. 91–2. See also Pelling, 'Older Women', p. 164.

70. Cf. J. E. Smith, 'Widowhood and Ageing in Traditional English Society', *Ageing and Society*, 4 (1984), 429–49, esp. p. 440. See also Pelling, 'Older Women'.

71. See Pound's full analysis: *Census*, pp. 13–15 and Appendix VIII (housing occupied by the poor owned by aldermen or common councillors).

72. Slack, *Poverty and Policy*, p. 130.

underlined in humanist theory, for example by Vives, who, following Pauline precedent, advocated the earning of bread according to health and age. The elderly, or the dull of intellect, could 'in the last resort' be given a range of arduous and less arduous jobs defined by the short period required for learning them: digging, drawing water, sweeping, pushing a barrow, ushering in court, carrying messages and letters, or driving horses in relays. Vives also made firm recommendations for hospitals, stressing that even the blind, men and women, could do useful work, saving them from pride and listlessness: 'no one is so enfeebled as to have no power at all for doing something'.[73] The census, taken just before the implementation of Norwich's poor-relief schemes, reveals some of the expedients adopted by the elderly poor themselves, as well as the inadequacy of what they were then receiving in alms according to traditional forms of charity.

73. Vives in Salter, *Some Early Tracts*, pp. 13, 15–16.

CHAPTER SEVEN

Older Women: Household, Caring and Other Occupations in the Late Sixteenth-century Town

As an historical actor, the older woman is perhaps more subject to stereotyping than any other.[1] She is able to achieve identity only if accused as a witch, or, more dimly, as a passive recipient of poor relief. Sometimes she gains brief authority as a witness in court, or fleeting notoriety as a scold, but in such contexts she is generically a woman, rather than specifically a woman of a certain age. Retrospectively, women of some substance can achieve a certain dignity as widows; the poor old woman, when she is visible at all, appears as either embittered, or helpless, or both. This is in spite of the fact that pre-industrial society had some use for the older woman at the level of wage-labour, albeit that the functions allocated to her were often double-edged, showing her to be as expendable – or at least replaceable – as she was useful. Some of these women – 'sober, ancient matrons', with 'ancient' carrying some of the connotations of the 'ritual strength' usually attributed to older men – may have been regarded as having the 'manly-hearted' character made most explicit, paradoxically enough, in respect of the early modern midwife. The midwife's work could not have been more 'womanly', but she had a public identity akin (although hardly equal) to that of men. Midwifery was identified long ago by Alice Clark as 'the most important public function exercised by women'.[2]

Twentieth-century typology does of course include a strong older female figure who might be seen also as matrilineal. The famous studies of families in

This chapter has been wholly rewritten and expanded from part of a paper first given in Oxford in June 1990. I am grateful to those present for their comments. Other sections of the Oxford paper, complementary to this chapter, have appeared as the essay 'Thoroughly Resented? . . .' cited in the first footnote.

1. In general, see the introduction, and references there cited, to M. Pelling and R. M. Smith (eds), *Life, Death and the Elderly: Historical Perspectives* (London, 1991), pp. 1–38. See also Pelling, 'Thoroughly Resented? Older Women and the Medical Role in Early Modern London', in L. Hunter and S. Hutton (eds), *Women, Science and Medicine 1500–1700* (Stroud, 1997), pp. 63–88. For important points of comparison, see P. Sharpe, 'Literally Spinsters: a New Interpretation of Local Economy and Demography in Colyton in the Seventeenth and Eighteenth Centuries', *Eco. Hist. Rev.*, 45 (1991), 46–65.

2. A. Clark, *Working Life of Women in the Seventeenth Century* (1919; London, 1982), p. 242. Clark's choice of language is particularly apposite. See M. Wiesner, 'The Midwives of South Germany and the Public/Private Dichotomy', in H. Marland (ed.), *The Art of Midwifery: Early Modern Midwives in Europe* (London and New York, 1993), pp. 77–94. On the manly-hearted midwife, see H. Marland, '"Stately and Dignified, Kindly and God-fearing": Midwives, Age and Status in the Netherlands in the Eighteenth Century', in Marland and Pelling, *Task of Healing*, pp. 271–305.

the East End of London in the 1950s by Young and Willmott, and of old people by Townsend, were concerned to counter the prejudiced view of working-class life as inadequate and uncaring.[3] Although these images of working-class kinship and solidarity were readily dismissed as atypical, one image which stuck was that of the working-class matriarch, the 'Mum' whose presence in the neighbourhood (definitely not in the home of her son or daughter) was such a source of strength and support for her married daughters in particular. However, Mum's durability, for these male authors, was based not on any role in the workplace but on its perceived opposite: the continuity of interest and responsibility for women represented by their families. For men, by contrast, retirement was a disaster: it was too difficult for them to adjust to circumstances so different from identities based on work outside the household. In spite of the positive tone of the East End studies, their effect has been criticised as perpetuating an individualistic focus on women's relational role within the family and at home.[4] There is a family resemblance between the East End studies and the much-noted findings of Anderson for the nineteenth-century industrial town of Preston, although Anderson stresses co-residence. His study, in seeking to demonstrate the perpetuation of kinship links after migration to such towns from the country, saw the older woman as taking a home- and childminding role which allowed the younger woman, her daughter or daughter-in-law, to go out to work.[5]

In general, however, late-twentieth-century society seems to shy away from focusing on the post-menopausal woman whose children have left home. Instead, there is, as in the early modern period, a preoccupation with weakness and dependency. Attention is currently drawn to the 'oldest old', the increasing proportion of those over 85, an agegroup dominated by women.[6] In this context, the woman in her fifties and sixties has a muted identity as a daughter, the only one available to care for her aged mother (and possibly also her own husband). Strenuous efforts are made to achieve recognition for this caring role, and an identity in the world of work for such carers, but these meet with little success. There is an obstinate refusal to conflate caring about, and caring for: the first concept honours relationships, but is informal, unpaid, open-ended, private, and divorced from economic calculations. The second is rationed, perceived as expensive, and public. In gender terms, there are of course considerable overlaps, since both functions are of low status and largely performed by women. The need to escape these dilemmas has led to so-far-unsuccessful suggestions that the problematic term 'caring' be replaced by some other, such as 'tending'.

3. M. Young and P. Willmott, *Family and Kinship in East London* (1957; London, 1987); P. Townsend, *The Family Life of Old People* (London, 1957).

4. J. Seabrook, *What went Wrong? Working People and the Ideals of the Labour Movement* (London, 1978), esp. pp. 122–6; idem, *Mother and Son: An Autobiography* (London, 1979). Cf. J. Swindells, 'Hanging up on Mum or Questions of Everyday Life in the Writing of History', *Gender and History*, 2 (1990), 68–78.

5. M. Anderson, *Family Structure in Nineteenth-Century Lancashire* (Cambridge, 1971); for a comment see the essay review by M. B. Katz, *Journal of Social History*, 7 (1973), 86–92.

6. This term was coined in America in 1984: R. Suzman and M. W. Riley, 'Introducing the Oldest Old', *Milbank Memorial Fund Quarterly*, 63 (1985), 182, 180. Interestingly, as the authors note (p. 184), there was in this special issue no single paper devoted to women.

In terms of affective relationships, studies from Townsend's onwards have pointed both to the role of older men in caring for their spouses, to inhibitions on certain caring relationships (for example daughter–father), and to situations showing the difference between moral responsibility for a dependent person, which might be taken by one relative, and caring for that person physically, which might be done by someone else. Such complexities have however done little to erode the standard equations between gender and caring.[7]

In what follows I wish to explore some of these issues by examining the households and occupational profile of older women in the late sixteenth century – something made possible by an unusual, if not unique source, the Norwich census of the poor of 1570. While not wanting to strain a comparative point, I would like the East End studies to be borne in mind for a number of reasons. Primarily, I think it is a useful method of examining our own preconceptions at the same time as asking questions of the historical evidence. It is also one way of approaching, with all due caution, the vexed issue of *longue durée* with respect to gender issues. Specific points of comparison include the following: first, both the communities in question are highly urban, but are (for observers at least) on a comparatively human scale. Secondly, the people concerned are all poor. Thirdly, these people are given their identities by outside observers with social policy concerns who were male. Fourthly, the proportion of those aged 60 and over in Great Britain in the 1950s was about the same, between 14 and 16 per cent, as those of this agegroup in the Norwich census population of 1570. This contrasts with the Wrigley and Schofield estimate for the English population of 1571 (based largely on rural parishes) of 7 per cent.[8] There are of course structural fallacies here, in that the Norwich population was one selected for poverty and deficient in certain of the younger agegroups; but it does at least mean that there are not the extravagant differences in the presence of elderly people associated with the twentieth-century demographic shift. Fifthly, the East End studies usefully stress both the problems of defining households in crowded and ill-housed urban communities, and the vital nature of the links *between* households, as opposed to within them. In respect of links between households, the East End studies contrast somewhat with our view of the early modern period, in that the links uncovered in the East End relate mostly to the extended family of more than two generations. Historians of early modern urban life increasingly focus on the importance of neighbourhood associations rather than kinship. Lastly, as already indicated, the East End studies especially celebrate older women, while concentrating on the nuclear family of the daughter or son. Influenced by anthropological work on non-western communities which would also be seen as poor, the authors gave to the wife's mother a crucial role. At the same time, however, this important figure is not approached

---

7. The modern literature on caring is large, but see C. Ungerson, 'The Language of Care: Crossing the Boundaries', in idem (ed.), *Gender and Caring. Work and Welfare in Britain and Scandinavia* (Hemel Hempstead, 1990), pp. 8–33; J. Lewis and B. Meredith, *Daughters Who Care* (London, 1988), esp. pp. 1–8; J. Finch, *Family Obligations and Social Change* (Cambridge, 1989), pp. 26–30. The cover chosen for Finch's book is a striking portrait of four female generations.
8. Pelling, 'Illness among the Poor', p. 278 and Table 2 (69, 71).

directly – she looms, but her own situation is relatively ill-defined. Later commentators detected a tendency in these studies to lump the later years together indiscriminately.[9]

Most significantly in the present context, the aspect of Mum's situation which is given least definition in the East End studies is whether she works or not and if so, what at. It could also be noted that not a great deal of attention is paid to the daughter's work. Stress is rather placed on the continuity between whatever work the adult daughter did do, and her work in the home. In this way the daughter, like the mother, will be at an advantage compared with her husband once he retires. Mum's employment situation is even less defined, but the support roles attributed to her mean that, in spite of her omnicompetence, it would hardly be possible for her to be absent from her house for any length of time during the day. For that matter, if she worked at home it could only be in some job that allowed interruption. In spite of the temporal distance between them, the attributes, present and absent, of this matriarchal stereotype can suggest both continuities and discontinuities with respect to women's work when placed alongside the working poor women identified in sixteenth-century Norwich.

The Norwich census provides an extremely rare opportunity for identifying the household situation and occupations of older women – as attributed to them by male writers.[10] (The latter proviso is true of virtually all early modern records, but has a particular pertinence in the present case.) Normally, sources do not give the ages of women, and these are difficult to determine even when reconstitution is an option.[11] As Barbara Todd and others have shown, it is usually much more rewarding to discuss widows, since widows have a legal and occupational salience denied to women of any other status.[12] Unfortunately, it is rarely possible to distinguish older widows from younger, an important issue

9. L. E. Troll, 'The Family of Later Life: a Decade Review', *Journal of Marriage and the Family*, 33 (1971), 276.

10. I share the indebtedness of later historians to Clark, *Working Life of Women*. In the growing literature on women's work in the early modern period, the later agegroups are not often specifically dealt with. An exception is P. Earle, 'The Female Labour Market in London in the Late Seventeenth and Early Eighteenth Centuries', *Eco. Hist. Rev.*, 42 (1989), 345–6. See also Pelling, 'Old Age, Poverty, and Disability', pp. 83–4 (142–4). Of particular value in the present context are B. Todd, 'Widowhood in a Market Town: Abingdon, 1540–1720' (University of Oxford DPhil thesis, 1983); M. Prior, 'Women and the Urban Economy: Oxford 1500–1800', in idem (ed.), *Women in English Society 1500–1800* (London and New York, 1985), pp. 93–117; S. J. Wright, '"Churmaids, Huswyfes and Hucksters": the Employment of Women in Tudor and Stuart Salisbury', in L. Charles and L. Duffin (eds), *Women and Work in Pre-Industrial England* (London, 1985), pp. 100–21; M. E. Wiesner, *Working Women in Renaissance Germany* (New Brunswick, 1986); M. Kowaleski, 'Women's Work in a Market Town: Exeter in the Late Fourteenth Century', in B. A. Hanawalt (ed.), *Women and Work in Preindustrial Europe* (Bloomington, IN, 1986), pp. 145–64; P. J. P. Goldberg, *Women, Work and Life Cycle in a Medieval Economy: Women in York and Yorkshire c. 1300–1520* (Oxford, 1992).

11. There are of course reservations to be expressed about the accuracy of ages given in the Norwich census. Nonetheless, they can be accepted for their approximate and also their comparative value: see Pelling, 'Old Age, Poverty and Disability', pp. 76–80 (135–6).

12. Todd, 'Widowhood.' On widows see also I. Blom, 'The History of Widowhood: a Bibliographic Overview', *Journal of Family History*, 16 (1991), 191–210; J. E. Smith, 'Widowhood and Ageing in Traditional English Society', *Ageing and Society*, 4 (1984), 429–49; L. Mirrer (ed.), *Upon My Husband's Death: Widows in the Literature and Histories of Medieval Europe* (Ann Arbor, MI, 1992); S. S. Walker (ed.), *Wife and Widow in Medieval England* (Ann Arbor, MI, 1993); C. M. Barron and A. F. Sutton (eds), *Medieval London Widows 1300–1500* (London and Rio Grande, 1994).

in periods of high adult mortality when young widows might be relatively com-mon.[13] Crude measures to do with ages of a woman's children are seemingly fallible in relation to poor populations, in that poor women seem to have had children (not necessarily their own) in their homes at a later stage of their own lives. For a later period, Sue Wright has demonstrated one way of getting round the problem of indeterminate age, by taking as her elderly population the long-term bereaved.[14] Both Wright and Todd make excellent use of the wills or in-ventories of widows, but these, like other attributes of widows which give them visibility in the historical record, are rarely available for very poor women. Sources giving the occupations of men usually do not give those of female householders, including widows.[15] Married women are in certain respects the least visible of any. Their husbands block the light and it is very difficult to dis-cover their ages or their true occupations.[16] For the sixteenth century onwards, historians have adopted the rule of thumb that women's work was increasingly confined to occupations which were an extension into the public arena, limited in scope, of tasks carried out in the household. This argument fits the known facts, and explains the invisibility of such work, but has a tendency to be circular. It is desirable, if possible, to particularise. Sicknursing (considered in detail in Chapter 8 in this volume) poses one kind of challenge: if there is such continuity between women's work inside and outside the home, did women go out to nurse the sick? If not, then what was the 'block' on the public performance of this most 'natural' of women's roles and did it always apply? Should we even assume the existence of a range of 'traditional' women's tasks which can be taken for granted then as now? If so, how would these break down at any given time into particular skills, and which of these could be sold outside the household? The Norwich census reveals some details of work women did purely for their families, but it provides a much greater body of information on paid work done by poor women, wives as well as widows, to keep their households alive.

In two earlier essays, reproduced in this volume, I looked at Norwich's population of elderly poor identified as a whole.[17] Their patterns of work, mar-riage and remarriage, household structure, and migration are seen as expedients aimed at survival in the presence of poverty, illness, and disability. The richness of the Norwich census allows these structural features to be explored in some detail.[18] Only an outline need be given here. The census recorded 2,359 men, women and children as belonging to approximately 790 households, selected

13. Todd, 'Widowhood', p. 137.

14. S. J. Wright, 'The Elderly and the Bereaved in Eighteenth-century Ludlow', in Pelling and Smith, *Life, Death, and the Elderly*, pp. 102–3, 105.

15. See however A. L. Erickson, *Women and Property in Early Modern England* (London and New York, 1993), pp. 14–15. P. Clark and J. Clark, 'The Social Economy of the Canterbury Suburbs: the Evidence of the Census of 1563', in A. Detsicas and N. Yates (eds), *Studies in Modern Kentish History* (Maidstone, 1983), Table 7.

16. Goldberg, *Women, Work, and Life Cycle*, p. 100; Todd, 'Widowhood', p. 84; M. Prior, 'Wives and Wills, 1558–1700', in J. Chartres and D. Hey (eds), *English Rural Society, 1500–1800* (Cambridge, 1990), pp. 201–25.

17. Pelling, 'Old Age, Poverty and Disability'; 'Illness among the Poor'.

18. Pound, *Census*. For an interesting discussion of the period of the census, see M. Roberts, 'Women and Work in Sixteenth-century English Towns', in P. J. Corfield and D. Keene (eds), *Work in Towns 850–1850* (Leicester, 1990), pp. 86–102.

for poverty but representing nearly a quarter of the native-born population of the city. As already indicated, its main abnormality is its low proportion of young people aged between 15 and 24.[19] As previously noted, its proportion of people aged 60 and over is about twice the estimated norm for the period. Adult women (aged 20 and over) outnumbered adult men by about three to two. There were 533 people definitely aged 50 and over, or 22.6 per cent of the census population, with women in about the same proportion (3:2) to men as among adults as a whole.[20] This predominance of women is characteristic of listings of the impotent poor, but is also found for major English towns from the later medieval period onwards.[21] Exceptions appear to be London and York around 1600, although a consciousness of being outnumbered by women was already developed in the minds of London men by the mid-seventeenth century.[22] Goldberg has persuasively suggested a chronology of shifts in urban sex ratios associated with economic change, but the late sixteenth century, which was in any case disrupted by plague and the crises of the 1590s, lacks definition and appears mainly as a phase of transition. Norwich's experience might well resemble that of London and York, but its total population can only be estimated and the sex ratio for any period is unknown.[23]

A vital factor affecting occupations, usually only glanced at by historians, is the force of disability. The Norwich census reminds us of the importance of this factor by giving details of state of health for men, women, and (to a lesser extent) children, and I have analysed these elsewhere: as might be expected, perceived sickness and disability increase towards the end of life, although also threatening the middle years to a significant extent. It is possible to estimate that a person aged 60 or over in Norwich stood between a one-in-three and a one-in-two chance of poverty at or after that age, and that, once aged, a poor person stood about a one-in-four chance of also being severely disabled. These are minimal estimates: the chances were in fact probably much worse than this.[24] The censustakers, like the poor themselves, took note only of levels of disability drastically affecting the capacity to work. However, for women especially, disability altered the extent of work done, rather than the fact of working. Very few older women are listed in the census as 'past work', and it is clear that such women had to be bedridden or otherwise totally disabled. A few were 'past work', yet still spinning.[25] There was no retirement from work, and little

19. Pelling, 'Old Age, Poverty and Disability', p. 77 (136–7). Also on the 'hole in the middle' characteristic of poor populations, see Clark and Clark, 'The Social Economy', p. 71.

20. Women are 61% of the whole adult group, and 63% of the older. Pelling, 'Illness among the Poor', Table 1 (70); idem, 'Old Age, Poverty and Disability', pp. 77, 97 (136, 143 n.31).

21. Clark and Clark, 'The Social Economy', p. 70; Goldberg, *Women, Work and Life Cycle*, pp. 288, 297ff, 342ff.

22. Goldberg, *Women, Work and Life Cycle*, p. 348; J. Graunt, *Natural and Political Observations . . . upon the Bills of Mortality*, 5th edn (1676), in C. H. Hull (ed.), *The Economic Writings of Sir William Petty*, 2 vols (New York, 1963–64), vol. 2, pp. 372–8, 386–6.

23. Pound, *Census*, p. 10, Appendix IX; Slack, *Impact of Plague*, p. 127; P. Corfield, 'A Provincial Capital in the Late Seventeenth Century: the Case of Norwich', in P. Clark and P. Slack (eds), *Crisis and Order in English Towns 1500–1700* (London, 1972), pp. 263ff.

24. Pelling, 'Illness among the Poor', pp. 282–3 (75–6).

25. For example Joan Brampton, a widow aged 74: Pound, *Census*, p. 69.

'unemployment' either, for older women, even if severely disabled.[26] There are of course ideological forces in action here, in that the authorities were concerned that the poor should not be idle even if they could not be self-supporting; with women there was the added concern that they should not be 'abroad in the streets'. The censustakers noted harlots, and other suspect women who were transient, but judgement was also passed on women who could be counted as resident poor.[27] An example of the non-approved woman was Katherine Bloker, 'nott maried ever, of 50 yer, that spynn white warpe when she wyll, & go abrode'; another was Margaret Fen, 'wedowe, of 60 yeris, a lame woman that worketh not but go about, & is an unruly woman'. The solution to Fen was to put her in the hospital.[28] Whether or not women could earn a *living* wage was in many respects secondary. Even so, the persistence of women in paid work is significant given the likelihood that older women, then as now, carried a heavier burden of disability than men even while living longer.[29]

Although it is recognised that little is known about the lives of women barely able to support themselves,[30] it is sometimes also assumed that extreme poverty, in terms especially of lack of goods, meant a minimum of household responsibilities for poor women. It is possible, of course, to make work simply by multiplying rooms and possessions, but this seems to me a far cry from the laboriousness of cooking, washing, sewing, caring, and cleaning in a dirty environment and in the absence of appropriate utensils, light, and water. Work is created by people eating, relieving themselves, menstruating, and getting ill, however 'simple' the surroundings. Moreover, Norwich's poor households, though not large, were more likely to involve a substantial amount of this kind of work for a greater proportion of the lives of poor women. This was in part an effect of other expedients adopted by the poor.

First, as examined in detail elsewhere, a surprising number of Norwich's elderly poor (taking 'elderly' in this case to mean those aged 50 and over) are recorded as married to a partner very different in age.[31] Overall, it was older men who were married to younger women, but the reverse was also true, only to a lesser extent. Among the poor as a whole, nearly 40 per cent of unions were between partners unequal in age (that is, an age difference of ten years or greater), of which over 70 per cent are to be found among those aged 50 and over. As already indicated, men were in the minority among the surviving elderly, but it is nonetheless striking that the number of elderly men living without women was very small, only 5 per cent of men aged 50 and over.[32]

26. For an example of a woman exhibited spinning with no hands and only one foot, see Wiesner, *Working Women*, p. 182; the Norwich equivalent may have been Elizabeth Mason 'of 80 yere, a lame woman of one hand, & spin & wynd with one hande': Pound, *Census*, p. 28.

27. For an in-between case in terms of residence, see Elizabeth Gaske, 'suspected of evell rule . . . & as she sayth she hath a dyseas in hyr leg': ibid., p. 78.

28. Ibid., pp. 26, 29.

29. In general see S. Payne, *Women, Health and Poverty: An Introduction* (Hemel Hempstead, 1991).

30. Todd, 'Widowhood', p. 337.

31. This paragraph is based on Pelling, 'Old Age, Poverty and Disability', esp. pp. 87–92 (147–51). On definitions of old age, see ibid., pp. 78–80 (137–8); Pelling and Smith, 'Introduction', pp. 5–8.

32. I hope to look more closely at the situation of poor widowers and others in a volume on widowhood being edited by Sandra Cavallo and Lyndan Warner.

Secondly, partly as a result of such unions, many of which must have been remarriages, many of the elderly were living with young children.[33] The 'empty nest' phenomenon that preoccupies late-twentieth-century commentary, and which to some extent encourages the use of older women as informal carers, was present among poor Norwich couples, but only to a limited extent, especially when the overall absence of adolescent children (which was more or less forced upon the poor) is taken into account. Of 215 couples of whom at least one spouse was 50 and over, two-thirds still had unmarried children in the house – although these could be various, including sometimes grandchildren, an alms-child they were looking after, or a poor maid or boy (it would be misleading to describe most of these as servants) looking after them. The possibility must also be envisaged that some of these unmarried children represent the survivors among those who had never been able to leave home because too severely disabled, mentally or physically. As the 'hole' in the census population implies, every effort was made to place even disabled young people in service or apprenticeship, but there must have been children whose survival represented long-term caring responsibilities for their mothers in particular. Such offspring are not easily identified, even in the Norwich census. Two possibilities are the 'long tyme syk' child, aged 12 or older, of the 54-year-old widow Johanna Welles; or the 44-year-old daughter, 'lame of bode', who was (still?) with her widowed mother, Katherine Waterday, aged 72.[34] Predictably, in the light of the above, the 'empty nest' couples tend to be closer together in age, although not necessarily aged as such. Nonetheless, for both the 'empty nest' couples and those with children, the phenomenon of unequal (or, preferably, symbiotic) marriage or remarriage does create differences with modern populations. In so far as such unions seem often to have been a symbiosis between the elderly, the disabled, and those burdened with children, they also involved continuing care responsibilities for women.

As already pointed out, a major advantage of the census is that it sheds some light on the work patterns of married women as well as widows. However, this is not to deny the importance of finding out more about poor widows, who, stereotypes apart, have their own problems of invisibility. The census amply illustrates the vulnerability of women to the combination of widowhood, poverty, and old age. If we turn to Pound's analysis[35] of marital structure for all those in the census aged 16 and over (a total of 1,433 individuals), 183 adults, or 12 per cent, are definitely identified as widowed. All of these are women: significantly, there is no category of 'widower' in Pound's own analysis. Besides the men who were married, there are a mere 30 'others'; the 'other' category for women is much larger (137). In addition, there are 46 deserted wives, of whom the

33. See Pelling, 'Old Age, Poverty and Disability', pp. 85–7 (145–6); for the poor as whole, see Pound, *Census*, pp. 16–17.

34. Pound, *Census*, pp. 49, 57. Welles had four older children also living with her, any of whom could have been the sick child meant.

35. With respect to ages, Pound's analyses included the round figure in the preceding rather than the ensuing decade. Although it causes problems of comparison, I have preferred the reverse, e.g. 50–59, rather than 41–50, on the grounds that someone described as 'around 50' is more likely to have belonged in age to the fifties than the forties. In what follows, those of unspecified age have been excluded.

highest proportion (taking into account how many women there were overall in a given agegroup) were aged between 31 and 40, the decade into which fell the highest proportion of women overall (25.23 per cent). For each decade from the age of 61 onwards, around half of women were widowed, these agegroups comprising 15 per cent of the total of 860 women aged 16 and over. Of those between 51 and 60, over one-third (36.1 per cent) were widowed; among the best-represented female agegroup (31–40), just over 15 per cent. Thus, presumed high adult mortality rates notwithstanding, the widowed (women only) do not exceed the married even – or perhaps, in the light of symbiotic marriage, especially – in this poor population until after the age of 60, although the proportion of 'others' must be noted as almost certainly including some widows as well as the never-married.[36]

Even given the phenomenon of symbiotic marriage, the situation of poor women in Norwich appears to bear out one enduring cliché, that older women found it more difficult to remarry than older men. At the same time, however, the Norwich census suggests reasons why this cliché should be re-examined to pay greater respect to decision-making by older women.[37] Of the total of 262 women over 50, calculation from Pound's analysis shows that 167, or 63.7 per cent, were spouseless, if all the 'others' are included.[38] If the calculation is remade for women 50 and over, 193, or 58.3 per cent of the total (331), were spouseless. This includes those whose husbands were away and providing no support, like Agnes Daniell whose husband Nicholas 'hath bene from hyr 1 quarter & comfort hyr with nothinge', or the 'skold' Agnes Gose whose husband was 'in the hospitall', or Margery Pallin, whose spouse was 'gon from hyr 6 yer, of whom she have no helpe'.[39] Although it is made clear that a husband might be away and still helping his wife (as the censustakers saw it), only a few possible cases of this type were noted. Examples among the younger couples are the husbandman Richard Rich, aged 35, who '[kept] not with his wyfe but at tymes & helpeth hyr lyttle', and Rafe Claxton, aged 43, 'botewright abrode at work, and comfort his wyfe to his poure'.[40] In some ways 'spouselessness' as evidenced by the census details offers a better definition of a woman's condition for present purposes than labels indicating marital status, as these tend to be deficient or ambiguous.[41]

It is much more difficult to decide whether a spouseless woman was living alone, or, if not alone, whether those around her or associated by the censustakers with her were dependants, sharers in the household with her, or isolated

36. Pound, *Census*, Appendix I.

37. For expansion of this point, see my paper 'Inequalities among the Poor: Men and Women in Early Modern Norwich', given at the ESSHC, Leeuwenhorst, May 1996, a revised version of which will appear in a volume on old age edited by Lynn Botelho and Pat Thane. On widows' decisions about remarriage, see B. Todd, 'Demographic Determinism and Female Agency: the Remarrying Widow Reconsidered . . . Again', *Continuity and Change*, 9 (1994), 421–50.

38. Pound, *Census*, Appendix I.

39. Ibid., pp. 49, 36, 81.

40. Ibid., p. 23.

41. In many documents 'wife of', or 'uxor', which was used for part of the Norwich census, is used of women known to be widows. Conversely, some poor women without visible husbands may have preferred to call themselves widows. See also the category of 'others' in Pound's analysis: ibid., Appendix I; and ibid., p. 7.

householders like herself. This issue is of course far more complicated than that of determining who shared the same roof, which might be of no significance at all. Among the Norwich poor, most roofs were shared. The censustakers were determined to find out not only how people were housed but also how people were supported and who was responsible for them, so the ambiguities found in most listings are kept to a minimum; they noted for example that the Whayberde couple, aged 40 and 26, with no children, 'have takyn in one Helen of Wyndham, wedow, about 40 yeris', or that the deserted wife Elizabeth Newman aged 40, left with two young sons, 'hav with her an olde wedow, Elizabeth Petis, of 68 yeris, veri syke & feble'.[42] Nonetheless, it is hard to decide on the significance of connectives like 'and' and 'also' between separately entered individuals, or between a group and an individual, who were recorded as under the same roof.[43]

This said, it is equally difficult to discover whether an isolated widow benefited by kinship or neighbourhood links outside her own household – or, whether, on the East End model, such a person benefited others.[44] Again, the census is unusually descriptive in this regard, albeit occasionally; Margaret Lamas, for instance, a widow aged 56, living alone but sharing a roof with two other poor widows, was 'a lame woman & worketh not but . . . now lyv upon hir fryndes'.[45] Of the spouseless older women, over one-third (127, or 38.4 per cent) were apparently living alone, of whom nearly two-thirds (79) were described as widows. Of the half-dozen or so elderly women described as 'never married', nearly all were alone; one, Katherine Downynge aged 60, lived with another 'never married' woman aged 40.[46]

Norwich's elderly poor, and the women among them, were scattered among the poor population as a whole, which formed a substantial proportion of the inhabitants of all but three of Norwich's city wards.[47] One cluster of lone women was located in the Normans, or Normanspitel, a group of buildings in Fyebridge, a ward in which Pound estimates 31 per cent of the population were poor.[48] One, a widow of 60 called Joan Bower, 'tend[ed] the allms' as well as spinning white warp. The 15 Normans women, many of whom were sick or disabled, seem to have lived each as a separate household; some worked, some were past work, and most but not all were elderly. Not all were alone: the younger ones lived with children, one aged 80 lived with 'a gerle of 14 yere', and another, aged 76, who was 'lame handad', lived with one of the oldest old, her husband, aged 88, 'nott hable to work & sykly'.[49] The Normans was reorganised specifically

42. Ibid., pp. 25, 47. The Petis entry was later crossed out.

43. I have usually taken these as separate households. Sometimes the connection may have been that of travelling to Norwich together.

44. An analysis of similar surnames, such as that carried out for Coventry, could not be attempted here. Phythian-Adams found putative links among craftspeople, even during crisis years, but the 'submerged' quarter of poorer households were 'very largely excluded' from such links: Phythian-Adams, *Desolation of a City*, pp. 154–7.

45. Pound, *Census*, p. 29. It is not of course clear who the friends were.

46. Ibid., p. 46.

47. Ibid., pp. 10–11. See also Phythian-Adams, *Desolation of a City*, pp. 163–6. On Norwich's topography, see Corfield, 'A Provincial Capital', p. 270.

48. Pound, *Census*, pp. 11, 91–2.

49. Ibid., pp. 11, 13, 91–2.

to support aged and infirm women in 1429; significantly, like many institutions of this type, it was diverted in 1571 from this purpose to more general uses as a bridewell.[50]

Whatever their invisible sources of support, the condition of many of the women living alone often emerges only too clearly. The censustakers did append to their entries a judgement as to the state of poverty of each household, but the litany of 'indifferent', 'poor' and 'very poor' is ultimately less revealing than the entries themselves. From the latter it is clear that of the widows living alone, just over one in five (20.2 per cent) were severely disabled, very ill, or permanently past work. However, among the others, including the deserted and the never-married, the proportion of those suffering disability was actually somewhat higher (32.5 per cent). As already suggested, their poor physical condition did not of course mean that these women were not working. Mental disability among elderly women, as opposed to moral defect, is referred to more rarely, or possibly by implication, as for Maud House, 'of 60 yere, a wedowe that is a desolete thinge & beggethe'.[51]

Among the spouseless who did not live alone, there is considerable variety with respect to living arrangements. The tendency of poor women to cluster together, noticed particularly by Hufton, is undoubtedly present, but what is also striking is the predominance of the mother–daughter link, marked in Willmott and Young's East End of the 1950s but little reflected there in co-residence.[52] Among the 64 older widows and other spouseless women who did not live alone, about half lived in specifically daughter or daughter-derived combinations; that is, with a daughter, or with a daughter (several deserted, one widowed, one noted as pregnant) plus the daughter's dependants, or with the daughter's dependants only.[53]

The remaining combinations tended to be with children of unspecified origin, although a few spouseless women lived with other, apparently unrelated adult women, and a few daughter combinations also involved such women. The husbands of both the daughters and the other adult women are conspicuously absent. The tendency for family responsibilities to revert to the older woman seems obvious, although it is important still to note that responsibility may have been two-way, if not in the other direction, given that in some cases the older woman was disabled. A marked instance is that of the heavily burdened Curstanc (?Constance) Harison, who at the age of 40 had been deserted by her husband, a hatter, leaving her with six children aged between one and 14.

50. W. K. Jordan, *The Charities of Rural England 1480–1660* (London, 1961), pp. 119–20; C. Rawcliffe, *The Hospitals of Medieval Norwich* (Norwich, 1995), chap. 2, pp. 153, 159; Pelling, 'Old Age, Poverty and Disability', p. 94 (153).

51. Pound, *Census*, p. 50. A younger widow, Thamison Pecke, is described as 'somewhat beside hyr selfe' (p. 62); another woman of 48, 'hyr husbond from hyr', was 'somewhat lunatick' (p. 73).

52. O. Hufton, 'Women without Men: Widows and Spinsters in Britain and France in the Eighteenth Century', *Journal of Family History*, 9 (1984), 361. For other observations of the mother–daughter link, see for example Goldberg, *Women, Work, and Life Cycle*, p. 141; Todd, 'Widowhood', pp. 86–7, 305; using wills, Todd finds a marked change in this direction in the later seventeenth century, prefiguring modern preferences. See Troll, 'The Family of Later Life', pp. 269–70, 277ff; Lewis and Meredith, *Daughters Who Care*.

53. It may be noted that many of the older women *not* called widows are recorded as having children.

In addition Constance was 'charged with hyr mother, Cysely Angell, of 80 yeris that lye bethred'. The Harisons may have sunk very suddenly into poverty: there were two servants (unusual in the census population) and the house, which they alone occupied, was 'in morgadge', but both Constance's family, and her mother (who had 4*d.* a week in alms) were 'veri pore'.[54]

Links specifically with sons were limited to: one woman who lived with a son and a daughter, three (all 60 or over and one of them disabled) who lived just with a son, and a small minority of eight women who followed the pattern more honoured in the breach than the observance, by being with a married son and his family. In at least one of these cases, that of Agnes Hollyns aged 80, the older woman had only recently arrived, and was to be sent away again by the city authorities.[55] In three other cases, the apparently dependent mother may in fact have had a caring role, temporary or otherwise, in spite of her age, since either her son or her daughter-in-law was sick or disabled.[56]

The primary occupations (taken as being those first mentioned) of married, spouseless, and lone women are set out in Table 7.1. The censustakers consistently use a syntax for occupations indicating that men *are* something, while women *do* something.[57] Similarly, a woman typically 'has no work', while a man has 'no occupation or exercise'. There are a few exceptions: women who acquired the status of being described as a spinster, a knitter, a lavender, a spinner of webbing, or of one who 'occupies sewing'. These might be stylistic aberrations, but they underline the fact that only two other women are similarly described: a tailor, and a midwife. Where all these women went to work remains unclear, but approval is reserved for those who neither 'went abroad', nor worked at home only for themselves. Thus Margaret Baxter, a widow of 70, 'spyn hir owne work in woollen & worketh nott'. The censustakers tended to use 'etc.' in relation to work most closely related to housework, indicating its unstructured and ill-defined character; this loss of work identity is also suggested by Agnes Welles, a widow of 76, who 'do no worke butt helpe others that have nede', or another Welles, Johanna, aged 54, 'that kepe wyves & spyn white warp at hom'.[58] On the other hand, although the recording of 'service' tasks outside the household is minimal even here, the census does imply some recognition of the role of such work, including caring, in the household economies of older women. The most remarkable feature is for how few cases the censustakers could find no work being done by an older woman.

---

54. Pound, *Census*, p. 60. As Wright has pointed out, servants were not luxuries in the early modern period and are to be found even in humble households: '"Churmaids"', pp. 102–3.

55. Pound, *Census*, p. 85. See also Agnes Barnarde, aged 60, 'to & fro' from her son's household over four years (p. 73).

56. See Margery Whittred (son in work but 'brusten'), Elizabeth Aldrich (son out of work, his wife lame and unable to work), and Marion Tyttle (son 'very syk & worke nott'): Pound, *Census*, pp. 45, 49, 30.

57. This was noted of the Norwich census by Michael Roberts in his valuable development of this issue: '"Words they are Women, and Deeds they are Men": Images of Work and Gender in Early Modern England', in Charles and Duffin, *Women and Work*, p. 139.

58. Pound, *Census*, pp. 28, 72, 49.

TABLE 7.1 *Norwich women aged 50 and over: primary occupations and household*

	Married women	Spouseless women	Women alone
spin white warp	53	25	50
spin & card	13	6	8
spin	6	2	8
spin white stuff	0	1	0
spin flax, linen	3	1	0
spin small stuff	2	1	4
spin stuff	0	1	0
spin tow	2	0	1
spin hemp	1	0	0
spin webbing	3	0	2
spin wool	2	2	4
spin white wool	0	0	1
spin mentle warp	10	3	2
spin mydleuse	0	0	1
spin cotton	2	1	0
twist yarn	0	0	1
weave lace	0	2	0
knit	3	4	8
knit hose	0	0	1
tailor	0	0	1
sow	4	1	1
work in twine	1	0	0
weave string	1	0	0
fill pipes	1	0	1
chop flocks	0	1	0
still aqua vitae	1	0	0
sell fish	1	0	0
dress meat	0	0	1
peddle	1	0	0
haberdashery	0	0	1
go on purchase	0	0	1
labour with husband	1	0	0
sell towels	1	0	0
wash, help to	3	2	0
help neighbours*	0	1	1
help to labour	0	0	1
midwife	0	0	1
keep	0	0	1
keep sick persons	1	0	0
tend alms	0	0	1

TABLE 7.1 *Cont'd*

	Married women	Spouseless women	Women alone
keep wives	1	1	1
keep women	0	0	1
unable	8	6	18
lack of work	3	2	6
not stated	6	2	4
Totals	134	65	132

* includes helping 'others'

Note: Each woman has been counted once. Married women are those living with their husbands, with or without children, etc. Some spouseless women had husbands alive, but absent.

Source: Pound, *Census*.

Given the dominance of spinning, especially of white warp, the differences between the three groups of older women in Table 7.1 are not marked.[59] More women who were alone, as we have already seen, were incapacitated for work, partly because of greater age. Additionally, lone women were slightly more likely to have no work. On the other hand, the occupations of the lone women were somewhat more diverse than those of the other groups; it is perhaps suggestive that the two older women with the most 'manly' work identity, the tailor and the midwife, belong to this group. That midwives were not necessarily widows rather than married women only underlines the point about recognition.[60] The spouseless had the least varied occupations, and are not represented at all among the food, drink, and petty retail employments.[61] Although the numbers are small, it seems reasonable to regard this group as the most hampered and least mobile of the three, with the important exception of those suffering greater disability among the lone women. The caring occupations are best represented among the lone women, although one of all three groups 'kept wives' and it was a married woman who 'kept sick persons'. The latter however, Grace Tooke, had a 'very syk' husband aged 80; she also spun wool. The censustakers clearly

59. Using Pound's figures, 33.5% of all poor women over the age of 20 spun white warp: *Census*, Appendix IV. In all three groups of those 50 and over, the proportion was slightly higher, at 39.2%, 38.5%, and 37.8% respectively. On women, wage labour, and textiles at this period, see Clark, *Working Life of Women*, chap. IV; M. E. Wiesner, 'Spinsters and Seamstresses: Women in Cloth and Clothing Production', in M. W. Ferguson, M. Quilligan, and N. J. Vickers (eds), *Rewriting the Renaissance* (Chicago, 1987), pp. 191–205. Anderson's Preston was also a textile town; on the later history of women in textile towns, see also Sharpe, 'Literally Spinsters'; G. Belfiore, 'Family Strategies in Essex Textile Towns, 1860–1895: the Challenge of Compulsory Elementary Schooling' (University of Oxford DPhil thesis, 1986).

60. For recent work on midwives, see Marland, *Art of Midwifery*; A. Wilson, *The Making of Man-Midwifery: Childbirth in England, 1660–1770* (London, 1995).

61. On these see Clark, *Working Life of Women*, chap. V; M. Wiesner, 'Paltry Peddlers or Essential Merchants? Women in the Distributive Trades in Early Modern Nuremberg', *Sixteenth Century Journal*, 12 (1981), 3–13; Kowaleski, 'Women's Work in a Market Town', pp. 147–9.

understood what they meant by terms like 'helping women', 'helping neighbours' and 'keeping wives'; it is unfortunately far less clear to us, although it
is highly probable that any reference to 'keeping' involved more of a tending
or at least supervisory role than 'helping'.[62] The service/caring occupations,
although hardly monopolised by older lone women, can at least be seen as
tempering their isolation, however hard the work may have been, and whatever
the social distance between carer and cared.[63] However, as the traditional negative stereotypes of gossiping busybody carers suggest, the community did not
necessarily approve. With respect to networking, women's problems may have
arisen less from their failures than from their successes.[64]

A comparison with Pound's table for the occupations of all women over the
age of 20 and in work shows that there are only four incidental spinning or
textile occupations which were not followed by the older women.[65] In Pound's
clothing, food and drink, and miscellaneous categories, the differences are limited to occupations followed by a single younger woman in each case, with the
exception of knitters of caps (two) and buttonmakers (four). It should be noted
however that Pound's main analysis lists primary occupations only and tends to
omit occupations which do not fall into the usual male-oriented categories.[66]
With women's work especially, it is desirable to look at multi-occupation, to which
the censustakers, owing to their brief, were as alert as could ever be expected
of male authors of an official document. It should be added that they did not
extract this information only for women. In general, the degree to which men
followed – as opposed to being defined by – more than one occupation is still
much underestimated, medicine itself being an example of this.[67] Nonetheless,
multi-occupation is by way of being an inherent feature of women's work. The
importance of by-employment in the working lives of women has been noted
by historians from Power onwards, but evidence is very often lacking.[68] Multi-
occupation is a more awkward term than by-employment, but in many respects
a more appropriate one. Another important issue is the tendency of women
to follow different employments at different stages in their lives: as the census
is a snapshot, this can only be approached by a comparison of different agegroups. Multi-occupation for all women aged 50 and over is set out in Table 7.2.
'Spinning and carding' has been treated as a single occupation (see Table 7.1).

---

62. Pound, *Census*, p. 57. On 'keeping', see also Pelling, 'Nurses'.

63. Cf. the interesting reconstruction of neighbourhood interaction by Clark and Clark, 'The Social
Economy', pp. 80–3, which finds that widows 'stood apart from the local network most of all', being able
at most to maintain links with other widows. Cf. also the authors' own reference to spinning (p. 80). On
older women as carers, see also L. A. Botelho, 'Provisions for the Elderly in Two Early Modern Suffolk
Communities' (University of Cambridge PhD thesis, 1995), pp. 342–3. I am grateful to Lynn Botelho for
access to her thesis.

64. On female networking around childbirth, see for example A. G. Hess, 'Midwifery Practice among the
Quakers in Southern Rural England in the Late Seventeenth Century' (pp. 49–76) and H. King, 'The Politick
Midwife: Models of Midwifery in the Work of Elizabeth Cellier' (pp. 115–30) in Marland, *Art of Midwifery*.

65. Pound, *Census*, Appendix IV. The four are bobbin filling, bone-lace making, wool carding, and hair
spinning.

66. See however the footnote to Pound's analysis: *Census*, Appendix IV.

67. See Pelling, 'Occupational Diversity'. See also Roberts, 'Words they are Women', pp. 136–44.

68. Goldberg, *Women, Work, and Life Cycle*, p. 4.

TABLE 7.2 *Norwich women aged 50 and over: multi-occupations*

Primary employment	Secondary employment
spins	& helps neighbours or others (2)/ knits/ washes (3)/ helps women in need/ sells fish
spins small stuff	& helps neighbours
spins white warp	& teaches youth*/ teaches youth to spin/ keeps alms children
knits	& washes/spins
sews	& spins
weaves lace	& washes
sells fish	& spins
dresses meat and drink etc.	& spins
goes on purchase	& turns spits
keeps sick persons	& spins wool
keeps women	& spins
tends alms	& spins
washes	& spins (2)/ helps women
helps to labour	& does business
Total multi-occupied women	26

* probably also means spinning

Note: The primary employment is taken to be that first mentioned. The combination of spinning and carding has been omitted (see Table 7.1). 'Washing and scouring' is treated as a single occupation. Working 'at home' has also been omitted.

Source: Pound, *Census*.

Apart from the occasional use of 'etc.', no older woman had ascribed to her more than two occupations. The multi-occupied represent 7.8 per cent of the older women. A comparison with the younger adult women in the census, that is those aged between 20 and 49 (inclusive), shows multi-occupation among them (again ignoring 'spinning and carding') standing at 56 instances, or just over 11 per cent. About half of the employments of the younger women involved a combination falling within the service/caring category, of washing, keeping wives, scouring, and the enigmatic 'helping others', or 'helping wives'. Of these the most numerous was washing.[69] The other combinations were largely between different kinds of spinning or textile work. The figure of 11 per cent is a minimum, but, as the calculation stands, the difference of 3–4 per cent is enough only to suggest, rather than establish, the possibility that older women were more likely to be in a single occupation than younger women. If Pound's figure for those women aged 21 and above and actually in work is used, the proportion

69. Washing at this period, albeit often invisible, could be described with little irony as a major exercise: see for example Pelling, 'Appearance and Reality', p. 92; also 'Nurses', pp. 191–3.

of younger women in multi-occupation rises to 14.2 per cent; the comparable figure for the older women (that is, excluding the unstated, out of work, and unable to work) is again lower, at 9.4 per cent.[70] Even if weight is placed on the equivalence of the two groups, rather than on the small differences, it is at least clear that multi-occupation was not a downgrading forced on women as they grew older and lost their husbands. Taking into account the added burden of disability among the older group, it is possible to infer from the figures a kind of return to the workforce, at least among able-bodied older women, married and otherwise – something usually seen as belonging, for demographic reasons, to the postwar years of the twentieth century.[71]

With respect to the incidence of multi-occupation as such, the proportions found for Norwich's poor women – which include lone women as well as the married and the spouseless – seem surprisingly small. As a comparison, Earle's listing of occupations of married couples in London over a century later yields a figure for multi-occupation among *wives* (of all ages) of 17.7 per cent.[72] Even this does not seem particularly high. As well as being later, Earle's population is less uniformly poor than that of the census. Another point of comparison is Kowaleski's figure of 18 per cent for the women of late-fourteenth-century Exeter.[73]

There are of course any number of contingent reasons why the extent of multi-occupation among Norwich's poor might be underestimated by the censustakers, although these would apply *a fortiori* to most other records. It might also be argued that older women had single occupations (albeit, it should be noted, ones very similar to those of younger women) because they could do no better; but in that case, the established approach to multi-occupation would be due for some revision. That is, it is conventionally assumed, under the influence of the male work model, that those doing only one thing necessarily had better work than those in multi-occupation. As we have seen, the Norwich authorities themselves give this impression, stigmatising women who went 'abroad' from one thing to the next, especially if it was not certain what they did. This applied to a few of those identified as harlots and 'gresse women' – Joan Abell, for example, aged 40, was 'a gresse mayde, that kepe wyves & do busyness' – but the 13 women so identified were more likely to be young, spinning, and/or returned pregnant from the country.[74] Because of the risks to which they were exposed, particularly pregnancy, it is mainly the younger women out of service and involved in casual caring and cleaning who attracted official

---

70. Table 7.2; Pound, *Census*, Appendix IV.

71. See for example M. Anderson, 'The Emergence of the Modern Life-Cycle in Britain', *Social History*, 10 (1985), 75. The present discussion develops a suggestion made in Pelling, 'Old Age, Poverty and Disability', pp. 83–4 (142–3).

72. This rises to 21.6% if washing and scouring are taken as two occupations. Earle does not discuss multi-occupation except as casual work: 'The Female Labour Market', p. 342; for the listing, see Appendix A. His model is the listing of Old Bailey witnesses, prisoners etc. by George, which yields (again for wives only) a figure for (simultaneous) multi-occupation of 8.9%: M. D. George, *London Life in the Eighteenth Century* (1925; Harmondsworth, 1979), Appendix VI.

73. Kowaleski, 'Women's Work in a Market Town', p. 148.

74. Pound, *Census*, pp. 38, 42. For 'gress' see *OED*, 'grass-girl' or 'grass-widow', though a 'grass-nurse' was a wetnurse.

attention, rather than the older.[75] The stereotypical disapproval of women's independent 'patchwork' employment outside the home, especially in nursing or
washing, which gave a licence to be outdoors as well as intimate access to the
houses of others, was best expressed by Firmin at the end of the next century.
Steady, year-round employment within doors, such as spinning, was preferred
for women.[76] However, it is not at all clear that women following this sequestered
pattern would have been better off financially. Moral approval was not tied
to economic reward. But given that what the Norwich censustakers recorded
must to some extent have reflected attitudes and expectations, then the differences between the younger and the older women become all the more
interesting. In terms of occupational identity, the older women, whatever their
disadvantages, look a little bit more like men. Nonetheless, the census also
reminds us of the social difference discerned between the patchwork activities
of women tied to home and family, who might still be criticised for gossiping
and scolding, and the dubious licence of those who went 'abroad'.

In spite of the census's unusual if not unique detail, it is not exhaustive
enough to be taken as proving a negative about any given occupation of poor
women. Apart from the particular character of Norwich as a textile town, the
censustakers were not recording everything a woman did or mentioned, but
only her main occupations, directed at economic survival and giving her the
moral status of working for her living, beyond if not actually outside the household. Certain absences may however be noted. One might, for example, expect
there to have been more midwives, in spite of the current view of them as
relatively prosperous.[77] There are no nurses, including wetnurses, explicitly identified as such, and no herbwomen, although for wetnurses and herbwomen
those serving the town may have more often lived outside it.[78] There are no
tallowchandlers, which underlines both the lack of reference to regulated crafts
in general, and the tendency for even humble crafts increasingly to exclude
women.[79] Most strikingly, since poor old women often resorted to it and it
became official policy as a means of supporting them, there are no alehouse-
keepers or tipplers – an occupation commonly associated, like tallowchandling,
with the lower levels of caring and medical practice.[80]

The phrase 'at need' or 'in need' used by the censustakers is some recognition of the occasional character of important areas of women's employment,
including much midwifery, but such employment was necessarily elusive. I
have considered in detail elsewhere how, in its poor-law schemes of the late
sixteenth century, the Norwich authorities employed poor women to keep and

75. See Wright, ' "Churmaids" ', pp. 104–5; Roberts, 'Women and Work', pp. 92–3; Kowaleski, 'Women's
Work in a Market Town', pp. 153–5.

76. Firmin was quoted in this context by Clark and has become a staple reference since: *Working Life of
Women*, pp. 135–7.

77. Marland, *Art of Midwifery*, p. 4.

78. Though for wetnurses see note 74 above; on sicknursing, see Pelling, 'Nurses'.

79. On women chandlers, see Goldberg, *Women, Work, and Life Cycle*, pp. 133–4.

80. Wright, ' "Churmaids" ', pp. 110–11. Pelling, 'Occupational Diversity', pp. 504 (tallowchandling),
505–6 (alcohol) (222, 223).

to cure the sick poor.[81] Although over a period the full spectrum of male and female practitioners were so employed, one-third were women, including widows, the wives of lazarhouse-keepers, or lazarhouse-keepers who were women. These, it should be stressed, were those involved in curing patients; often they were paid for keeping as well, but the proportion of women employed would significantly increase if all those paid simply for keeping in the course of a cure were added. A good example of the older woman practitioner in the context of occasional occupations is widow or mother Waterman, variously paid by Norwich in the 1570s for 'healing', her patients including Margaret Cowper of Berstreet ward, who had a scald head.[82] The census records, under the one roof in St Michael's parish in Berstreet ward, both Gillian Waterman, a widow of 60 who did no work, and Margaret Coper, a widow of 47, who spun white warp. If these are the same people, the Norwich authorities clearly discovered a range of medical skills in mother Waterman which supported her, and were of value to the city. It may not have been the case, in fact, that mother Waterman 'did no work' before being employed by the city as a practitioner. It may be noted that the curing of scald head was very much a woman's specialty at this time.[83] However, in spite of the comparative flexibility of the language of the censustakers, it is hard to imagine how they could have described what mother Waterman did.

If we return in conclusion to the 'Mum' of the East End in the 1950s, we can see both similarities and differences. In each case, the older woman does not live with her adult children, unless they remain unmarried or their families break down in some way. In each case, the older woman is observed to have some kind of independent existence, although this is differently expressed. In the later case, her work identity is very weak; in the earlier, it is surprisingly strong. Some of the differences of course arise from the fact that Young and Willmott wanted to prove affective factors, while the Norwich censustakers, albeit with a moral purpose, were investigating the world of work. However the Norwich material does provide a substantial reminder of the importance of work in the lives of older women. Comparison with the younger agegroups suggests a continuity of work throughout the lifecycle of poor women, as well as continuity in terms of relationships. Older women defending their activities outside the household often stressed how long these had been carried on: this anecdotal evidence should perhaps be taken as indicating some kind of truth. Such women also underline their breadwinning role and their support of sick or disabled dependants.[84]

The lifecycle approach to poverty, dating from LePlay in the nineteenth century, has encouraged a view of older women, especially lone women, as uniquely

81. Pelling, 'Healing the Sick Poor'.

82. Pelling and Webster, 'Medical Practitioners', pp. 222–3.

83. Pound, *Census*, p. 37. Pelling, 'Appearance and Reality', p. 102.

84. L. Roper, *The Holy Household: Women and Morals in Reformation Augsburg* (Oxford, 1989), p. 47; Wiesner, *Working Women*, pp. 176, 181–2; Marland, 'Stately and Dignified', pp. 288–90. I have found similar claims by unlicensed women practitioners in London: Pelling, 'Thoroughly Resented?', p. 76.

helpless and dependent. Although women in living longer and suffering higher rates of debility could be in great danger of a miserable and protracted end to their lives, this should be balanced by a recognition of the ingrained work habits of poor women. Such work histories help to explain why widows, for example, were, as one historical sociologist has put it, *'unexpectedly* capable of self-support'.[85] Among older women it may indeed have been the lone woman who came closest to achieving the occupational identity accorded to men. Historians normally look for such status among more prosperous widows who carried on their husband's trade, often for short periods, but the relatively low incidence of multi-occupation among Norwich's poor older women is at least suggestive. This trend might confirm Roberts's view of the stronger definition of occupations seen as 'women's work' in the later sixteenth century, although the narrow range of occupations actually identified may qualify this argument somewhat.[86] The older woman, spouseless or alone, needs also to be seen as a head of household more or less to the day of her last decline. That this semi-independence could be double-edged from the point of view of authority is obvious from the Norwich evidence. Moreover, far from being 'safely' confined to a suburban purlieu, the older women of Norwich were at work in almost every area of the city. However, recalling the point made already about prostitution among younger women, it is at least interesting that in Coventry unmarried women over 50 were by implication permitted to live by themselves.[87]

Early modern women were paid below subsistence level even when demand was high for their product and even when they did the same work as men, so the fact that the older women of Norwich were so often poor and needing alms – or, later, poor relief – should not be allowed to dictate their occupational status. Women were given few special advantages by the providers of private charity.[88] Their right of entry to sheltered accommodation was often on the basis of their providing caring services, and a similar quid pro quo was extensively used by the poor-law system. 'Tending' is, incidentally, a word commonly used in the early modern period for such services. Women are known to have used the rhetoric of dependency which was expected of them, but their sense of entitlement to relief is just as likely to have come from their awareness of themselves as people who worked hard all their lives for little reward.

As already indicated, the occupations of Norwich's older women obviously confirm points made by other historians about the narrowing of women's opportunities in the visible labour market in this period. Although nearly all worked, the range of their employment was very limited. It was not, however, appreciably different from that of the younger female agegroups.[89] The census further confirms that wage-earning for women meant doing 'women's work' – a somewhat backhanded recognition, historically, of the continuity of work within and

85. Smith, 'Widowhood and Ageing', p. 446. (My italics.)
86. Kowaleski, 'Women's Work in a Market Town', pp. 156–7. Roberts, 'Women and Work', p. 93.
87. Cf. Goldberg, *Women, Work, and Life Cycle*, pp. 316–18; ibid., p. 317. The relevant ordinances are from 1492.
88. Todd, 'Widowhood', pp. 228–32.
89. Note also the similarities with towns at an earlier period: Goldberg, *Women, Work, and Life Cycle*, pp. 93ff.

outside the household. (It should be noted however that, in the textile category particularly, 'women's work' was also children's work.)[90] The census reveals, especially in the details of multi-occupation, a few of the unsung many who washed, scoured, 'kept wives', and helped other women, presumably at home. Although it is going much too far to infer any collective work identity among women from such details, a web of work-related contacts is at least implied. Lurking within the detail is some extrapolation into the labour market of the caring role, although, as in the present, a high level of invisibility remains, compared with information on women carers who were paid out of the public purse. Living arrangements imply a continuation for older women of caring roles; the standard practice of poor-relief authorities of paying women to care for even close kin is probably prefigured in private arrangements between older women working for their living, and their kin and neighbours. The contrast with the present is that these women are likely to have been paid, in cash or in kind, even by their kin.[91]

90. See also Wright, '"Churmaids"', p. 102.
91. Cf. Ungerson, *Gender and Caring*, pp. 5–6.

PART III

OCCUPATIONS

CHAPTER EIGHT

Nurses and Nursekeepers: Problems of Identification in the Early Modern Period

One of the best indications of the difficulty of defining nursing in the past must be the problems it still faces in the present. This is not by way of contrast with any ideal of straightforward, linear development over time, but simply to suggest the persistence of difficulties very hard to remove. Nursing in developed western societies has no assured status, though this is not for want of effort on the part of nurses. Although a proportion of nurses have gained some of the attributes of a profession, a greater proportion of the nursing workforce have been left behind, while at the same time the bulk of the nursing task continues to be carried out as a domestic responsibility, and one still largely assumed by women. The ambiguous status of nursing epitomises both the positive and the negative ways in which western society has preferred to regard women's work.[1]

In a review of historical sociology on the sexual division of labour published in 1989, Harriet Bradley argued against a single sociological theory of gender relations, preferring instead a 'joint orientation' which combined the materialist interpretation of women's work, which tended to stress aspects of production, for example women's role as a reserve army of labour, and the connection of female employment with de-skilling, and the reproductive approach, which sees the determinants of women's work more in terms of the effects of child-bearing and child-rearing, even where these are taken to be culturally rather than biologically determined. For Bradley, aiming at a more comprehensive analysis, the key concepts linking the productive and the reproductive approaches are patriarchy and male dominance, which in a number of obvious ways can

A version of this chapter was first given in February 1988 in Oxford. A version emphasising evidence from apprenticeship was given in London in September 1993. I am grateful to both audiences for their comments. I should also like to thank Paul Griffiths, Jane Lewis, Anne Laurence, Mary Prior and Emma Smith for valuable information.

1. On the recent history and enduring problems of nursing, see M. L. Fitzpatrick, 'Nursing' [review essay], *Signs*, 2 (1977), 818–34; R. Dingwall, A. M. Rafferty and C. Webster (eds), *An Introduction to the Social History of Nursing* (London, 1988); C. Davies, *Gender and the Professional Predicament in Nursing* (Buckingham and Philadelphia, 1996). A conspectus of current work on the history of nursing was provided by the international conference, 'Nursing, Women's History and the Politics of Welfare', organised by Jane Robinson and Anne Marie Rafferty at the Department of Nursing and Midwifery Studies, University of Nottingham, in September 1996.

be seen as common to the household and the workplace.[2] All of the orientations summarised by Bradley have been freely deployed by medieval and early modern historians in the flow of excellent writing on women's work which has appeared in recent years. It is noticeable, however, that nursing has not been a point of reference for the earlier period as it has for the later. The 'reproductive' approach has guaranteed some interest in what might be regarded as the definitive form of nursing in the early modern period, that is wetnursing, monthly nursing and infant care.[3] Wetnursing and infant care have also been of interest to historical demographers, because of their connections with such issues as birth-spacing, infant mortality, and the differential survival of male and female children. Sicknursing, on the other hand, seems to lack definition altogether. Even for historians of the family, sicknursing is subsumed within a range of domestic responsibilities, and possesses neither the interest of women's involvement in other healing tasks, nor wetnursing's affective implications and visibility outside the household.

There is a similar blank with respect to the 'productive' approach. Among the many reasons for this is the difficulty of isolating nursing personnel, let alone the nursing task, its 'product', or its effects, all of which tend to evade the categories used by economic historians. Both economic historians and historians of the professions depend upon a certain degree of nominal visibility among those carrying out the task in question: that is, it is as important to be, as to do. Sicknursing has been tackled for Catholic countries, where large institutions and sisterhoods call for attention, but for pre-industrial England it has been particularly neglected.[4] On the present basis, it is quite difficult to decide whether the early modern sicknurse existed in England at all before the late seventeenth century.

There are however advantages to this lack of definition. It is possible to get away from the most worked-over questions of the politics, institutionalisation, and professionalisation of nursing simply because these conceptions are almost entirely anachronistic for the period between 1500 and 1700. It is certainly not the case that the existing literature is devoid of valid insights with respect to nursing in the earlier period. There is however an inevitable tendency to place over the unknown earlier terrain, a map of the battleground of the nineteenth century, and to arrive at contrasts by that route. With respect to the professions we also tend to imply the existence of a Britanno-centric *ancien régime* or traditional society ending, as industrialisation is firmly established, around 1800. This periodisation is exemplified by Abel-Smith's standard history of nursing, which begins without embarrassment around 1800 and deals with the political and the professional. As Abel-Smith himself explicitly states, he avoided the

2. H. Bradley, *Men's Work, Women's Work* (Cambridge, 1989), pp. 23–6.

3. For an extensive bibliography, see V. Fildes, *Wet-nursing: A History from Antiquity to the Present* (Oxford, 1988). Of great interest is the study of 'lying-in maids' (who tended to be post-menopausal women) by Lyndal Roper: 'Witchcraft and Fantasy in Early Modern Germany', repr. in her *Oedipus and the Devil* (London and New York, 1994), pp. 199–225.

4. See esp. C. Jones, *The Charitable Imperative: Hospitals and Nursing in Ancien Régime and Revolutionary France* (London and New York, 1989). On the roles of women in pre-Reformation hospitals, see C. Rawcliffe, *Medicine and Society in Later Medieval England* (Stroud, 1995), pp. 205–13.

nature of the nursing task and even the content of nursing education, and was able fairly legitimately to avoid the problem of continuity altogether. Nonetheless, he did make important and relevant points needing investigation, for example, the greater degree of overlap, before his starting date, between the nursing and the medical functions, as well as the connection between nursing and domestic service, with the vital related point about the magnitude of service in relation to the size of the labour force as a whole. With respect to the division of labour between the sexes, this question is in a sense begged for Abel-Smith because the restructuring of nursing took place, as Bradley puts it, 'while Victorian separatist ideologies of gender were at their most powerful'.[5]

Similar points are made in a contrasting way, and very forcefully, by Margaret Versluysen in one of the few recent attempts to connect nineteenth-century nursing with a longer time scale. For Versluysen, adopting the reproductive rather than Abel-Smith's productive orientation, the emergence of nursing in the nineteenth century signals failure, rather than success. Nursing only emerges as a separate occupation at all, because women lose to men their traditional control of the healing task, which she sees holistically. In a different version of Abel-Smith's point, she stresses that statistically the bulk of both care and cure was the work of women, and that in their hands care and cure were indistinguishable. This is a reminder of a characterisation formulated about the post-industrial context, but also applied to earlier periods, which is that men's work was specialised (for which read skilled), while women's tended to remain generalised and open-ended. Not surprisingly, Versluysen also calls for less stress to be placed on whether work was paid for as part of the cash economy.[6]

In spite of their contrasting approaches, both Abel-Smith and Versluysen convey the same major implication, which is that the nursing task belonged to women. Versluysen indeed makes the remark that 'before the late seventeenth century, the male impact on the everyday healing experience of most people was minimal'.[7] This is a defensible statement historically, but one with a number of disadvantages. First, it implies a golden age of female dominance of health and healing, which came to an end with modernisation. Secondly, even if one were to give the crucial words 'everyday' and 'most people' their full literal value, the statement also seems to suggest a traditional form of society in which no person was ever far from home and the helping hands of his or her women-folk. This is questionable on a number of counts, beginning with the mobility of early modern English populations, old as well as young. Thirdly, I should also like to suggest the need to consider the implications of equally traditional, male-dominated work environments – ships, armies, monasteries, mines, even building and some forms of agriculture – where mutual assistance was likely on an everyday basis and where age was probably as important as gender in determining who helped whom. More generally, doubts arise on the basis of

5. B. Abel-Smith, *A History of the Nursing Profession* (London, 1960, repr. 1970), pp. xi, 4–6; Bradley, *Men's Work, Women's Work*, p. 195.
6. M. C. Versluysen, 'Old Wives' Tales? Women Healers in English History', in C. Davies (ed.), *Rewriting Nursing History* (London, 1980), pp. 175–99, esp. 175, 187–8, 185.
7. Versluysen, 'Old Wives' Tales?', p. 185.

the practices of a hierarchical society in which men were as often bodyservants as were women, and therefore as likely to have to take on a nursing role.[8] Don Juan, that is, was more likely to be nursed by Leporello than by any of the women he was busily exploiting. If nursing is defined as being inseparable from beds, then men can be found at the bedside as well, especially as beds were often shared by people of the same sex. A related issue is the suspicion of incest or other sexual misbehaviour which could arise when men were nursed by women; this was an important consideration even in hospitals.[9] My own impression of the seventeenth century, which Versluysen would also see as a period of transition, is that gender divisions with respect to sicknursing were both rigid and fluid, depending upon context and the nature of the nursing task.

Versluysen's account was influenced by the pioneering work of Alice Clark, first published in 1919 and lately more than once reprinted.[10] Clark's work is still, I think rightly, a major starting point for this area of discussion, whether explicitly or not. Clark had Liberal, suffragist, and Quaker connections, and acknowledged debts to Charlotte Shaw, Lilian Knowles, Eileen Power, and Dorothy George, who clearly influenced her choice of sources.[11] Just as significantly, Clark was involved in her father's firm, the Clark shoe company, and as a girl served an apprenticeship designed to be equivalent to that of her brothers. During World War I, she trained as a midwife.[12] She followed the line of her intellectual circle in seeing the seventeenth century as a watershed created by the rise of capitalism and the accelerated decline of the domestic system of labour, in which the family worked as an economic unit, wage labour was minimal, and production was based on the household, not a separate workplace. Within this context she identified damage done by the secularisation of women's work after the Reformation, the progressive exclusion of women from all offices although not from all functions, their continued lack of any institutional base or collective representation, and their exclusion from the male science which transformed the medical role during the Enlightenment. What can be overlooked is that her assessment of the work of women outside the home needs to be balanced by the fact that she reserved discussion of marriage, education, service, and apprenticeship, as well as the mental world of women and its effects on society, to a later volume which never appeared. In this context she was particularly influenced by the sexual politics of Olive Schreiner.[13]

8. A complex example of the effects of hierarchical distance on gender roles is William Ogilvie, tutor (and sicknurse) in the 1760s to the children of the Duchess of Leinster, and later their stepfather. Note, however, that the children appear to have taken their meals next door, with their aunt: S. Tillyard, *Aristocrats: Caroline, Emily, Louisa and Sarah Lennox 1740–1832* (London, 1995), pp. 246–9.

9. The obligation to nurse a family member could be cited as a defence. For an instance in which incest was suspected and the daughter asserted she was nursing her father, see A. Giardina Hess, 'Community Case Studies of Midwives from England and New England, *c.* 1650–1720' (University of Cambridge PhD thesis, 1994), p. 82. On indiscipline in hospitals, see C. Daly, 'The Hospitals of London: Administration, Refoundation, and Benefaction, *c.* 1500–1572' (University of Oxford DPhil thesis, 1994), pp. 179–80, 293–4; Webster, *Great Instauration*, pp. 296, 298.

10. A. Clark, *Working Life of Women in the Seventeenth Century* (1919; London, 1982).

11. Ibid., Preface.

12. See the introduction by M. Chaytor and J. Lewis: ibid., pp. ix, xi.

13. Ibid., Preface; pp. xvi–xx, 1–2, 4, 306–7.

Clark's strengths and limitations are particularly interesting with respect to nursing, which she ranked, in theory if not in practice, among the professions.[14] She was aware of her own historical context, especially in recognising many features of what she described as the post-scientific point of view, and was specifically arguing for historical relativity rather than absolutes with respect to women's work. Nonetheless, she did write prescriptively, and her ideals were very much professional, post-Nightingale, and middle-class, combined with a form of guild socialism. She deplored, at one end of the social spectrum, the absence of a sense of religious duty in the post-Reformation period which might have induced the increasingly idle upper-class woman to devote herself to nursing. Her adherence, at the other end of the spectrum, to the middle-class vocational ideal is shown in her repeated regrets that the seventeenth-century sicknurse did this work only to earn her bread – the consequence being that the occupation attracted only the lowest class of woman, who lacked a sense of social responsibility. Clark's own social location was thus defined by her despising useless upper-class women but also in her not approving women who were only useful.

Clark was partly influenced by her sources. She has been criticised as overly empirical, but her materialist approach was deliberately adopted for her first book because she felt there was a huge gap, prejudicial to women, between contemporary theoretical assumptions about women's capabilities, and the historical record.[15] It is a vindication of Clark's research that even in her short section on nursing she located areas which have only recently been further explored – poor-law nursing and plague nursing, for example. It is not surprising, however, that having found them, she saw these forms of employment outside the household as a degraded form of wage labour. Nursing which was not religiously inspired, not middle-class, not institutional, and yet pursued outside the household for money, had to be a low-grade occupation, and could only be carried out by poor women. The bluntness of Tudor and Stuart sources on poor relief and plague must have encouraged this disparaging conclusion. Clark's analysis of the work of nursing suggested to her that only the glamour (her own word) of religion, or of secure social status, could make it palatable. She was led to make other, related assumptions about early modern nursing, for example that paid nurses tended to be brought in only if the proper system of social obligation had broken down, as for instance when the sick person was a stranger.[16] From this point of view, poor-law nursing and plague nursing could also be seen as expedients which had to be adopted when the moral values of the productive *and* reproductive self-supporting household unit were undermined by disaster or economic change.

However individual her interpretation of her apparently literal material might have been, it has to be admitted that there was a neglect after Clark of sources deriving from local government, guilds, and other agencies connecting the family with organised society. Feminist historians, Clark's editors have noted,

14. Ibid., pp. 243–65.
15. Ibid., Preface and p. xvi.
16. Ibid., pp. 243–4, 249, 253.

have concentrated instead on sexuality, inheritance, and the intergenerational reproduction of family relations.[17] Consequently, while it may be surprising that the nursing function has not been singled out within the context of the early modern family, it is less surprising that nursing as an occupation remains ill defined. It is frequently mentioned by historians who are now turning to the kinds of sources used by Clark, but the occupation is allowed to exist chiefly as a matter of presumption. Nursing is of course affected by the deficiencies which stand in the way of conventional occupational analysis of all forms of women's work. Guild or company records, apprenticeship indentures, and freemen's rolls are of very limited relevance. Wills and inventories are fewer for women and rare for women dying before their husbands; the wills even of recognised female medical practitioners tend simply to give marital status.[18] In any case women's work tended almost by definition to lack equipment or other property of capital value which could be detected in testamentary records. Even where women's work had a major public dimension, as in the case of midwives, English midwives remain comparatively elusive.[19] Nor, in English sources, do midwives often lead one to nurses, of any kind. Filiation records, for example, may indicate the presence at a birth of half-a-dozen women at least, but apart from the midwife herself these other women are known only by their names or those of their husbands.[20] In general, the forms of women's work which are closest to those of men – which tends to mean that they have a nominal existence in re-cords – have proved the most accessible. Nursing fails to enter this category until the seventeenth century at the earliest, and even then possibly only in London.

A fairly basic attention to definitions seems desirable not only because nursing outside hospitals tends to be taken for granted, but also because occupational designations often crop up in early modern sources without any other relev-ant context and can thereby mislead.[21] Some of Clark's reasons for concentrat-ing on the seventeenth century as a watershed for women's occupations seem to be justified when we notice that the term 'nurse' itself changes, or rather enlarges, its meaning at this time. Pre-modern usage of the term and its deriv-atives seems to have had no specific reference to sickness, but was instead dominated by the idea of upbringing – the nourishment or tending necessary at the earliest stages of life, and especially where upbringing was by proxy, or at least non-parental. Hence of course wet- and drynursing, but also cognate words for foster-father and foster-child.[22] Some later applications relate to preserves

17. Ibid., pp. xii, xxi.

18. An example is Alice Glavin, employed in her own right by Norwich in the late sixteenth century, and the wife and mother of surgeons: M. Pelling, 'Tradition and Diversity: Medical Practice in Norwich 1550–1640', in Istituto Nazionale di Studi sul Rinascimento, *Scienze Credenze Occulte Livelli di Cultura* (Florence, 1982), pp. 166–7 (for her will: NRO, NCC, 140 Andrewes).

19. On midwives in England and continental Europe, see H. Marland (ed.), *The Art of Midwifery: Early Modern Midwives in Europe* (London and New York, 1983).

20. Good examples of declarations made by women present at births of illegitimate children can be found in Norwich's municipal records: NRO, Mayor's Court Proceedings, 1603–15, fols 159ff.

21. A vindication of this point with respect to classical sources is the excellent discussion by Helen King: 'Using the Past: Nursing and the Medical Profession in Ancient Greece', in P. Holden and J. Littlewood (eds), *Anthropology and Nursing* (London and New York, 1991), pp. 7–24.

22. See *OED*.

which were entirely male, but retain the connotation of care by proxy or early stage of life, as in the expression 'nursing a benefice'. There were 'nursery theatres' in London in the 1660s for training actors.[23] These metaphors clearly have nothing to do with sickness, but relate to imitations of kinship obligations towards the young and the social responsibilities of a head of household. This is reflected in the much later statement by a member of the Courtauld family to his offspring that he had been 'a nursing father to all of you'.[24] It is not surprising that in the sixteenth century one of the new applications of the word referred to the raising of plants, as in 'nursery-garden', and 'nurse-plants', which were strong plants grown alongside to shelter young ones in the first stages of growth.

Thus Nashe's description in 1596 of an opponent as rushing in 'bluntly with thy washing bowle and thy nursecloutes under thy cloake' has no positive connotation of urgency towards the sick, even though the opponent is being portrayed as a barber, but is a more scathing reference to degrading service and nappy-changing.[25] Shakespeare with typical ambiguity appears to be referring to sicknursing in the *Comedy of Errors*, when he has Adriana say of her supposed husband:

> I will attend my husband, be his nurse
> Diet his sickness, for it is my office
> And will have no attorney but myself
> And therefore let me have him home with me.[26]

Adriana is possessively and mistakenly contending for mastery with the Abbess Emilia who is equally determined to nurse the man in question in her nunnery. At the same time however Shakespeare seems to be playing with post-Reformation sentiment in allowing Adriana to assert the superior 'health and sickness' rights of a married woman over a religious.[27] The ambiguity arises in that the man in question is not ill, but mad, a condition which could legally as well as physically reduce an adult to child status, warranting subjection to a nurse. Subjection is also stressed in a speech Jonson puts in the mouth of Subtle in *The Alchemist*: 'A man must deale like a rough nurse, and fright / Those, that are froward, to an appetite'.[28] In general in sixteenth- and early seventeenth-century sources a nurse should be regarded as a wet or dry children's nurse unless proven otherwise, as for example in such London parish register entries

23. R. Latham and W. Matthews (eds), *The Diary of Samuel Pepys*, Vol. X, Companion (London, 1983), p. 304.

24. L. Davidoff and C. Hall, *Family Fortunes: Men and Women of the English Middle Class, 1780–1850* (London, 1992), p. 330. It is worth noting here that Davidoff and Hall also find some middle-class fathers of their period sicknursing their children, and (exceptional) sons their parents: pp. 330, 345–6.

25. Thomas Nashe, *Have with You to Saffron-walden* (1596), in R. B. McKerrow and F. P. Wilson (eds), *The Works of Thomas Nashe*, 5 vols (Oxford, 1966), vol. 3, p. 15.

26. *Comedy of Errors*, V, i, 98–101, Arden edn, ed. R. A. Foakes (London and New York, 1984), pp. 92–3.

27. Playing, because Emilia is in fact a wife and mother, and her abbey a site of reconciliation: ibid., pp. xlviii–xlix.

28. Jonson, *The Alchemist*, II, v, 89–90.

as 'norsse with Mr Malory' (1554) and 'Mr Daniell's nurce' (1569).[29] As with 'doctor', the *medical* version of nurse, which now seems so predominant, was in the pre-industrial period the minority rather than the majority case. References to nurses in medieval sources remain ambiguous but, where 'nurse' is used, are more likely to refer to children's nurses. Testamentary evidence suggests services rendered, rather than an occupation.[30] Other kinds of medieval evidence are complicated by commentary on the seven works of mercy; these included not nursing as such, but the optional, charitable activity of visiting the sick.[31]

Sicknurses around the turn of the sixteenth century can however be recognised by name under the heading of 'keepers' and 'nursekeepers'. 'Keeping' was a generic function involving some form of custodial responsibility analogous to that of a head of household; as might be expected, 'keepers' could as often be male as female.[32] As a reminder of this bias, 'keepers' of a later date tend to be male.[33] It is of interest here to note the gender shifts in the term 'housekeeper'; as this meant someone of a standing sufficient to be officially responsible for a house, early modern 'housekeepers' were mainly male.[34] It is only later that the 'housekeeper' becomes predominantly a salaried upper servant, the feminised equivalent of a steward; the ambiguous status of housekeepers is reflected in the frequency with which (in middling households) they were related to the master of the house.[35] Subsequently of course 'housekeeping' degrades even further down the gender scale of values.[36]

Nursekeepers, whose name was apparently a neologism of the early seventeenth century, seem on the other hand to have been female (and subject to stereotyping) from the outset, as in a reference of 1602 (by a physician, admittedly) to 'chattering char-women, and Nurs-keepers'.[37] This is effectively a literary reference, but the term is also found in such official sources as a return of divided houses of the 1630s, made during a preoccupation with overcrowding

29. W. B. Bannerman (ed.), *The Registers of . . . St Pancras Soper Lane, London*, Harleian Society Registers XLIV (1914), p. 286; idem (ed.), *The Registers of St Olave Hart St, London*, Harleian Society Registers XLVI (1916), p. 108.

30. P. J. P. Goldberg, *Women, Work, and Life Cycle in a Medieval Economy* (Oxford, 1992), pp. 134–5.

31. See N. Boymel Kampen, 'Before Florence Nightingale: a Prehistory of Nursing in Painting and Sculpture', in A. Hudson-Jones (ed.), *Images of Nurses: Perspectives from History, Art and Literature* (Philadelphia, 1988), pp. 16–29.

32. This is illustrated by the keepers of the lazarhouses around London, Norwich, and other towns: Pelling, 'Healing the Sick Poor', esp. pp. 126–35 (91–100).

33. The most obvious, and related, context is that of lunacy: see W. L. Parry-Jones, *The Trade in Lunacy: A Study of Private Madhouses in England* (London and Toronto, 1972), pp. 74–5.

34. See *OED*. Thus Face, the 'house-keeper' in Jonson's *Alchemist*, is male, although not the master of the house.

35. For examples see B. Hill, *Servants: English Domestics in the Eighteenth Century* (Oxford, 1996), pp. 115ff, 125, 215.

36. Hence the transformation of matrons from housekeepers into nurses is identified as a key Nightingale reform: E. Gamarnikow, 'Nurse or Woman: Gender and Professionalism in Reformed Nursing 1860–1923', in Holden and Littlewood, *Anthropology and Nursing*, p. 111.

37. *OED*, citing a translation of Johannes Oberndoerffer, with an additional essay, by the collegiate physician, anti-Paracelsian and writer on plague, Francis Herring: *The Anatomyes of the True Physition, and Counterfeit Mounte-banke* (London, 1602), p. 4. See also, in Herring's own essay, references to 'Patients and Nurses' (p. 34), and 'misdemeanours of the friends of Patients, especially Women, Nurse-keepers, Servants, Cookes, Surgions, and Apothecaries' (p. 35). For Herring, see *DNB*.

and in-migration. In one parish the officers found 'Thomas Wright dwelling in another house in the said street and ward with his wife and family hath Inmates now also dwelling in the same house viz Thomas Waller and his wife she is a nurse keeper and Thomas Clarke and his wife who have one child with them'.[38] It may be that Mrs Waller's occupation is singled out for mention because she was in the house as a result of it, whereas the Clarke family were more culpably subtenants. Similar references can be found: the College of Physicians, for example, recorded a report by 'Jone Cornish the Nurse Kepper' of medical practice by Mrs Nokes of Wapping, a midwife.[39] A few years later, the College's registrar was using 'nutrix' to mean a sicknurse.[40]

It would be wrong, however, to conclude that either the gender or the occupational definition of such terms was settled at this time. The Joan Cornish example is a reminder of the difficulty of distinguishing one form of nursing from another, given that Mrs Nokes, though practising medicine, was also a midwife, and her patient a married woman. Other possible complications are epitomised by an entry of 1590 from the diary of John Dee: 'Nurse Anne Frank most miserably did cut her owne throte, afternone abowt four of the clok, pretending to be in prayer before her keeper'. It can perhaps be inferred, largely from negative evidence, that Frank was a (dry) children's nurse, not a sicknurse; the use of 'keeper' for a mentally ill patient is a reminder of the masculinised, custodial aspect of this role; but the keeper on this occasion was in fact a 'mayden'. Here, the use of 'keeper' was still occasional rather than occupational.[41]

It should be noted in any case that these sources relate to London, where occupational differentiation was likely to be at its greatest. As we have already seen, parish registers, especially of burials, are valuable, where they mention occupations at all, in being likely both to give actual rather than nominal occupations and to mention part-time or menial employments; London's registers especially exemplify this. Outside London the likelihood of nominal definition may be less. In England's largest provincial city, Norwich, the census of the poor of 1570 which tried to identify occupations for a quarter of the town's native-born population located the activity, as in 'keeps sick persons', but did not recognise any such occupational identity by using the noun form.[42] It could be argued that the general contemporary tendency to describe women as doing, but not being, was particularly strong in the case of the poor. However, even the verb 'to nurse' was not in general use for sicknursing at this time. In 1631, for example, the London College took evidence from Margaret Woodman, 'who kept Mr Turner in his sicknes'.[43] A Rose Jones buried in St Margaret

38. London, Guildhall Library, L06/2, T. C. Dale, 'Returns of Divided Houses in the City of London 1637, [bound typescript, ?1937], p. 114. Contractions have been expanded.
39. CPL, Annals, 7 April 1623, p. 164.
40. Translated after some hesitation as 'nurse': CPL, Annals, 5 March 1630, pp. 275, 276 ('cum nutrice et ancilla' and 'per nutrice eius' in original).
41. John Dee, *The Private Diary*, ed. J. O. Halliwell, Camden Society XIX (1842; repr. New York and London, 1968), 29 September 1590, p. 36. See earlier references to 'Ann my nurse' from 2 August 1590.
42. See Pelling, 'Older Women'.
43. CPL, Annals, 17 October 1631, p. 321.

Moses parish in London in 1625 was identified as 'an old woman that tended Ellen Robinson, widow'.[44] 'Tending', a term favoured by some modern analysts of the caring role performed by women because it can comprehend the public as well as the private, was in the early modern period a widely used generic term which could refer to male as well as female social obligations.[45] Fathers could be expected to be 'tender' towards their sons, or brothers towards their brothers, and similarly for connections which imitated these relationships.[46] By the mid-seventeenth century, someone called a nurse could apparently be either a wetnurse *or* a sicknurse, and the verb is also used in some poor-law records instead of the earlier alternatives such as 'keeping' or 'looking to', at least from the early eighteenth century.[47]

As already indicated, there is little point for this period in hankering after institutional certainties to resolve these vaguenesses of gender and terminology. Nevertheless, although the term 'nurse' did not derive from the hospital context but rather was brought to it from outside, it is possible that the usage adopted for Christ's Hospital in London helped to bring about change. This returns us to the wider, child-related meanings of nursing already considered. As is well known, Christ's was refounded in the mid-sixteenth century not as a sick-hospital or even a hospice but as an asylum for poor children.[48] It had some provision for sick inmates, but serious cases were sent away to St Bartholomew's or St Thomas's. At these two major sick hospitals, the female attendants were initially called not nurses but matron, sisters, or keepers. At Christ's, on the other hand, because it had to do with children, the female attendants were called nurses or keepers.[49] Thus it was 'keeper' which was initially common to both types of hospital, not 'nurse'. Christ's fairly rapidly turned from a poor-relief agency into a school, and by the 1650s St Bartholomew's had added helpers to the female staff who were to be known as nurses.[50] As well as more 'tender'

44. W. B. Bannerman (ed.), *The Registers of . . . St Margaret Moses Friday St, London*, Harleian Society Registers XLII (1912), p. 79. See also, for Suffolk *c.* 1610–38, L. A. Botelho, 'Provisions for the Elderly in Two Early Modern Suffolk Communities' (University of Cambridge PhD thesis, 1995), p. 341. I am grateful to Lynn Botelho for giving me access to her thesis.

45. C. Ungerson, 'The Language of Care: Crossing the Boundaries', in idem (ed.), *Gender and Caring. Work and Welfare in Britain and Scandinavia* (Hemel Hempstead, 1990), p. 11.

46. See for example CLRO, MC6/197A (1666). By the eighteenth century, at least in Ireland and some regions of Britain, 'nurse-tender', or 'nurse-tending', was used specifically to mean sicknursing, by men or women: *OED*. This may have accompanied the use in Ireland of 'nurse-keeper' to mean monthly nurse: Tillyard, *Aristocrats*, pp. 231–2, 266. Cf. earlier references (*c.* 1571) to French- or Dutch-born 'keepers of women in childbed': R. E. G. and E. F. Kirk (eds), *Returns of Aliens Dwelling in the City and Suburbs of London*, Huguenot Society X, 2 Pts (1900–2), Pt 1, pp. 429, 430; Pt 2, p. 105.

47. Clark, *Working Life of Women*, p. 251. London poor-law usage of 'nurse', some of it ambiguous, may date from the 1650s: see the parish records cited by A. Wear, 'Caring for the Sick Poor in St Bartholomew's Exchange: 1580–1676', *Medical History*, Supplement No. 11 (1991), pp. 48, 59. On later poor-law nursing see also M. Fissell, *Patients, Power, and the Poor in Eighteenth-Century Bristol* (Cambridge, 1991), pp. 67–8.

48. See most recently C. Kazmierczak Manzione, *Christ's Hospital of London 1552–1598: 'A Passing Deed of Pity'* (Selinsgrove and London, 1995). On the London refoundations in general, see P. Slack, 'Social Policy and the Constraints of Government, 1547–58', in J. Loach and R. Tittler (eds), *The Mid-Tudor Polity c. 1540–1560* (London and Basingstoke, 1980), esp. pp. 108–14; Daly, 'The Hospitals of London'.

49. Daly, 'The Hospitals of London', pp. 179, 216, 253, 357.

50. N. J. M. Kerling, 'A Seventeenth-century Hospital Matron: Margaret Blague', *Transactions of the London & Middlesex Archaeological Society*, 22, iii (1970), 33.

associations, this term could bring with it from the nursery connotations to do with discipline, surveillance, custody, and 'upbringing' (or re-training) which were seen as appropriate to an institution seeking to solve the moral as well as physical problems of the poor. It was not until the term was applied to an orphanage, however, that it was adopted by poor-relief institutions concerned with medical care. In 1623, the town of Salisbury made William Waterman and his wife keepers of its workhouse; his wife was made 'laundress and nurse of the house and to be at the steward's command for the cleanly keeping and usage of those in the house'.[51] An important reference point for the mid-century with respect to hospitals is William Petty's practical and detailed scheme of 1648 for a teaching hospital as a pre-eminent part of his 'Nosocomium Academicum'. This remodelling of one of the old hospitals was to include nurses, of whom the 'ordinary' were to be paid £4 per annum and their subsistence. Petty effectively followed almshouse practice in prescribing 'honest carefull ancient Widowes' to be nurses; it was the medical staffs who had to be (relatively) young and unmarried. Although Petty gave some scope to the nurses' powers of observation, his plan otherwise showed little respect for them.[52] Petty also seems to have envisaged (sick)nurses as belonging in the nation's proper complement of medical practitioners.[53]

In terms of their real importance, the female staffs of the refounded hospitals bear the same molehill-to-mountain relation to the whole of the nursing task as the London College of Physicians did to the whole of medical practice. The hospitals can also be misleading in structural terms. Nonetheless, they may offer suggestions as to the content of the nursing task. The refounded St Bartholomew's began with a ratio of one sister to about ten patients, making a female complement of a matron, eleven sisters, and a 'fool' or 'innocent'. Norman Moore's rather 'merrie Englande' explanation of the fool was that she was kept to entertain the sisters, but it seems more likely that she was employed as an auxiliary, according to the widely used practice of paying the poor to help the poor, as well as the practice (adopted in Christ's Hospital and elsewhere) of finding suitable work even for the disabled. The inclusion of the fool is perhaps indicative of the nature of some of the work involved.[54] The subordinate class of nurses, added as already mentioned in the mid-seventeenth century, was eventually supplemented in the following century by a class of 'watchers' (who lived out), to do the night duty.[55] The activity of 'watching' was widely referred to before the eighteenth century, but 'watcher' seems to have been shortlived

51. P. Slack, *Poverty in Early Stuart Salisbury*, Wiltshire Record Society XXXI (1975), p. 87.

52. W. Petty, *The Advice of W. P. to Mr Samuel Hartlib* (London, 1648), pp. 10–11, 14, 16–17; Webster, *Great Instauration*, pp. 294–5. The nurses were to receive considerably less than even the surgeons' apprentices of the hospital (paid £10). 'Extraordinary' nurses were to be taken in as need arose, at a rate of 3s. per week. There was no matron, but a male steward, skilled in mathematics (paid £80).

53. W. Petty, *A Treatise of Taxes and Contributions* (1662), in C. H. Hull (ed.), *The Economic Writings of Sir William Petty*, 2 vols (New York, 1963), vol. 1, p. 27.

54. N. Moore, *The History of St Bartholomew's Hospital*, 2 vols (London, 1918), vol. 2, pp. 758–9; Pelling, 'Child Health', pp. 160–1 (129–30).

55. Moore, *History of St Bartholomew's*, vol. 2, pp. 764–5, 768. There was some overlap initially between 'nurse' and 'helper', the nurses being subordinate to the sisters.

as an occupational designation connected with the sick.[56] The matron – one is reminded of the sober or ancient matrons referred to in other official specifications – supervised the other women, and unlike the sisters and nurses she could be married.[57] She thus stood in a relation to them similar to that of a mistress of servants; as with most female servants, the implication was that sisters and *a fortiori* nurses (unlike nursekeepers) would be young. As in apprenticeship, the menial tasks tended to be allocated to the younger entrants.[58] The role of the matron in the institution was such that she was liable to set up in business for herself in various minor ways: medicine went together with the food and drink trades for women as well as for men.[59]

St Bartholomew's took serious cases and had an infectious ward for venereal disease, but, as in other refounded post-Reformation institutions, the incurable, as well as major operations like amputations, seem to have been transferred out of the hospital, often to the outhouses or lazarhouses which were placed in a ring around London alongside the main routes into the city.[60] This reduction of the sisters' task helps to explain why it was necessary to lay down that, when otherwise unoccupied, they were to spin and weave, not only for the hospital's needs but also to increase its income.[61] The regime imposed in principle on the sisters is usually seen as conventual, but it is little different from what was required from the poor inmates of hospitals themselves or from apprentices and servants. Incidents in and around the hospital make it clear that the buildings were an anthill of small traders and craftsmen, as well as serving in part as lodgings, so that the contact of the staff with daily life was greater than might be imagined; the same temptations were open to them as were worried about for apprentices and servants. Like the latter, the sisters were meant to stay in at night, but were apparently allowed out in an emergency, like attending wounded men, a practice which led to some bending of the rules.[62] The right to go abroad, to be on the streets, especially at night, was restricted as much as possible, particularly for women and young people, yet it was an essential aspect of many female employments including sicknursing, midwifery, laundering, marketing, and petty retailing.[63] The restrictions placed on the sisters and nurses of hospitals suggest less a true image of contemporary sicknursing, than something of its opposite: that is, regulations can be seen as an attempt to

56. *OED*'s example relating to sicknursing, of 1764, refers to women watchers in hospitals picking the pockets of their patients – significant in this context as a kind of continuation of the stereotype of the plague nurse (see below).

57. For a list of matrons from 1552, see Moore, *History of St Bartholomew's*, vol. 2, pp. 772–3. See also N. J. M. Kerling, 'Nursing in St Bartholomew's Hospital in the 17th Century', *St Bartholomew's Hospital Journal*, 74 (1970), 279.

58. Moore, *History of St Bartholomew's*, vol. 2, p. 763; Kerling, 'Nursing', pp. 278–9. In the mid-seventeenth century, some of the sisters and nurses could be widows and of mature age.

59. Moore, *History of St Bartholomew's*, vol. 2, pp. 759, 766–7; Pelling, 'Occupational Diversity', pp. 505–6, 509 (223, 227); Pelling, 'Trade or Profession', pp. 104–6 (244–5).

60. Moore, *History of St Bartholomew's*, vol. 2, chap. 17, esp. p. 278; Pelling, 'Appearance and Reality', pp. 97–8.

61. Moore, *History of St Bartholomew's*, vol. 2, pp. 269, 759.

62. Ibid., vol. 2, pp. 270, 280, 294, 310, 313.

63. On curfews and the young, see P. Griffiths, *Youth and Authority: Formative Experiences in England 1560–1640* (Oxford, 1996), pp. 78, 156, 177, 208–10.

redefine and reduce the independence characteristic of women engaged in such activity in the outside world. Such restrictions were most realistically applied to the young.

St Bartholomew's may be compared with a more typical institution, the refounded provincial hospital known as St Giles or God's House in Norwich.[64] This was more like an almshouse; during a reform period around 1620 it had male and female sick rooms, and a woman 'keeper of the sick', but it tended to send the seriously or terminally ill either to their homes or, as in London, to Norwich's own ring of outlying lazarhouses.[65] The post-Reformation God's House began in the late 1540s with specifications for a man, his wife, four 'matrons' or keepers, and 40 inmates. Later this ratio steadily worsened.[66] The male keeper or guider was indentured to provide a certain level of subsistence which was the same for the women keepers (who were apparently resident) as for the inmates. In contrast to later provisions, under which poor inmates were meant to nurse other inmates for nothing, the keepers were paid over and above their board by the institution. Included in their subsistence was a certain quality of bread, and in general meat, drink, firing, and washing 'meet and convenient for allmes people'.[67] Later in the sixteenth century the hospital's staff included a cator/steward, a porter/butler, and one person to be cook, baker, and brewer; these positions can more or less be matched to the working parts of the hospital indicated in a detailed inventory, including a firehouse, kitchen and pantry, brewhouse, wellhouse, millhouse, malthouse, buttery, little buttery, and pigs' house, leaving the washing house (and part of the cloisters where there was a rain-water tank and poles for drying) as the domain of the keepers.[68] The inventory goes into great detail of the bedding, blankets, coverings, and pillows in the hospital, naming also as assets 13 sheets brought in by poor people and in the keeper's hands for winding sheets; it also mentions two close stools and 21 chamber pots.

The material details of God's House are a reminder not only of the capital value of clothing, linen, and bedding, but also of their importance for health and the essential role of laundrywork. As the Salisbury appointment of Mrs Waterman also indicates, a major part of a female attendant's duty was to keep the almspeople, and *a fortiori* the sick, 'sweet and clean', and this was undoubtedly done more by washing coverings than by washing bodies. Washing clothes and linen, when soft soap was still a luxury and water not on tap or easily heated, was extremely laborious, physically uncomfortable and ultimately even disabling,

64. See C. Rawcliffe, *The Hospitals of Medieval Norwich* (Norwich, 1995), chap. 3, esp. pp. 102–3, 122, 125; W. K. Jordan, *The Charities of Rural England 1480–1660* (London, 1961), pp. 115–19.

65. NRO, Mayor's Court Proceedings, 1615–24, 30 October 1619, fol. 363verso; 25 December 1618, fol. 272recto. Pelling, 'Healing the Sick Poor', pp. 125–6 (900).

66. E. M. Leonard, *The Early History of English Poor Relief* (Cambridge, 1900), p. 209; NRO, Case 24, shelf b, no. 36, covenants with keepers of the Hospital, 1575–1627; W. L. Sachse (ed.), *Minutes of the Norwich Court of Mayoralty 1630–1631*, Norfolk Record Society XV (1942), pp. 161–2 (1631).

67. NRO, Case 24, shelf b, no. 36, covenant with William Oliver, 1556. The keeper of the sick appointed in 1619 was waged only until she could become an inmate: NRO, Mayor's Court Proceedings, 30 October 1619, fol. 363verso.

68. NRO, Case 24, shelf b, no. 36, covenant with Richard Durrant, 1582; NRO, Case 24, shelf b, no. 39, Inventory [n.d.]. Cf. Rawcliffe, *Hospitals of Medieval Norwich*, p. 115.

likely to involve exposure to strong chemicals as well as infection, and as a disruptive process often resented by those for whom it was being done.[69] The Norwich hospital's washing house contained at the time of the inventory one small copper, one great bucking tub, three great rinsing tubs, three washing tubs, two old pails with iron bills or spouts, one coalrake, one firefork of iron, one stool that the tub stood on, and one beating stool.[70] The term 'bucking', or washing with lye, occurs repeatedly in St Bartholomew's in connection with the duties of a nurse, and adequacy in this area was apparently the first technical as opposed to moral qualification to be explicitly laid down for sisters.[71]

This does not mean that attendants on the sick were not valued for qualities of gentleness and good conversation, or that laundresses were not employed for that task alone. Rather it needs to be stressed that the connection between washing and nursing was a serious one in personal, medical, and economic terms. On the one hand, washing was heavy labour, involving fires, equipment, and access to water-sources and outside ground; on the other it was extremely personal, allowing knowledge of the body's secrets, especially as cloth itself was not regarded as disposable. The stereotypes attached to laundresses (and to nurses) reflect the mixed, 'inside' and 'outside' character of their work. They were 'low life' but strong, and only too inclined, in their regular contacts with customers of higher social status, to assert their independence.[72] In the early seventeenth century two St Bartholomew's sisters beat some sheriff's officers who had come to arrest the hospital's steward for debt.[73] It is perhaps not surprising either that 'nurse' and 'laundress' were euphemisms for whore or bawd, or that Charles II as Prince of Wales was alleged to have escaped from the battle of Worcester disguised as a washerwoman.[74]

Although laundresses were made to bear many connotations of adult sexuality, they also reminded their employers of childishness, the dependency of infants, and the extreme loss of status involved in nappy-washing.[75] Thus, along with

69. On the labour of washing, see Mary Collier, 'The Woman's Labour', in *Poems on Several Occasions* (Winchester, 1762); C. Davidson, *A Woman's Work is Never Done: A History of Housework in the British Isles 1650–1950* (London, 1982), pp. 136–63.

70. NRO, Case 24, shelf b, no. 39, Inventory.

71. See Moore, *History of St Bartholomew's*, vol. 2, chap. 28, esp. p. 773 (1653). Soap (as opposed to wood ashes), which required hot water, was first mentioned in 1558, as the prerogative of the matron: ibid., vol. 2, p. 760.

72. See Pelling, 'Appearance and Reality', p. 93; Pelling, 'Older Women', pp. 170–2. Manningham took the trouble to record (*c.* 1602) the neat riposte of a laundress whom he accused of being saucy: J. Manningham, *Diary*, ed. J. Bruce, Camden Society XCIX (1868), p. 81. Cf. the 'real cleaners' of modern hospitals: L. Hart, 'A Ward of my Own: Social Organisation and Identity among Hospital Domestics', in Holden and Little-wood, *Anthropology and Nursing*, p. 93.

73. Moore, *History of St Bartholomew's*, vol. 2, p. 760.

74. James Shirley, *The Lady of Pleasure* (1635), ed. R. Huebert, Revels Plays (Manchester, 1986), p. 95; J. Raymond, 'The Daily Muse; or, Seventeenth-century Poets Read the News', *The Seventeenth Century*, 10 (1995), 193.

75. Luther used nappy-washing effectively as an extreme case to illustrate the blessedness of fatherhood under God: M. Prior, 'Reviled and Crucified Marriages: the Position of Tudor Bishops' Wives', in idem (ed.), *Women in English Society 1500–1800* (London and New York, 1986), p. 119. For an English response to Luther on this point, see M. Roberts, '"Words they are Women, and Deeds they are Men": Images of Work and Gender in Early Modern England', in L. Charles and L. Duffin (eds), *Women and Work in Pre-Industrial England* (London, 1985), pp. 149–50. Nappy-washing also represented an extreme in terms of (alleged) role reversal: L. Roper, *The Holy Household: Women and Morals in Reformation Augsburg* (Oxford, 1989), pp. 187, 259.

their physical strength, they threatened other forms of dominance over the body, as well as the dangers of pollution.[76] A much later, highly negative example illustrates the laundress's association with strength and with 'outside' and puts her in juxtaposition to the children's nurse:

Nurse was one of the race of tale-telling nurses, and whenever we were naughty she used to say a witch would come and take us off. . . . There was a most horrid old woman named Grassy, with a fearful front tooth like an elephant's tusk, who used to come and help in the wash house, and her husband, a frightful man called Long Peter (for he was quite a giant) who used to brew. And with these two dreadful people Nurse used to terrify us.[77]

Association with soap could imply not cleanliness, but pollution, damp, and a susceptibility to plague shared by soap boilers and soap sellers.[78] The link between nursing and washing needs to be explored outside as well as inside institutions, and points to the necessity of paying attention to the content of nursing at any period.[79]

One approach to this is invited by the Norwich census for the poor already quoted. The nature of the census is such that one might hope at least to identify a number of women in the expedient, wage-labouring category stigmatised by Alice Clark. In practice however matters are not so simple, even though the census freely uses the language of 'doing' as well as 'being' for occupations. Of the total of 838 women aged over 20, 112 (13.4 per cent) were unemployed or had no occupation ascribed to them.[80] Spinning and textile-related employments aside, the picture is one of diversity. Women who washed, or helped neighbours and wives to wash, comprised one of the larger groups, particularly since this was also a common secondary occupation.[81] However, only one woman (Joan Wattes) was described as a midwife, and only one as specifically engaged in sicknursing – Grace Tooke, a woman of 60 who had a very sick husband aged 80, and who was described as keeping sick persons and spinning wool.[82]

76. For controls in fifteenth-century towns over use of water-supplies by washerwomen, see Goldberg, *Women, Work and Life Cycle*, p. 135. For a washerwoman of Lyons accused of causing illness by sorcery (1554), see N. Z. Davis, 'Women in the Crafts in Sixteenth-century Lyon', in B. A. Hanawalt (ed.), *Women and Work in Preindustrial Europe* (Bloomington, IN, 1986), p. 195. Elizabeth Jackson, the old woman accused in the celebrated Mary Glover witchcraft case (1602), was a charwoman: M. MacDonald (ed.), *Witchcraft and Hysteria in Elizabethan London: Edward Jorden and the Mary Glover Case* (London and New York, 1991), p. xli.

77. A. Fairfax-Lucy (ed.), *Mistress of Charlecote: The Memoirs of Mary Elizabeth Lucy [1803–1889]* (London, 1985), p. 16.

78. Nathaniel Hodges, *Loimologia: or, an Historical Account of the Plague in London in 1665* [1665], trans. J. Quincy (London, 1720), p. 182; A. Brown, *The First Republic in America* (Boston and New York, 1898), p. 131.

79. On nursing, bodily excretion and the 'management of boundaries', see J. Littlewood, 'Care and Ambiguity: Towards a Concept of Nursing', in Holden and Littlewood, *Anthropology and Nursing*, pp. 170–89.

80. Calculated from Pound, *Census*, Appendices I, IV.

81. For greater detail on what follows, see Pelling, 'Older Women'. In general see also S. J. Wright, '"Churmaids, Huswyfes and Hucksters": the Employment of Women in Tudor and Stuart Salisbury', in Charles and Duffin, *Women and Work*, pp. 100–21; P. Earle, 'The Female Labour Market in London in the Late Seventeenth and Early Eighteenth Centuries', *Eco. Hist. Rev.*, 42 (1989), 328–53.

82. Pound, *Census*, pp. 30, 57.

Other formulae used in the census make it clear that the censustakers were not counting Grace Tooke as a sicknurse simply because she looked after her husband. Where this was a major feature of a household from the censustakers' point of view, it was recognised and recorded in formulae like 'looks to' and 'has the charge of'. It is hard to accept either that midwifery among the poor was limited to the scale indicated by Joan Wattes, or that sicknursing was carried on among this working population of over 700 women only by Grace Tooke. There is however a quite large group of women, about one in 20 of the female census population, who could superficially be written off as engaged simply in domestic wage labour but whose occupations may be seen as a continuum including nursing and washing. Some of them were specifically engaged in washing as well. The formulae used were various – the woman 'keeps wives', 'helps neighbours at need', 'keeps women', helps others or helps women, helps women 'in need', or 'washes and works abroad'. One woman, a widow of 60, spun white warp and 'tend[ed] the allms'. To this group could be added a man, a labourer of 56 (also, interestingly, with a sick family) who 'kept prisoners'.[83] Obviously it is a misrepresentation to describe this fairly large group of poor women as sicknurses or nursekeepers. Nevertheless, as we have already seen, it is within terms like 'keeping' and 'helping' that the activity of nursing may be found, and in most communities at this time the kind of labour pool represented by these women is the most likely source of occasional outside help. Most of them were aged 40 or older, but many still had family responsibilities of their own. The actual work of spinning, washing, and tending done by these poor women was little different from that of the unmarried sisters of St Bartholomew's who tended the London poor – or of the 'nurse Hilton' who supervised a spinning school for the children of Christ's in the late 1560s.[84] Whatever the exact content of their work, the implication of the Norwich census is that these poor women were not simply being neighbourly but were doing paid work outside the household.

The women keepers and helpers of the census would provide a reasonable representation of the providers of care in many poor-law contexts, and it could be assumed that they would be affordable (in cash, or kind). Whether or not they could fairly be regarded as 'unskilled' depends on our decision as to what skills were most essential. Interestingly, it is also in the poor-law context that one finds evidence suggesting a continuum of nursing and medical skills. For certain major surgical cases, such as cutting for the stone, the Norwich authorities were prepared to pay both a medical practitioner and another person, usually a woman, who would 'keep' the patient during the cure. In other cases however the keeping and curing roles were combined. I have discussed elsewhere the range of functions carried out in Norwich by the keepers of the lazarhouses, who took over serious, contagious, and incurable cases in the way already indicated.[85] Centres other than London and Norwich remain to be investigated, but much smaller towns such as Great Yarmouth had several of

83. Ibid., pp. 91, 56.
84. Daly, 'Hospitals of London', p. 328.
85. Pelling, 'Healing the Sick Poor', pp. 126–35 (91–100).

these vestigial lazarhouses and seem to have used them in a similar way. The keepers both cured and kept; they clearly had a partly custodial role; they were sometimes unmarried men, but were more often married men, or the widows of such men who carried on the business independently and could continue to do so in the event of remarriage. That is, the female keepers continued to be given keeping and curing or just curing contracts whether they were married or widowed. They did not subside into an auxiliary keeping role as a result of marriage. It is of course possible that in practice these keepers used the other inmates of their houses as a source of nursing care; they might also have employed one or two servants, likely to have been women.

A connection hard to escape in the available evidence on sicknursing by women is the connection apparently made by contemporaries between women and infectious disease. The nature of this connection would bear considerable examination, but it is at least possible that the sicknurse identified as such emerged from contexts involving the major infectious diseases of the period — plague, smallpox, typhus, and syphilis. Such conditions entailed the separate establishment (however small in scale, and whether under a different roof or not), and the custodial function, implied in 'keeper'; it is possible that such roles were seen as 'natural' extensions of the equally 'natural' responsibilities of children's nurses, children being seen as especially subject to infectious disease. It is possible also that older women were regarded as 'seasoned' by their contacts with children earlier in life.[86] Moreover, these major diseases provided the economic opportunities for the emergence of this kind of nursekeeper, especially in London.[87] Finally, the fairly short life of the term 'nursekeeper' could similarly be explained by its being too closely associated with some of the most contaminating diseases. 'Nurse' may have acquired some poor-law connotations, but retained the wider, more positive context of subordination to masculine social responsibility already described.[88]

With respect to plague, the difficulty arises of the relationship of emergency arrangements with common practice. Although 'opportunity' seems too positive a term, especially in this context, there is no doubt that conditions that spelt economic disaster for many provided chances for others prepared to take great risks. Paradoxically, incidents in which one member of a family bribed another to care for him or her, by promising legacies and other material incentives, may have been closer to normal practice involving nursekeepers than the

86. Some contemporary observers noted, pejoratively, that women keepers rarely died during epidemics: F. P. Wilson, *The Plague in Shakespeare's London* (Oxford, 1927), p. 67. Generally, women, especially pregnant women, were regarded as susceptible because of their overplus of 'excrementitious humours'; older women, and 'milch-nurses' were less so: S. Bradwell, *Physick for the Sicknesse, Commonly called the Plague* (London, 1636), pp. 9, 11. Whether men's susceptibility arose from residues of menstrual blood received from the mother's womb was also debated: S. Kellwaye, *A Defensative against the Plague* (London, 1593), fol. 39.

87. For instances of this kind of activity by private households from the fifteenth century, and criticism of it, see Slack, *Impact of Plague*, pp. 40, 290; F. M. Getz, 'To Prolong Life and Promote Health: Baconian Alchemy and Pharmacy in the English Learned Tradition', in S. Campbell, B. Hall and D. Klausner (eds), *Health, Disease and Healing in Medieval Culture* (Basingstoke, 1992), p. 148; Pelling, 'Appearance and Reality', p. 97.

88. For the range of occupational terms in use in London 1695–1725, including 'nurse-keeper', see Earle, 'The Female Labour Market', esp. p. 340, Appendix A.

elaborate administrative arrangements attempted by the authorities.[89] Following continental precedent, local bodies in time of plague were instructed to conscript a small army variously described as viewers, searchers, keepers, watchers, surveyors, examiners, collectors, providers, deliverers, and buriers. Only the richest parishes could make anything like such provision and the various functions, if carried out at all, tended to be combined in few people.[90] Many of these functions were not alien to what later came together as the occupation of nursing. Ipswich, in a plague outbreak in 1579, recruited women 'fitt to be kepers' and these keepers were to be responsible for fumigation of both premises and patients. In the same plague period Ipswich paid one Elkoke's widow 12 pence – about a week's maintenance – for 'wyndyng of Crawforde's douter' (i.e. in her winding-sheet) and for bringing her down from her chamber.[91] Laying-out continued to be a job done by freelance nurses at least into the nineteenth century, and was still being done by nurses in and outside hospitals in the twentieth.[92] This contrasts with the ideal, at least, of the role of men at the graveside.[93] In an interesting instance from the 1670s, a porter and his wife looked after a 'corpulent' man dying of 'the pox and a acancerated finger'; the division of labour appeared to be that the woman 'was nurse to' the patient throughout his last sickness, and present at his funeral; her husband 'watch[ed] with him day and night to help and torne him in his bed' especially in the final stages, and 'helped to lay him out'.[94] In the 1660s a 'nurse' of Christ's Hospital in Abingdon (a group of almshouses), was given charge of a funeral pall donated to the parish; she probably also washed it.[95]

The appointment of plague nurses in London parishes has been dated by Wilson to 1578, reinforced by the unique Act of Parliament of 1604.[96] Those working in pesthouses were still likely to be called keepers. Women actually described as plague 'nurses' were apparently appointed in some English urban parishes from the 1610s.[97] A case before Cheshire quarter sessions is valuable in giving some detail of plague nursing, and also in indicating the terminology being used by the later date of 1648. Two plague nurses of Manchester petitioned for arrears of pay owed to them by Middlewich, a salt town about 21 miles east

89. Slack, *Impact of Plague*, pp. 40, 288–90.

90. Ibid., pp. 270–83.

91. J. Webb, *Poor Relief in Elizabethan Ipswich*, Suffolk Record Society IX (1966), pp. 110–11. The Ipswich accounts used 'attending upon', 'looking to', and especially 'keeping' for the nursing task. 'Nurse' was still reserved for children: ibid., p. 116.

92. See B. Todd, 'Widowhood in a Market Town: Abingdon 1540–1720' (University of Oxford DPhil thesis, 1983), p. 59; Botelho, 'Provisions for the Elderly', pp. 339, 343; P. Sharpe, 'Literally Spinsters: a New Interpretation of Local Economy and Demography in Colyton in the Seventeenth and Eighteenth Centuries', *Eco. Hist. Rev.*, 44 (1991), 60–1. Hart, 'A Ward of my Own', p. 98. Mary Prior, personal communication.

93. See a complaint of 1550 that the male inmates of God's House in Norwich 'wylle nat help to bere them to ther gravys but make excusys and lat the women do ytt': Hudson and Tingey, *Records*, vol. 2, pp. 387–8.

94. CLRO, MC6/289B. Both man and wife were in their forties; the man was probably by trade a 'citizen and weaver' who had had to take on the more menial employment of portering. For similar examples see Pelling, 'Old Age, Poverty, and Disability', pp. 82–3 (141–2).

95. Todd, 'Widowhood', p. 322; for Christ's see pp. 20, 230ff.

96. Wilson, *Plague*, pp. 60, 67. On the Act (1 James I c. 31), see Slack, *Impact of Plague*, pp. 211–13 and *passim*. The Act refers to 'keepers', not 'nurses'.

97. Wilson, *Plague*, p. 181; Slack, *Impact of Plague*, pp. 271, 282.

of Chester. The women had been sent for by the constables and other inhabitants of Middlewich 'to be nurses to tende sicke persons', and claimed to have carried out their side of the bargain in dressing meat, keeping clean the clothes of the infected people, and cleansing and making habitable their houses, 'soe far as God should Enable them'. For this they were meant to receive 7*s.* a week and their diet, but they had only been paid in total £7 between them. This money they said had hardly been enough to buy victuals because of scarcity and high prices, and they had no other recourse or help, being as they put it 'far from their friends and where their Imployment most lyeth' – presumably Manchester.[98] What is not clear from this interesting example is whether the impression given by the women of being in regular employment as nurses meant just that, and it was incidentally that they were willing to nurse plague cases; or whether their employment would last only as long as the plague – which might explain part of their frustration at being stranded; or whether their usual employment was in fact something quite different. On the surface, the petitions of these Manchester women give an almost professional impression, supporting the possibility that this kind of nurse evolved as a result of the disease environments of major towns.

It may be a reflection of this form of female independence that a negative stereotype so rapidly developed in the vernacular plague literature – the predatory nurse or night-crow, who either spread infection by taking in strangers and nursing them for cash, or who robbed her patients while they were on their deathbeds and spread infection by selling their clothes and bedding. Thomas Dekker perhaps did most to establish this stereotype, playing on 'keeper' and bringing in other terms like 'nurse' and 'char-woman', although he also praised 'motherly' attendants, 'good Nurses indeed'. By 1665, Dekker's 'gnawers of linnen' were being abused by an unnamed writer as 'nurses', 'the off-scouring of the City', 'dirty, ugly, and unwholsome Haggs', 'a cunning Succuba'.[99] The nurse's right to dispose of clothing and linen may have been customary – one of the few privileges due to a woman attendant or a servant for remaining by the patient until death or recovery, and one of the few means of payment or inducement available even in the most exigent circumstances.[100] However, it could lead to conflict where there was (or was seen to be) considerable social distance between nurse and patient, and it obviously became a most problematic right in the context of infectious disease.[101] The stereotypical plague nurse long antedates Dickens's Mrs Gamp (who was a nurse as well as a midwife) and

98. J. H. Bennett and J. C. Dewhurst (eds), *Quarter Sessions Records . . . for the County Palatine of Chester 1559–1760*, Record Society of Lancashire and Cheshire XCIV (1940), pp. 127, 137. Cf. Clark, *Working Life of Women*, pp. 249–51.

99. Dekker, *English Villanies . . . discovered by Lanthorne and Candle-light* (London, 1638), sigs K2–3; Anon., *The Shutting up Infected Houses As it is practised in England Soberly Debated* (n. pl., 1665) [Wing 3717], pp. 9–10.

100. See for example C. M. Barron and A. F. Sutton (eds), *Medieval London Widows 1300–1500* (London and Rio Grande, 1994), p. 127; Todd, 'Widowhood', pp. 61–2; Slack, *Impact of Plague*, p. 289; Wright, '"Churmaids"', p. 107; Hill, *Servants*, p. 214.

101. Plague orders and tracts routinely insisted on measures to combat the pre-eminent role of clothing (including leather and fur) and bedding: see for example *Orders, thought meete by her Majestie* (London, 1593), sig. Aiii. Two of the 75 ways by which one observer thought people caught plague in 1665 were 'By a Chair woman' and 'By the Rakers or Ragg women': *Shutting up Infected Houses*, pp. 8, 14.

foreshadows many of her characteristics, in particular that of making a profit from a role which (as Mrs Gamp at least knew) society expected her to play out of charity or strictly according to the requirements of her community.

Plague was an obvious focus for ruminations upon the structure of social obligation, so that plague records can also include details of what was done in such testing circumstances by private individuals. Slack mentions the case of a London gentleman who dealt with the illness of a servant by boarding her up in a separate part of the house and employing a stranger to look after her.[102] This master was observing the letter of his obligation towards his servant but not its spirit: hence the stress on his having employed a stranger. Similar lines of action involving outsiders to the household were developed with respect to smallpox, and argue connections between at least some level of nursing care and the exchange economy. Such practices would have been needed first in large towns; the most likely victims of smallpox were young immigrants, servants or apprentices whose illness threatened the security of the master's own family.[103] Moreover, a 'bad sort' of smallpox could grossly affect the surface and mucous membranes of the body, covering the head, face, and hands and even the inside of the mouth as well as the body with weeping, blackening pustules; nursing such a case was infinitely unpleasant and unrelenting. Among a number of cases brought over the breakdown of apprenticeship in seventeenth-century London, in only one is a woman tending a sick or injured apprentice explicitly called a nurse, and she is brought in specifically to deal with smallpox.[104] The apprentice had a doctor to him for about three weeks, who advised convalescence in the country, which the apprentice's father also desired.[105] The master asked the apprentice's family to send a nurse out of the country for the apprentice, and part of the argument was because he paid her only 5s., and the father was forced to pay her 25s. more. This nurse may have supervised the recovery of the apprentice, whom the father felt obliged to accommodate in a separate house half a mile from his own. He had a numerous family and was obviously terrified of infection, besides the fact that the master was legally responsible for caring for the boy. As I have suggested elsewhere, the ubiquity and horror of smallpox among young immigrants to London may have had a considerable role in reshaping the conventions of apprenticeship and thereby the contemporary structure of social obligation.[106] It may be also that this disease created a demand, similar to but more persistent than in the case of plague, for establishments separate from either the parental or the master's household, supervised by women who came to call themselves nurses, or where the apprentice could be placed in charge of a nurse. The use of the term 'nurse' to describe such a woman is likely to have been encouraged by the comparative

---

102. Slack, *Impact of Plague*, p. 288.

103. See Pelling, 'Child Health', pp. 158–9 (127–8); Pelling, 'Apprenticeship', esp. p. 45.

104. CLRO, MC6/222A–B (1669).

105. The doctor, who (reticently) gave evidence, was a physician, Nathaniel Hodges of London – probably the author of *Loimologia*, which included a diatribe against plague nurses: ibid., pp. 8 ff, 26, 188, 216.

106. Pelling, 'Apprenticeship', pp. 45–6, 51.

youth of her most usual patients, and by the devolving to her of quasi-parental responsibilities.[107] Thomas Sydenham, part of whose reputation as the 'English Hippocrates' was based on his studies of smallpox, referred to 'nurses' in connection with this disease in 1668; Gideon Harvey in his critique of academic physicians of 1683 implied that nurses effectively competed with physicians in the management of smallpox. By the 1730s, one male practitioner at least could express guarded approval of the 'sober, thoughtful, and long experienced' smallpox 'nurse'.[108]

Greater detail is required before it is possible to determine how much autonomy was enjoyed by the sicknurse or nursekeeper. However it will already be evident that, in most of the circumstances discussed here, there is little reason to expect a dependent relationship between the person acting as nurse, and the medical practitioner. Medical sources tend to be vague about those tending the sick, while often giving the impression (as was traditional) that these friends and representatives were numerous and often unreasonable in their expectations as well as heedless of instruction.[109] A major exception should be made here in respect of the apprentices of barbers and barber-surgeons, who were nearly always male.[110] In the period in question, probably a majority of these practitioners did *not* take on apprentices, but where they did, and where this was connected with a medical role rather than one in some other occupation, the apprentices must have functioned in some respects as nurses.[111] Sometimes it seems that they were made to live with a patient for a time, although this was frowned upon as a form of neglect by the master. According to the satirists, the true surgeons, having fewer cases than other practitioners, made each of them last a long time. The satirists were thinking especially of accidents and woundings.[112] However the new diseases, especially syphilis, and more drastic treatments, could also involve lengthy hands-on procedures in which the surgeon had either to act a modern nurse's role himself, or depend upon someone else to do so with strict conformity to instructions. Thus, perhaps surprisingly for later commentators, it is the early modern male surgeon for whom care

107. Tracts linking smallpox and plague, both as diseases and as creating a similar need for advice, include Kellwaye, *Defensative against the Plague* (1593), and Thomas Sherwood, *The Charitable Pestmaster* (London, 1641). Kellwaye gave advice 'for that often times the face and handes which is the beautye and delight of our bodies are . . . disfigured' (fol. 43). Sherwood deplored mistaken measures taken by 'tender mothers' but also by 'women' who managed smallpox cases (pp. 7, 13).

108. A. Cunningham, 'Thomas Sydenham: Epidemics, Experiment and the "Good Old Cause"', in R. French and A. Wear (eds), *The Medical Revolution of the Seventeenth Century* (Cambridge, 1989), pp. 178, 187; Wear, 'Caring for the Sick Poor', pp. 56–7 (syphilis, smallpox); T. Lobb, *A Treatise of the Smallpox* (London, 1731), pp. iv–v. See also Lobb's reference to 'our good Women' (p. xxvi). Lobb also implied that there were two main schools of thought (hot and cold) among smallpox nurses (p. iv). Note, however, Lobb's record of a devoted father acting as nurse, who was otherwise typical in having been himself exposed to the disease as an apprentice (p. xxxiv).

109. A relevant example is the surgeon William Clowes, who warns of 'evil keepers': *A Brief and Necessarie Treatise, Touching the Cure of the Disease called Morbus Gallicus* (London, 1585), fols 16–18. His 'lewd and filthy . . . good and honest nurses' are clearly wetnurses: fols 2–3.

110. See also King, 'Using the Past', pp. 18–19.

111. Pelling, 'Occupational Diversity', pp. 497–503 (215–19).

112. See for example John Earle's 'Surgeon': H. Morley (ed.), *Character Writings of the Seventeenth Century* (London, 1891), pp. 192–3.

was inseparable from cure.[113] For the Elizabethan surgeon William Clowes, the mode of management of a syphilis cure was what made the difference between himself and a quack using the same specific. Diseases like smallpox, syphilis, and plague, in which the patient had to be 'sweated', meant a rigorous regime of giving drinks and keeping the patient in bed, covered, warm, and even, in certain phases, awake. Keepers or watchers in the patient's household would have been essential for such cases, as well as for other fevers, but the continued existence of (male) apprentices would have limited pressure for any other group of attendants under the control of the practitioner. However the apprentice, even if left with the patient, is very unlikely ever to have had to carry out tasks like washing linen and scrubbing floors. This gendered division of labour probably pertained even where males carried out other parts of the nursing task.[114]

Some 'acute' situations involving infectious disease contrast with the range of expedients which continued to be adopted in time of illness: servants carried out first aid,[115] servants (male as well as female) could be paid extra for extra 'pains',[116] washerwomen were brought in, travellers were lodged with those whom the parish could pay to take them in,[117] former servants could be taken back into the household on a semi-permanent basis as carers,[118] relatives were offered inducements or placed under pressure, and households in general were restructured to cope with chronic illness or disability.[119] Although wives undoubtedly had much to do with nursing members of their households – and the nursing of a sick husband was, as we have already seen, a duty attracting various forms of comment, satirical and otherwise[120] – it is often very unclear exactly who carried out the actual work involved. The terminology used for the poor women of Norwich suggests that outside help was often brought in even

113. Clowes tells a number of stories from his own practice illustrating these points: see F. N. L. Poynter (ed.), *Selected Writings of William Clowes 1544–1604* (London, 1948), pp. 56–70, 107–9; Clowes, *Brief and Necessary Treatise*, fols 38ff. A model for surgeons of the period was provided by Ambroise Paré; a success story involving his taking over the diet, bedding, and hair care of a case is rightly quoted by older nursing historians: see M. A. Nutting and L. L. Dock, *A History of Nursing*, 4 vols (New York and London, 1907–12), vol. 1, pp. 481–2.

114. This would also be true of medical students if not orderlies in hospitals, but distinctions between 'clean dirt' and 'dirty dirt' can also of course make divisions among women themselves. See above, p. 193; Hart, 'A Ward of my Own', pp. 95–6, 103–5.

115. See for example the actions of Judith Butcher, maidservant: CLRO, MC6/141A–B (1662).

116. For one among many examples, see the accounts generated during an outbreak of smallpox in the Archer household in 1711: J. O. Halliwell (ed.), *Some Account of a Collection of Several Thousand Bills, Accounts and Inventories* (Brixton Hill, 1852), pp. 76, 82, 92, 119 and *passim*. These well illustrate the sources of confusion, since as well as paying 'Betty' for nursing him – one of several possible 'Bettys' during the short period involved – Archer also employed a nurse for his child, who was paid extra for looking after 'dear Willy' in the smallpox, and he further paid 'a nurse' to care for one of his servants.

117. T. R. Forbes, *Chronicle from Aldgate: Life and Death in Shakespeare's London* (New Haven, CT, and London, 1971), pp. 224–8.

118. See Mr Waver, 'a sickly man' who took in a former servant and her husband: Dale, 'Returns of Divided Houses' (1637), p. 119.

119. See the residual household of Sir Richard Martyn, alderman and bankrupt, which included a surgeon to dress Martyn's leg, an 'innocent', and a Mrs Dale who paid board but was 'a stay and comfort': M. B. Donald, *Elizabethan Monopolies* (Edinburgh and London, 1961), p. 47.

120. See for example Thomas Smith, *De Republica Anglorum* (London, 1583), p. 104; for one grateful husband, see Barron and Sutton, *Medieval London Widows*, p. 131. See also Rawcliffe, *Medicine and Society*, pp. 182–3, 185.

by relatively poor families, even if only for the major task of washing. By contrast with the nursekeepers, none of these practices could be expected to produce a stable occupational identity, although they might prompt its development. Gender identity seems also to have remained fairly fluid, partly because of the role of contingent circumstances – where the person fell ill, for example. Probably most revealing here are the deathbed and funeral expense accounts which survive for the later period along with other testamentary documentation. An example of 1676 involved male and female personnel: the account itemised lodging, a shroud, comforts like mutton, tobacco, pipes, and ale, a fee to the women searchers of £1/0/6, bread with a posset and other drinks costing 8s., clerk's fees of 19s., a washerwoman paid 1s. 2d., and 5s. paid 'for the man that lookt after him in his siknes' – the total bill coming to £4/12/0.[121]

It is tempting in conclusion to stress the enduring sameness of low-status women's work, a continuity which might link the Magota Spynster alias Lavender glimpsed in late-fourteenth-century Exeter, through the Norwich women, to . Mary Collier, the eighteenth-century washerwoman-poet who gained a patron by night-nursing a sick gentlewoman.[122] However, although this is a necessary emphasis, the implications of terminology are only one reminder of the need to respect the involvement of men in some aspects of the nursing task. It also seems clear that Alice Clark was correct to identify the seventeenth century as a period in which significant shifts in respect of women's work took place, of which nursing provides a telling example. This is not to say that Clark's account of nursing can be allowed to stand. Her approach may be compared with that of the monumental history of nursing by Nutting and Dock, first published from 1907 but apparently not consulted by Clark. Like Clark, these authors located the 'dark ages' of nursing in the two centuries following the Dissolution, and found England before the nineteenth century particularly deficient. Unlike Clark however, Nutting and Dock dissociated nursing from vocational institutions, commenting that 'something in the nature of nursing service naturally eludes strict monastic forms and is resistant to solemn vows'; they also saw nursing as contributing to the movement of women towards economic equality.[123] Although the perspective of Nutting and Dock is probably closer to the truth for the English context, it is ironic that they should also stigmatise the very period in which nursing for women may have come closest to having a visible occupational identity outside hospitals. This is however hardly accidental, or unfaithful, in one way, to the sources. If it is true that infectious disease did most to provide this 'opportunity', it is not surprising that the gains for women were both extremely precarious and double-edged. Outside the household, the connotations of upbringing, surveillance, and control included in 'nursing' and 'keeping' could in any case have been lent to women only on sufferance and under limiting conditions, such as those obtaining in poor relief or in the care of apprentices and servants. An association with infectious disease was not simply

121. Halliwell, *Some Account*, pp. 18–19.

122. M. Kowaleski, 'Women's Work in a Market Town: Exeter in the Late Fourteenth Century', in Hanawalt, *Women and Work*, p. 153; Collier, *Poems*, p. iv.

123. Nutting and Dock, *History of Nursing*, vol. 1, pp. 450, 460, 470, 499–503, 259.

limiting, but corrosive. The circumstances in which nursekeepers were most needed, were also those which aroused the most fear and distaste; as we have seen, negative stereotypes leapt into being almost immediately. 'To lye at the mercy of a strange woman is sad . . . but who can express the misery of being exposed to their rapine that have nothing of the woman left but shape?', wrote one seventeenth-century author in plague-time, with unconscious resonance.[124] The services of 'strange women' were essential on an everyday basis for most men in early modern towns, were taken for granted, and indeed exploited; this was not in itself evidence of the breakdown of social obligation. However the short-lived 'nursekeeper' had to carry the burdens not only of the normal dislike of female independence, but also of the mistrust associated with devolved responsibility, fears of loneliness, helplessness and loss, and, in an exaggerated form, connotations of contamination and decay.

---

124. *Shutting up Infected Houses*, p. 9. On fear of loss of control as an aspect of nursing, see also King, 'Using the Past', p. 13.

CHAPTER NINE

Occupational Diversity: Barber-surgeons and Other Trades, 1550–1640

Our historical investigations into health and medicine in the early modern period have not yet passed the early stages. Possibly more has been achieved for England than for elsewhere (Italy excepted), but our knowledge is still, in many respects, deficient and unbalanced. On the medical side, a small elite of academically qualified physicians continues to represent 'the profession'; with respect to the topic of health, a recent burgeoning of interest has been confined largely to the major plague epidemics and their effects on general trends in mortality. Some notable attempts have been made to move into unexplored territory,[1] but we are still largely ignorant of the routine experience of ill health of ordinary people in the past, just as we are uncertain of the character of those who gave them medical attention once health problems emerged which called for treatment outside the family circle.

The main theme of the present chapter is the interdigitation of medicine with other trades in the period 1550–1640. However, this diversification should not be taken as an indication that there was a low level of demand for medical advice. On the contrary, there is every sign of a consistently high demand for medical services in the early modern period, probably at every level of society, and irrespective of the usual criteria of effectiveness. The phenomenon requires further investigation, but some suggestions may be advanced. Historians of literature have long been aware that, among the literate classes at least, a high incidence of mortality did not lead the individual to look on the prospect of death with the indifference or resignation suggested by some historians of the family. Similarly, there seems good reason for supposing that a higher incidence

The first version of this chapter was given at the Spring 1981 meeting of the Society for the Social History of Medicine in Oxford. I am particularly grateful to Michael MacDonald and Charles Webster for their comments.

1. See K. Thomas, *Religion and the Decline of Magic* (Harmondsworth, 1980); Webster, *H, M & M*; M. MacDonald, *Mystical Bedlam: Madness, Anxiety and Healing in Seventeenth-Century England* (Cambridge, 1981); R. Porter (ed.), *Patients and Practitioners: Lay Perceptions of Medicine in Pre-Industrial Society* (Cambridge, 1985); L. M. Beier, *Sufferers and Healers: The Experience of Illness in Seventeenth-Century England* (London and New York, 1987); R. Porter and D. Porter, *In Sickness and In Health: The British Experience 1650–1850* (London, 1988); D. Evenden Nagy, *Popular Medicine in Seventeenth-Century England* (Bowling Green, OH, 1988); B. Duden, *The Woman Beneath the Skin: A Doctor's Patients in Eighteenth-Century Germany* (Cambridge, MA, and London, 1991); B. Harvey, *Living and Dying in England 1100–1540: The Monastic Experience* (Oxford, 1993).

of disease and deformity caused individuals to feel a proportionate acuteness of anxiety. It is rare in any correspondence of the period for the writers not to mention health problems. At the same time, concern was not reserved for major threats to health; there is little sign of stoicism even about minor defects or discomforts. These were undoubtedly augmented in this period by different kinds of dietary deficiency and as a result of infestation by external and internal parasites. The contemporary definition of disease, which emphasised symptomology, recognised the ever-present possibility that a minor symptom might herald a major decline. The enduring 'regimen of health' tradition reflected the need for constant vigilance. The individual had every reason for closely observing his or her own bodily functions and for demanding expertise in prognosis as well as cure. Economic as well as spiritual issues could be at stake – risks to property and posterity as well as to the health of the soul. To state of body was linked state of mind, and much attention was given to problems such as sleeplessness. For both men and women the generative functions, even when normal, constantly led to the need for advice on such questions as fertility and pregnancy. Of the senses, that of sight caused almost obsessive concern and, as in the third world today, was easily threatened; institutions and specialisms arose accordingly.

In the early modern period, human beings were seen as continuously interacting with their environment, so that health, even if attained, was a matter of a carefully preserved equilibrium rather than a state of permanency. Given a humoral view of disease which emphasised a process of resolution at either the inner surface of the body (the gut) or the outer (the skin), it is not surprising to find emphasis both on monitoring the excretions, and on sores, boils, and other cutaneous appearances which might now be regarded as superficial. It is possible that few individuals would have called themselves healthy, but this did not mean that they lacked ideals of health and of beauty which stressed, against all the odds, the clean, straight, unmarked body which the searchers were seemingly to have in mind during witchcraft trials. In fact, unblemished skin in men as well as women must have been a rarity. As well as local infections, several major diseases of the time – leprosy, scurvy, syphilis, smallpox, and certain forms of tuberculosis – manifested themselves strikingly on visible parts of the body such as the face, neck, and hands. The barber's attentions to these parts would therefore have had considerable significance, and a good appearance and health itself must have been seen partly as interchangeable.

The maintenance of health, and the relief of anxiety about health, were thus daily preoccupations the irreducibility of which was universally acknowledged. Illness was accepted as an excuse for disobeying the most urgent summons, even though it must often have been used as a ploy. Traditional medicine had evolved a scale of treatments, fees, and even illnesses according to the status of the patient so that having the means to pay was not decisive in seeking treatment. For their part, laypeople reserved the right to treat themselves, to drive bargains (they bought 'cures' rather than treatment), and not to trust themselves to any single practitioner. Medicine's sacerdotal aspect may be seen in its provision of a rich source of psychological support commensurate with the individual's state of anxiety. In other respects, however, medicine at this time appears as an item of consumption, a daily necessity which could be treated with irreverence, bought in the marketplace, and publicly consumed. In its double nature, sacred and profane, medicine resembled food and drink; there was no dividing line between medicines and nourishment. This had its economic consequences: physicians dominated the emergent Distillers' Company in London, and, as we shall see, medical practitioners were closely connected with the food and drink trades at all levels.

Few of the economic aspects of medicine have received the serious attention they deserve from historians. This is particularly true of the period 1550–1640, when medicine's claims to status, professionalisation, and institutionalisation all appear uncertain. Although guided by very different assumptions, economic historians have conspired with historians of medicine to minimise the role played by medical practitioners in the wider social and economic context.

This neglect has not been remedied by the enthusiasm among general historians for occupational analysis. Such analysis transfers the role of work in defining industrial society primarily to the early modern town, offering insights into its economic and social state previously thought unobtainable. Occupations provide a common language for urban, economic, social, and local historians, a language regularly translatable into quantitative terms and therefore meaningful also to demographers. Earlier writers, in analysing the growth of capitalism, gave prominence to the guilds.[2] More recent discussion, while relying on similar types of information, tends to hinge on broad divisions of occupations into functional categories (for example, service, retail), or categories based on the raw materials of production.[3] That the accepted forms of occupational analysis have definite limitations has been increasingly recognised by historians, but a state of dependency persists, partly because of the need to make comparisons between centres of economic activity.[4] The argument continues to concentrate on identifying the best single source for analysis, a restriction of view encouraged by the emphasis on quantification.[5] Sources other than the freemen's rolls of citizens of towns or members of companies have largely been used only in towns where these records happen to be absent, or with respect to rural areas.[6]

2. For earlier studies see E. E. Le P. Power, 'English Craft Gilds in the Middle Ages: Historical Revisions, 12', *History*, 4 (1919–20), 211–14.

3. The models most commonly used are those of W. G. Hoskins (see especially his essays published in 1955 and 1956, and reprinted in his *Provincial England* [1965]); or Hoskins via Pound (J. F. Pound, 'The Social and Trade Structure of Norwich, 1525–1575', *P & P*, 34 (1966), 49–64).

4. A. J. and R. H. Tawney, 'An Occupational Census of the Seventeenth Century', *Eco. Hist. Rev.*, 5 (1934), 25–64; D. M. Woodward, 'Freemen's Rolls', *Local Historian*, 9 (1970), 89–95; J. Patten, 'Urban Occupations in Pre-industrial England', *Transactions of the Institute of British Geographers*, 2 (1977), 296–313; also the stress by Pound on giving the contents of larger occupational categories: e.g., in his 'Government and Society in Tudor and Stuart Norwich, 1525–1675' (University of Leicester PhD thesis, 1974), chap. 3. See lately H. Swanson, *Medieval Artisans* (Oxford, 1989); J. Barry, 'Introduction', in Barry (ed.), *The Tudor and Stuart Town: A Reader* (London and New York, 1990), esp. pp. 8–9; P. J. Corfield, 'Defining Urban Work', in Corfield and D. Keene (eds), *Work in Towns 850–1850* (Leicester, 1990), pp. 207–30.

5. J. F. Pound, 'The Validity of the Freemen's Lists: Some Norwich Evidence', *Eco. Hist. Rev.*, 34 (1981), 48–59.

6. For a tabulation of analyses including the sources used, see L. A. Clarkson, *The Pre-Industrial Economy in England 1500–1750* (London, 1974), pp. 88–92. See also, with respect to parish registers, E. A. Wrigley, 'The Changing Occupational Structure of Colyton over Two Centuries', *Local Population Studies*, 18 (1977), 9–22.

In this context medical practitioners have so far played a very minor role. In an analysis of occupations, if they are lumped together under services, they appear as an aspect of consumption. Otherwise, physicians and surgeons appear as high-status professionals along with clergy and officials, apothecaries appear sometimes as professionals but usually as retailers, and barbers and barber-surgeons are listed as either dealing and retail, or services, or miscellaneous.[7] The numbers registered are usually minute, although such groups as school-masters are often no more numerous and yet receive separate treatment.

Medical practitioners have been neglected in occupational analysis partly because trades and professions in the early modern period have tended to be studied from very different points of view. Trades were numerous and are seen as the index to economic development. Professions are regarded as culturally important but numerically insignificant, and of limited value as economic indic-ators. Lawyers, schoolmasters and medical practitioners are primarily studied not because of the role they played in the economic life of the community, but because they represent various stages of the process of professionalisation.[8] This approach has tended to enforce a distinction between tradesmen and professionals and to obscure important features of so-called professional groups. This has had several consequences. First, the number of those engaged in different branches of the relevant activity has been concealed. Second, partly as a result of this, their importance within the community has been greatly underestimated. It is still common, for example, to come across statements in the literature that the vast majority of inhabitants of early modern towns either treated their own ills or were not treated at all; or that medical poor relief remained rudimentary or non-existent until a later period when the growth of the medical profession allowed it to be developed.[9] Third, there is a failure to recognise the range and complexity of the economic activities of medical prac-titioners. Last, as a consequence of this, the degree of comparability between occupational and professional groups in towns, especially in the case of medicine, is unrecognised, as is the extent of shared economic ground and of the inter-weaving of occupational activity. Thus one study of the town of Worcester, which places some emphasis on economic diversification, finds little evidence of the activity of physicians in its single main source (inventories), and therefore con-cludes that 'the medical profession – if it deserves such a distinguished title at this date – was an occupation of only modest importance in the city'.[10]

The literature on this period generated by medical historians, on the other hand, deals with medical practitioners in isolation, but it has, usually uninten-tionally, contributed to the effect of undervaluation by seeking to place medicine

7. Less conventional are D. Charman, 'Wealth and Trade in Leicester in the Early Sixteenth Century', *Transactions of the Leicestershire Archaeological Society*, 25 (1949), Table III, who includes both 'barber' and 'medicus' in 'General Trades', and C. Phythian-Adams, 'The Economic and Social Structure', in *The Fabric of the Traditional Community*, Open University Course Book (Milton Keynes, 1977), p. 40, who deliberately omits the categories 'professional' and 'miscellaneous' from his general discussion altogether.

8. K. Charlton, 'The Professions in Sixteenth-century England', *University of Birmingham Historical Journal*, 12 (1969), 20–41. See also Pelling, 'Trade or Profession'.

9. See Pelling, 'Healing the Sick Poor', p. 115, n. 1 (79, n. 1).

10. A. D. Dyer, *The City of Worcester in the Sixteenth Century* (Leicester, 1973), pp. 145, 146.

unequivocally among the professions. National legislation and institutional events in London have been made a suffficient basis for showing medicine in England as having by right an independent status as one of the learned professions, although this status might be regarded as some way off achievement. Separate institutionalisation is thus said to reflect a sense of responsibility and the desire to enforce essential educational standards. The craft element of surgery is seen as ensuring the lesser status of surgeons and barber-surgeons. The tripartite division of the profession into physicians, surgeons and apothecaries is depicted as at last asserting itself in this period, if it is not seen as a priori. One result of this approach has been that the provinces are described only in a negative way, as having fewer resources and lower standards.[11]

There is an obvious need for a re-examination of the role of medical personnel in the occupational structure of provincial towns which brings to bear on the problem the various categories of available evidence. With an inclusive approach a more organic idea can emerge of the working of the guild system and of the functioning of an occupational group: at the same time, light will be cast on the operations of other groups. A modified case-study approach will allow a detailed analysis to be made of a particular example of the occupational group as a whole, both within and outside the guild structure.

The provincial capital of Norwich has often served as a basis for analysis, both because its enduring role in the important and populous region of East Anglia has ensured the survival of a wide range of sources, and because the numbers involved could be assumed to be sufficient for statistical as well as illustrative purposes.[12] It was on not-dissimilar grounds that Norwich was seen by the London College of Physicians in the sixteenth century as the only town outside the metropolis where the College had a real prospect of regulating unlicensed practice, at least by certain types of practitioner. (It will become clear that there was every reason for these hopes also to be groundless.) In the present context, Norwich alone supplies more than enough information to suggest that a reassessment of occupational groups is needed, but this examination will be strengthened by reference to medical practice in provincial towns in general.[13]

11. See for example J. H. Raach, 'English Medical Licensing in the Early Seventeenth Century', *Yale Journal of Biology and Medicine*, 16 (1944), 267–88; G. Clark, *A History of the Royal College of Physicians of London*, 2 vols (Oxford, 1964–66); E. Shelton-Jones, 'The Barber-Surgeons' Company of London and Medical Education 1540–1660' (University of London MPhil thesis, 1981). Far more suggestive is R. S. Roberts, 'The Personnel and Practice of Medicine in Tudor and Stuart England', *Medical History*, 6 (1962), 363–82 and 8 (1964), 217–34.

12. See especially the work of Pound (see notes 3, 4, 5, 47); of P. Corfield, for example, 'A Provincial Capital in the Late Seventeenth Century: the Case of Norwich', in P. Clark and P. Slack (eds), *Crisis and Order in English Towns 1500–1700* (London, 1972), pp. 263–310; P. Slack, for example, *Impact of Plague*; J. T. Evans, *Seventeenth-Century Norwich* (Oxford, 1979); P. Griffiths, *Youth and Authority: Formative Experiences in England 1560–1640* (Oxford, 1996).

13. The basis for what follows are the biographical indexes of medical practitioners, 1500–1720, held at the Wellcome Unit for the History of Medicine, University of Oxford. These indexes are derived from a wide range of primary and secondary sources, with reference principally to East Anglia (including Cambridgeshire and Essex), the University of Oxford, and London, as indicated elsewhere: Pelling and Webster, 'Medical Practitioners', esp. p. 167, n. 1; p. 192, n. 63; p. 208, n. 83; and Pelling, 'A Survey of East Anglian Medical Practitioners 1500–1640', *Local Population Studies*, 25 (1980), 54–5. No attempt will be made in the present chapter to duplicate index entries for all sources in respect of each point or identity. Additional, more specific sources for individuals are given where appropriate.

The results obtained from an investigation of Norwich from 1550 to 1640 contradict the idea of the small, emergent professional group. A great diversity of practice is found within the main medical guild of the town, and large numbers of different types of practitioner involved themselves in some way with guild and municipal procedures. At the same time, the discovery of a very large group in Norwich who lay outside the formal procedures of freedom, or membership, apprenticeship, and officebearing in the guild or company confirms that the size of an occupational group cannot be accurately estimated from official sources alone, or indeed from any single alternative source. In addition, the range of economic diversification displayed by a significant number of practitioners at the time further demonstrates that, in the expanding English towns, occupational affiliations were far less restrictive than it has been convenient to believe. Individuals followed more than one line of economic activity, not only sequentially but also simultaneously, and it is not clear that this occurred only as an aspect of economic decline.[14] Diversification varied with the locality and occupation concerned.

Any examination of the organisation of medical practice in the English provinces at this period must concentrate on the barber-surgeons. No distinct body of physicians is known outside London, and the College of Physicians had merely the will, not the ability, to play a credible role outside the capital. Similarly, there were no recognisably separate surgeons' companies, and even the London surgeons failed to maintain an identity separate from that of the numerically superior barbers. The associations of the apothecaries were with the mercantile trades, and, for this reason, less will be said about them here. It should, however, be stressed that the apothecaries were collectively, among those practising the medical crafts, of higher status, more wealthy, and very much more likely than barber-surgeons to bear civic responsibilities; the London apothecaries' company did not separate off from the grocers until 1617, and associations of apothecaries with barber-surgeons' companies belong rather to the later seventeenth century. Nonetheless, it must be emphasised that examples are readily found of Norwich apothecaries engaging in medical practice, and that the formation of a separate company in London was related to the involvement of apothecaries in physic.[15]

Efforts to determine the complexion of barber-surgeons' companies in terms of distinct groups of barbers, surgeons and barber-surgeons seem doomed to failure. This is not to deny that there were many barbers who concentrated on barbering, with its washing, shaving, and minimum of medical skills,[16] or that there were, even in official records, individuals who emerge as the equivalent

14. Cf. Dyer, *City of Worcester*, p. 145. Swanson has lately argued this point for York in the late medieval period, but with the effect of depriving the guilds of economic functions: *Medieval Artisans*.

15. See Pelling and Webster, 'Medical Practitioners', pp. 177–9, 220–2. See also R. S. Roberts, 'The London Apothecaries and Medical Practice in Tudor and Stuart England' (University of London PhD thesis, 1964); T. D. Whittet, 'The Apothecary in Provincial Gilds', *Medical History*, 8 (1964), 245–73; L. G. Matthews, 'The Spicers and Apothecaries of Norwich', *Pharmaceutical Journal*, 198 (1967), 5–9; Pelling, 'Apothecaries and Other Medical Practitioners in Norwich around 1600', *Pharmaceutical Historian*, 13 (1983), 5–8.

16. In this chapter the term 'medicine' is used to include surgery. Where surgery is excluded, the term 'physic' is used.

of surgeon-specialists. Rather, the situation was a fluid one. Barbers were particularly prone to diversification in their careers, and they were notorious for diversifying in the direction of physic as well as surgery. As one sixteenth-century satirist complained,

> O *Esculape*! How rife is Phisicke made
> When ech Brasse-basen can professe the trade.[17]

Complaints by other practitioners of the intrusion of barbers were commonplace. Some barbers went to the trouble of obtaining licences to practise from the ecclesiastical authorities, a fact denied by some later surgeons anxious to stress their own connections with the learned physicians.[18] In Norwich the barber-surgeons' company explicitly included physicians and had among its officebearers physicians (including MDs), surgeons, lithotomists, bonesetters, and surgeon-physicians, but was familiarly known as the barbers' company.[19] As has been shown elsewhere, the barbers, barber-surgeons and surgeons carried the main burden of general practice in the towns;[20] in order to convey more accurately this range of activities, the term 'barber-surgeon' will be used here. The term 'barber', which was more routinely used in the sixteenth century, has too narrow a connotation for the modern reader, even though some twentieth-century barbers have been found practising a form of medicine.[21]

Barber-surgeons' companies have been located in 26 English urban centres outside London, and it is not surprising that this list roughly coincides with the top half of a ranking of the foremost English corporate towns of the early modern period.[22] However, the examples of Kings Lynn (ranked eighth in 1523–27), Colchester (ranked eleventh) and Great Yarmouth (ranked twentieth), where no company is known but where barber-surgeons existed in appreciable numbers, are a reminder that separate companies are only one indication of activity. In northwestern towns especially, barber-surgeons were included in conglomerate companies.[23] It might have been expected that persons calling themselves barbers would only proliferate outside towns subsequent to the diversification of trade in rural areas, but this is not true of well-populated regions at least. A single source for East Suffolk, an area less disturbed than Norfolk

17. A. Davenport (ed.), *The Collected Poems of Joseph Hall Bishop of Exeter and Norwich* (Liverpool, 1949), p. 54.

18. See James Paget's introduction to J. F. South, *Memorials of the Craft of Surgery in England*, ed. D'A. Power (London, 1886), p. xii; cf. for example NRO, Diocesan Archives, VSC/2 Consignation Book No. 4 (1636), fol. 31 (George Watts).

19. See Pelling and Webster, 'Medical Practitioners', pp. 211, 217; C. Williams, *The Masters, Wardens and Assistants of the Guild of Barber-Surgeons of Norwich . . . 1439–1723* (Norwich, 1900).

20. Pelling and Webster, 'Medical Practitioners'.

21. R. S. and H. M. Lynd, *Middletown* (New York, 1929), p. 435.

22. For the ranking, based on subsidies of 1523–27, see W. G. Hoskins, *Local History in England*, 2nd edn (London, 1976), pp. 238–9. On provincial barber-surgeons' companies, see G. Parker, 'The History and Powers of the Barber-surgeons in Great Britain', in *International Congress of Medicine (History of Medicine Section)*, 23 (1914), 285–95, esp. p. 286; S. Kramer, *The English Craft Gilds* (New York, 1927), esp. pp. 18, 57–9; [E. P. Dickin], 'Barbour-surgeons of Sandwich', *British Medical Journal*, ii (1906), 960; Phythian-Adams, *Desolation of a City*, pp. 45, 101; J. McNee, 'Barber-surgeons in Great Britain and Ireland', *Annals of the Royal College of Surgeons of England*, 24 (1959), 1–20.

23. For example, Lancaster, Ripon, and Kendal.

might be thought to be by the presence of large towns and cities, shows barbers to be present before 1640 in such smaller centres as Brentham, Coddenham, Framlingham, Botesdale, Beccles and Woolpit. This echoes the distribution of other kinds of medical practitioner in the same period. Patten has been able to demonstrate the distribution of barbers and surgeons in smaller rural centres as early as 1522.[24]

As with so many companies, the most copious constitutional information on the Norwich barber-surgeons' company derives not from the sixteenth century, but from the defensive and antiquarian petitions and ordinances presented to town authorities in the 1670s and 1680s.[25] The Norwich company is also known by a petition of 1561, which underlines the inclusion of physicians (a feature dating formally at least from 1550), and an increase in officebearers (dating from 1554) to a complement of a headman and two wardens, instead of only two 'masters'. In its complaints about unqualified practice and its provision for regular lectures to members, this petition appears to represent the struggle of an emergent professional group to establish itself, as well as to ensure standards of care.[26] However, these features, as well as demands such as for the regular employment of journeymen, are equally characteristic of the complaints of other trades. Moreover, the petition should be seen as part of a process by which all crafts were required by the city to bring forward new sets of orders for ratification, following the abandonment of the principle of a single set of rules for all occupational groups. After the suppression of chantries and the confiscation of much guild property, attempts had been made to regroup crafts and to provide secular (and preferably cheaper) versions of guild ceremonies. That the petition and associated ordinances were regarded as ambitious, may be indicated by the fact of their being accepted to stand for only one year in the first instance. The first years of a monarch's reign normally saw a temporary suspension and renewal of a city's liberties; in addition, the 1550s continued the rush of industrial legislation which was codified in 1563. Similar procedures affecting barber-surgeons were being followed at this time by, for example, Salisbury, Lincoln and Preston.[27]

The petition of 1561 is balanced by a previously unnoticed set of ordinances of 1605.[28] In its succinctness (11 articles) this set contrasts not only with the inflated sets of the late seventeenth century, but also with some other sets of

24. M. E. Grimwade and W. R. and R. K. Serjeant, *Index of the Probate Records of the Court of the Archdeacon of Suffolk 1444–1700*, 2 vols, Index Library XC, XCI (1979–80); Pelling and Webster, 'Medical Practitioners', p. 225 (map); J. Patten, 'Village and Town: an Occupational Study', *Agricultural History Review*, 20–21 (1972–73), 12, 13.

25. For those of the Norwich barber-surgeons of 1684 (33 articles), see C. Williams, 'The Ordinances of the Gild of Barber-surgeons of Norwich', *Antiquary*, 36 (1900), 274–8, 293–7 (reprinted from NRO, Case 17, shelf d, Byelaws of Trades 1683–1719). See also NRO, Case 10, shelf b, Documents Relating to Trade and Merchandise.

26. The petition is reprinted from the Norwich Assembly Books in C. Williams, *The Barber-Surgeons of Norwich*, 2nd edn (Norwich, 1897), pp. 6–10.

27. C. Haskins, *The Ancient Trade Guilds and Companies of Salisbury* (Salisbury, 1912), p. 49; J. W. F. Hill, *Tudor and Stuart Lincoln* (Cambridge, 1956), pp. 80–1; W. A. Abram, *Memorials of the Preston Guilds* (Preston, 1882), pp. 20–2.

28. NRO, Case 16, shelf c, Assembly Minute Book No. 5, 1585–1613, fols 311–12 (31 May 1605). Barber-surgeons' ordinances are recorded for only eleven provincial towns before 1600: see Parker, 'History and Powers of the Barber-surgeons', pp. 293–5; [Dickin], 'Barbour-surgeons of Sandwich'.

its own period such as the famous 'ordinary' of York.[29] The Norwich set was drawn up on the initiative of the city, which was interested in selecting from the barber-surgeons' company's books only what was still useful and relevant to the responsible running of the company from the city's point of view.[30] The company still explicitly included physicians in its activities but barbering was also provided for. The ordinances make minimal reference to the social and charitable functions of the company, but this lack was also a feature of the 1561 petition. Also like the 1561 petition, these later ordinances sought to regulate the commercial life of the craft – that is, practice, shops, and bills – but differed both in specifying a seven-year apprenticeship for practitioners, and in a strong emphasis on strict officebearing, record-keeping and attendance at meetings. There is no specification of lectures or anatomies.

Even less than the petition of 1561 did this tidying-up operation reflect a situation unique to the medical crafts.[31] At the turn of the century, the city authorities were engaged in a general revision of regulations which produced at this time new sets of ordinances for the hatters (17 articles), cordwainers (46 articles) and cobblers (8 articles). The preamble to the barbers' set was the same as that used for the raffemen (tallowchandlers), and as a part of the much more urgent plea for active regulation which prefaces the ordinances for the comparatively new and struggling hatters' craft.[32] It is clear from this activity that the city's attempt to delegate some of its responsibilities to reconstituted craft companies and their officebearers had been a failure. On the national level, the Statute of Artificers was belatedly having some effect, and the new reign was seeing further industrial legislation prompted by anxieties over the state of overseas trade.

A major feature of Norwich civic life is that of those eligible only a comparatively low proportion took out their freedoms or rights to follow a trade. This contrasts with comparable towns such as York, where the proportion was much higher, and possibly also with smaller towns where conditions of entry were easier. Even with respect to York it has been asserted that 'the size of the freeman class in any town was directly related to the rigour with which its city authorities enforced that condition'.[33] It may be assumed that both the will and the means of enforcement must have varied not only with locality but also with time and even the occupation involved. Around the turn of the century Norwich was attempting with both bribes and threats to increase the numbers of those taking out the freedom.[34] Ordinarily, however, the Norwich authorities were more concerned with apprenticeship than with enforcing the freedom,

29. Reprinted in Furnivall, *Vicary*, pp. 269–87.
30. See Assembly Minute Book No. 5, 1585–1613, fol. 305verso (8 January 1605).
31. O. J. Dunlop and R. D. Denman, *English Apprenticeship and Child Labour* (London, 1912), p. 75; A. J. Willis and A. L. Merson, *A Calendar of Southampton Apprenticeship Registers, 1609–1740*, Southampton Record Series XII (1968), p. xiii.
32. See Assembly Minute Book No. 5, 1585–1613, fol. 313.
33. Pound, 'Government and Society', pp. 55, 67–9; Woodward, 'Freemen's Rolls', p. 91; R. B. Dobson, 'Admissions to the Freedom of the City of York in the Later Middle Ages', *Eco. Hist. Rev.*, 26 (1973), 16; H. Swanson, 'The Illusion of Economic Structure: Craft Guilds in Late Medieval Towns', *P & P*, 121 (1988), 29–48.
34. See below for an ordinance of 1600.

although the two could be related. The medical crafts took full advantage of these conditions. In most towns the freedom was used as a means of adjusting supply and demand, of encouraging crafts in short supply and discouraging others where there was an excess, of conferring favours, and of making bargains with individuals, including medical practitioners, whose services were required or who were prepared to take on a city responsibility such as the care of a blind girl or the free treatment of the poor, as in Kings Lynn in the 1640s.[35] It is perhaps significant that in Norwich medical practitioners bargained with the city in terms not of the freedom but of fees or contracts.

Ultimately, however, the whole effect of a flexible approach to the old rules by all concerned became so unsatisfactory as to result in a total reorganisation of all the crafts in Norwich. This was effected by a set of ordinances published in 1622.[36] The craft-by-craft approach adopted two decades previously had evidently had little success. Records, especially those relating to apprenticeship, remained ill-kept or non-existent. Guild officebearers had failed to make proper searches, especially for apprentices, and some crafts had made excuses for going without officebearers or ordinances altogether. The city had admitted freemen in secret, without telling the relevant craft; too few were taking out their freedom or paying a sufficient fee for it; many entrants either could not prove their apprenticeship or presented false papers; and masters were unable to enrol apprentices without paying extortionate fees. Most of these practices, regarded on this occasion as abuses, find some reflection among the barber-surgeons; their total effect was to facilitate the intrusion of 'foreigners'.[37]

The remedy agreed upon in the ordinances of 1622 was a more onerous system of fines, and a drastic increase in the supervision of occupations by the city's executive. Seventy-eight trades and crafts were regrouped into 12 so-called grand companies, each headed by one of the important crafts or mercantile trades, such as the brewers, worsted-weavers, goldsmiths, grocers, or apothecaries.[38] The officebearers of the craft of each grand company were actively supervised (and if necessary substituted for) by the two aldermen of a given ward, who were called Masters, and by Assistants chosen annually by the officebearers from among themselves. This new arrangement, in which the companies acquired permanent officials who represented the city's interests, resembled not so much the true grand companies of London, which were based on alliances of kindred crafts, but rather the usual division of city business among the aldermen of the 12 city wards.[39] Only the worsted- and russell-weavers were exempt.

35. See *A Calendar of the Freemen of Lynn 1292–1836* (Norwich, 1913), p. 161. For examples (including a woman surgeon) in which the city simply bypassed normal procedures on behalf of certain practitioners, see G. A. Auden, 'The Gild of Barber-surgeons of the City of York', *Proceedings of the Royal Society of Medicine*, 21 (1928), 1402–3. For further discussion of apprenticeship, see Pelling, 'Child Health'; 'Apprenticeship'.

36. *Ordinances and Regulations concerning Apprentices and Freemen by the Mayor and Corporation of Norwich* (n. pl., [1622]).

37. Throughout this chapter the term 'foreigner' will be used for those of English birth but coming from outside the town, and the term 'stranger' for those not of English birth.

38. On this type of amalgamation in the history of guilds and companies, see Kramer, *English Craft Gilds*, and T. H. Marshall, 'Capitalism and the Decline of the English Gilds', *Cambridge Historical Journal*, 3 (1929–31), 23–33.

39. Hudson and Tingey, *Records*, vol. 2, p. lvii.

There is no sign in the new arrangements of any recognition of the medical crafts as an emergent professional group.[40] The barber-surgeons' company was included in the first grand company with the scriveners, haberdashers of small wares, pinmakers and joiners, and was led by the mercers. As we shall see later, there was a certain rough rationality in this seemingly random assortment.

The other major change imposed showed little expectation of an increase of orthodox admissions to the freedom. The fee normally paid by the person taking out his freedom was instead required to be paid by the master at the time of sealing the indenture, unless his apprentice was a poor child or the freeborn son of a citizen. This practice resembled that of the mercers and drapers of Coventry.[41] For their part the city officers agreed to admit annually no more than four freemen, 'for any fine or fee whatsoever', without consent of the officebearers of a particular occupation. This system lasted for only six years, but was sufficiently threatening to cause a flurry of freedoms around the decade of the 1620s, among the barber-surgeons at least.[42] This prudence was probably in part induced by action taken in 1618 to increase the effectiveness of fines by distraint and the distribution of the proceeds of distraint among informers.[43] These measures taken by the city authorities in the late sixteenth and early seventeenth centuries make it difficult to use official records either to determine the effects of losses caused by plague, or to describe accurately secular increases in occupational strength.

The variable practice suggested by this background is borne out by an analysis of the barber-surgeons' company with respect to apprenticeship, freedoms and officebearing in the company. The Norwich company, like most others, has to be reconstructed because it failed to preserve its own records of its activities. For the period 1550–1640, a group of about 150 individuals can be said to have belonged to the company because they are known to have been enrolled as an apprentice, taken out their freedom, enrolled an apprentice themselves, or held office in the company. This group will be referred to as Group A.[44]

The barber-surgeons occupied a middling position among the trades in most towns, below the apothecaries and the rest of the mercantile sector. Like physicians and surgeons, but unlike the apothecaries, they are very rarely found in any provincial representative or municipal office between 1550 and 1700.[45] However, with barber-surgeons as with most trades, on closer examination of a range of sources the notion of a kind of occupational caste system bears little relation to reality. The status of barber-surgeons varied greatly from being rich

---

40. Other reorganisations (e.g., Ipswich, Reading) divided the medical crafts among two or more amalgamated companies: Whittet, 'The Apothecary in Provincial Gilds', pp. 253, 255. See also above, p. 209.

41. M. D. Harris, 'Craft Gilds of Coventry', *Proceedings of the Society of Antiquaries*, 16 (1895–97), 18, n.

42. See NRO, Case 17, shelf c, Foreign Receiver's Account Books, 1555–1727, year 1627–28; Evans, *Seventeenth-Century Norwich*, p. 8, n. 6.

43. Transcribed in NRO, Byelaws of Trades 1683–1719.

44. It may be noted here that numerical analyses of Norwich freemen's lists and apprentice indentures taken as a whole are provided by Pound, 'Government and Society'.

45. See for example Evans, *Seventeenth-Century Norwich*, p. 32. Cf. F. F. Foster, *The Politics of Stability: A Portrait of the Rulers in Elizabethan London* (London, 1977), Appendices. Barbers were apparently more prominent in urban affairs before 1550: instances occur in Norwich, Chester, Stamford, and Great Yarmouth.

to being very poor. An appreciable number were householders;[46] by contrast two barbers appear in the 1570 Norwich census of the poor.[47] Physicians were not necessarily better off than barbers. Thus it is scarcely possible to develop a typical life-history for a member of the barber-surgeons' company. It will become clear that the conventional figure of the apprentice who serves his term, takes out his freedom, and then enrols apprentices of his own was in Norwich the exception, not the rule.

The apprentice barber-surgeon's father was likely to pursue almost any trade; none of the major economic sectors failed to produce a father.[48] Similarly, the sons of barber-surgeons showed at this period no great tendency to imitate their fathers: they became bladesmiths, blacksmiths, worsted-weavers, dornix-weavers, painters, bakers, innholders, scriveners, and saddlers, as well as barber-surgeons and surgeons. Norwich apprentice barber-surgeons were typical of Norwich apprentices in general in that they were as likely to come from outside Norwich as from Norwich itself, and in that some were attracted from more distant counties such as Westmorland, Lancashire and Durham.[49] London sent comparatively few apprentices to Norwich, although these included a barber, James Cox, son of Leonard. Leonard Cox, barber, was warden and later master of the London barber-surgeons' company. It should, however, be stressed that for Group A from 1550 to 1640, as for all Norwich apprentices from 1510 to 1625, those of unknown origins exceed in number those whose place of origin is known.[50]

Once indentured, the Norwich barber-surgeon's apprentice had before him the conventional prospect of a seven-year term.[51] Conformity in this respect increased after 1605 and became virtually total after the reorganisation of 1622.[52] The anomalies relating to the term of apprenticeship among the enrolled indentures of barber-surgeons had consisted of terms of greater, rather than lesser, length.[53] Terms of ten to twelve years persisted among grocers, apothecaries, and elsewhere in the mercantile sector. At the end of his term the barber-surgeon's

46. Twelve barbers, seven apothecaries, two surgeons and one bonesetter appear in a register of householders of 1589: NRO, Aylsham Collection 156.

47. Pound, *Census*, index of occupations.

48. Information on Norwich apprenticeship has been made available in P. Millican (ed.), *The Register of the Freemen of Norwich 1548–1713* (Norwich, 1934) and in W. M. Rising and P. Millican (eds), *An Index of Indentures of Norwich Apprentices*, Norfolk Record Society XXIX (1959). However, the original sources (NRO, see note 54 below; also Case 16, shelf d, Proceedings of Assembly, Book 4, 1583–1587, which contains indentures 1625–1719) have also been used here, as the apprenticeship enrolments in particular contain details mostly excluded from the *Index*. It is important to note that the *Register* includes as an Appendix all the indentures of apprentices enrolled in Norwich who were also admitted to the freedom there. These are silently excluded from Rising and Millican's *Index*. In addition Millican's Appendix omits 210 enrolments from Register D (1583–1625); these have been interleaved in the NRO's copy of the *Register*.

49. See J. Patten, 'Patterns of Migration and Movements of Labour to Three Pre-industrial East Anglian Towns', *Journal of Historical Geography*, 2 (1976), 121–2.

50. Cf. for example Southampton: Willis and Merson, *Calendar of Southampton Apprenticeship*, pp. xxix–xxx.

51. Hudson and Tingey, *Records*, vol. 2, p. 307.

52. In Southampton this trend was more gradual: Willis and Merson, *Calendar of Southampton Apprenticeship*, p. xix.

53. However, this was also the case elsewhere: see ibid.

apprentice could expect from the master the middling sum of 10–25s., although he was sometimes allowed to keep customers' gratuities in lieu of this.[54] The convention of endowing the apprentice with money was dying out among Norwich enrolments at the end of the sixteenth century, and had disappeared among the barber-surgeons by 1607.[55] There is no evidence of the admittedly more covert practice of paying premiums to the master, which may have established itself first in towns where admission to the freedom was a factor of greater consequence.[56]

It was relatively common in the Norwich crafts for enrolments to specify that tools of the trade be given by the master to the apprentice at the end of his term.[57] Among the barber-surgeons, nearly one in three was due to receive, in descending order of frequency, the 'accustomed' barber's case or bag with razors or knives, barber's basin (of latten), scissors, shaving cloths, a (latten) ewer, combs, barber's pot, aprons, looking-glass, napkins, and a 'thone' or stone. These basic tools appear later, improved in variety and quantity, in the inventories of the more prosperous. By the time of his death in 1608 Robert Blome senior had added to this range of equipment a warming basin, curling irons, casting-bottles, brushes, caps, and instruments for drawing teeth. However, as we shall see, Blome's shop also contained stock for other purposes, and the shop of a much poorer barber, Edward Goodman, contained such stock to the exclusion of barber's gear.[58]

There is almost no check possible on whether the apprentice completed his term, because most apprentices in Norwich were never freed and many of those freemen who later claimed apprenticeship were not enrolled. The movements and ultimate fate of apprentices remain one of the most difficult but interesting areas of investigation. A start can be made with smaller centres where it can be argued that the catchment area was smaller and families more easily reconstituted. These methods may not be applicable to Norwich.[59] It is hardly surprising, however, that in Norwich some of those otherwise known only by their enrolments as apprentices are later to be found in residence in the

54. End-of-term payments of £3 or more occurred among butchers, mercers, brewers, glaziers and embroiderers. See also Willis and Merson, *Calendar of Southampton Apprenticeship*, pp. xxvi–xxvii. Five pounds was to be paid to a Southampton surgeon's apprentice (son of a gentleman and the surgeon's stepson) in 1563: ibid., pp. xxvii, 42. For the retention of gratuities, see the Norwich cases, 30 years apart, of Thomas Bretton and Robert Dickerson: NRO, Case 17, shelf d, Enrolments of Apprenticeship Indentures 1548–1581, fol. 24; 1583–1625, fol. 38.

55. Again, this is somewhat earlier than elsewhere: Willis and Merson, *Calendar of Southampton Apprenticeship*, p. xxvi.

56. Ibid., p. xviii. Willis and Merson find no evidence in Southampton of premiums paid for apprenticeship to handicrafts as opposed to mercantile trades. But compare, with respect to barber-surgeons, a Newcastle petition c. 1620: D. Embleton, 'The Incorporated Company of Barber-surgeons and Wax and Tallow Chandlers of Newcastle-upon-Tyne', *Archaeologia Aeliana*, 15 (1892), 234; and a Birmingham instance of 1629: S. C. Ratcliff and H. C. Johnson (eds), *Warwick County Records, Vol II. Quarter Sessions Order Book* (Warwick, 1936), p. 69.

57. Cf. Willis and Merson, *Calendar of Southampton Apprenticeship*, p. xxv.

58. NRO, NCC, Inv. 22/75 (1608); Inv. 7/154 (1590/1).

59. See esp. P. Clark, 'The Migrant in Kentish Towns 1580–1640', in Clark and Slack, *Crisis and Order*, pp. 117–63. For analyses of Norwich indentures, see Pound, 'Government and Society', esp. pp. 56–7, and Patten, 'Patterns of Migration'. See also Pelling, 'Child Health', p. 151, n. 69 (120, n. 69).

town and in the same occupation.[60] With respect to the medical crafts in particular, travelling from town to town may not have been limited to practitioners attached to households, itinerant specialists, purveyors of balsams, and those wishing merely to finance a journey from one place to another. For example, the Newcastle barber-surgeons' company not only made charitable payments to poor travelling (and shipwrecked) barber-surgeons and surgeons: in addition, even though the obligation to travel laid upon the apprentice or journeyman by continental guilds was not usual in England, the Newcastle company licensed apprentices to travel and practise with or without their masters, partly as a means of reducing oversupply within the craft.[61]

There was in Norwich a lack of continuity between apprenticeships and freedoms, just as the city lacked full knowledge of the training of many of its freemen. Two-thirds of Group A were either apprentices or claimed a background in apprenticeship. This appearance of good rule is undermined by the fact that more than one-third of the total were apprentices of whom nothing more is known. The second chief distorting factor in the appearance of regular progress from apprenticeship to freedom is the large number (24) of freemen whose indentures were never authenticated. A general ordinance of 1600 requiring those who had served an apprenticeship to claim their freedoms within two years of notice being given or else lose their claim to it except by 'composition' as a foreigner, may have caused a bulge that is observable around the three-year point, but probably had a greater effect in swelling the numbers of those freemen alleging apprenticeship in the absence of an indenture, or giving the appearance of being foreigners by entering by composition.[62]

All those delaying their freedom more than seven years after the end of their term had been apprenticed to major 'employers of labour', of whom more will be said later. John Woods's freedom, postponed for 18 years, was one among the flurry generated during an amnesty of 1622–23, following the 1622 ordinances;[63] Woods had been living as a barber and raising a family in the parish of St Peter Mancroft since the end of his term. The most extreme case was Francis Beales (32 years), who conformed to the ordinances only under the stricter conditions of the 1630s, when his own apprentice came to be admitted freeman. In the meantime, Beales had four times been warden of the barber-surgeons' company. It was also in the 1630s that foreign practitioners paid the highest fees on entry to the freedom.[64] Apart from Beales, the only other cases among the barber-surgeons of non-freemen penalised for occupying as freemen belong to the 1550s.[65]

60. Examples are the barbers Robert Pygeon (St Peter Mancroft), William Mason (St Stephen's), and the barber and porter of Bishopsgate, Edmund Smyth.

61. Embleton, 'Barber-surgeons of Newcastle-upon-Tyne', pp. 246, 247, 253 and *passim*.

62. Assembly Minute Book No. 5, 1585–1613, fol. 235 (17 October 1600).

63. *Ordinances of Norwich*, p. 15.

64. For example, Henry Plumer, surgeon, who paid £4 in 1638 although he was already in possession of an ecclesiastical licence, and was being paid by the city to treat the poor; he became 'surgeon to the poor in the hospital' in 1639. James Pumfrett, barber, also freed in 1638, paid £5.

65. For example, Thomas Reynoldes, surgeon, fined in 1554 and 1555; still a surgeon in Norwich at his death in 1558. Robert Goodwyn, barber, was also fined in 1555.

The apparent plethora of apprentices should not be allowed to obscure the fact that, even in Group A, the taking-on of an apprentice was not common. More than half of Group A never took on an apprentice; a quarter again had only one in the course of their working lives. The numbers are made up by a few 'employers of labour' who enrolled many apprentices. It does not seem that the general level of abstention can be attributed to defective enrolment of indentures, or early death of masters due to plague, or a dearth of apprentices due to the same cause, although some masters with many apprentices undoubtedly had long working lives. An inducement *not* to take on an apprentice had existed from early in the sixteenth century, when it was laid down that a non-citizen artificer was exempt even from fines if his occupation was one he could exercise without help.[66] It seems probable that the medical crafts took full advantage of this.

Taking on an apprentice was one of the few circumstances which could induce a barber-surgeon to take out his freedom. Most of those who indentured an apprentice before taking out their freedoms, became free between sealing the indenture (a more private matter), and having it enrolled by the city. All of these cases save one relate to the period after 1590; in times of greater strictness, the visibility of apprentices constituted one point at which conformity to civic regulations could be enforced. John Buttefant, for example, was probably taking no great risk in indenturing his first apprentice the day before becoming free; but for three out of four, freedom preceded indenturing, sometimes by as little as two weeks; a third of these went through both formalities within one year.

Enrolment, when it occurred at all, was carried out within about a year – that is, in conformity with the practice of London as recommended by the Statute of Artificers, but also as laid down in Norwich craft regulations from 1449 to 1580.[67] Attempts to enforce enrolment within a shorter period proved too ambitious, even with the threat of heavy fines.[68] In five cases of delay the belated enrolment took place in January to March 1623, just before the expiry of the amnesty on defaulters. The instances of delays longer than two years, in all but one case, relate to indentures sealed after 1598. The concentration of anomalous cases after 1600 indicates an improved detection rate, with a moment of panic on the part of the masters after the reorganisation of 1622. Default (or detection of default) tended to run in families, and was also concentrated among masters who were 'employers of labour'.

Figure 9.1 compares the life histories of two of the chief employers of labour, Robert Hennant and Barthaby Carter (senior). Hennant's career, although unusually long and including many apprentices, was orthodox except that he indentured his first apprentice, Goose, ten months before taking out his freedom, cautiously deferring Goose's enrolment until two months after becoming free. Hennant may never, even furtively, have had more than two apprentices at one time; by contrast, Carter, between 1615 and 1630, often had three, and staggered

66. Hudson and Tingey, *Records*, vol. 2, pp. 300–1; cf. p. 289 (1449).
67. See also Willis and Merson, *Calendar of Southampton Apprenticeship*, pp. xv–xvi.
68. *Ordinances of Norwich*, p. 5. Cf. Millican, *Register*, p. xvii.

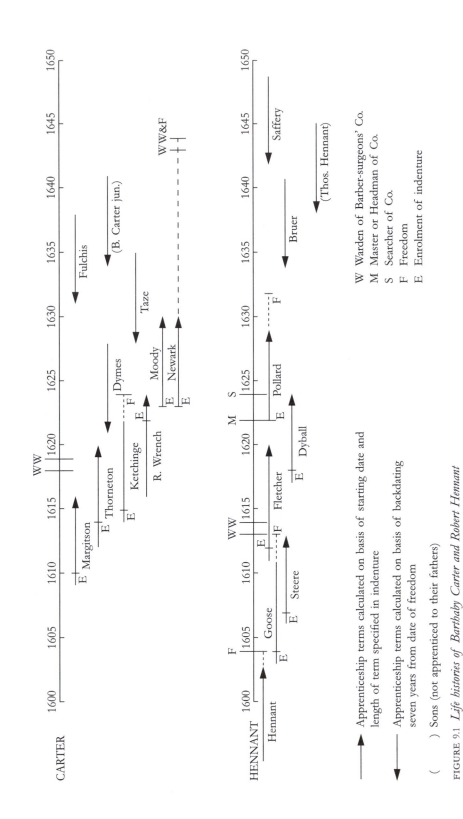

FIGURE 9.1 *Life histories of Barthaby Carter and Robert Hennant*

his enrolments to avoid admitting having four. Three apprentices at one time, with a brief overlap, was the traditional allowance in Norwich, although this varied for different trades; the tailors, for example, being allowed only two in 1543, and the worsted-weavers regularly being allowed more.[69] Also, the evidence suggests that the practice of different trades must have varied even more radically: one Thomas Jackson was said in 1561 to have as many as 17 journeymen and apprentices.[70] Officebearers of companies were sometimes allowed more leeway;[71] both Carter and Hennant held office in the barber-surgeons' company, and although not dominant in the headship, the employers of labour appear in office with increasing frequency from the late sixteenth century.

As we have seen, the decision to take on an apprentice could oblige the master to take out his freedom. The example of Carter, for whom there is no record of either freedom or apprenticeship, may indicate defects in the Norwich freemen's roll. The tendency, already noticed, of those who delayed but eventually took out their freedoms to be apprentices of employers of labour could indicate the retention by these masters of their apprentices on a journeyman basis. It may be significant that in one of these cases, one of the apprentices, in a manner unusual among barber-surgeons and the non-mercantile crafts, was indentured on the basis that his master would cause him to be made free within three months of the end of the term. The explanation of Carter's assemblage of labour seems to be his combination of barbering and slaymaking, a feature of the indentures of his apprentices Fulchis and Ketchinge – the latter later being freed merely as a barber. Other employers of labour combined 'barberscraft' with 'heavelmaking' and slaymaking. Such diversification may explain the presence in other centres of a minority who 'specialised in apprentices'.[72]

Although it may have been desirable for an employer of labour to hold office in a company, and, sooner or later, necessary for him to take out his freedom, a man's free or unfree status had little relevance to officebearing in the company, just as it had none to the employment or consultation of a practitioner by the city. One-third were not free on first taking office in the company. This is less a measure of the autonomy of the craft, than an indication of the range of activity which could be detached from the freedom.[73] It was common early in the sixteenth century for a headman of the barber-surgeons (who had usually first served as a warden) to serve for two years running, but repeated re-election only began in the 1550s. After 1560 a tendency developed for the same individuals to hold one of the different offices each year. Only eight individuals served as headman between 1570 and 1620; the penalties for not taking office in the ordinances of 1605 were prompted by the company's inability to find a headman from 1597 to 1602. A faltering revival thereafter was only stabilised by the longest-ever incumbency, that of the surgeon John Hobart (1612–21).

69. Hudson and Tingey, *Records*, vol. 2, p. 307. Dunlop and Denman, *English Apprenticeship*, pp. 45–6, 89–90.

70. NRO, Case 16, shelf a, Mayor's Court Proceedings No. 7, 1555–1562, p. 548.

71. Dunlop and Denman, *English Apprenticeship*, p. 46.

72. See Willis and Merson, *Calendar of Southampton Apprenticeship*, p. xxxiv.

73. The 1622 ordinances optimistically specified that freemen were to elect the officebearers of a company: *Ordinances of Norwich*, p. 9.

Following the formation of the grand companies in 1622, the revival was somewhat more convincing. This pattern may have been aggravated, but was probably not caused, by losses due to plague. No vacancies occurred in the wardenships over the same period (1570–1620).

A summary and illustrative decadal analysis of aspects of apprenticeship and freedom is given in Figure 9.2. The limitations of such an analysis, even in a city with such good records as Norwich, have already been indicated, and the numbers are too small for firm conclusions. Although valuable as an expression of one end of the spectrum, it is not (as will be re-emphasised below) representative of the whole occupational group. Within its own terms, however, this analysis indicates the lack of a one-to-one relation between apprenticeships and freedoms, and also the minimal role played numerically by those progressing smoothly from one to the other. Admission to the freedom was for Norwich barber-surgeons most affected by events surrounding the reorganisation of 1622, including the amnesty offered up to March 1623. Apprenticeships were most affected by failure to enrol c. 1560-80 and by plague.[74] The comparative evenness of the freedoms taken out over the plague period perhaps indicates the small proportion of freemen compared with Group A as a whole.[75]

Earlier in the chapter, I suggested that much occupational analysis implies a kind of specific classification of those capable of work. The natural-historical metaphor can readily be extended. Medical historians, it could be said, have favoured a Linnaean classification of fixed, clearly defined species; any gradation or mingling appears as unnatural and to be resisted. Other historians are interested in a wider range of organisms but see those capable of work in vulgar Darwinian terms. Thus, changes in the habitat, whether natural or artificial, seem to cause different species to evolve, dominate or become extinct. Wastage is inevitable, since most organisms are committed to a particular niche and must fail when this disappears. To both of these descriptions of the economic and social world of the early modern period, there may be opposed an interpretation which emphasises the natural flexibility of some occupational populations in the face of changing circumstances. In such a view, the specific differences decrease in importance; diversification ceases to seem exceptional.

Occupational designations become increasingly common in records of the fifteenth and sixteenth centuries, along with the desire shown for the crafts to separate out into self-regulating groups. This could involve the individual in arbitrary decisions; in Beverley each man was told to assume the clothing of the craft 'he most gets his living by'.[76] Alternatively, the *status quo* could be recognised and a man charged for each of his occupations, as at Norwich in 1543. For Norwich, at least, it is clear that occupational diversification was recognised in regulations and indentures. After 1550 indentures were sealed linking a range of groups including: grocers with apprentice raffemen or chandlers; grocers with apothecaries; hosiers with mercers; gentlemen with bakers, hosiers,

---

74. Norwich indentures as a whole display congruent features: Patten, 'Patterns of Migration', p. 119.

75. Cf. Dobson, 'Admissions to the Freedom of York', pp. 11, 17.

76. J. F. Scott, 'Limitations of Gild Monopoly', *American Historical Review*, 22 (1916–17), 588; Hudson and Tingey, *Records*, vol. 2, p. 309. See also Swanson, *Medieval Artisans*, 'Illusion of Economic Structure', pp. 38–9.

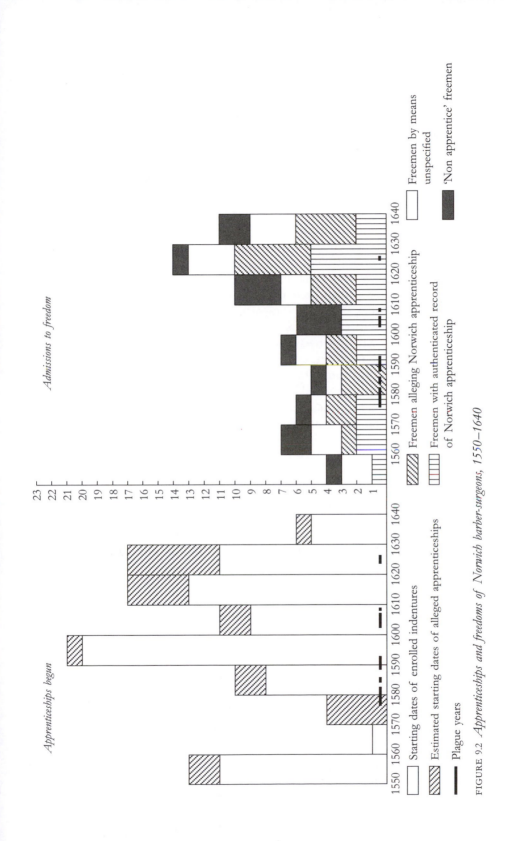

Admissions to freedom

▨ Freemen alleging Norwich apprenticeship

▤ Freemen with authenticated record of Norwich apprenticeship

☐ Freemen by means unspecified

■ 'Non apprentice' freemen

Apprenticeships begun

☐ Starting dates of enrolled indentures

▨ Estimated starting dates of alleged apprenticeships

▬ Plague years

FIGURE 9.2 *Apprenticeships and freedoms of Norwich barber-surgeons, 1550–1640*

parchment-makers, and worsted-weavers; reeders with thaxters; grocers with pinmakers; cappers with hatters; armourers with crossbowmakers; innholders with tailors; hosiers with tailors and worsted-weavers; and barbers with surgeons. As we shall see, rather more unexpected combinations existed, which on examination have their own tradition and rationality.

Of the trades commonly connected with barbering, perhaps the best known is chandling, wax or tallow. Companies combining the two occurred in Sandwich, Newcastle, Chester, and (rather later) Worcester and Shrewsbury. In Norwich, Henry Holden, three times headman of what was then, in the 1540s, called the 'Barbers, Surgeons, Physicians, and Waxchandlers Co.', was admitted and readmitted to the freedom alternately as barber and grocer. He later indentured an apprentice in 'grocers craft and raphmans craft and other faculties that he useth'. This latter formulation is very common in Norwich indentures.[77] In the later sixteenth century waxchandling declined and was absorbed by the grocers. By 1614 the Chester chandlers were complaining that the barbers were deserting them for other trades.[78] Another long-standing activity of barber-surgeons was netmaking. In 1686 Richard Blome told his gentleman readers to obtain materials for making their own game nets from barbers, for 'almost every Barber is a proficient therein'. Behind Blome's confidence were barbers like Clement Bolton of Norwich, who in 1544 agreed to instruct his apprentice in barbering, waxchandling and the making of nets, and Ralph Elmeham, who instructed his nephew and apprentice John in barberscraft and especially in shaving and nets-knitting.[79]

Even better established, and common throughout Europe, was the association of barber-surgeons with music.[80] The instruments most commonly provided in barber-surgeons' shops for the use of customers were the cittern and the lute; these, and other instruments more likely to be for private use, like virginals, are more common in barber-surgeons' wills and inventories than among the population at large.[81] The barber's cittern, as well as his chair and his brass basin, were well-worn sources of satirical metaphor in plays of the period.[82] Although 'barber's music' came to mean an impromptu performed by amateurs, barber-surgeons themselves were often skilled in music.[83] During the 1630s, John Adkin, barber of Norwich, indentured three apprentices in the art and science of music and barbering. Similarly, in 1618 Thomas Vyall, barber of Yarmouth, was to instruct Philip Stedman 'in and upon all such instruments of musicke as he [Vyall] nowe use or . . . shall use'.[84] William Pickering, barber of Norwich,

---

77. This was clearly more than a form of words. Cf. Willis and Merson, *Calendar of Southampton Apprenticeship*, pp. xxi-xxii.

78. L. M. Clopper (ed.), *Chester* (London and Toronto, 1979), pp. 280–1.

79. R. Blome, *The Gentleman's Recreation* (London, 1686), p. 195. For examples in Great Yarmouth of barbers making (?) fishing nets, see J. Patten, 'Freemen and Apprentices', *Local Historian*, 9 (1971), 232.

80. C. Engel, *An Introduction to the Study of National Music* (London, 1866), p. 281.

81. I am grateful to Jonathan Barry for confirming this with respect to Bristol inventories.

82. R. Nares, *A Glossary or Collection of Words*, ed. J. O. Halliwell and T. Wright, 2 vols (London, 1859), vol. 1, pp. 53–4, 59, 163.

83. J. Hawkins, *A General History of the Science and Practice of Music*, 5 vols (London, 1776), vol. 2, p. 768; S. Pepys, *Diary*, ed. H. B. Wheatley, 8 vols in 3 (London, 1962), vol. 1, p. 159.

84. I owe to David Galloway both this information and a transcript from the Great Yarmouth Borough Court Rolls (C4/311).

left to a grandchild, son of another barber Lawrence Wright, 'my virginals and all my books with lute lessons'. Thomas Hooke, a pious and prosperous citizen, householder, and barber of Norwich, combined these attributes with musicality in a different context, finally bequeathing his quarter's wages (perhaps more than 10s.) as a singingman to his fellow singingmen at Christ Church. The barber-surgeon's use of music points most importantly, however, to his shop as a place of resort, thereby providing a natural and reciprocal link with the inn and the alehouse, where music was also usually available on request. Barber-surgeons' shops could also have curiosities on show for the diversion of customers.[85]

Another important (and integral) area of diversification was the making and selling of alcoholic drink. Malting, brewing and the retailing of drink were areas into which all occupations (including the clergy) were always likely to diversify, but barber-surgeons were involved in them to an unusual extent.[86] In Norwich, Robert Pleasance, barber, Richard Durrant, bonesetter, Richard Fisher, surgeon, and the singingman-barber Hooke, all men of substance, were among those who were parties to licences relating to drink. Other barbers and surgeons kept alehouses for extended periods or were fined for unlicensed tippling. John Elvyn, barber and later warden of the Norwich barber-surgeons' company, was imprisoned in 1598 for unlicensed tippling at a time when he had two apprentices in barberscraft.[87] A tippling house, if strictly kept, served its customers outside; 'good rule' had to be maintained within doors, but no food, drink, or unlawful games were allowed. Tippling was thus a retail business requiring little accommodation, which could readily be combined with another business, or resorted to at time of need. Those involved in licences and recognisances to do with drink tended to guarantee each other, and this mutual backscratching could lead to a fluidity in occupational designation.[88] In their turn, those most closely connected with the food and drink trades also engaged in medicine; in Rye in 1602, 17 persons taxed for occupying as barber-surgeons included three brewers, two victuallers, two butchers, and an innkeeper. Eight of the 17 were also involved in tippling beer.[89]

It should not be assumed that the barber-surgeon's more medical activities were conducted any more privately than in his shop, or that his shop was irrelevant or even a hindrance to this side of his enterprise. The confidential consultation was an aspect of gentility and, in general, a comparatively late

85. NRO, NCC 78 Adams (1598); NCC 138 Clearke (1593). R. V. French, *Nineteen Centuries of Drink in England*, 2nd edn (London, [1891]), pp. 149–50; P. H. Scholes, *The Oxford Companion to Music*, 9th edn (London, 1963), pp. 84–5; Embleton, 'Barber-surgeons of Newcastle-upon-Tyne', p. 232.

86. D. M. Palliser, *Tudor York* (Oxford, 1979), p. 167; Dyer, *City of Worcester*, p. 140; examples from Devizes, Salisbury and Warminster in N. J. Williams (ed.), *Tradesmen in Early Stuart Wiltshire, A Miscellany*, Wiltshire Archaeological and Natural History Society, Records Branch XV (1960), see index. For a substantial barber-innkeeper, see Swanson, 'Illusion of Economic Structure', p. 35. Other examples could be given.

87. NRO, Case 17, shelf d, Book of Innkeepers and Tipplers, *c.* 1580–90; Mayor's Court Proceedings No. 13, 1595–1603, p. 278.

88. See the suspicious example of Robert Olden or Oldom of Warminster, surgeon and alehousekeeper, 1620: Williams, *Tradesmen in Wiltshire*.

89. East Sussex Record Office, RYE 1/7, 404verso–405recto: personal communication from Stephen Hipkin. I am grateful to Dr Hipkin for this information. In addition to the 17, a tallowchandler, a basketmaker and one other were taxed for occupying as physician-surgeons.

development; the insistence of later medical men, especially physicians, on the decorum and exclusiveness of the doctor–patient relationship can be seen in part as a means of dissociation from older craft origins. Much consultation would have taken place in the presence of the 'friends' who are later found as parties, with the patients, to legal proceedings arising out of failed contracts with medical practitioners. Given this more public aspect of medicine in the early modern period, it is not surprising that barber-surgeons' shops employed different means to attract, entertain, and possibly distract customers and their friends. If barber-surgeons' shops offered drink, music, curiosities, gaming, and conversation as well as the usual services, it is easy to explain the long-established and much-repeated prohibitions against barbering on Sundays, as well as the imposition of curfews on barbering in times of social disruption. Sabbatarians accused barbers' shops of being outlets of Sunday newspapers and centres of political discussion as late as the nineteenth century.[90]

As well as these regular associations of trades, it is to be expected that diversification should also occur according to local circumstances, and barber-surgeons are to be found making a trial of trades new to Norwich such as hatting. As we have seen, Norwich barber-surgeons, especially the employers of labour, were overtly involved in slaymaking and heavelmaking.[91] Others rented space in churchyards for twistering. In York, barbers also made bowstrings.[92] Elsewhere, barber-surgeons made alliances which may have been more than formal: with ropemakers (Durham, 1658) and with cooks and later silkweavers (Salisbury). Some London barber-surgeons also engaged in trades relating to silk.[93] The Oxford barbers were at an earlier period in association with razor-grinders, waferers, and makers of 'singing bread', as well as with surgeons; by 1499 they were allied to the hurers or cappers, with knitting the possible bond between them. Like the cooks and to some extent the brewers, they were under the control of the university, rather than the town.[94] The most common alliance later in the seventeenth century was with perukemakers; barbers are recorded as attending to wigs from at least the 1640s.[95]

90. See for example D'A. Power, *A Precept of the Archbishop of Canterbury* [n.pl., n.d.; repr. from *The Lancet*, 23 January 1909], relating to London; W. A. Leighton, 'The Guilds of Shrewsbury', *Shropshire Archaeological and Natural History Society Transactions*, 5 (1882), 265, 267, 272, 274, 290; P. H. Ditchfield, 'The Gilds of Reading', *Reliquary*, 4 (1890), 145. 'THEOLOGOS, M. A. Cantab.', *Shaving: A Breach of the Sabbath* (London, 1860).

91. For slays see *OED*. Slaymakers or slaywrights existed independently in Norwich, but in small numbers: Millican, *Register*, p. xxii. Heavelmaking is presumably related to ME 'hefel' or 'heveld', meaning the weft or woof in weaving: *Middle English Dictionary*, ed. Kurath and Kuhn (I owe this explanation to Suzanna Harris). If 'heavels' is equivalent to 'heddles' (cords set before the reeds of a loom, for dividing up the warp threads), then slaymaking and heavelmaking are closely related. In addition to heavel yarn, 48 ready-made heavels, 22 cloth heavels and 'one iron with a strykinge shafte to make wollen hevells', Robert Blome's inventory included 300 'cann readds': NRO, NCC Inv. 22/75 (1608).

92. NRO, St Margaret's Parish, PD 153/43, Churchwardens' Accounts 1552–1642, typed transcript, pp. 14, 41; Swanson, 'Illusion of Economic Structure', p. 37. Barbers engaged in clothmaking in other textile towns: see Dyer, *City of Worcester*, p. 104.

93. See for example (1557–1606) Henry Billidge, John Browne, and Robert Mudesley: Wellcome Unit Biographical Index (see note 13 above), London Barber-surgeons' Company Minutes Section.

94. H. E. Salter (ed.), *Records of Medieval Oxford* (Oxford, 1912), pp. 70–6. J. L. Bolton, 'The Barbers' Company. A University Gild', *Oxoniensia*, 28 (1963), 84–6.

95. Embleton, 'Barber-surgeons of Newcastle-upon-Tyne', p. 250.

Barber-surgeons also contributed to the growth in the indigenous production of small consumer goods.[96] In the case of Edward Goodman, who made lace, silk fringes and purses, this may have been an aspect of poverty; but the combination into one Norwich pageant of 'Barbours, Wexchaundelers, Surgeons, Fisicians, Hardewaremen, Hatters, Cappers, Skynners, Glovers, Pynners, Poyntemakers, Girdelers, Pursers, Bagmakers, Sceppers, Wyerdrawers, Cardmakers' was clearly more rational than at first appears.[97] The medical crafts were often placed with the small-wares crafts for administrative and social purposes. Nor was the relation one-sided: bagmakers, glovers, and others also intruded into medicine.[98]

Many of the various activities of Norwich barber-surgeons are epitomised in the inventory of the barber Robert Blome, officeholder in the barber-surgeons' company and father of a barber. As already indicated, Blome was prosperous and he died possessed of a great amount of barber's gear, including musical as well as surgical instruments. However, his greatest asset, besides his bedroom furniture and some debts of obligation, was wax valued at £42. In addition, the contents of his shop show that Blome made and sold plover nets and shake nets as well as heavels.[99] When one recalls in addition the better-known tendency of physicians and surgeons also to be schoolmasters and divines, it is not surprising that the town of Chester, in employing the surgeon Alexander Harrison to treat the poor, required him 'not to trade any other arte, trade, sciens, nor occupacon, but only surgery.'[100]

So far, I have been concerned primarily with Group A, a group of about 150 practitioners active in Norwich between 1550 and 1640 who bore some part in the formalities and responsibilities of the city and the barber-surgeons' company. Group A included physicians, surgeons, barber-surgeons, lithotomists, bonesetters, and many to whom it would be difficult to give a single occupational designation. It might be expected that this large and diverse group would, together with the apothecaries, exhaust the personnel engaged in medicine. However, use of an extended range of sources reveals the existence of another, similarly various group, Group B, of approximately 120 practitioners for whom there is no evidence of connection with the barber-surgeons' company. It should be stressed that there is no reason why a large part of Group B should not also have been, like Group A, members of the company, albeit unrecorded, although this degree of uniformity would in the circumstances be surprising. Group A and Group B do not differ radically in composition, except in two important respects: that is, the presence in Group B of the bulk of the two important minorities regularly missing from formal records used for occupational

96. On this subject in general see J. Thirsk, *Economic Policy and Projects* (Oxford, 1978).

97. Hudson and Tingey, *Records*, vol. 2, p. 230. For a similar combination in Kendal in 1578, see Kramer, *English Craft Gilds*, p. 18.

98. See, for example, note 89 above; or 'Charles the Bagmaker' who was paid by the Norwich authorities in 1580 for healing a boy: NRO, Case 18, shelf d, Books of the Clavor's Accounts, 1550–1601, fol. 51. (Note that these accounts are not clavors' accounts but rather the 'Hamper' or 'Hanaper' Accounts referred to by earlier writers on Norwich.)

99. NRO, NCC Inv. 22/75. Shake nets were also for game birds.

100. R. H. Morris, *Chester in the Plantagenet and Tudor Reigns* (Chester, n.d.), pp. 357–8.

analyses, women and 'strangers'. Peripatetic practitioners (known names are included in Group B) could be regarded as a third such minority. When the apothecaries (about 40 individuals) are added to Groups A and B, a group is formed large enough to justify the conclusion that for Norwich at this period the ratio of practitioners to population was in the region of 1:200.[101] It should be noted that none of the present totals, especially with respect to Group B, can be regarded as exhaustive, so that the true ratio may well have been higher.

In Group B are to be found the better-known physicians: William Blomfild, Sir Thomas Browne, William Cuningham, Arthur Dee, Isaac Delaune, or Tobias Whitaker.[102] Among such practitioners, but previously almost unknown, is the much-travelled Helvetian physician John Ghesel who, having published an English translation of his *Regimen Salutatis* in Oxford in 1631, obtained a licence to practise medicine from the Bishop of Norwich and settled in Norwich in St Mary Coslany.[103] In Norwich, any omission of the strangers is important because they formed a large minority of the population at this period and because medical practice was a favoured recourse among immigrants.[104] The stranger practitioners in Norwich included midwives, and they ranged in respectability from 'Poor Peter' Astoe, a Dutch surgeon charged with drunkenness and wife-beating in 1608, to Ghesel and John Cropp, a Walloon surgeon who founded in St Michael at Plea the family which later produced the well-known surgeon William Cropp and his less respectable surgeon nephew John Browne, as well as a number of London merchants. John Cropp himself may have merchandised in figs and other commodities.[105] The examples of John Cropp and his son, a surgeon-physician, show that stranger practitioners could prosper and also obtain (like Ghesel) a range of formal qualifications confirming their status and extending their right to practise, although they may have done this under pressure.

The total for all women practitioners, including midwives, is 37. Excluded are numerous women recorded in bastardy cases as 'standing instead of a midwife' at the birth, one of whom was the wife of a barber. (Medical personnel play a seemingly major role in bastardy cases, perhaps as a reflection of the greater opportunities for intimacy provided by medical practice: John Carr, barber, John Pickering, surgeon of Cromer, and Thomas Carter, son of Thomas

101. M. Pelling, 'Tradition and Diversity: Medical Practice in Norwich 1550–1640', in Istituto Nazionale di Studi sul Rinascimento, *Scienze Credenze Occulte Livelli di Cultura*, Convegno Internazionale 1980 (Florence, 1982), p. 165.

102. For Blomfild and Delaune, see C. H. Cooper and T. Cooper, *Athenae Cantabrigienses (1500–1609)*, 3 vols (Cambridge, 1858–1913); F. N. L. Poynter, *Gideon Delaune and his Family Circle* (London, 1965), p. 10, and *passim*. For the remainder see *DNB* on Dee; see also papers by J. H. Appleby in *Ambix* and *Slavonic and East European Review*.

103. John Ghesel, *A Facsimile of the Rule of Health* (Ann Arbor, MI, 1932), reproduced from a unique copy in Christ Church, Oxford; NRO, VSC/2, Consignation Book No. 4 (1636), fol. 4. An 'Album Amicorum' of Ghesel apparently survives: BL MSS Add. 28,633 (Ralph B. Weller, personal communication).

104. This was equally the case in London: see Pelling and Webster, 'Medical Practitioners', p. 185.

105. Pelling and Webster, 'Medical Practitioners', pp. 224–5; K. F. Russell, 'John Browne, 1642–1702: a Seventeenth-century Surgeon, Anatomist and Plagiarist', *Bull. Hist. Med.*, 33 (1959), 393–414, 503–25; P. Rutledge and D. L. Richwood, *Great Yarmouth Assembly Minutes . . . Norwich Accounts*, Norfolk Record Society XXXIX (1970), p. 96.

Carter apothecary, who debauched his father's servant in his father's house and may also have been a medical practitioner, were all adjudged reputed fathers in Norwich.)[106] Supposing the same number of midwives to have been active in each period of 20 years as have been located for one ten-year period, the total of women practitioners could rise as high as 70. The role of women as general practitioners and surgeons in Norwich has been described elsewhere.[107] Needing emphasis here is the vital role played by women as keepers of poor-houses. By the end of the sixteenth century, Norwich was using at least five so-called lazarhouses at the city gates for the custody, employment, and medical treatment of the poor.[108]

Not all women practitioners lacked formal qualifications or status in official records. In addition to obtaining licences in physic and surgery, they were also involved in apprenticeship. Some industrial legislation of the sixteenth century sought to exclude women; the practice of barber-surgeons' companies was, in general, more tolerant, although in Norwich women also joined their husbands in indenturing apprentices in such trades as grocery. The greater participation of women was a further point in common between medicine and the food and drink trades.[109]

Group B also tends to include those who are known primarily as clerics, or schoolmasters, or both, but who diversified into medicine or surgery. William Stinnet, graduate and benefactor of Christ's College, Cambridge, was rector of St John Maddermarket in Norwich for at least 20 years; he obtained a licence to practise medicine and surgery from the Bishop of Norwich shortly after going there in 1614.[110] Stinnet's contribution to the welfare of Norwich people may well have been greater than that of the better-known physicians, few of whom would have been so long resident in the town. Another example, the prominent Puritan divine John Yates, probably combined all three vocations. His son John graduated MD from Leiden, took orders, and settled in Great Yarmouth. John Yates and his son, the Norwich physician Duncan Burnet, and Burnet's son Alexander (also an academically qualified physician) were all connected with Emmanuel College, Cambridge, but the fathers were also linked by friendship with the surgeon John Fary. The choice of college for Fary's own nephew, namesake, and heir, to whom he left all his books 'of surgery and divinity', can be traced to Fary's brother-in-law, the Norwich schoolmaster and

---

106. Mayor's Court Proceedings No. 14, 1604–1615, fol. 285recto; No. 13, 1595–1603, pp. 31, 48; ibid., pp. 2, 308, 329. For contemporary criticism of a libertine practitioner, see A. Sorsby, 'Richard Banister and the Beginnings of English Ophthalmology', in E. A. Underwood (ed.), *Science, Medicine and History*, 2 vols (London, 1953), vol. 2, p. 252. See also Pelling, 'Compromised by Gender'.

107. Pelling and Webster, 'Medical Practitioners', pp. 222–3.

108. For more detail on the lazarhouses, see Pelling, 'Healing the Sick Poor'.

109. See L. Fox, 'The Coventry Gilds and Trading Companies with Special Reference to the Position of Women', in *Essays in Honour of Philip B. Chatwin*, Birmingham Archaeological Society Transactions, LXXVIII (1962), pp. 13–26; cf. Phythian-Adams, *Desolation of a City*, pp. 87–98, 272–3; Palliser, *Tudor York*, p. 150. See also Swanson, 'Illusion of Economic Structure', pp. 34ff; idem, *Medieval Artisans*, esp. chap. 2; Pelling, 'Food, Status and Knowledge'; Pelling, 'Older Women'.

110. J. Venn and J. A. Venn, *Alumni Cantabrigienses. Part I. From the Earliest Times to 1751*, 4 vols (Cambridge, 1922–27); NRO, Diocesan Archives, VSC/2, Consignation Book No. 3A (1633), p. 2; Consignation Book No. 3B (1635) [unpag.]; Consignation Book No. 4 (1636), fol. 3.

cleric Matthew Stonham, whose connections with Caius College also determined the educational backgrounds of such Norwich practitioners as the physician John Lescallet. Lescallet himself was the son of a Norwich weaver and his own son reverted to this trade. Also at Caius were Paul Gold, who later combined schoolteaching and medicine in Norwich, and the son of Nicholas Shaxton, a well-known Norwich schoolmaster. The elder Shaxton obtained a licence to practise surgery in 1620 and was paid by the city to teach children in the new children's hospital in the same year.[111]

The example of Norwich shows that particular legislation affecting barber-surgeons, physicians, and surgeons reflected general developments in industrial legislation, just as the barber-surgeons' company was affected by local legislation covering all occupations. However, all forms of regulation, like the various licensing systems for medical practice, had a limited effect on the occupational group as a whole. Among the Norwich barber-surgeons, the duly enrolled apprentice who sought admission to the freedom as soon as he was eligible – that is, the craftsman who could be regarded either as ideal or as epitomising restrictive practice, depending on one's point of view – was the exception, not the rule. For certain barber-surgeons and surgeons, apprenticeship remained important; a few specialised in it, probably as a result of diversifying their occupation in particular directions. The employers of labour emerge as a special type, often paying the penalty of visibility but deeply entrenched, especially in the company. The integration of diversity in companies should also modify the assumption that apparently incongruous combinations are always a sign of weakness, of minor or threatened trades clinging together for support.

More generally, it should be noted that medical practitioners are not the only group to be inadequately represented by official sources. A single parish register for Norwich reveals the occupations of tennis-court-keeper, lanthorne-maker, combteethmaker, ostler, conyseller, tapster, bookseller, matmaker, tippler, hatdresser, fringeseller, drummer and horserider, none of which appear in the freemen's rolls.[112] These may be dismissed either as subsumable under other designations or as irrelevant to larger economic issues, but the example of medicine shows that when an occupational grouping is fully examined, a substantial increase in both numbers and diversity of occupation may be expected. A single occupational group may also contain extreme differences in wealth and status. On many counts, therefore, caution should be exercised before locating major economic or social changes in such appearances as the number of freemen for a particular occupation. The size of the medical group gives it a greater natural significance in the structure of the Norwich community; it is relevant to stress that the barber-surgeons were numerically the largest of the London companies in the sixteenth century, and, on a proportional basis, appear among the twelve leading trades in half (Coventry, Chester, Leicester, Bristol) of a recent sample of

111. See especially, for John Yates senior, *DNB*; for his son, 'Will of Dr John Yates, 1657', *East Anglian Miscellany* (1934), 18–19, 23–4; for Burnet, PRO, PCC Wills, 81 Evelyn (1641); for Farr, PCC Wills, 92 Skynner (1627); for Shaxton, VSC/2, Consignation Book No. 3A (1633), p. 2, and Mayor's Court Proceedings No. 15, 1615–1624, fol. 324.

112. NRO, NRO 70/3, Register of St Peter Mancroft 1538–1736.

provincial towns. On the same basis in Norwich (over the period 1548–1713), freemen barber-surgeons and surgeons were as numerous as the carpenters and were exceeded in numbers only by the worsted-weavers, tailors, cordwainers, grocers and bakers.[113]

A constant high demand for medical services could be fulfilled in a great variety of ways by a wide range of practitioners, and the individual practitioner was likely to be engaged in other activities as well. Medicine may thus be seen as one aspect of economic and social flexibility, and the high incidence of part-time activity allows the persistence of very high ratios of practitioners to population. These conclusions also point to the correspondences between medical practice and other enterprising occupations, rather than to the narrow and isolating concept of professional development which is usually applied. Far from being a rare species, requiring a specialised environment for evolution and survival, medical practitioners emerge in the Lamarckian sense as a major occupational population in which specific definitions may be arbitrary or temporary, and which had within it the capacity to survive as a whole by adaptation to environmental pressures. It is possible that such Lamarckian populations may be found to underlie the small, mutually exclusive groups hitherto made to represent other occupational areas.

There is no evidence of a massive increase in the number of medical practitioners from decade to decade in the period under discussion, and it seems more probable that the population maintained within itself the capacity to provide any amount of medical care. However, the nature of the demand, and the means by which it was supplied, must have altered according to circumstances, the most obvious factor being the distinction between urban and rural areas. Similarly, part-time activity can be seen as a regular aspect of medicine which varied with prevailing conditions. Thus, around 1600, the Norwich authorities, concerned with the increase of poverty, vagrancy and disaffection, likewise acted to prevent the spread of bodily corruption among the poor, by paying for medical services. Greater poverty can increase the demand for such consolations as alcohol, gambling – and medicine. The late sixteenth-century explosion in the number of alehouses, which can be seen as a local expression of need at the lower levels of subsistence, may have had parallels in medicine which are less visible. Similarly the barber's shop, like the alehouse, may have emerged more strongly as another of the fragmented, commercialised alternatives to the parish church as a centre of communal activity.[114] The large numbers of respectable practitioners who seem suddenly to become visible in the late seventeenth century, may have had their real origins in adverse circumstances a hundred years before.

113. Young, *Annals*, p. 19; Phythian-Adams, 'The Economic and Social Structure', p. 17; Millican, *Register*, pp. xxi–xxii.
114. See P. Clark, 'The Alehouse and the Alternative Society', in D. Pennington and K. Thomas (eds), *Puritans and Revolutionaries* (Oxford, 1978), pp. 47–72.

CHAPTER TEN

Trade or Profession? Medical Practice in Early Modern England

The success of the medical practitioner in recent times has done much to arouse and inform the professionalisation debate. Medicine's apparently unique combination of cognitive and ethical values has given ample scope for discussion, and it is medicine which provides the most striking contrasts in historiography. Positivist and conspiratorial interpretations of professionalisation alike see the modern medical practitioner as a powerful figure in society, thrown up by changes associated with industrialisation or urbanisation. Both sides have inherited terms of debate from nineteenth-century struggles and discussions, and the nineteenth century is still regarded as the main period of transition. Part of the fascination with medicine lies in the late and dramatic change from comparatively humble origins. The exact point at which scientific knowledge became effective in medicine now tends to be placed at the end of the nineteenth century or even later. However, even where growth of knowledge and/or competence is not seen as in itself conferring professional status, attention is given to the cultural or non-technical value of knowledge in achieving social legitimacy and independence for marginal groups within the nascent nineteenth-century profession.[1] Some perceptive analysts have raised the possibility that professionalism represents an ideal, rather than reality, in all historical situations, including the present day.[2] In this chapter I hope to show that a broader approach to medicine in the early modern period reveals continuities which enlarge the discussion as a whole. Further, I hope to point to areas of neglect which have relevance to more recent periods in which professionalisation can be better defended as a full interpretation of historical events. Definitions of

I am grateful for the comments of Jonathan Barry, Irvine Loudon, Wilfrid Prest and Charles Webster on this chapter, the first version of which was given in a Society for the Social History of Medicine lecture series in 1983.

1. For discussion and references see S. E. D. Shortt, 'Physicians, Science and Status: Issues in the Professionalization of Anglo-American Medicine in the Nineteenth Century', *Medical History*, 27 (1983), 51–68. See also P. Wright and A. Treacher (eds), *The Problem of Medical Knowledge: Examining the Social Construction of Medicine* (Edinburgh, 1984); J. H. Warner, 'Science in Medicine', *Osiris*, 2nd ser., 1 (1985), 37–58; and more recently, J. V. Pickstone, 'Ways of Knowing: Towards a Historical Sociology of Science, Technology and Medicine', *British Journal for the History of Science*, 26 (1993), 433–58, esp. pp. 436–7, arguing for a more varied typology of medical science.

2. M. S. Larson, *The Rise of Professionalism: A Sociological Analysis* (Berkeley, 1977), p. xi.

professionalisation are still remarkably exclusive. Their lack of historical value with respect to the whole occupation of medicine is simply more striking for the early modern period; it is not that such definitions are unproblematic with respect to later contexts.

It is not surprising that medicine as a profession in the early modern period has received relatively little critical attention. A few have been confident: Bullough's reason for taking the sixteenth century as his termination date was that 'medicine was recognised as a profession' by that time.[3] Most such claims have been made on the basis of the overriding importance of tiny elites, usually physicians, but occasionally (as in the work of Gottfried for the fifteenth century) surgeons.[4] In some cases the numbers involved hardly exceed single figures. Clark's supremely confident justification of the (Royal) College of Physicians was compatible with the view of physicians adopted by Raach, but was predicated on an even greater degree of selection.[5] The physicians gained in importance through being seen as the top of a pyramid otherwise composed of (barber-) surgeons and apothecaries; little doubt is felt about their position, while that of the latter two of the 'three orders' of practice is more uncertain. The tripartite division of medicine into physicians, surgeons and apothecaries derives from modes of organisation developed in continental Europe. Such a division appears to some to support two related criteria of professionalisation: specialisation and the division of labour. That the division was effectively observed in England at some time continues to be implied, even though this traditional phase of development becomes increasingly hard to locate chronologically as more detailed studies are made of different periods.[6]

The significance of small groups is heightened by reference to their institutional context. Bullough made all professional organisation in European medicine dependent upon the evolution of medical faculties in the universities, even while admitting that the latter were crucial only in Italy, France and England. The College of Physicians of London continues to attract attention as an institution, while Gottfried, writing of the period before its foundation, has made rather less defensible claims for the connections of medical men with fifteenth-century hospitals.[7] This stress on institutions means that discussion has had to concentrate on urban centres, but there is no sign of reluctance on this point,

---

3. V. L. Bullough, *The Development of Medicine as a Profession. The Contribution of the Medieval University to Modern Medicine* (Basle, 1966), p. 3. Throughout this chapter I shall use 'medicine' to refer to all parts of practice, and not simply to 'physic' as opposed to surgery.

4. R. Gottfried, 'English Medical Practitioners 1340–1530', *Bull. Hist. Med.*, 58 (1984), 164–82.

5. G. N. Clark, *A History of the Royal College of Physicians of London*, 2 vols (Oxford, 1964–66); J. H. Raach, *A Directory of English Country Physicians 1603–1643* (London, 1962); see also Raach, 'The English Country Doctor in the Province of Canterbury, 1603–1643' (Yale University PhD thesis, 1941).

6. See for example J. F. Kett, 'Provincial Medical Practice in England 1730–1815', *Journal of the History of Medicine*, 19 (1964), 17; M. Jeanne Peterson, *The Medical Profession in Mid-Victorian London* (Berkeley, CA, 1978), pp. 5ff; I. Waddington, *The Medical Profession in the Industrial Revolution* (Dublin, 1984), p. 1; M. T. Walton, 'Fifteenth-century London Medical Men in their Social Context' (University of Chicago PhD thesis, 1979), pp. xiiff.

7. Bullough, *Development of Medicine*, pp. 86–7; Gottfried, 'English Medical Practitioners', p. 165. For stress on the College of Physicians, see W. J. Birken, 'The Fellows of the Royal College of Physicians of London, 1603-1643: a Social Study' (University of North Carolina PhD thesis, 1977); H. J. Cook, *The Decline of the Old Medical Regime in Stuart London* (Ithaca, NY, 1986); and subsequent publications by these authors.

in spite of Raach's demonstration of the presence of qualified medical men in country areas.[8] The existence of local forms of control of medical activity (including civic control) has hardly been admitted by recent writers: only pretensions at the national level, such as those of the College of Physicians, are seen as significant, however unsuccessful. The same selected institutions have also been made to serve the function of providing suitably lengthy training, and of dividing the professional from the layman in terms of knowledge and experience. Apprenticeship is not seen as serving these purposes. Obsolescence is said to be built into this mode of transmission of knowledge, but not into textbook-based instruction.[9]

It is important to stress the degree to which the historiography of medicine – and thus of the professions – has followed, for the early modern period, lines of interpretation established by nineteenth-century apologists and antiquarians.[10] The chosen few memorialised in Munk's *Roll* of the Royal College of Physicians are presented, from the first fellow to the last, as literary gentlemen. Munk also found it fitting that he could say little of the actual practice of his subjects. He asserted not only a norm of social status, but a legitimacy based on the private transactions between patient and practitioner, which were of necessity hidden from public view. *Public* statements were made through *publications*, literary or scientific. Yet private transactions may not have been a major part of medicine in the early modern period, although they are assumed to be integral, not only to the forms of authority now enjoyed by the medical profession, but also to the face-to-face, 'patronage' relations said to be characteristic of medicine before 1800.[11]

Other nineteenth-century writers exaggerated the credulity and eccentric behaviour of earlier practitioners in order to distance the educated or scientific medical man from superstitious practices; and perhaps, also, to justify his sometimes notorious (or alleged) lack of religion. Past raffishness was contrasted with present ideals of propriety. Some painted a picture of the lowly barber or apothecary of earlier periods in order to contest the claims of rival groups

8. Cf. Walton, 'Fifteenth-century London Medical Men', p. viii.

9. K. Charlton, 'The Professions in Sixteenth Century England', *University of Birmingham Historical Journal*, 12 (1969), 27. Cf. C. M. Cipolla, 'The Professions. The Long View', *Journal of European Economic History*, 2 (1973), 39.

10. There are historical reasons for this: see C. Webster, 'Medicine as Social History: Changing Ideas on Doctors and Patients in the Age of Shakespeare', in L. G. Stevenson (ed.), *A Celebration of Medical History* (Baltimore, MD, 1982), pp. 108–9.

11. W. Munk, *The Roll of the Royal College of Physicians of London . . . 1518 to . . . 1825*, 2nd edn, 3 vols (London, 1878), vol. 1, p. iv. The interpretative stress on the private relationship between practitioner and patient in the modern profession goes back at least to publications of the 1940s: see Larson, *Rise of Professionalism*, pp. 22–3, 25; J. Woodward and D. Richards, 'Towards a Social History of Medicine', in Woodward and Richards (eds), *Health Care and Popular Medicine in Nineteenth Century England* (London, 1977), pp. 36–7, 53. For shrewd comment on different attitudes towards the individual client and to the community, see A. M. Carr-Saunders and P. A. Wilson, *The Professions* (Oxford, 1933), pp. 471–7. That medicine in the eighteenth century was dominated by patronage relationships was asserted by S. W. F. Holloway, and developed by N. D. Jewson; see more broadly J. V. Pickstone, 'The Biographical and the Analytical: Towards a Historical Model of Science and Practice in Modern Medicine', in I. Löwy (ed.), *Medicine and Change: Historical and Sociological Studies of Medical Innovation* (Paris, 1993), pp. 23–47. Different stresses on 'low demand' have been placed by, for example, Holloway, Freidson and, especially, Starr: see sources cited in Waddington, *Medical Profession*, pt III.

within the nineteenth-century profession. Whatever the trend towards uniformity in the nineteenth century, the level of internecine warfare was very high. Other writers, who, like the nineteenth-century antiquarians, were aware of how many remnants of the sixteenth and seventeenth centuries their own period had swept away, saw earlier craftsman ancestors more romantically, but as impossibly far away in the past.[12] By and large, later commentators have followed these leads and emphasised the novelty and uniqueness of the nineteenth century with respect to medicine. Thus, we are told that before 1800 or the onset of industrialisation (often kept vague as to exact timing), most of the population depended on a ragbag of lesser and lay expedients. The university-trained physician was learned, but may not have practised much, and then almost exclusively among the elite. He had an immense scarcity value, but at the same time demand for his services was low, and medicine was consequently of little importance in economic terms. Professional autonomy was out of reach even of the qualified practitioner, because he was subject to lay and local control within the patronage relationship. Even when demand for medical services rose, as a result of commercialisation or the 'consumer revolution', the qualified practitioner was unsuccessful in distinguishing himself from his unqualified rivals.[13]

The well-regarded account of Augustan England by Holmes set itself to break this mould by boldly shifting the chronology of professional development back as early as 1680, with particular reference to the medical profession.[14] Claims are made not simply for a small elite of medical men, but for a substantial and uniform body serving the needs of a large and prosperous proportion of the population. In Holmes's golden age, the links connecting professionalisation with industrialisation (though not, significantly, with urbanisation) are broken. However, Holmes's interpretation is nonetheless an extrapolation backwards, locating in the eighteenth century the middle-class intellectual and economic vigour which nineteenth-century writers saw as belonging to their own age. (Similarly, but even more radically, Gottfried makes a claim for medicine as part of the rising middle class more than two centuries earlier.)[15] Holmes's framework is also notable for a reassertion of the distinction between works of brain and hand reminiscent both of Clark's history and of Victorian ambitions for medicine.

The failure until recently to explore medicine in the earlier period on its own terms has had a number of identifiable effects. First, and perhaps most

12. Cf. T. J. Pettigrew, *Medical Portrait Gallery* (London, 1840); idem, *On Superstitions Connected with the History and Practice of Medicine and Surgery* (London, 1844); C. Allbutt, *The Historical Relations of Medicine and Surgery to the End of the Sixteenth Century* (London, 1905); J. F. South, *Memorials of the Craft of Surgery in England*, ed. D'A. Power (London, 1886).

13. See note 11 above. The work of Roy Porter takes as its framework the commercialisation of the 'long eighteenth century': see esp. his *Health for Sale: Quackery in England 1660–1850* (Manchester and New York, 1989).

14. G. Holmes, *Augustan England: Professions, State and Society, 1680–1730* (London, 1982), esp. chaps 6 and 7.

15. Gottfried, 'English Medical Practitioners', pp. 166–7, 181. This argument is put more cautiously, and with respect to continental cities, by Cipolla, 'The Professions', pp. 37–52. Cf. W. J. Birken, 'The Royal College of Physicians of London and its Support of the Parliamentary Cause in the English Civil War', *Journal of British Studies*, 23 (1983), 47–62.

importantly, by far the larger part of medical activity remained undescribed, at least for England. Secondly, there is a disguising of the more negative elements of continuity before and after 1800, so that the modern profession comes to approximate to the 'ideal'. Thirdly, there is persistent understating of the connections between medicine and other economic and social activity, except as a reflection of medicine's failure to establish its professional credentials. This defect is also carried through until the present day, albeit in a different form. The 'medical market', for example, is drastically and artificially limited to transactions involving qualified practitioners. Fourthly, in order to provide a contrast with middle-class solidarity and professional uniformity (whether of the nineteenth century or after 1680), medicine in the earlier period is made to look like a series of battlegrounds, largely lacking in standards or centralised control, and yet at the same time over-rigidly stratified into the three parts of practice represented by apothecaries, surgeons and physicians.[16] Those writers for whom professional values exist before professional development can actually be identified, find such values then in the guardianship of tiny elites. Other important effects have tended to follow from this depreciation of the earlier period: for example, civic control of medicine has been disregarded; and conflicting accounts have been given of apprenticeship and of specialisation. The growth of specialisation is conventionally seen as a sign of increasing knowledge and professional maturity, but the resistance to this development has until recently received scant attention, and its existence in practice in the earlier period is regarded as an aspect of quackery.

We have already seen that writers on the earlier period lay stress on institutional developments. This reflects the fact that the focus for many points of definition of medicine post-1800 is the institution, and in particular the hospital.[17] Professions are also seen as communities, and doubt has been expressed whether even modern medicine would appear as a community outside the institutional context.[18] In a more whole-hearted return to traditional views, Holmes has seen the voluntary hospital movement of the eighteenth century as generating 'intimacy', co-operation and unity among previously divided callings.[19] This interpretation seems open to considerable reservations, as the hospital movement itself had many divisions, and was under lay control until a late date; the hospital has also been the means of consolidating elite privileges within the profession.[20] But the undoubted importance of institutions, thrown back on the earlier

16. Holmes adopts this approach: cf. *Augustan England*, pp. 169, 202ff. For an earlier example, see R. Shryock, 'Public Relations of the Medical Profession in Great Britain and the United States, 1600–1870', *Annals of Medical History*, new ser., 2 (1930), 310.

17. The stress on institutions received a new lease of life from the still-influential work of Michel Foucault, especially his *Naissance de la clinique: une archéologie du regard médical* (Paris, 1963); *Folie et déraison* (Paris, 1961); *Surveiller et punir* (Gallimard, n. pl., 1975). Cf. E. H. Ackerknecht, *Medicine at the Paris Hospital, 1794–1848* (Baltimore, MD, 1967). See in general C. Jones and R. Porter (eds), *Reassessing Foucault: Power, Medicine and the Body* (London, 1994). M. E. Fissell, *Patients, Power, and the Poor in Eighteenth-Century Bristol* (Cambridge, 1991), successfully connects institutional and extra-institutional circumstances within a Foucauldian framework.

18. Larson, *Rise of Professionalism*, p. x.

19. Holmes, *Augustan England*, pp. 183–4, 199–202.

20. Cf. C. Webster, 'The Crisis of the Hospitals during the Industrial Revolution', in E. Forbes (ed.), *Human Implications of Scientific Advance* (Edinburgh, 1978), pp. 214–23; F. Honigsbaum, *The Division in British*

period, has caused much medical practice to become invisible, since it took place largely outside them, and even out of sight of the qualified medical practitioner. As already suggested in the context of the 'medical market', it is not clear how historically useful a definition can be which excludes so much relevant activity. The excluded areas involve qualified as well as unqualified practitioners, especially the common round of provincial practice, and the long-standing arrangements whereby some access to qualified practitioners was given to patients in receipt of poor relief. The neglect of the sick after the Reformation likewise has been inferred principally from the loss of provision of bricks and mortar.[21]

As we have already seen, selected institutions of the early modern period and before have been made to carry a considerable burden of interpretation. The reality of the tripartite division of medicine in England depends on the universal significance of certain well-known developments in the institutionalisation of medicine in London: the foundation of the College of Physicians (not 'Royal' until the late seventeenth century) in 1518; the merging of the Barbers' Company with the tiny elite of the Surgeons in 1540; and the splitting off of the Apothecaries from the Grocers' Company in 1617.[22] Older writers, more sympathetic to the guilds, noted the extensive organisation of barber-surgeons' and apothecaries' companies in the provinces, and the numerical strength of the Barbers' Company in London.[23] Later occupational analysis, based largely on formal records such as freemen's rolls, has revealed as a by-product that barbers appear among the twelve leading trades in important towns such as Coventry,

Medicine: A History of the Separation of General Practice from Hospital Care 1911–1968 (London, 1979). Poor-law (later municipal) hospitals and specialist hospitals represented further divisions within the profession: see M. A. Crowther, *The Workhouse System 1834–1929* (London, 1981), chap. 7; Peterson, *Mid-Victorian Medical Profession*, pp. 259–82; I. S. L. Loudon, *Medical Care and the General Practitioner 1750–1850* (Oxford, 1986), chap. 11 and pp. 189–93; R. Stevens, *Medical Practice in Modern England: the Impact of Specialization and State Medicine* (New Haven and London, 1966); idem, *American Medicine and the Public Interest* (New Haven, CT, 1971).

21. Still-useful exceptions are J. J. Keevil, 'The Seventeenth-century English Medical Background', *Bull. Hist. Med.*, 31 (1957), 408–24; R. S. Roberts, 'The Personnel and Practice of Medicine in Tudor and Stuart England', *Medical History*, 6 (1962), 363–82 and 8 (1964), 217–34; R. M. S. McConaghey, 'The History of Rural Medical Practice', in F. N. L. Poynter (ed.), *The Evolution of Medical Practice in Britain* (London, 1961), pp. 117–43. See also Webster, *H, M & M*; I. S. L. Loudon, 'The Nature of Provincial Medical Practice in Eighteenth-century England', *Medical History*, 29 (1985), 1–32; Pelling, 'Healing the Sick Poor'; R. Porter (ed.), *Patients and Practitioners: Lay Perceptions of Medicine in Pre-Industrial Society* (Cambridge, 1985). The debate over the effects of the Dissolution is of long standing: see for example S. and B. Webb, *English Local Government: English Poor Law History Part 1: The Old Poor Law* (London, 1927), pp. 17–19. A more pragmatic view is now generally taken by historians: see J. Youings, *Sixteenth-Century England* (Harmondsworth, 1984), pp. 256–9, 264; S. Brigden, *London and the Reformation* (Oxford, 1992), pp. 477–83.

22. See Clark, *History*; Young, *Annals*; C. R. B. Barrett, *The History of the Society of Apothecaries of London* (London, 1905); H. C. Cameron and C. Wall, *A History of the Worshipful Society of Apothecaries of London, Vol. 1, 1617–1815*, ed. E. A. Underwood (London, 1963). Cf. R. S. Roberts, 'The London Apothecaries and Medical Practice in Tudor and Stuart England' (University of London PhD thesis, 1964); R. T. Beck, *The Cutting Edge. Early History of the Surgeons of London* (London, 1974).

23. See for example G. Parker, 'Early Bristol Medical Institutions, the Mediaeval Hospitals, and Barber Surgeons', *Transactions of the Bristol and Gloucestershire Archaeological Society*, 44 (1922), 155–78; F. C. Pybus, 'The Company of Barber Surgeons and Tallow Chandlers of Newcastle-on-Tyne', *Newcastle Medical Journal*, 9–10 (1928–30), 147–63; F. Simpson, 'The City Gilds or Companies of Chester, with Special Reference to that of the Barber-surgeons', *Journal of the Chester Archaeological Society*, 18 (1911), 98–203; D. Embleton, 'The Incorporated Company of Barber-surgeons and Wax and Tallow Chandlers of Newcastle-upon-Tyne', *Archaeologia Aeliana*, 15 (1892), 228–69; W. A. Leighton, 'The Guilds of Shrewsbury', *Shropshire Archaeological and Natural History Society Transactions*, 5 (1882), 265–97; Furnivall, *Vicary*, esp. pp. 243–87.

Chester and Bristol.[24] The apothecaries, though fewer in number and usually in combinant guilds, were commonly further up the civic hierarchy than barber-surgeons in the early modern period, yet this status is disregarded in accounts of their rise from humble origins to become the 'general practitioners' of the late eighteenth century. Where apothecaries are given higher status for the earlier period, this is by virtue of their connections with medicine and particularly with physicians, rather than because of their equality with goldsmiths and mercers.[25] In a kind of bastard remnant of this situation, apothecaries may be given precedence above surgeons in the medical hierarchy simply because non-manual trade is assumed to be of higher status than any manual craft.

In the nineteenth century, the guilds were idealised primarily in order to prove either that they were or that they were not the precursors of trade unions.[26] Later commentators stressed the decline of the guilds as an acceptable face of the 'rise of capitalism' hypothesis, and have adopted a similar line in distinguishing the professions as of higher status than the crafts, as possessing an ideal of service, and as excluding occupations purely commercial, agricultural and mechanical. From this point of view, the only organisational institution of importance in the early modern period was the College of Physicians.[27] The guilds are also bypassed by those who have seen the origins of the ideals of professionalism in the post-Reformation work ethic.[28] This latter view has the advantage of drawing attention to major social and religious changes, and is at least preferable to the interpretation which sees the qualified medical practitioner before 1800 as a mere appendage of the landed elite. The notion of (some) physicians as feudal lackeys has its attractions, but, as well as concentrating on a small minority, it leaves out of account a vast range of social and economic fluctuations, notably the early development of socio-economic independence of towns. By implication it supposes a uniform persistence of an ill-defined 'traditional' form of society up until the major upheavals of eighteenth-century industrialisation.

The views just noted seem to take too little account of the social and ethical traditions of the craft and mercantile guilds. The relevance of the guild tradition even for the physicians is perforce recognised by Clark, in a backhanded way, in his discussion of the possible models for the foundation of the College. Clark was concerned to stress that the College, a pre-Reformation body, had a distinctive character which was related to the role of the profession as a 'beneficent and civilising force'. After describing the rules under which physicians were required to renounce personal gain in the public interest, Clark notes that

24. C. Phythian-Adams, 'The Economic and Social Structure', in *The Fabric of the Traditional Community*, Open University Course Book (Milton Keynes, 1977), p. 17.

25. T. D. Whittet, 'The Apothecary in Provincial Gilds', *Medical History*, 8 (1964), 245–73; cf. Holmes, *Augustan England*, pp. 184–92, 210–13; Charlton, 'Sixteenth-century Professions', pp. 24–5.

26. See J. Toulmin Smith, *English Gilds* (London, 1870). See also G. Unwin, *The Gilds and Companies of London*, 3rd edn (London, 1938); E. Power, 'English Craft Gilds in the Middle Ages. Historical Revisions, 12', *History*, 4 (1919–20), 211–14.

27. G. Unwin, *Industrial Organization in the Sixteenth and Seventeenth Centuries* (Oxford, 1904); T. H. Marshall, 'Capitalism and the Decline of the English Gilds', *Cambridge Historical Journal*, 3 (1929–31), 23–33; Holmes, *Augustan England*, p. 3; Clark, *History*, vol. 1, pp. 7–11.

28. Larson, *Rise of Professionalism*, pp. 61–3.

'up to a point, no doubt they are generally the same as the rules of the fraternities or companies of craftsmen and traders; but, if we consider how much of human good or ill hinged upon them, we see that they stood on an altogether different, a much higher, plane'. The weakness of this is apparent, the more so as the two new bodies which Clark found most similar in England to the College were Doctors' Commons and the College of Arms, neither of which had the crucial ethical pretensions he ascribed to the College of Physicians.[29]

Clark also underestimates the presence of physicians in urban craft companies, going so far as to say that 'there seems to be no clear case in Tudor England of a boy or youth bound by indentures to a master to serve him and to learn the mystery of physic'.[30] The formal presence of physicians in civic life at this period is certainly minor, as there were few of them in towns compared with other medical groups, but they are necessarily under-represented in most official sources to a degree for which Clark does not allow. Even on the formal level, however, physicians were included in medical guilds in Bristol, Norwich, York and Canterbury. At a later date in York it was assumed that outsiders practising physic and surgery in the city would be contributory to the barbers' guild.[31] With respect to apprenticeship, by this time a proportion of many occupations, including the medical crafts, were working without being apprenticed, being made free, or ever having an apprentice of their own, so that it is less remarkable to find no such records in the case of physicians. However, one example which could be quoted against Clark's statement is that of John Potell of Leicester, physician and apothecary, whose apprentice was made a freeman in 1594. It was relatively common at this period for a craftsman to be indentured to learn more than one craft, so this feature of the Potell instance is not sufficient to disqualify it as an example.[32]

Inconsistent views have been taken of apprenticeship, reflecting its later history of social devaluation. Ironically, in view of Clark's comments, apprenticeship of an increasingly formal (but 'private') kind was to become an important part of medical education in the nineteenth century. In this context as well, it is necessary to break out of the inherited framework of Victorian social distinctions. Clark's view here may be contrasted with that of Holmes, whose writing is otherwise often reminiscent of Clark's: Holmes sees apprenticeship as providing in the eighteenth century an inexpensive uniform education without recourse to the universities.[33] Several points can be noted here: in the sixteenth

---

29. Clark, *History*, vol. 1, pp. 34, 62–3. Cf. A. Clark, *Working Life of Women in the Seventeenth Century* (1919; London, 1982), pp. 260–1; C. Webster, 'Thomas Linacre and the Foundation of the College of Physicians', in F. R. Maddison, M. Pelling and C. Webster (eds), *Linacre Studies: Essays on the Life and Work of Thomas Linacre* (Oxford, 1977), pp. 198–222.

30. Clark, *History*, vol. 1, p. 16.

31. Pelling, 'Occupational Diversity', pp. 490–2, 504, 507 (209–10, 222, 225); D. M. Palliser, *Tudor York* (Oxford, 1979), p. 177; C. F. Bradshaw, 'The Craft Gilds of Canterbury', *Good Books* [Canterbury Central Library], 5 (1948), 8–11; Furnivall, *Vicary*, p. 274; Keevil, 'Medical Background', p. 410.

32. Whittet, 'The Apothecary in Provincial Gilds', p. 256. Clark himself cites the example of a physician and mercer of Colchester: *History*, vol. 1, p. 16, n.

33. Holmes, *Augustan England*, pp. 17–18. I have considered medical apprenticeship further in an unpublished paper, 'How Apprenticeship was Discredited: the Case of Early Modern Medicine', given at Cambridge and Sheffield.

century at Cambridge, as at Oxford in the eighteenth century, students of medicine practised outside the university under the guidance of an experienced physician; the assistants of physicians often set up practice on their own account; and famous practitioners like Richard Napier attracted pupils eager to learn their special skills. In the mid-seventeenth century, Thomas Sydenham, whose systematic practical writings and example did much to revive the reputation of physicians, recommended apprenticeships in physic to the exclusion of any attendance at universities, and acted on this principle in his own career.[34]

Although enormous changes had taken place in the guilds since the high middle ages, the trades were not further from the guilds in the sixteenth century, than the term 'profession' was from its religious context. The guilds showed many of the features later thought to be definitive of the professions: for example, they specialised, they were self-regulating, they were recognised both by the public and by authority, and they were the source of criteria of qualification. Two features which the craft companies were careful to preserve after the Reformation were the requirement of confidentiality about the secrets of the craft and the company's affairs, and the regulation within the company of disputes among members. Company members were usually forbidden to resort to law without first bringing their case before senior officials of the company. This internal regulation covered a very wide range, from personal behaviour to serious disputes, and is perhaps still an underestimated factor among the forces in early modern society directed at controlling the behaviour of the male sex in particular.[35]

The guild's sense of responsibility towards the public was expressed in its supervision of standards of production, which was at least partly performed in public, and in the signs by which the craftsman visibly declared his qualification: his distinctive dress and accessories, his shop sign and his shop window. These traditional methods of control were indeed those which the College of Physicians sought to impose on the apothecaries of London. The College has been given credit for its pursuit of incompetent practitioners, but this activity was routine in other occupations, and it could also be argued that the College was primarily concerned to eliminate competition.[36] It is important to stress the generality of the guilds' codes of conduct because it is often implied that such standards were peculiar to the select institutions of medicine. It could be suggested, on the contrary, that the oaths which continued to be taken within the

---

34. Pelling and Webster, 'Medical Practitioners', p. 203; K. Dewhurst, *Dr Thomas Sydenham* (London, 1966), pp. 17, 47–8, 56–9; Webster, 'Medicine as Social History', p. 109; A. Cunningham, 'Thomas Sydenham: Epidemics, Experiment and the "Good Old Cause"', in R. French and A. Wear (eds), *The Medical Revolution of the Seventeenth Century* (Cambridge, 1989), pp. 164–90. I am grateful to Ronald Sawyer for allowing me to consult his thesis on the physical medicine of Napier: 'Patients, Healers, and Disease in the Southeast Midlands, 1597–1634' (University of Wisconsin-Madison PhD thesis, 1986).

35. C. Phythian-Adams, 'Sources for Urban History. 3: Records of the Craft Gilds', *Local Historian*, 9 (1971), 267–74. For the persistence of provincial guilds in particular up to the eighteenth century, see D. Palliser, 'The Trade Gilds of Tudor York', in P. Clark and P. Slack (eds), *Crisis and Order in English Towns 1500–1700* (London, 1972), pp. 86–116; Young, *Annals*, pp. 423–30.

36. Cameron and Wall, *Worshipful Society of Apothecaries*, pp. 13–14, 41–57; W. L. Sachse (ed.), *Minutes of the Norwich Court of Mayoralty 1630–1631*, Norfolk Record Society XV (1942), pp. 39–41 and *passim*; Palliser, 'Trade Gilds of Tudor York', pp. 95–6, 101–2.

guild or company context have been far more a living part even of medicine in England than the Hippocratic oath, itself a memorial to the compatibility of religious, philosophical and craft principles.[37] Clark's contrived dismissal of the guilds and companies also ignores the extent to which the regulation of crafts and trades, especially but not only the food trades, was concerned with public health as an aspect of the public interest. This regulation was exerted internally, within the companies, as well as by municipal authorities.[38] With respect to health and medicine it is likely to have done more for the protection of the consumer than any university training, however lengthy. The role of guilds and municipal authorities in this respect has been diminished by the assumption that effective control of standards can be maintained only within the professional peer group as organised on a national basis independently of all forms of local authority.[39]

As an institution, the London College undoubtedly (although perhaps tauto-logically) comes closest to the criteria selected by modern commentators as defining a profession. As we have seen, however, it was not uniquely endowed with a sense of moral responsibility about its activities. Other features of the College, which suit modern definitions, actually militated at the time against its success in modern terms. It does not quite fit the modern vocational criterion, as there is nothing to suggest that its members were any more full-time than any other practitioner of the period; but with respect to the important criterion of autonomy, the College seemed to achieve a good deal. Its strongest obliga-tions seem to have been to the crown; its relations even with the universities were limited and often negative, and it was not subordinated to the City author-ities. On the other hand, this degree of autonomy often worked out in practice as a weakness rather than a strength, and the College certainly failed to achieve the public recognition and control over the practice of physic on which the analysts of the professions insist. The continued viability of the guilds as com-panies is instanced by the greater degree of integration into civic life of the London Barber-Surgeons, and then of the Society of Apothecaries, as com-pared with the College.[40]

37. Although the assumption is repeatedly made, it has not been clearly established that the Hippocratic oath was taken in any context in either England or Scotland in the sixteenth or seventeenth centuries. Clark implies its relevance to the ideals of London physicians without establishing any actual connection: Clark, *History*, vol. 1, pp. 32–4. I am grateful to Charles Webster for his guidance on this point. The most author-itative discussion in print of the oath is L. Edelstein, *The Hippocratic Oath, Text, Translation and Interpretation* (Baltimore, MD, 1943). See also S. V. Larkey, 'The Hippocratic Oath in Elizabethan England', *Bull. Inst. Hist. Med.*, 4 (1936), 201–19; V. Nutton, 'Beyond the Hippocratic Oath', in A. Wear, J. Geyer-Kordesch and R. French (eds), *Doctors and Ethics: the Earlier Historical Setting of Professional Ethics* (Amsterdam, 1993), pp. 10–37; W. H. S. Jones, *The Doctor's Oath* (Cambridge, 1924), Appendix, reproduces versions from Montpellier, and nineteenth-century Glasgow. For examples of guild and municipal oaths, see Hudson and Tingey, *Records*, vol. 2, pp. 313, 315–16, 382ff; Young, *Annals*, pp. 142, 254; S. Rappaport, *Worlds within Worlds: Structures of Life in Sixteenth-Century London* (Cambridge, 1989), pp. 298–9.

38. Cf. J. H. Thomas, *Town Government in the Sixteenth Century* (London, 1933); A. Everitt, 'The Marketing of Agricultural Produce', in J. Thirsk (ed.), *The Agrarian History of England and Wales, Vol. IV: 1500–1640* (Cambridge, 1967), pp. 577–86; Sachse, *Minutes of the Norwich Court of Mayoralty 1630–1631*, pp. 39–43, 46–8 and *passim*; and under the heading of 'nuisances' in S. and B. Webb, *English Local Government: The Manor and the Borough* (London, 1908). See also Pelling, 'Medicine and the Environment'.

39. See, for example, Waddington, *Medical Profession*, pp. 183–5.

40. Pelling and Webster, 'Medical Practitioners', pp. 168–77; Webster, *Great Instauration*, pp. 308–14; Pelling, 'Compromised by Gender'.

There are major features of medicine in the early modern period which seem to point to the value of shifting the emphasis away from the conventional definition of a profession as a full-time, autonomous activity, and towards other crafts, trades and occupations. As we have seen, the tendency in the past has been to take the claims of certain minorities at their own valuation. Raach's approach had the merit of looking beyond London institutions to reveal the high incidence of academically qualified physicians even in small rural centres. This is confirmed by, for example, the finding that more than half of sixteenth-century medical graduates of Cambridge, and a larger proportion of the licentiates and unlicensed practitioners from the university, settled in the provinces.[41] However, it is not clear that this is definitive of professional activity when many such graduates may have practised only sporadically. Much has been gained historically by taking Raach's quantitative approach further, to make an assessment of the occupation of medicine as a whole. This has involved both the adoption of a generic category of 'medical practitioner' in place of the conventional tripartite distinctions, and the inclusion in this category of any individuals recognised by their contemporaries as involved in the care of the sick. Behind this approach lies the assumption that 'any balanced view of medicine in the early modern period, or in non-western societies, must take into account all practitioners involved in dispensing medical care'.[42] The inclusive view is also warranted on the grounds of the lack of historical justification for most criteria of selection:

the difficulties involved in framing consistent and historically fruitful criteria for isolating responsible medical practitioners from empirics and quacks have often not been fully appreciated. Terms such as empiric tend to be used without consistency or sound historical justification. Adoption of technical criteria for the isolation of empirics based on the legal code, professional attachments, or educational attainment is practicable, but it tends to generate a trivial and unrealistically narrow conception of legitimate medical practice. Reference to more meaningful criteria related to professional efficiency, reliability and responsibility, or the ideal of service rather than pecuniary gain, is difficult to operate because of lack of evidence, but if applied objectively it is likely to reinforce the use of a broader rather than narrower conception of responsible medical practice.[43]

Even if fairly strict criteria are adopted, a high ratio of practitioners to population emerges. An estimate for London in the late sixteenth century, which is consistent with estimates of later date, leads to a ratio to population of at least 1:400. This body of *c.* 500 practitioners comprised: 50 fellows, candidates and licentiates of the Physicians' College; 100 members of the Barber-Surgeons' Company, including those prosecuted by the College; 100 apothecaries, some of them also the subject of prosecutions; and 250 practitioners (of all descriptions

41. Pelling and Webster, 'Medical Practitioners', p. 205. For Raach, see above, note 5.
42. Ibid., pp. 188, 186.
43. Ibid., p. 166.

but excluding midwives and nurses) lying outside the London institutions except for (in some instances) the possession of licences. At the parish level, where occupational realities are often best reflected, a single London parish at the same period contained a barber-surgeon of some repute; a grocer free of the Barber-Surgeons' Company; two unlicensed practitioners and one immigrant practitioner; a 'professor of physic and other curious arts', and a poor man who also professed physic; and a woman described as a 'counterfeit' physician and surgeon.[44] A similar quantitative approach applied to Norwich over the period 1550–1640 revealed a group of 150 physicians, barber-surgeons, surgeons, lithotomists and bonesetters, all of whom had some formal connection with the barber-surgeons' company of the city; and an additional group of 120, apparently lacking any such connection, which included physicians, women practitioners, immigrant practitioners, midwives, clerical practitioners, practising schoolmasters, and keepers of lazarhouses (male and female) who practised medicine. Even though the apothecaries were excluded, this more exhaustive assessment produced an even higher ratio of practitioners to population. That the present estimates are minimal rather than over-high is indicated by the fact that many of the practitioners have been identified by their being prosecuted for unlicensed practice, by the College or by the ecclesiastical authorities. Other evidence suggests strongly that prosecution by either authority was far from exhaustive. These estimates have led to the conclusion that medicine was a much more significant occupation in the early modern period, both economically and culturally, than previous analysis had suggested.[45]

What was there for so many practitioners to do? There seem to be a variety of answers to this question. Perhaps most importantly, all the evidence suggests that the 'patient' in the early modern period was extremely 'active', being critical, sceptical and well-informed to a degree not anticipated in analysis of the professions, except in the extremely limited context of the pre-professional patronage relationship. This latter phenomenon is, as already indicated, assumed to go with low demand. However, it seems clear that the critical consumer of the early modern period absorbed enormous quantities of medical care, of all kinds, and that this consumption probably increased at crisis periods such as the later sixteenth and early seventeenth centuries, just as the consumption of similar consolations such as alcohol also increased.[46] Poverty did not inhibit the consumption of certain forms of medicine at least; in periods of economic difficulty, loss of health or mobility was more threatening than ever. Not only was a scale of payment generally adopted, from pennies and payment in kind to high fees; there is some evidence to suggest that high fees failed to deter many patients, and that municipalities and parishes regarded medical expenses as being as legitimate an object of charity as losses by fire, or shipwreck.[47] Poverty could also be seen by authority and the poor alike as a justification for practising medicine, especially in the case of women, and this suggests there were

44. Ibid., p. 166.
45. Pelling, 'Occupational Diversity', esp. pp. 495, 507–8 (213, 225–6).
46. P. Clark, *The English Alehouse: A Social History 1200–1830* (London, 1983), chaps 4–7.
47. Pelling, 'Healing the Sick Poor'.

grounds for confidence that poverty could be alleviated by such means. There are parallels here with the granting of alehouse licences. One example was Adrian Colman, the widow of a practitioner of physic, who was licensed at Whitehall in 1596 to practise on women and children in Norfolk, because she had no other means of support.[48] Clerics also pleaded poverty as an excuse for practising medicine. Poverty could thus increase both supply and demand. At the same time, by 1600 medical care was already an aspect of the consumption of services in towns like Norwich and York, which early became centres for professional and social life.[49] Holmes attributes the 'rise of the doctor' in the early eighteenth century to increased middle-class prosperity, along with a generalised tendency for towns to become service centres.[50] This argument was previously applied to the nineteenth century, along with the assumption of a shift from patronage to commodity relations associated with industrialisation. As already suggested, with respect to medical personnel this interpretation has not been precisely articulated in historical terms, and tends to be based on minorities, rather than on the whole occupational group. Here it should be stressed that prosperity was not the only engine either of consumption or of the proliferation of medical practice.

This phenomenon of high but fluctuating consumption is complemented by a characteristic which increasingly is being shown to apply to a wide range of other occupational groups, and which may not be irrelevant to later periods when the professions seem firmly established. Both formally and informally, a great many medical practitioners either practised medicine part-time, or combined it with a range of associated activities.[51] This was a feature of urban as well as of rural life, where it is more familiar. Barber-surgeons traditionally diversified into tallowchandling, knitting, netmaking and wigmaking; in towns dominated by the textile trades they also engaged in these in a minor level. Particularly strong and widespread was their involvement in music, which was one aspect of the social and public context represented by the shops of barbers and barber-surgeons. The latter offered a range of personal services which, in sophisticated urban environments, led to a natural intermingling with other tradesmen concerned with dress and adornment, such as dyers and perfumers. As well as continuing their traditional diversifications, medical practitioners showed themselves highly responsive to new economic opportunities. Among these, in the seventeenth century if not earlier, were the manufacture of small consumer goods relating primarily to dress and accessories, the selling of tobacco, and distilling. An enterprising surgeon of the early seventeenth century was William White of Midhurst, Sussex, a small centre near Chichester. White possessed a wide range of surgical instruments but also barber's gear, distilling equipment, apothecary drugs, a considerable library of books, a stock of wine, and tobacco. The alertness of the apothecaries to new botanical discoveries, and

48. Pelling and Webster, 'Medical Practitioners', p. 209.
49. Palliser, *Tudor York*, p. 20; J. T. Evans, *Seventeenth-Century Norwich* (Oxford, 1979), p. 6.
50. Holmes, *Augustan England*, pp. 11–18.
51. See Pelling, 'Occupational Diversity'; 'Appearance and Reality'.

the growth in imported drugs are both well-established developments, although the latter is under-explored.[52] Barber-surgeons and physicians as well as apothecaries were involved in distilling of various kinds. Such flexibility could be formal: a citizen waxchandler around 1660 could accept an apprentice in 'the several arts of chirurgery and distillation'. When distilling reached the level of an industrial process, thus prompting attempts to monopolise it under the sponsorship of the crown, objections were heard from the barber-surgeons as well as from the apothecaries and the vintners. Distilling related to the production of new drugs as well as of strong liquors.[53] The association of medical practitioners with alcohol took many forms, and involved all kinds of practitioner. For Holmes, on the other hand, convinced of the difference between 'patient' and 'customer', the provision of alcohol by a practitioner after bloodletting around 1730 is simply a quaint relic of the 'curious hybrid' of barbery and surgery.[54]

Practitioners of physic diversified as well as surgeons and barber-surgeons. At one extreme there is the 'professor' of physic of London already mentioned who also practised 'other curious arts'; at the other is the well-known tendency of schoolmasters and clerics also to be physicians. Scriveners and physicians enjoyed close relations, and were sometimes (as with surgeons) combined in one person, possibly because of the congruence of skills and occasions. The latter could include attendance at the time of will-making, if not the actual deathbed.[55] In the country, John Crophill could be both bailiff and medical man.[56] Also striking as a characteristic response to economic opportunities is the involvement of practitioners in the Muscovy Company, which was founded in an attempt to dominate trade with Russia in the mid-sixteenth century. Physicians as well as surgeons and midwives formed part of the diplomatic commerce between England and Russia, which tended to focus on the person of

---

52. F. W. Steer, 'The Possessions of a Sussex Surgeon', *Medical History*, 2 (1958), 134–6; R. S. Roberts, 'The Early History of the Import of Drugs into England', in F. N. L. Poynter (ed.), *The Evolution of Pharmacy in Britain* (London, 1965), pp. 165–86.

53. T. R. Forbes, 'Apprentices in Trouble: Some Problems in the Training of Surgeons and Apothecaries in Seventeenth-century London', *Yale Journal of Biology and Medicine*, 52 (1979), 230. Webster, *Great Instauration*, pp. 253–4; Young, *Annals*, p. 338; Cameron and Wall, *Worshipful Society of Apothecaries*, p. 57. See also M. Berlin, *The Worshipful Company of Distillers: A Short History* (Chichester, 1996).

54. Holmes, *Augustan England*, p. 197.

55. During a period in Ipswich Richard Argentine, a sixteenth-century physician and divine, and graduate of Cambridge, practised medicine, held ecclesiastical appointments, and taught at the grammar school: *DNB*; Pelling and Webster, 'Medical Practitioners', pp. 227–8. See also McConaghey, 'History of Rural Medical Practice', pp. 118–21; D. W. Amundsen, 'Medieval Canon Law on Medical and Surgical Practice by the Clergy', *Bull. Hist. Med.*, 52 (1978), 22–44; C. Webster, 'English Medical Reformers of the Puritan Revolution: a Background to the "Society of Chymical Physitians"', *Ambix*, 14 (1967), 21–3; C. H. Talbot, *Medicine in Medieval England* (London, 1967), p. 196; D. Harley, 'James Hart of Northampton and the Calvinist Critique of Priest-Physicians', *Medical History* (forthcoming). In the sixteenth century, the London Barber-Surgeons' Company included citizen-scrivener-surgeons: Furnivall, *Vicary*, pp. 200–1. On relations between continental medical personnel and notaries, see Cipolla, 'The Professions', p. 50.

56. See J. K. Mustain, 'A Rural Medical Practitioner in Fifteenth-century England', *Bull. Hist. Med.*, 46 (1972), 469–76. Cf. the case of Edward Rigby, distinguished provincial physician/surgeon/lithotomist/farmer and agricultural writer, d. 1822: *DNB*; A. Batty Shaw, 'The Norwich School of Lithotomy', *Medical History*, 14 (1970), 247–8. See also F. Neale, 'A Seventeenth-century Country Doctor. John Westover of Wedmore', *Practitioner*, 203 (1969), 699–704; Waddington, *Medical Profession*, pp. 187, 189–90.

the monarch, and many of these took the opportunity to engage in trade, one leading example being Arthur Dee, the son of the astrologer John Dee.[57]

Taken as a whole, medical practice in early modern England was neither well organised nor firmly controlled. No system of surveillance had more than a partial application. The tripartite structure more strictly adopted in continental Europe remained the aim of minority groups. This intermittent kind of regulation is compatible with the occupational flexibility just described, which seems entirely at odds with the full-time, self-sufficient, life-long commitment characteristic of the professional as usually defined. For Bullough, full-time dedication had to be the inevitable consequence of the protracted training in medicine developed by the medieval universities, but neither the training nor its aftermath was necessarily so specific. Where occupational diversity in medicine has been recognised previously, it has been assumed to signify simply low status, low demand for qualified practice, poverty, and other features outside the professional pale, including too great a degree of integration into local communities.[58] To put it into metaphorical terms, explored in more detail elsewhere: medical historians who have tended to favour what might be called a Linnaean classification of medical practitioners into fixed, clearly defined species, see any merging or mingling as unnatural and something to be resisted.[59] Historians of the professions are perhaps closer to a kind of vulgar Darwinism in seeing the professions as a highly evolved but rare species, extremely successful (according to certain criteria) but peculiar to a specialised environment. Historians of occupations in general have the advantage of being interested in a wider range of organisms but have in some respects a similarly Darwinian point of view. They see different species evolving, dominating, or becoming extinct according to changes in their habitat, whether natural or artificial. The picture of a large but versatile occupational population defined by part-time activity and intimate relations with other social and economic areas suggests instead a more Lamarckian situation in which specific differences may be arbitrary or temporary, and which allows adaptation to environmental pressures, favourable or unfavourable.

There were other intimate associations which raise issues fundamental to the medical art. We have already seen that early modern medical practitioners were involved in the drink trades at various levels. In selling drink in alehouses and tippling houses they were inevitably also involved in the food trade.[60] In addition, strong drinks were often flavoured with grocery items like dates and raisins, and these and similar food items were also indistinguishably part of an

---

57. On Dee, see J. H. Appleby, 'Dr Arthur Dee: Merchant and Litigant', *Slavonic and East European Review*, 57 (1979), 32–55; idem, 'Some of Arthur Dee's Associations before Visiting Russia Clarified, including Two Letters from Sir Theodore Mayerne', *Ambix*, 26 (1979), 1–15.

58. Bullough, *Development of Medicine*, pp. 2, 5; Waddington, *Medical Profession*, pp. 186–91.

59. Pelling, 'Occupational Diversity', pp. 503, 511 (220, 229).

60. Pelling, 'Occupational Diversity', pp. 505, 506 (223, 224). Little attention has been paid to the connections between medicine and the food trades, but see J. O'Hara May, *Elizabethan Dyetary of Health* (Lawrence, Kansas, 1977); C. Webster, 'The College of Physicians: "Solomon's House" in Commonwealth England', *Bull. Hist. Med.*, 41 (1967), 406, 407; Webster, *Great Instauration*, pp. 248, 249; Pelling, 'Food, Status and Knowledge'.

apothecary's goods.[61] Another connection is that both the food and drink trades and medicine were notable as employments of women.[62] Apart from the actual difficulty of telling the difference between food and medicines, there are many parallels on both the material and the spiritual planes which reflect on the nature of medicine as a transaction.[63] On the more profane side, each can be seen as an item of consumption, a daily necessity which could be bought in the market-place and publicly consumed. The range of diversions – food, music, drink, tobacco, games, conversation, news and displays of curiosities – which could be found in the shops of early modern medical practitioners was undoubtedly deployed to attract as well as to divert their clientele. The breadth of activities which could be encompassed in the shop of a medical practitioner has been obscured by the efforts of nineteenth-century commentators who were think-ing primarily in terms of emancipating the practitioner from the retailing of drugs. Thus the connection has been effectively severed between the shop of the earlier period and the 'surgery' of the modern general practitioner, which, as in the former case, was almost always part of the practitioner's own house.[64]

The range of provision within shops also draws attention to the delivery of medicine at this period as a public rather than private act. Mountebanks and itinerants obviously sold their cures in public places, and in an urban context especially, the practitioner's shop could be a place of resort. Even at home, however, the patient and the practitioner were unlikely to be alone together. Many consultations took place by letter or by proxy, a reflection of the kind of services offered, but also of the important role played by the patient's friends or relatives. The stress on privacy and confidentiality can be seen as an aspect of later phases of social differentiation, although persistent restrictions on the examination of patient's bodies may owe less to Victorian prudery than the con-tinued presence during the consultation of other people, including friends and servants, overlapping with changes in attitudes to the body. The face-to-face

---

61. See for example the inventory of Samuel Newboult of Lichfield (1666): D. G. Vaisey (ed.), *Probate Inventories of Lichfield and District 1565–1680*, Staffordshire Records Society, Collections, 4th ser., V (1969), pp. 155–61; M. Rowe and G. E. Trease, 'Thomas Baskerville, Elizabethan Apothecary of Exeter', *Transactions of the British Society for the History of Pharmacy*, 1 (1970), 3–28. See also the complaints made by the Grocers' Company of London against the claims of the apothecaries: Cameron and Wall, *Worshipful Society of Apothecaries*, p. 37.

62. Clark, *Working Life of Women*, pp. 197–235, 242–89; D. Willen, 'Guildswomen in the City of York, 1650–1700', *The Historian* [USA], 46 (1984), 204–18; Palliser, *Tudor York*, p. 150; M. Prior (ed.), *Women in English Society 1500–1800* (London, 1985), pp. 70–1, 106–7; Pelling and Webster, 'Medical Practitioners', pp. 183–4, 186–7 and *passim*; A. L. Wyman, 'The Surgeoness: the Female Practitioner of Surgery 1400–1800', *Medical History*, 28 (1984), 22–41; D. Evenden Nagy, *Popular Medicine in Seventeenth-Century England* (Bowling Green, OH, 1988), chap. 5; Pelling, 'Occupational Diversity', pp. 508–9 (226–7); Pelling, 'Food, Status and Knowledge', p. 56. Women barbers appear in their own right in formal records to the end of the fifteenth century: L. Fox, 'The Coventry Gilds and Trading Companies with Special Reference to the Po-sition of Women', *Birmingham Archaeological Society Transactions*, 78 (1962), 17. See also C. Rawcliffe, *Medicine and Society in Later Medieval England* (Stroud, 1995), chaps 8 and 9.

63. J. O'Hara May, 'Foods or Medicines? A Study in the Relationship between Foodstuffs and Materia Medica from the Sixteenth to the Nineteenth Century', *Transactions of the British Society for the History of Pharmacy*, 1 (1971), 61–97, esp. pp. 61–8.

64. See Holmes, *Augustan England*, p. 215; Waddington, *Medical Profession*, pp. 187–9. On surgeries as such, see A. Digby, *Making a Medical Living: Doctors and Patients in the English Market for Medicine, 1720–1911* (Cambridge, 1994), *passim*.

but mostly unequal contact posited as characteristic of the patronage relationship in medicine before 1800 emerges as too limited a description of contact with practitioners on a number of counts.[65]

On the less profane side, medicine, again like food or drink, could be and often was given for nothing, an aspect which became a feature of the voluntary hospitals, survives to the present day, and is relatively unexplored except as an aspect of institutionalised philanthropy.[66] Medicine in the early period thus shows a variety of types of exchange. At one extreme, the mountebank Valentine Raseworme, having cut a woman for the stone, handed the alleged stone to the woman's husband with one hand, and received the large sum of £10 from him with the other.[67] More widespread at different levels of practice was the conditional contract, in which the terms defining the disease and the 'cure' were agreed on, and the practitioner was first paid something on account, and the balance when the cure was completed. The conditional contract seems to have had a long life through the late medieval period to at least the late seventeenth century.[68] The patient could be dominant to the point of hiring a particular practitioner to cure the form of disease as he or she, the patient, had diagnosed it; the 'cure' was usually defined as an agreed outcome, something which was an improvement on the *status quo*, rather than a return to perfect health. With respect to high-risk cures, where things were most likely to go wrong, the terms of the agreement were (ideally) overseen either by civic authorities or by senior members of the craft under civic authority.[69] Given the nature of these contracts, it is not surprising that, when they did not go according to plan, patients first sought to get their money back, and only secondarily went into the difficult area of damages. The case of Susanna Levine, brought to the London Mayor's Court in 1687, is one in point. Susanna's witnesses, medical and otherwise,

65. The major shifts proposed by Jewson and others (e.g. from 'bedside' to 'hospital' medicine) are essentially based on medical ideas: see note 11 above; N. D. Jewson, 'The Disappearance of the Sick-man from Medical Cosmology, 1770–1870', *Sociology*, 10 (1976), 225–44; M. Nicolson, 'The Metastatic Theory of Pathogenesis and the Professional Interests of the Eighteenth-century Physician', *Medical History*, 32 (1988), 277–300. N. Elias, *The History of Manners*, trans. E. Jephcott (Oxford, 1983), pp. 163–8, is suggestive, but Elias does not deal with the conventions of sickness. Adrian Wilson stresses the public (but all-female) and ritual aspects of midwifery, most recently in his *The Making of Man-Midwifery: Childbirth in England 1660–1770* (London, 1995), pp. 25–30; on the Victorian period, see for example M. Poovey, '"Scenes of an Indelicate Character": the Medical "Treatment" of Victorian Women', *Representations*, 14 (1986), 137–68. On the nature of consultations, see also M. MacDonald, *Mystical Bedlam: Madness, Anxiety and Healing in Seventeenth Century England* (Cambridge, 1981); G. Smith, 'The Physiology of Air: Eighteenth-century Fever Therapy in the Advice Literature', *Bull. SSHM*, 35 (1984), 22; D'A. Power, 'John Halle and Sixteenth-century Consultations', *Proceedings of the Royal Society of Medicine (History of Medicine Section)*, 11 (1918), 60.

66. See Furnivall, *Vicary*, pp. 208–9, 274; Pelling and Webster, 'Medical Practitioners', p. 213; W. D. Foster, 'Dr William Henry Cook: the Finances of a Victorian General Practitioner', *Proceedings of the Royal Society of Medicine (History of Medicine Section)*, 66 (1973), 47–8. See in general J. Barry and C. Jones (eds), *Medicine and Charity before the Welfare State* (London and New York, 1991).

67. W. Clowes, *A Brief and Necessarie Treatise, touching the Cure of the Disease called Morbus Gallicus* (London, 1585), fol. 10. The operation took place 'in the presence of divers honest persons'.

68. On contracts, see E. A. Hammond, 'Incomes of Medieval English Doctors', *Journal of the History of Medicine*, 15 (1960), 154–69; Talbot, *Medicine in Medieval England*, p. 138; Pelling, 'Healing the Sick Poor', pp. 122–3, 129 (88–9, 93–4); M. McVaugh, *Medicine before the Plague: Practitioners and their Patients in the Crown of Aragon 1285–1345* (Cambridge, 1993), pp. 174–81 and *passim*; Pelling, *Strength of the Opposition*.

69. For ordinances and examples, see Young, *Annals*, pp. 182 and *passim*; Furnivall, *Vicary*, p. 255; C. Williams, *The Barber-Surgeons of Norwich* (Norwich, 1897).

described not so much her injury and its treatment as the details of the financial agreements between the patient and her practitioner. Susanna was trying to avoid paying her bill by claiming that the practitioner had neglected her over the two years of her cure. She further claimed that during this period she, as the owner of a painting business, had painted one of the practitioner's houses. Cases of this sort tend to be labelled malpractice suits simply because they relate to medicine, rather than because this is an accurate description of proceedings which could occur in other circumstances.[70] Again the effect is to sever the connection between medicine and other areas of economic life.

A cure at this period could thus be more or less material, but it was still in many respects bought as an item. This contrasts with a definition of the 1830s, which stated confidently – or perhaps aggressively – that the professions dealt with 'men as men', whereas trades dealt with 'external wants or occasions of men'.[71] It also casts doubt on the idea that 'commodity relations' in medicine began only in the nineteenth century with the increased market said to be created by industrialisation – or in the long eighteenth, as a result of commercialisation.[72] With respect to hospitals and the medical treatment of the poor, the practitioner of the earlier period could be paid for unspecified cures on unspecified patients as an extension of the system of paying certain sums yearly to retainers of households. This 'retainer' system proved very enduring, and became increasingly rather than less competitive. The conditional contract was of course in its very essence competitive. Failure to recognise the effects of competition, for example in the use of a practitioner from a more distant centre, or the desire of a town authority to obtain the services of a highly qualified practitioner or specialist by compounding for a lump sum, has been one factor behind the assumption that substantial practitioners were not numerous in the early modern period. Compounding for a lump sum also occurred with respect to specific individuals, where the practitioner gambled on effecting a permanent cure of his or her patient's condition. This particular kind of arrangement bears some relation to the 'maintenance' agreements of the later medieval period, and may have faded out in the course of the seventeenth century.[73] The retainer system, on the other hand, which consisted of a kind of contractual bulk buying, with a similar calculation on either side of the balance of probabilities, is familiar in the poor-law context in the eighteenth century, and also occurs later in factories, schools, collieries, sick clubs and other institutions. However,

---

70. For the Levine case, see T. R. Forbes, 'The Case of the Casual Chirurgeon', *Yale Journal of Biology and Medicine*, 51 (1978), 583–8. For other examples see Young, *Annals*, pp. 316, 319; C. H. Talbot and E. A. Hammond, *The Medical Practitioners in Medieval England. A Biographical Register* (London, 1965); references as given in J. B. Post, 'Doctor versus Patient: Two Fourteenth Century Lawsuits', *Medical History*, 16 (1972), 296–300. Cf. M. P. Cosman, 'Medieval Medical Malpractice: the Dicta and the Dockets', *Bulletin of the New York Academy of Medicine*, 49 (1973), 22–47; Walton, 'Fifteenth-century London Medical Men', pp. 150–65.

71. *OED*, s.v. 'profession', citing a lecture on middle-class education by F. D. Maurice.

72. Cf. Larson, *Rise of Professionalism*, pp. 14ff, 209–19; K. Figlio, 'Sinister Medicine? A Critique of Left Approaches to Medicine', *Radical Science Journal*, 9 (1979), 14–68. There is a lack of connection between such views, and those of early modernists like Harold Cook and Roy Porter who stress 'the medical marketplace' and pre-industrial commercialisation.

73. See Pelling, 'Healing the Sick Poor'; 'Old Age, Poverty and Disability', pp. 86–7 (146); E. Clark, 'Some Aspects of Social Security in Medieval England', *Journal of Family History*, 7 (1982), 307–20.

it also persisted to a very late date in the arrangement whereby a practitioner was paid a certain sum *per annum* for attendance on all members of a particular family. This similarly provided the practitioner with an assured minimum income, but also involved an 'actuarial' estimate of risks. Competitive tendering, with the advantage lying with the buyer, was possibly last seen in the conditions under which medical officers of health and poor-law medical officers were employed by local authorities and Boards of Guardians. Organised resistance to this disadvantageous version of a 'commercial' system was not wholly successful until the 1920s. The persistence of commercial characteristics was exemplified in the panel system of National Health Insurance, and even in the systems of payment favoured by medical practitioners themselves for the National Health Service.[74]

Opposition to some aspects of such systems was being offered in the earlier period by physicians and some surgeons.[75] Both saw the advantages of aiming at the kind of unconditional, disembodied or verbal transactions with their clients which were usually associated with lawyers and the clergy. Thus, at its most extreme, there was neither substantial nor even visual contact between the physician and his patient: advice was given through intermediaries. Even in hospitals, the physician was by his own definition to be more distant from his patients than the surgeon or the apothecary. At the refounded St Bartholomew's Hospital in London, under the regulations proposed by William Harvey in 1633, the physician (who was not resident) attended once a week and sat at a desk in the great hall flanked by the other officers of the hospital. The patients were then brought before him; there was no provision for his seeing the bedridden in their beds.[76] The collaborations entered into for mutual benefit by some apothecaries and physicians are in some ways reminiscent of the lawyer's use of his clerk, who still protects his principal from the material side of each transaction.

So far, many of the criteria of professionalisation under discussion – except, perhaps, occupational diversity – may seem to relate to conditions in towns rather than to rural life. As has already been suggested, this is not surprising given that for some authors, stressing institutional developments as a basis for professional achievement, this becomes a matter of definition. Yet any discussion of professions in the early modern period must take into account the fact

---

74. On the incomes and conditions of medical practitioners in the later period, see Peterson, *Mid-Victorian Medical Profession*, chaps 3 and 5 (where 'tendering' is mentioned only in passing); Loudon, *Medical Care and the General Practitioner*; Digby, *Making a Medical Living*. See also H. Marland, *Medicine and Society in Wakefield and Huddersfield 1780–1870* (Cambridge, 1987), chap. 7; M. A. Crowther, 'Paupers or Patients? Obstacles to Professionalisation in the Poor Law Medical Service before 1914', *Journal of the History of Medicine*, 39 (1984), 33–54; D. Watkins, 'The English Revolution in Social Medicine, 1889–1911' (University of London PhD thesis, 1984). On incomes and fees in the earlier period, see Walton, 'Fifteenth-century London Medical Men', pp. 171–92; W. R. LeFanu, 'A North Riding Doctor in 1609', *Medical History*, 5 (1961), 178–88; McConaghey, 'History of Rural Medical Practice', pp. 126–9; Raach, 'The English Country Doctor', chap. 5; C. Rawcliffe, 'The Profits of Practice: the Wealth and Status of Medical Men in Later Medieval England', *Social History of Medicine*, 1 (1988), 61–78; and note 68 above. On contracting, tendering and 'farming' in poor relief from the eighteenth century, see S. and B. Webb, *English Poor Law History Part I*, pp. 277–313.

75. In relation to the serious conditions caused by syphilis, Clowes can be seen attempting to modify the usual contractual terms: Clowes, *Morbus Gallicus*, fols 39recto, 42verso.

76. J. Paget, *Records of Harvey* (London, 1846), p. 16. On avoidance of contact, see also Pelling, 'Compromised by Gender'.

that around 1500 only about 6 per cent of the population could be classified as urban, and, even in 1700, only 20 per cent of the population were living in towns.[77] Without forgetting that a town also served those in the surrounding area to a greater or lesser degree, and that the population as a whole was relatively mobile, it must still be assumed that in considering urban conditions one is concerned very much with the minority rather than the majority. Although evidence is much harder to find than in respect of the largest centres, it has at least been demonstrated that orthodox practitioners were not uncommon even in small towns – which must be taken into account in conclusions about changing social conditions for the professions in towns in the early eighteenth century – and that, on the same quantitative basis already described, medical practitioners were present in well-populated rural areas at least, on a similar ratio to population of *c.* 1:400.[78]

The complexion of rural practice was of course different from that of towns. Although barbers could be present even in small villages, barbers, barber-surgeons and apothecaries did not form the dominant groups, and unlicensed practitioners were more common than the licensed. A major resource in the countryside (although they also flourished in London) were the cunning men and women who often used ritual, magic and prayer, leading in some cases to charges of witchcraft or conjuring. As might be expected from the changing structure of rural economies at this period, medicine was very often practised either simultaneously or alternately with other employments, by, for example, blacksmiths. Both the clergy and the gentry were likely to be involved in medicine, balancing the idea of rural practice as being necessarily of low status. The influence of women of all classes on their sons is an under-explored aspect of medicine. An interesting example is Thomas Tyrell, a younger son of a strongly Protestant gentry family based at Gipping Hall in Suffolk. Tyrell was apprenticed to an apothecary in Norwich and made his life there in the same occupation, but when he died in 1644 he left bequests to his mother at Gipping which indicate that his choice of business could be seen as a commercial and urban extension of his mother's influence in a rural setting.[79]

Work by Ronald Sawyer on the case records of the Bedfordshire clergyman-physician Richard Napier (d. 1634) confirms the extent to which rural medicine proceeded outside the usual terms of historiographical definition.[80] Among Napier's wide circle of medical acquaintances, many moved through the different

77. P. Clark and P. Slack, *English Towns in Transition 1500–1700* (London, 1975), pp. 11–12. See pp. 5ff for definition of towns. These percentages are based on populations of around 4,000 and over. On rural medical practice, see McConaghey, Sawyer, MacDonald, Neale, Raach and Mustain (notes 21, 34, 65, 5 and 56 above). Except for McConaghey these sources are dealing primarily with the comparatively prosperous practitioner of physic; cf. Pelling and Webster, 'Medical Practitioners', pp. 230–4; K. Thomas, *Religion and the Decline of Magic* (Harmondsworth, 1980), esp. pp. 209–27.

78. Pelling and Webster, 'Medical Practitioners', p. 235.

79. See Pelling, 'Apothecaries and Other Medical Practitioners in Norwich around 1600', *Pharmaceutical Historian*, 13 (1983), 5–8. On the Tyrell family, see W. E. Hampton, 'Sir James Tyrell: with some Notes on the Austin Friars', *The Ricardian*, 4 (1978), 9–22; for Tyrell's will, see NRO, NCC 129 Amyson (1644). On the mother-son connection, see M. Pelling, 'The Women of the Family? Speculations around Early Modern British Physicians', *Social History of Medicine*, 7 (1995), 383–401.

80. See above, note 34.

categories of practice in their own lifetimes. Sawyer identifies unofficial women practitioners as providing the most important stratum of care in Jacobean England. His finding that proximity was an important factor in choosing a practitioner reinforces the suggestion already made that even in rural areas practitioners were likely to be present in large numbers. Many of these were provided from the 'internal resources' of rural communities, and Sawyer stresses the role of community sanction in the emergence of practitioners. This situation tended to create a 'system of competences', with the scope of practice defined largely by what the practitioner's skills were perceived to be.[81] Thus lay participation was even greater than in towns, and, while differences in levels of education might be very large, there was a more obvious role for shared traditional knowledge. Rather than the unbridled conflicts between practitioners which have been assumed to be typical of an allegedly deeply divided but less 'civilised' (and extra-institutional) medical system, Sawyer finds that in one rural area at least there was considerable harmony and co-operation among those engaged in medicine. This is a particularly striking finding for the area of Napier's practice, as one of his medical rivals was John Cotta, author of a well-known diatribe against unlicensed practitioners, which undoubtedly drew upon his own experience.[82] Sawyer's findings about rural practice reinforce points already made: harmony among members of an occupation is not necessarily dependent upon an institutional context or on 'uniformity', and local forms of control have their own historical importance.

One area of identifiable conflict detectable in Napier's circle was the hostility of London to provincial practitioners, a feature indicating both the extreme competitiveness of practice in the capital, and the frequency of interchange between London and the surrounding counties. Another source of conflict emerged when the accepted division of labour was not respected. This tendency to specialisation did not, however, place much restriction on patients. Napier's practice provides ample confirmation of the high level of consumption of medical care in the earlier period. Sick people 'shuttled' (Sawyer's term) ceaselessly from one kind of practitioner to another in search of relief, according to their own and their friends' judgement of their condition, and its persistence. Specialisation as a 'refinement of skill' certainly existed at this time, just as specialisation as an indication of limited (or entrepreneurial) skills is not unknown at later periods.[83] Among the more traditional specialists were the bonesetters, ophthalmologists, lithotomists and those specialising in the diseases of women and children. These could be itinerant but nonetheless respectable, travelling according to occasion from a fixed base. Many specialisms were recognised in licensing, although here restriction, expediency, and recognition of special skills could overlap.[84] Licensing could also be a way of ensuring that useful skills

---

81. Cf. William Clowes's observation made in an urban context, quoted below, p. 255.
82. For Cotta, see *DNB*.
83. See Peterson, *Mid-Victorian Medical Profession*, pp. 259–82.
84. See Young, *Annals*, pp. 178, 313, 317, 324, 325, 329, 331, 340. Men as well as women could be licensed specifically for the treatment of women: ibid., pp. 330–1 (male practitioner, generative parts of women, including midwifery, 1611); Pelling and Webster, 'Medical Practitioners', p. 209 (female practitioner, the art of physic on women and children and others, 1596).

could be practised among the population without interference from other practitioners. It is important to stress that neither experience nor formal education in medicine was likely to produce uniformity at this time. The products even of a single university tended to be heterogeneous, partly because of the influence of the 'informal curriculum'. At the same time many aspects of medical culture, far from 'emancipating' the educated medical practitioner from the layman, formed part of a common philosophy which partly explains the level of lay knowledge of, and interest in, medicine.[85]

So far this chapter has stressed what seem to be neglected features of the larger part played by the whole population of medical practitioners in the earlier period. These features stress the interrelation of medicine with other occupational groups, and point to some of the defects in the contrasts usually drawn between the earlier and the later periods. It is perhaps desirable, finally, to pay some attention to the various contexts in which contemporaries showed that they themselves perceived a difference between 'professions' and trades or crafts. The term itself had a wide range of meanings derived from its use in the religious context. A member of a religious order 'professed' when he or she took in public the final vows of commitment to the religious life. After the Reformation the term rapidly acquired a range of secular applications, having as their common denominator the theme of public commitment or open avowal. The term 'professor', implying public teacher, passed into English use as opposed to Latin in connection with Henry VIII's Regius professorships (one of them in physic). A neat summary of the history of the term is contained in a recommendation of the nineteenth-century Royal Commission on Oxford which was trying to establish prestigious lecturing posts in 'liberal' (not applied) science in the university. The Commissioners expressed the hope that in future a professorship would become a recognised profession.[86] Given the sense of change in sixteenth-century society, it is not surprising that the word almost immediately acquired a range of connotations implying insincerity or a distance between spoken commitment and actual performance. This creates a difficulty for the modern reader in distinguishing the literal and satirical meanings in such sources as plays.

Undoubtedly literal is the reference of the printer and author Robert Copland, who wrote in 1541 that 'the parts of the art of medicine (that is to wit dietetic, pharmaceutic, and surgery) be in such wise coupled and connected together that in no wise they cannot be separated one from the other without the damage and great detriment of all the medicinal profession'. However modern this may sound, it seems clear that Copland was referring in effect to all who *professed* medicine, and that his usage was affected by proximity to the Reformation. Francis Bacon, writing at the beginning of the seventeenth century, used the

85. Pelling and Webster, 'Medical Practitioners', p. 198; C. Webster, 'Alchemical and Paracelsian Medicine', in Webster, *H M, & M*, pp. 301–34; C. Webster, *From Paracelsus to Newton: Magic and the Making of Modern Science* (Cambridge, 1983), introduction.

86. See *OED*, s.v. 'profession'; E. Freidson, *Professional Powers. A Study of the Institutionalization of Formal Knowledge* (Chicago and London, 1988), pp. 20ff. Cf. on 'occupation', P. Corfield, 'Defining Urban Work', in idem and D. Keene (eds), *Work in Towns 850–1850* (Leicester, 1990), pp. 216–18.

term 'profession' in a fairly pragmatic way to mean 'occupation'. An example from *The Advancement of Learning* serves as a reminder of points made earlier in this chapter, as well as pointing to the relatively low social status and reputation of physicians:

For in all times, in the opinion of the multitude, witches and old women and impostors have had a competition with physicians. . . . And therefore I cannot much blame [them], that they use commonly to intend some other art or practice, which they fancy more than their profession. For you shall have of them antiquaries, poets, humanists, states-men, merchants, divines, and in every of these better seen than in their profession; and no doubt on this ground, that they find that mediocrity and excellency in their art maketh no difference in profit or reputation towards their fortune; for the weakness of patients, and the sweetness of life, and nature of hope, maketh men depend upon physicians with all their defects.[87]

It is easy for the modern reader to understand a shift from a declaration made in the religious context to a different kind of public declaration based on learning and the verbal skills of the lawyer, clergyman, or even the physician. It is less easy to remember that in the earlier period, and to some extent even to the present day, learned men also declared themselves in public by their dress and accessories, and therefore that, as we have seen, they shared this mode of declaration with other occupations and trades. Thus a Shakespearean character *c.* 1601 could demand of an anonymous passer-by,

> you ought not walk
> Upon a labouring day without the sign
> Of your profession, . . . what trade art thou?[88]

The terms used in apprenticeship do not seem to have included 'profession', but it may not be too far-fetched to suggest that 'profession' referred to a state which had been achieved and could be publicly declared, rather than to what had to be learnt. It should be emphasised that, as has already been suggested in relation to guilds, the wearing or displaying of 'signs of profession' was not only necessary but honourable: individuals without identity were suspect. Im-portant social changes had to occur before such signs were seen as demeaning, and 'self-advertisement' as a breach of the professional code.[89]

The self-consciousness of physicians in particular is illustrated by the physi-cian Edward Jorden in the context of his treatise, published in 1603, claiming that the subject of a celebrated witchcraft trial (Mary Glover) was naturally, not

87. R. Copland, *The Questyonary of Cyrurgyens* (London, 1541), sig. [2]Ai verso; F. Bacon, *The Advancement of Learning*, ed. G. W. Kitchin (London, 1965), Book 2, X, 2.

88. *Julius Caesar*, I, i, 3–5. Cf. the reference in 1755 by Henry Bracken, surgeon, physician and man-midwife, to 'the businesses I do profess': quoted in D. Harley, 'Provincial Midwives in England: Lancashire and Cheshire, 1660–1760', in H. Marland (ed.), *The Art of Midwifery* (London and New York, 1993), p. 40.

89. L. Edelstein, 'The Professional Ethics of the Greek Physician', *Bull. Hist. Med.*, 30 (1956), 410; cf. Holmes, *Augustan England*, pp. 194, 197; Peterson, *Mid-Victorian Medical Profession*, pp. 252–9.

supernaturally, afflicted. Jorden considered that people had the wrong view of such cases, that is, cases of hysteria or suffocation of the mother, because they were either too little learned or lacked the humility to consult physicians. In a passage stressing the role of public avowal as made by the possessors of the whole range of manual and intellectual skills, Jorden asked:

if . . . we do depend upon those which have been trained up in other particular subjects, believing men in their own professions: why should we not prefer the judgements of physicians . . . before our own conceits; as we do the opinions of divines, lawyers, artificers, etc., in their proper elements.[90]

The College, of which Jorden was then a fellow, was in the event unable to present the kind of united front implied by Jorden with respect to Mary Glover's case. Jorden also implies not only that the clergy and the lawyers were in a more favourable position to suppress competition than physicians, but that physic was less organised even than the trades.

The campaign for the reform of the learned professions conducted in the first half of the seventeenth century is significant not only for the increasing trend towards social polarisation, but also as indicating how the ideal of the full-time professional might have been strengthened later in the century as one result of the forces of reaction. In spite of its stress on idle and elaborate learning, this campaign, like other major moves affecting the regulation of the medical profession at this period, should be seen in a wider economic and social context: in this case, the continuing struggle against monopolies, which were, like the College of Physicians, dependencies of the crown. Contemporary critics saw a symmetry of exploitation in which the clergy monopolised an individual's rights in his soul, physicians his body, and the lawyers his property and land. Physicians were put together with the clergy as Latin-speaking and heathenish. As with the clergy, learning had made physicians idle. In the previous century, both Vesalius and Paracelsus had strongly criticised physicians for abandoning their most useful and basic skills to uneducated artisans, who had subsequently, though still despised, become much more useful and reliable as practitioners. However necessary learning might be, to regard it as the only necessary qualification was to deny the role of divine grace, without which learning itself became a mere trade. Lawyers were particularly criticised for elaborating the law to such a degree that it had become a full-time occupation, inaccessible to those whom it was designed to serve. Thus, occupational diversity, with the emphasis on 'honest' trades, was elevated to a moral principle. Moreover, any form of 'specialism' which involved the monopoly of knowledge or the hoarding of esoteric lore was to be deplored.[91]

90. E. Jorden, *A Briefe Discourse of a Disease called the Suffocation of the Mother* (London, 1603), Ep. Ded., sig. A2. On Jorden, see M. MacDonald (ed.), *Witchcraft and Hysteria in Elizabethan London: Edward Jorden and the Mary Glover Case* (London and New York, 1991).

91. See Webster, 'English Medical Reformers'; Webster, *Great Instauration*, section IV, 'The Prolongation of Life'; C. Hill, 'The Medical Profession and its Radical Critics', in idem, *Change and Continuity in Seventeenth-Century England* (London, 1974), pp. 157–78. See also W. Eamon, *Science and the Secrets of Nature: Books of Secrets in Medieval and Early Modern Culture* (Princeton, NJ, 1994).

Puritan reformers also suggested that the clergy should combine useful work with their vocation, and further that the clergy could themselves become the basis of an evenly distributed and responsible medical service.[92] The College of Physicians was hostile to the involvement of the clergy in medicine, but there was a convenience about transferring from one occupation to the other which had spiritual meaning, as well as the material justifications already mentioned. The sanitary reformer Thomas Southwood Smith is one example from the nineteenth century who deliberately combined the two vocations in the context of Unitarian belief. Smith practised as physician and minister in Yeovil around 1815, and his medical studies in Edinburgh, themselves partly motivated by his renunciation of a career as a Baptist minister, were supported by the Unitarian Fund. It seems implausible that the College of Physicians, whatever its ambitions in the professional direction, and whatever its envy of the established state of the clergy in settled times, would ever have wished to create the equivalent of the church's wide-flung administrative hierarchy, with its army of underbred and often impoverished underlings. The College's indifference to the periphery, although striking from the mid-eighteenth century onwards, was hardly anything new.[93]

Thus on the one hand physicians in particular were criticised for having achieved a state of empty scholarship – in Bacon's words, 'more professed than laboured'. They assumed social graces, and despised 'the meaner sort'. As part of this critique there was an attempt to 'rematerialise' the transactions between physicians and patients. Physicians should cease to hide behind their apothecaries, they should do their own prescribing, and their prescriptions should be written in English, so that the patients knew what they were getting. That is, the transactions of physicians should be made to bear a greater resemblance to the purchase of an agreed cure. This may hark back to the familiar use of the conditional contract. At the same time, critics pointed to discrepancies between the medical practitioners' professed claim to belong to a higher calling, and their economic behaviour. Clergy, lawyers and physicians were all abused as having the profit motives of tradesmen.[94] This charge had particular application in the context of early modern London, as the capital became increasingly a trading rather than a manufacturing centre, and a focus for the activities of middlemen. The upheavals of the first part of the seventeenth century thus lent great complexity and political significance to the concepts of trade and profession.

The surgeons, particularly the surgeons of London, were not exempt from similar criticism, especially with relation to high fees and a tendency to distance themselves from their patients. Nonetheless, the generation of London surgeons that was dominant towards the end of the sixteenth century does provide a contrast with the physicians in respect of the means to be adopted to raise professional standards. These surgeons spoke strongly against idle knowledge and

92. Webster, *Great Instauration*, pp. 259–60, 282–3.

93. F. N. L. Poynter, 'Thomas Southwood Smith – the Man (1788–1861)', *Proceedings of the Royal Society of Medicine*, 55 (1962), 383–5. See above, note 55, and Pelling, 'Compromised by Gender', pp. 105–7.

94. Bacon, *Advancement of Learning*, Bk 2, X, 3; Webster, *Great Instauration*, pp. 256ff.

were conspicuous by their use of the vernacular, a move usually regarded as prejudicial to professional status as now defined.[95] Nor did surgeons like William Clowes, who was copious in his denunciation of intruders into surgery from other trades, necessarily despise the unlearned operator. In his indictment of Raseworme as lithotomist, Clowes was careful to make clear that he was speaking against 'this proud ambitious golden ass, and false deceiver' but not against 'any honest man which cutteth for the stone and ruptures'. It could not be denied, he stated, that many of these had performed 'honestly, carefully, painfully, and skilfully, to their great praise, and to the comfort and health of their patients, and to the honour and praise of almighty God'. At the same time,

every science and faculty hath his own bonds and limits, in the which, good order willeth . . . men to keep themselves without confusion, disorder or mingle mangle. Therefore I exhort all such, of what trade or faculty so ever they be, to profess only that art wherein they have most knowledge, best judgement, and greatest experience.

Clowes and his friends denied all motive for discrediting rival practitioners, 'for it is the comfort of every honest artist, to see the professors to flourish, and especially being of one body, and company, for one member not doing his duty, all the rest fareth the worse'.[96] Clowes proceeded to back up his attitude by making available to young practitioners instructions in the vernacular, both from the best sources, and as he had had experience of them himself. The surgeons and barber-surgeons, whose social utility took many forms, and whose practice best fitted the tangible, contractual model of patient–practitioner relations, continued to be regarded as useful, much more certain in principle, and less precarious in success.[97]

In a well-known article Lawrence Stone plausibly defined the period from 1550 to the mid-seventeenth century as one of great social mobility, characterised by a rise in population and an expansion of educational opportunities. He saw both the trades and the professions as rising in status relative to the landed classes. After the Restoration, land transfer was greatly reduced and opportunities for advancement through the professions were, more and more, open only to those with access to the educational ladder. This interpretation was compatible with Everitt's thesis concerning the rise of the 'pseudo-gentry' in towns, which has been expanded, notably by Borsay, into the notion of an 'urban renaissance'. It also seems a plausible framework for the evolution of the numerous, competitive, self-improving and extremely various body of medical practitioners

95. On different attitudes to the vernacular, see Bullough, *Development of Medicine*, p. 4; Larson, *Rise of Professionalism*, pp. 3–4. Cf. Pelling and Webster, 'Medical Practitioners', pp. 176, 177; Webster, *Great Instauration*, pp. 256–73. See also P. Slack, 'Mirrors of Health and Treasures of Poor Men: the Uses of the Vernacular Medical Literature of Tudor England', in Webster, *H, M & M*, pp. 237–73. On the literacy of barber-surgeons, see also Walton, 'Fifteenth-century London Medical Men', pp. 72–7; Young, *Annals*, pp. 309–10, 312; Talbot, *Medicine in Medieval England*, pp. 186–97. On increasing literacy among apprentices in general in the sixteenth century, see Palliser, 'Trade Gilds of Tudor York', p. 99; Rappaport, *Worlds within Worlds*, pp. 298–9.

96. Clowes, *Morbus Gallicus*, fols 10recto, 13verso–14recto; George Baker, 'The Nature and Property of Quicksilver' in ibid., fol. 49recto.

97. Holmes, *Augustan England*, p. 194.

which emerges against a background of population increase and economic and social crisis in the period before 1660, and the relatively more uniform and familiar situation which was developing at the end of the seventeenth century. Stone also pointed to various features of the period before 1660 which analysts have regarded as concomitant with the emergence of the professions in the nineteenth century: increasing secularisation, population expansion, increases in demand, and a trend towards literacy. Further changes with respect to the medical profession after the Restoration identified by Holmes confirm the other half of Stone's interpretation: the increased incidence of medical 'dynasties'; the payment of high premiums; the greater uniformity of more expensive education. To these may be added the lessening of women's chances of practising medicine reputably outside the household. Other changes underline the importance of social polarisation: in spite of their real usefulness and general viability, the barber-surgeons lost ground, as the concept of utility itself became discredited.[98]

In spite of the importance of these social changes, the degree of continuity into the eighteenth century was considerable. Uniformity was not a characteristic of the medical practitioners of even the nineteenth century.[99] The connections with the wider economic and social world changed but did not disappear. Even where these later connections have been recognised by historians, they tend still to be seen as deviations from professional norms.[100] It is a curious feature of much discussion of the professions which concentrates firmly on the industrial period that it has established little about medical personnel as full members of an industrial society. Economic language and concepts are used, but only as a different way of describing medicine itself.[101] In such an interpretation there is only one view taken of such cases as the Tunbridge and London practitioner William Henry Cook, who was essentially supported by the unearned income of his wife's mother and sister, and also in part by the income earned by his wife in writing, teaching and lodging children who needed a good Christian

98. L. Stone, 'Social Mobility in England, 1500–1700', *P & P*, 33 (1966), 16–55; A. Everitt, 'Social Mobility in Early Modern England', ibid., pp. 56–73. M. Espinasse, 'The Decline and Fall of Restoration Science', ibid., 14 (1958), 71–89.

99. This is rightly stressed by Peterson, *Mid-Victorian Medical Profession*, and has been emphasised since by historians concerned with general practice, public health, and the poor-law medical service. For a reassertion of the professional differences between the 'ordinary practitioner' of the eighteenth century (in France) and the nineteenth-century general practitioner, see T. Gelfand, 'The Decline of the Ordinary Practitioner and the Rise of a Modern Medical Profession', in M. S. Staum and D. E. Larsen (eds), *Doctors, Patients, and Society: Power and Authority in Medical Care* (Waterloo, Ontario, 1981), pp. 105–29.

100. This is true even of Peterson, Loudon and Digby, who are unusually broad and detailed in their coverage of the economic circumstances of the profession.

101. There have consequently been only certain kinds of response to Inkster's charge of 'neglect of the economic function of the profession': I. Inkster, 'Marginal Men: Aspects of the Social Role of the Medical Community in Sheffield 1790–1850', in Woodward and Richards, *Health Care and Popular Medicine*, p. 154. Hence the vagueness in application of terms such as 'supply', 'demand' and 'market', and the lack of reference to areas outside medicine itself. Similar limitations apply to the criticism made by Paul Starr, and to his own attempt to supply the deficiency, even though his interpretation would be regarded by many as extreme: P. Starr, 'Medicine, Economy and Society in Nineteenth-century America', in P. Branca (ed.), *The Medicine Show* (New York, 1977), p. 47; P. Starr, *The Social Transformation of American Medicine* (New York, 1982). An exception in moving outside 'professional' issues in this respect is J. Pickstone, 'The Professionalisation of Medicine in England and Europe: the State, the Market and Industrial Society', *Nihon Ishigaku Zasshi* [*Journal of the Japan Society of Medical History*], 25 (1979), 520–50; see also *passim* in his 'Ways of Knowing'. Marland, *Medicine and Society*, provides a convincing contrast between an old corporate town and a centre of industrialisation.

upbringing while their parents were in the colonies. There is even less room for other examples, such as William Budd, physician and distinguished epidemiologist, who, at a time when he could earn less than £500 per annum for his practice, apparently lost £3,500 in an investment in shares. A strong believer in water carriage as a cause of disease, Budd was a member of the first Board of Directors of the Bristol Water Works Company. William Farr, the medical statistician, made extensive and usually unfortunate commitments in the world of commercial insurance. John Snow, anaesthetist to Queen Victoria, was prompted to enter this line by the example of a druggist who boasted to him of having built up an 'ether practice'. Disinfection was another area of combined medical and commercial enterprise.[102] These examples are not specially selected, but they do indicate that there was more to the economic life and occupations of even nineteenth-century men than remote and gentlemanly investment in land or consols, or desperate and ungentlemanly selling of pills and ointments.

It is usually assumed that it is professionalisation which must be continuous: that, having once begun (whether, as has been variously proposed for medicine, in the middle ages, the eighteenth century, or the nineteenth), its progress is inevitable. The persistence of institutions (universities, hospitals) seems to provide a tangible basis for this. Yet, if professionalisation is to be linked to these institutions, its course must likewise be one not of linear development but of periodic weakness and strength. For example, the revival of Cambridge in particular as a centre of medical education in the sixteenth century must be contrasted with the nadir of English university faculties in the eighteenth century. Growth in the university context could take place largely outside the 'training' curriculum, as in the mid-seventeenth century at Oxford; and such 'training', as already suggested, could help maintain a common cultural experience, rather than dividing the layman from the professional. Similarly the College of Physicians of London could claim greater pretensions to professional leadership in the early sixteenth or early seventeenth centuries, than by the eighteenth, when religious tests had created separate nonconformist establishments rivalling the older institutions, and when fragmentation was a permanent feature of social life. By this time the College had cut itself off from the sectors of society most likely go into medicine. The contrasting notions evolved during the Commonwealth did not simply disappear. As we have seen, medicine, with its combination of mental and manual skills, was peculiarly likely to reflect changing or conflicting attitudes to hierarchy and class structure.

Even historically-based accounts of the rise of medicine since the nineteenth century end by presenting a kind of immutable monolith. Seen in this way,

102. Foster, 'Dr William Henry Cook'; William Budd to Richard Budd, 16 November 1845, Autograph Letter Collection: William Budd, Wellcome Institute for the History of Medicine, London; E. W. Goodall, *William Budd* (Bristol, 1936), p. 64; *DNB*, art. 'Farr, William'; J. Snow, *Snow on Cholera*, ed. W. H. Frost (New York, 1965), p. xxxi; D. Palfreyman, *John Jeyes . . . The Making of a Household Name* (Thetford, 1977). For other possible examples, see Holmes, *Augustan England*, p. 222; Inkster, 'Marginal Men', p. 162. On Farr, see J. M. Eyler, *Victorian Social Medicine: the Ideas and Methods of William Farr* (Baltimore, MD, and London, 1979). For some aspects of the link between medical practitioners and the growth of insurance, see M. A. Crowther and B. M. White, 'Medicine, Property and the Law in Britain 1800–1914', *Historical Journal*, 31 (1988), 853–70. Snow's career is under investigation by Stephanie Snow of the University of Manchester.

becoming a profession is a goal, and once this is achieved, it is not clear what happens subsequently. But is it actually true, as has been suggested, that 'the modern professions – whose archetype is medicine – fostered group solidarity, loyalty, and exclusiveness, regardless of differences in general education, ascribed social rank or economic standing'?[103] Or is medicine even in the twentieth century a larger field, more various, less controlled, and more fragmented in socio-economic terms than this suggests, and thus recognisably the product of much earlier developments?

103. Peterson, *Mid-Victorian Medical Profession*, p. 287.

Index

Note: the names of the poor have had to be omitted, except where they are mentioned in more than one place, or if they are identifiable as practitioners.